MODERN HEBREW FICTION

JEWISH LITERATURE AND CULTURE

SERIES EDITOR, ALVIN H. ROSENFELD

MODERN HEBREW FICTION

GERSHON SHAKED

TRANSLATED FROM THE HEBREW BY YAEL LOTAN

EDITED BY EMILY MILLER BUDICK

BIBLIOGRAPHY COMPILED BY JESSICA COHEN

INDIANA UNIVERSITY PRESS • BLOOMINGTON AND INDIANAPOLIS

This book is a publication of

Indiana University Press
601 North Morton Street
Bloomington, IN 47404-3797 USA

http://www.indiana.edu/~iupress

Telephone orders   800-842-6796
Fax orders   812-855-7931
Orders by e-mail   iuporder@indiana.edu

Library of Congress Cataloging-in-Publication Data

Shaked, Gershon.
    [Siporet ha-Qvrit, 1880–1970. English]
    Modern Hebrew fiction / Gershon Shaked ; translated from the Hebrew by Yael
Lotan ; edited by Emily Miller Budick ; bibliography compiled by Jessica Cohen.
        p.   cm. — (Jewish literature and culture)
Includes bibliographical references and index.
ISBN 0-253-33711-9 (cloth: alk. paper)
    1. Hebrew fiction—History and criticism.   2. Israeli ficton—History and
criticism.   I. Budick, E. Miller.   II. Title.   III. Series.

PJ5029 .S5413 2000
892.4'3609—dc21   99-054356

1   2   3   4   5   05   04   03   02   01   00

Indeed, the kind of literature which is an everlasting structure, built up slowly by the generations, a literature which is a self-sustaining entity, which develops naturally and draws its vitality from the many readers who are influenced by it, which includes a variety of currents, mores and tendencies, while being animated by a distinctive national spirit—such a literature we do not have, we have not had and cannot have. . . . But there are writers, a handful of talented Hebrew authors, divinely inspired, living in the midst of their people and writing —intermittently and against all odds. Each of them offers his mind's work for the Hebrew-Jewish reader. These profound writers, who strive to express themselves despite the external literary reality, resemble flies trying to climb a slippery pane of glass. Such writers we do have today!

—YOSEF HAIM BRENNER

CONTENTS

ACKNOWLEDGMENTS

The present book is an abridgment and translation of my Hebrew study *Hebrew Fiction 1880–1980* [*Hasiporet Ha ʿivrit 1880–1980* (Jerusalem: Keter and Hakibutz Hameuchad, 1977–1999)], which encompassed five volumes and was highly detailed and annotated. In the present book I try to summarize that history of Hebrew fiction in a single volume, leaving out whatever is not essential to a reader seeking a general picture of modern Hebrew narrative. I discuss internal literary developments in the tradition of Hebrew prose and the interaction between social processes and the writing. I focus on the most notable writers and their best works. Most chapters include brief summaries of individual writers, but in the final chapters of the book, which deal with writers of the contemporary period, I have incorporated observations about individual writers and works within expanded general surveys of trends and issues. My reason is simply that most of these writers are still in the prime of their creativity, and any summary written today is almost certain to be obsolete tomorrow.

Methodologically speaking, my historical survey does not apply one particular literary theory. Rather, as the academic reader will readily discern, it makes use of several theories. In an undertaking as broad as a literary history that attempts to cover a multitude of different writers, writing in different countries and within different time frames and social contexts, it seemed to me prudent to be as flexible as possible in bringing forward the salient features of the literary works under discussion.

A list of works cited and a glossary are provided, but those wishing more detailed information should consult the footnotes of my original Hebrew work. Biographical material about each of the authors is incorporated in the index. Information about English translations of the texts under discussion is included in the list of works cited.

My thanks to several people who have helped prepare this manuscript for publication: to Tammy Hess, who helped to adapt the book for its intended readership and who checked and double-checked materials for accuracy; to the translator, Yael Lotan; to Janine Woolfson, who proofread early copies of the manuscript; and to Chava Burstein Rothenberg, who proofread the manuscript at later stages, retyped the glossary, and checked various bibliographical materials; to Nilli Cohen and Haya Hoffman of the Institute for the Translation of Hebrew Literature, who read the manuscript before its translation, contributed useful comments, and supported me throughout; and, last but not least, special gratitude to Emily Miller Budick, who edited and adapted the translated manuscript and helped prepare it for publication. David Patterson read the manuscript and was very helpful and reassuring. The editors at Indiana University Press—Jane Lyle, Kate Babbitt, Kendra Boileau Stokes, and especially Janet Rabinowitch—with extraordinary skill and grace guided this project through to its proper culmination. To them also, my sincere gratitude.

This work was translated thanks to the generous support of the Research Fund of the Hebrew University of Jerusalem. Research assistance was also subsidized by the Faculty of Humanities of Hebrew University.

EDITOR'S FOREWORD

Literary historians face a double challenge. As literary critics they must present works in their uniqueness and aesthetic integrity. In the final analysis, literary texts engage us because of some quality of creative power that distinguishes one text from another. Unless the critic can convey the aesthetic dimensions of the work of fiction, its historical and cultural affiliations seem largely insignificant. At the same time, literary historians confront an equally important, if somewhat contradictory, task. They must reveal just those continuities and informing contexts that may seem to detract from the singularity of the single text.

In *Modern Hebrew Fiction,* Gershon Shaked, one of the leading scholars of Hebrew literature today, treads the fine line between these two separate, sometimes mutually exclusive activities. In so doing, he skillfully produces that magical combination we call literary history. Through detailed explications of particular works, Shaked captures the alchemy by which these literary texts cast their spell, stylistically as well as thematically. At the same time, through biographical sketches, historical surveys, and socio-cultural and political analyses, he illuminates the equally important conditions of the works' production within the ongoing development of Hebrew literature. In this way, Shaked locates the relationship between the aesthetic and the socio-political, cultural, and historical contexts of Hebrew fiction. He pulls into view the ultimate intertext: the play between literature and life.

But Shaked performs another function as well, one not usually required of literary historians, at least not those who write about the major Western traditions. He conveys those features of the canon of modern Hebrew fiction that qualify it to enter onto the arena of contemporary cultural and literary study. Equally important, he provides the tools by which students of other literary traditions can begin to take into account the important example of Hebrew writing.

In many ways the tradition of Hebrew literature is unique. As Shaked points out early in his study, the literature took its inception not only without the benefits of national, geographical borders and the existence of political or cultural autonomy, but virtually without a usable language. That is, despite the antiquity of Hebrew as a language of sacred discourse and prayer, until the twentieth century, the writers of Hebrew fiction did not possess a non-sacred literary language (spoken or written) with which to produce modern secular literature. By simultaneously constructing both a literary tradition and a language, the writers of Hebrew fiction remind us of the centrality of language in the construction of the literary text. This importance is not only aesthetic but ideological as well. For in forging a language, writers of Hebrew fiction implicitly and explicitly affirm the necessity of possessing a language as a condition of cultural, if not national, self-expression. At the same time, however, as they avail themselves, not only of their own Jewish heritage of texts and folk traditions, but also the broader world of Western thought, the authors impress upon us the heteroglossic, mutually constructed nature of all culture and all writing.

For this reason, modern Hebrew literature provides a kind of laboratory for observing how culture and literature happen, in particular how they happen in conditions of human extremity. Excluded from the centers of cultural production in the countries in which they lived and wrote, turn-of-the-century and early-twentieth-century Hebrew writers could not write without a commitment to the construction of a specifically Jewish culture. At the same time, however, they were critical of traditional Jewish life and its rejection of secular culture. Therefore they could not simply celebrate Jewish (religious) life and use it as the basis for the budding literary tradition. To complicate matters even further, even after the writers inhabited shores of their own—both before and after they had acceded to genuine cultural authority in a national homeland—they could not simply forget the marginalization and annihilation of the Jews of Europe. Nor could they ignore threats to the Jewish *Yishuv* (settlement) in Palestine or, after 1948, to the newly emergent Jewish State.

They also could not be oblivious to the role of nationalism and cultural politics in the marginalization, annihilation, and continuing assault against Jewish life, both within Israel and outside its borders, that compelled their attention. For the Hebrew writer, then, writing could not be a straightforward vehicle of social critique. Within the context of international culture, the Jews were not accorded equal status. By the very fact of its existence, Hebrew writing proclaimed voice and identity against the denial by others of its right to exist. But in creating a literature that would declare the existence of a people and its culture, the writers also had to beware of turning the literature into a mirror of the ideological imperatives of nationalism and cultural hegemony that had once marginalized and disempowered the writers themselves.

Embodying the tension between the dangerous power to create and the equally fraught resistance to that power, which just might return a people to voicelessness and disenfranchisement, the canon of modern

Hebrew fiction, as explicated by Shaked, provides potent insights into some of the major dilemmas confronting human societies, especially in the modern period. Hebrew literature pulls into focus the complex relationship between ideology and culture, both as a phenomenon of minority literatures struggling to achieve cultural autonomy and as a feature of national cultures pursuing their social and political agendas. For the Hebrew writers who dreamed of Eretz Yisrael (the land of Israel) at the turn of the century, or who ventured there in the early decades of the century, or who witnessed the birth of the nation, nationhood promised the possibility of Jewish secular culture unburdened by the necessities of ideological argumentation. Secular Jewish culture represented the possibility of individual psychological and spiritual growth and genuine social critique. As Shaked tells the story of Hebrew fiction in the modern period, there were those writers who could not keep literature clear of political indoctrination. However, there were also the large majority of cultural figures who succeeded brilliantly in achieving that quality of linguistically mediated individual voice that we recognize as literature. This is the voice that expresses struggle and irresolution and insoluble dilemma as the essential enactments of human creativity.

It was Yosef Haim Brenner who first referred to the project of producing Hebrew literature as being "against all odds." This phrase, which informs the opening chapter of Shaked's book, nicely sums up the historical conditions of the tradition's emergence. But it captures as well, I think, the far greater accomplishment of the Hebrew literary canon to which Shaked's study directs us: its resistance to the powerful pull toward polemic and didacticism. In so doing, Hebrew fiction teaches us what all literature teaches us: that in the contingent, non-transcendental struggles of human beings is contained the whole of human knowledge—moral, psychological, political, and otherwise. Such knowledge does more than suffice. In the hands of great writers, it does nothing less than inspire. Gershon Shaked's *Modern Hebrew Fiction* illuminates the inspiration that is the tradition of Hebrew literature.

E. M. B

MODERN HEBREW FICTION

1

A LITERATURE "AGAINST ALL ODDS"
THE ADVENT OF MODERN HEBREW LITERATURE

In tracing the development of modern Hebrew literature, the present work takes as its point of departure the 1881 pogroms in Russia. The history of Jewish persecution from the 1880s on does not differ radically from that of the previous decades. Nonetheless, beginning in 1881, proceeding through the rise of anti-Semitism between the two world wars, and culminating in the Holocaust itself, some features of that history move into prominence. These caused a variety of responses within the Jewish community, some of which had great influence on the production of modern Hebrew writing.

The pogroms and blood-libels (including the famous Beilis Trial of 1913), which continued throughout the early twentieth century, caused many members of the Jewish intelligentsia to abandon the hope, fondly nurtured during the Haskalah (the Hebrew Enlightenment), that European culture and the assimilation of the Jewish community into that culture would produce social freedom for Jews. The motto of the Haskalah had been "Be a Jew at home and a man in the world." The repudiation of the Jews by European society caused widespread disillusion and fear. Many Jews emigrated from Europe to the United States, their numbers swelling some years to one hundred thousand. Many of those who remained joined revolutionary movements. The specifically Jewish organizations consisted of two groups: The Bund was comprised of those who demanded social and cultural, but not national, autonomy; Hibbat Zion was comprised of those who laid the groundwork for national Zionism.

These political positions corresponded to equally strong cultural tendencies. Most of the Jews of Eastern Europe were polyglot. Among themselves they spoke Yiddish. Hebrew was the language of prayer and sacred discourse. And the national vernacular languages, such as Russian, Polish, and Ukrainian, served as the instruments of their communication with the surrounding society. In keeping with their general philosophy concerning the interpenetration of national and Jewish culture, the assimilationists of the Haskalah favored writing in the vernacular. The Bundists and the Zionists, more oriented toward the creation of a specifically Jewish culture, emphasized Yiddish and Hebrew, respectively.

The decision to write in the non-vernacular Jewish languages was facilitated during this period by the expansion of the Hebrew press and by the appearance in the 1890s of "penny books" or *sifrei 'agorah*, cheaply produced pocket books. These developments created a platform for the writers who would shape the new literature. Some of the early creators of the emergent tradition had previously contributed to the literature of the Haskalah. Most notable among them was Mendele Mokher Sefarim (the pen name of S. Y. Abramowitz), who at this time stopped writing in Yiddish and began to write in Hebrew. Other writers who had contributed to the periodicals of the Haskalah and who now became pioneers of the new revival in Hebrew literature included I. L. Peretz; D. Frischmann, whose early stories appeared in periodicals such as *Hamelitz* [*The Advocate*], *He'asif* [*The Harvest*], and *Hayom* [*The Day*]; and the young M. Y. Berdyczewski, who had also published his earliest stories in *He'asif*.

In the latter decades of the nineteenth century, concomitant with other internal and external transformations, the religious foundations of Jewish community life began to disintegrate. Hasidic and traditional communities continued to exist, but the religious congregation as the all-encompassing unit of Jewish solidarity fell apart. Hebrew literature, as a result, had to concern itself not only with the failure of the ideology of the Haskalah vis-à-vis the cultural assimilation of European Jewry but also with the further tensions within the Jewish community itself between secular and religious identities. This issue of identity informs early-twentieth-century Hebrew literature, including essays by such important figures within the Hebrew literary tradition as Ahad Haam, Berdyczewski, and Yosef Haim Brenner. It also circulates within the poetry of Haim Nahman Bialik and in the fiction of Berdyczewski, Mordechai Zeev Feierberg, and Brenner. However disillusioned Jewish intellectuals might have been with the failure of the Haskalah to alter the status of Jews in Christian countries, the effects of the Enlightenment and of secular humanistic and scientific education on traditional Jewish beliefs and community life could not be reversed.

The increased migration of Jewish authors to Palestine after the First World War also transformed the linguistic, political, and cultural agendas of the literature. Just as the Jews of Eastern Europe had become an immigrant society in the early years of the twentieth century, so also had their literature become vagabond. It was born in the villages of Russia, Poland, and Galicia, but together with its authors and readers it abandoned the villages for the cities and the cities for countries overseas: the New World and Palestine. Wandering and migration, which marked the Jewish experience, shaped the literature. While Jewish texts from the United States and Western Europe reflected the distress that had driven the Jews to those places, the literature of the migration to Palestine, which was generally motivated by Zionist ideology, told a different story. Even more important, it told its story in Hebrew.

In the late nineteenth and early twentieth centuries, the majority of Jewish writers wrote both in Yiddish and in Hebrew, sometimes using the two languages interchangeably. In the early years of the twentieth century these two languages and their respective literatures struggled for supremacy, a struggle which in Palestine was dubbed "the war of the languages." As in the early days of the revolutionist rejection of the ideology of the Haskalah (by the Bund and Hibbat Zion), language and politics were inextricably linked. The proponents of national autonomy in the diaspora (primarily the members of the Jewish socialist movement, the Bund) preferred Yiddish. As a living dynamic language, rich in folk idiom, Yiddish had certain advantages over Hebrew, which offered an impressive written canon but little in the way of contemporary local reference. Furthermore, to choose Hebrew implied support for the Zionist conviction that Jews could have no permanent home outside of Palestine, or Eretz Yisrael (the Land of Israel). Even in Palestine, however, Hebrew did not immediately triumph as the language of choice. Only when the immigrants of the Second Aliyah (the second wave of Jewish immigration to Eretz Yisrael, between 1904 and 1913) decided on Hebrew as their spoken language did it establish itself as the national language of letters. Even into the 1930s, each of the contending languages had its own educational system and press.

In the 1930s, however, Hebrew emerged as the literary language of the Jews, and Eretz Yisrael as the center for the production and publication of Hebrew writing. The beginnings of a Hebrew literature industry are evident even earlier. Periodicals such as *Hapoʿel hatzaʿir* [*The Young Worker*], founded in 1907, which published Second Aliyah writers such as Brenner and Devorah Baron, were already in place in Eretz Yisrael. Nonetheless, from the 1890s and into the 1920s, the literary center was not Eretz Yisrael but Odessa, which was a kind of Russian Jerusalem, replete with Hebrew publishing houses, schools, and periodicals. Many Hebrew authors lived there, such as Mendele, Ahad Haam, Shaul Tchernichowski, Bialik, and later Yaacov Rabinowitz, Shlomo Zemach, and Yehuda Karni. In the

1920s, however, after the Bolshevik Revolution and the outlawing of Hebrew study and the Zionist movement, Hebrew literature began its precipitous decline in Europe. For a brief period early in the decade, Germany replaced Russia as the center, when such writers as Bialik, Shmuel Yosef Agnon, Tchernichowski, and several young Jewish scholars, namely Gershom Scholem, Martin Buber, and Yaacov Klatzkin, resided there. But this was a transitory shift that was about to yield to the final relocation of the literature to Palestine. Thus, Hebrew literature was transformed from a wandering entity to a fixed cultural expression with its own national center. This center presented its own problems. Nonetheless, it at least provided a stable readership and a natural locale. As it distanced itself from Eastern European and Orthodox religious influences, its links with traditional Jewish culture and Yiddish literature grew fainter.

Like most literary histories, the history of Hebrew literature concerns two interrelated tensions. The first is the tension between, on the one hand, the definition and development of shared themes and subjects, linking members of a single generation and functioning intergenerationally to produce something we call literary tradition, and, on the other hand, its opposite: the radical opposition to or deviations from those same themes and subjects (and, thereby, the introduction of different themes and subjects) that distinguish between generations and between writers within a single period of literary composition. The second literary pressure, which follows from the first, is the question of literary form; namely, *how* the writer represents the subject of his or her fiction: mimetically—through the devices of literary realism or naturalism; or non-mimetically—romantically, impressionistically, expressionistically, symbolically, and so on.

To these standard dilemmas of the literary text, modern Hebrew fiction presented two other unique problems: namely, how to produce literature in the absence of a geographically, temporally contiguous population with political, or at least, cultural, autonomy; and how to write that literature in an ancient language that lacked even basic terms for contemporary experience. Throughout the centuries, Hebrew had functioned (brilliantly, some might claim) as a written language of liturgical and philosophical discourse. But it had not served as a vehicle of spoken communication. Furthermore, within the various nations where Jews dwelt, it existed as an anomalous and foreign body, even to many Jews themselves.

In a 1908 essay in the periodical *Revivim* [*Showers*], Yosef Haim Brenner described the uniqueness of the Hebrew literary situation this way:

> Indeed, the kind of literature which is an everlasting structure, built up
> slowly by the generations, a literature which is a self-sustaining entity,
> which develops naturally and draws its vitality from the many readers who

are influenced by it, which includes a variety of currents, mores and tendencies, while being animated by a distinctive national spirit—such a literature we do not have, we have not had and cannot have. . . . But there are writers, a handful of talented Hebrew authors, divinely inspired, living in the midst of their people and writing—intermittently and *against all odds*. Each of them offers his mind's work for the Hebrew-Jewish reader. These profound writers, who strive to express themselves despite the external literary reality, resemble flies trying to climb a slippery pane of glass. Such writers we do have today!

To produce this literature *against all odds* modern Hebrew literature was nothing if not eclectic. The novels and poems of the Haskalah in the 1860s and 1870s had tended to be both melodramatic and didactic: Villains exploited unfortunate and innocent victims, tense plots were arbitrarily and unexpectedly resolved, and characters reflected the ideas and moral values of the author. Most of these works called for the reform of Jewish society, which, in the view of the writers, had become petrified and stagnant. As faith in the Haskalah weakened, and as the literature opened itself to new theories of literary production, so too did its concerns and modes of representation undergo transformation. Thus, modern Hebrew literature, remaining attuned to the major developments of modern literature, enacted its own internal self-revision, both in relation to European paradigms and in relation to Jewish materials.

The continued strong influence of Western culture on Hebrew writing can be glimpsed through the proliferation of translated texts from the nineteenth century on. Indeed, some of the best Hebrew writers were themselves translators, producing in Hebrew a broad variety of literary works, from Dostoyevsky, Chekhov, Stendhal, and Maeterlinck to Cervantes, Goethe, Whitman, Peter Jens Jacobsen, and Knut Hamsun; and later from Alexander Bek, Mikhail Sholokhov and Fyodor Gladkov to Ernest Hemingway and Max Frisch. The major European influences on Hebrew literature might be summarized as nineteenth- and early-twentieth-century Russian literature, Soviet literature of the 1930s and 1940s, late-nineteenth- and early-twentieth-century Western European writings (German, Scandinavian, and French), and Anglo-Saxon literature. The Hebrew writers did not hesitate to imitate everything from typical syntactical patterns to the modern genres (such as the novel, novella, and short story). Nor was the Western influence on Hebrew literature synchronous or directly affected by relative geographic proximity. Thus, for example, the writers of the Second Aliyah (1904–1913) were for some reason influenced by Scandinavian literature (mainly by Hamsun), whereas the native-born writers were strongly influenced by Soviet literature and American writings of the 1920s and 1930s.

At the same time, of course, that Hebrew writing adopted ideas and techniques from the canon of Western literature, it also drew on its own reserves of Jewish history and culture. Indeed, from the Haskalah to the present, Hebrew literature evidences the conflict between ancient Jewish sources and the humanist secular culture of Europe. Some of the fiction is, to be sure, more imitative of European than Jewish forms. Much of it, however, stays fairly close to traditional Jewish narrative structures, such as the tales of piety and the Midrashim (early glosses on and elaborations of biblical stories; for example, Agnon's "Forsaken Wives" ["'Agunot"]). To a large extent this incorporation of elements from an old religious tradition into a new secular literature is what gave Hebrew writing its distinctive character. Indeed, it is possible to say that the greater the tension between traditional and contemporary elements, the more complex and interesting the fiction became. Traditional materials often served as external symbols of the stories' themes (as, for example, Mendele's parody of the allegorical interpretation of Song of Songs in his tale "The Nag" ["Susati"]). Sometimes they lent a deeper spiritual or mythical resonance to a motif or figure (as, for example, in Berdyczewski's *The Secret Place of Thunder* [*Beseter Ra'am*]).

Although the tension between European and Jewish literary models characterized Hebrew literature even before its translocation to Palestine, nonetheless the new national setting radically altered the writing's relationship to Jewish tradition. The principal themes of Hebrew writing changed from the diaspora's preoccupation with the Jewish spirit to the struggle for the future of the nation in the new land. The literature affirmed, even as it questioned, the nature of the new society, both as it existed and as it might evolve. In place of the familiar characters of diaspora literature—persecuted immigrants with their troubled relationship to tradition—came new figures: the pioneer and the fighter; native-born sabras and their heroic founding fathers, the two generations poised in inter- and intragenerational conflict; and a host of pragmatic rootless disappointed intellectuals and dreamy-eyed unrealistic idealists. To present its new Jewish reality the writing secularized traditional materials and celebrated secular ones, often using religious motifs and themes to infuse secular values with religious significance. Bialik, Berdyczewski, and Agnon sanctified art; many other writers did the same with nature, labor, and love. The Zionist imperative supplanted the religious commandments, and even atheism was perceived by some writers as a form of religious expression.

Structurally, Hebrew fiction from the late nineteenth century on pursued two principal currents. One strand, which began with Mendele (who constitutes a "group" by himself and who every group could claim as its progenitor) and proceeded through Abraham Laib Ben-Avigdor (originally Shaikovich), Bialik, Shlomo Zemach, Yehudah Burla, Yitzhak Shami, and Moshe Shamir, is marked by its emphasis on social context. These writers sought to directly engage and represent the socio-economic and political world, and therefore tended toward the writing of social novels, as defined by a critic such as Northrop Frye. The other, starting with Frischmann and Berdyczewski and continuing through such figures as Brenner, Uri Nissan Gnessin, Elisheva Bikhovski, David Vogel, Yaacov Horowitz, and Pinhas Sadeh to Amos Oz and A. B. Yehoshua, veered toward more romantic or expressionist modes of representation. The writers within this trajectory of Hebrew fiction were also less concerned with configuring social reality than with exploring the human psyche. Their characterizations focused on the protagonists' inner worlds, tending toward the genres of romance and of confession (Frye's terminology again).

Needless to say, the boundaries between these two categories of Hebrew prose fiction, with their alternative modes of expression, are often blurred (as in Brenner's writings, for example). This is especially the case as the emphasis in the writing begins to shift from socio-typological representation to more psychologically informed fiction. In this already variegated field of Hebrew writing, Agnon constitutes a category unto himself. Balancing exquisitely between social context and the inner worlds of his protagonists, reflecting both a real world and its psychic emotional transformations, Agnon produced a style uniquely his own. As we shall see, Agnon stands at the crossroads of the new Hebrew literature. Through his writings all the various currents and continuities of Hebrew literature intersect and achieve powerful representation.

In the literature of Eretz Yisrael the tension between realism and romanticism and between mimetic and non-mimetic modes of representation produced two contending genres. One of these genres, which was actually dubbed by Brenner "the Eretz Yisrael genre" (*janer' eretz Yisra' eli*), attempted to depict the new society in its idealized form, as if the aspirations of the community had already been met and were already in place. The other oppositional genre, which I will call "anti-genre," insisted on representing the actual conditions of Palestine, human, social, and otherwise. Among the writers who pursued more realistic representations were two distinctly different groups: those who endeavored to reproduce the patterns of more natural, everyday speech (Ben-Avigdor and, later, Shamir, Yigal Mossinsohn, and Aharon Megged); and those who wrote a formal, stylized Hebrew prose, called "formulation."

Formulation is a phenomenon unto itself. From the latter part of the nineteenth century on, Hebrew writers had devised strategies for dealing with the intransigencies and archaisms of the ancient language. For the most part, the fiction of the Haskalah had been written in an elevated pontific Hebrew style, derived largely from biblical and rabbinical Hebrew. Post-Enlightenment writers such as Mendele and Bialik effected radical transformations on the language, formulating a new Hebrew suitable, in their view, for the writing of enlightened, contemporary Hebrew prose. Like older Haskalah diction, this formulated language, or formulation, as it came to be known, also transplanted idioms directly from canonical sources. It did so, however, in unexpected ways and in new contexts.

This strategy of direct importation of biblical and later canonical sources (Midrash, for example) into otherwise non-biblical structures continued to characterize one form of response to written Hebrew, used by such various authors as Y. D. Berkowitz, Haim Hazaz, and Amalia Kahana-Carmon, who used such classical sources to give symbolic depth to their prose and/or to parody traditional meanings. By altering the connotations of the language, either by changing one of the components of a particular construct or by rearranging them, these writers succeeded in defamiliarizing the ancient tongue and appropriating it to contemporary purposes without losing the balanced and symmetrical character of classical Hebrew style.

Another way of taming the elevated tradition of classical Hebrew for contemporary usage was to borrow from other languages. Most writers turned to Mishnaic Hebrew, which seemed to them more prosaic than the exalted diction of the Bible itself; others to Aramaic, which denoted "common" speech; while still others borrowed words and phrases from Yiddish, English (as in the works of Rachel Eytan), Arabic (Shamir), and other languages, often adding appealing local color to the tale. Later on, in modern Israeli literature, such linguistic blends marked a natural transition from high literary language to standard or colloquial speech.

Indeed, modern Hebrew writing is distinguished by the general infiltration of non-Hebrew language patterns into the literature. By importing idioms verbatim from Yiddish and other languages or by Hebraizing them (as in the writings of Brenner), writers not only augmented the vocabulary of the language but altered its syntax, which began to take on a Western hypotactic form (the stories of Gnessin are a good example of this). The great turning point came, of course, when Hebrew became the spoken language of Eretz Yisrael. "We are now in a new era," wrote the critic and author Yaacov Rabinowitz in the journal *Heidim* [*Echoes*] in 1922:

> We have carried the language from the text to the mouth . . . and that has its own laws. . . . The mouth will not obey us meekly. We may be able to weaken it, to help it or to disturb it, but the mouth and the ear are fully alive. It is absurd to fear illegitimate and barbaric speech. We have resurrected the dead, and he has risen and is developing in his own way.

> The language will be neither biblical nor Mishnaic, neither European nor Oriental Hebrew, neither Ashkenazi nor Sephardi Hebrew, nor yet Yemenite Hebrew, but something new, unlike any of these but with something from them all.

Even before the spoken language had quite materialized, the advocates of formulation had protested the corruption and hybridization of Hebrew. But, just as they were powerless to stop the process then, so they were powerless now. In the 1930s and 1940s neologisms and irregular constructs spilled from the spoken language into prose writings and translations, and canonical purity was lost. All that native-born writers such as Mossinsohn, Shamir, and Hanoch Bartov had to do was listen to the way people around them talked and introduce elements from the spoken dialect into their writings. It was a slow process that succeeded in producing a literary language only in the 1960s—if, indeed, it has yet succeeded in this endeavor.

* * *

The past ninety years of Hebrew literary production are best organized around four different generations of writers. The authors within each group share something of the same biography, even if they nonetheless distinguish themselves from each other and certain members from different generations have more in common with each other than with their compeers. The first generation covers the period between the 1880s and the 1920s. Most of its writers lived in the diaspora and experienced the pogroms and mass migrations that drove both Jewish history and its literature. They tended to write in Yiddish as well as in Hebrew. Mendele, Frischmann, Peretz, Berdyczewski, and Ben-Avigdor belong to this generation. Coexisting with this generation of European figures was a Palestinian community of First Aliyah and "Old Yishuv" (the original settlements in Palestine) authors (e.g., Y. Barzilai-Eisenstadt and M. Smilansky), who wrote about the experience of Eretz Yisrael.

The second generation made its appearance at the turn of the century and includes several groups. Their best writings were produced in the diaspora, but most of these authors eventually settled in Palestine, where they created the new Hebrew literary center that would come to define the new, national (Israeli) Hebrew literature. The leading figures were Bialik and Brenner. Others included Berkowitz, Gershon Shoffman, Uri Nissan Gnessin, Yaacov Steinberg, Elisheva Bikhovski, and Devorah Baron. Members of this group of writers, whose literary careers began in Palestine rather than in the diaspora, were Zemach, Aharon Reuveni, Dov Kimhi, Lev Arieh Arieli-Orloff, Agnon, and the native-born Burla and Shami.

The third generation enters the literary stage at the end of the First World War. Most of these writers—Nathan Bistritski, Aharon Ever-Hadani,

Yitzhak Shenhar, Yehoshua Bar-Yosef, Horowitz, and Hazaz—arrived in Palestine with the Third and Fourth Aliyot, when Zionist enthusiasm reached its peak. The dominant experiences of their lives were the two world wars, the Holocaust, and the settlement in Eretz Yisrael, the pioneering experience emerging as their primary collective experience (the notable exception to this is David Vogel). This generation had an American branch, led by Shimon Halkin and Reuven Wallenrod.

The fourth generation, encompassing two main groups—those born in the 1920s and those born in the 1930s and 1940s—is predominantly native born. The older ones made their literary appearance in the late 1930s, and the younger in the late 1950s. The annihilation of the Jews of Europe, the War of Independence, and the creation of the state of Israel dominated their lives. The writers of this generation tend to be more critical of Jewish tradition than do their predecessors, and sometimes also of Zionist ideology. To this generation belong S. Yizhar, Benjamin Tammuz, Moshe Shamir, Yonat and Alexander Sened, Yehuda Amichai, Pinhas Sadeh, Aharon Appelfeld, Amalia Kahana-Carmon, Yoram Kaniuk, Amos Oz, A. B. Yehoshua, Yehoshua Kenaz, and others.

There is no way that a single literary history can do justice to the richness and diversity of Hebrew literature over almost a century of its production, as the Jewish people moved from diasporic consciousness to national identity and, "against all odds," not only created for itself political nationhood but virtually narrated itself ex nihilo into cultural, linguistic, and literary existence. The following story of Hebrew literature is a story of revival and revision—of an ancient language, of a history, and finally of a people. It is not simply a story of the struggle of the Jewish people against an inhospitable and oft-times punishing non-Jewish world (as in much non-Israeli Jewish fiction and in some Israeli fiction as well). Rather, it deals as well with internal divisions: a people's hesitancy and uncertainty, not always sure of what it wants or how to get it or how to represent such human striving in the full complexity of its privacy and collectivity. The story of modern Hebrew literature, in other words, is the story in the people's own words (and language) of a people's struggle within itself as it takes upon itself, for the first time in its history, full responsibility for a hard-won and sometimes very painful cultural and, finally, political autonomy.

2

MENDELE MOKHER SEFORIM
FORMULATION AND THE
STIRRINGS OF HEBREW SOCIAL REALISM

> If two Jews were to be shipwrecked on one
> of those desert islands, where there was
> not one other human being, there is no
> doubt that one of them would open a
> shop, and the other would start some little
> business of his own, and they would give
> each other credit.
>
> —THE BOOK OF BEGGARS, P. 100

Mendele Mokher Seforim ("Mendele the Book Peddler") began his literary career in the 1860s, writing in Hebrew as one of the *maskilim* (expo-
nents of the Haskalah). He later switched to Yiddish, and in the 1880s,
following his arrival in Odessa, returned to Hebrew writing. This return
to Hebrew was decisive for the future course of modern Hebrew literature. It was marked by his writing a series of short stories. He then proceeded to translate his own Yiddish novels into Hebrew. These translations themselves constituted a major contribution to Hebrew fiction and
were welcomed as such by figures such as Ahad Haam and Bialik. Those
writers who opposed Mendele, no less than those who followed his example, had to contend not only with the intellectual and aesthetic challenge of his writings (Brenner credited him with setting the criteria for
Jewish social critique) but with his linguistic example as well. Dubbing
him "the formulator," Bialik put it this way in his book on Mendele: "If
ever the wheel comes round again and literature returns to the biblical
style, it will be a totally different one—a post-Mendele biblical style."

Mendele's stylistic solutions to the problems of Hebrew writing determined the course of Hebrew literary history, his two major inheritors being Agnon and Hazaz. In refusing the goals and assumptions of the Haskalah, Mendele also rejected the dominant style of Hebrew fiction, as characterized by its major representative, Abraham Mapu.

Inspired by positivist Russian critique, notably that of Belinsky, Mendele abandoned fiction's elevated plots, characterizations, and canonical language, with its lavish use of biblical phrases. He strove instead for a more realistic depiction of everyday Jewish existence. He might, in this endeavor, have returned to writing in Yiddish, which afforded the unmediated immediacy between writer and reader that Mendele sought. Unlike Hebrew, Yiddish was largely independent of canonical sources. It abounded in colorful and comical phrases, drawn largely from common folk speech, which could be directly cited in the text. Instead Mendele made the artistic move that would redefine the entire literature. In an effort to achieve something of the vitality of Yiddish, he mined all the historical layers of the Hebrew language, from biblical to rabbinical texts to commentaries. He played fast and loose with classical Hebrew, pitching Hebrew words and phrases against reality and constructing a new linguistic medium for the literature.

The following passage, which opens the story "Shem and Japeth in the Train" ["Shem vaYefet ba'agalah," 1890], serves as a useful introduction to Mendele generally and, in particular, to the linguistic revolution Mendele launched in his wild bid to produce a secular Hebrew fiction:

> There, in haste and confusion, our brethren press on, with bundles of every size and shape in their hands and on their shoulders; women too, encumbered with pillows and bolsters and wailing infants; all jostling one another as they perilously hoist themselves up the ladder to the third-class compartments, where a fresh battle will be fought for places in the congested train. And I, Mendele the Bookseller, burdened with my goods and chattels, join manfully in the fray: I climb, stop, and jostle my way through as one of the crowd. Yet, while we Jews hustle and work ourselves into a state of frenzied irritability, lest, Heaven forbid, someone should get ahead of us in the crush and while we gaze beseechingly upon the railway employees, as if the fact that we are traveling at all indicates an unrequited act of grace on their part—all this while, the gentile passengers are strolling up and down the hallway in front of the station with their luggage and waiting until the bell rings for a second or even a third time, when they will mount the train at leisure, and each proceed to his appointed place. (p. 19)

In the Hebrew, these lines do not achieve their satiric force simply, as in the English translation, from the sufficiently humorous comedy of overly encumbered poor Jews awkwardly managing their way onto a train (a familiar enough scene of Jewish self-parody). Rather, the play derives from the juxtaposition between the biblical events, conjured in the allusions and linguistic rhythms of the text, and the commonplace events of the scene. Some of this biblical reference functions in the manner of general literary allusion. References to various passages from the Torah, the Prophets, the Book of Esther, some of which constitute unique appearances in the classical materials, produce the mutual interrogation of later and earlier texts. This results in everything from interpretive depth to sheer comedy.

But the intertextuality of Mendele's description extends further than thematic evocation. It linguistically constructs the passage itself. And this produces a kind of linguistic rather than thematic allusion, which, in the case of Hebrew writing, does nothing less than create a new, secular, literary language. For example, the opening phrase of the English—"in haste and confusion"—achieves a much fuller and more complex rendering in the Hebrew. The passage begins and is structured by a particular phraseology which appears in Exodus 32:18–20, when Moses and Joshua are descending to the camp of the Israelites after the people have built the golden calf. "There is a noise of war in the camp," Joshua has said to Moses; and then he continues (the structural elements being picked up by Mendele's Hebrew text appearing in italics): "*It is not the voice of them that shout* for mastery, *neither is it the voice of them that cry* for being overcome, *but the noise of them that sing* do I hear" (p. 19) (in Mendele a literal translation of the opening phrases would be: "It was not the voice of them who are being driven out by fire, nor the voice of those escaping thieves, just the voice of Jews gathering at the railway station").

Setting his contemporary narrative into an ancient mold, Mendele does more than produce parody and satire. He marks the Jewishness of this text (and, one might extrapolate, of Jewish secular literature in general) as a linguistic as much as a thematic entity; and he provides his subject, which is Jewish folly and grotesquerie, with its internality within Jewish history and culture. However much Jewish behavior (like all human behavior) might serve as universal allegory, it also has a specifically Jewish density of meaning. This feature emerges not only through telling the story of Jewish experience but also through the literary and cultural tradition that his text reproduces as language itself. Mendele creates a new Hebrew language, grounded in tradition and yet capable of producing a contemporary fictional literature.

In secularizing canonical texts, Mendele was able to expose the hollowness of ancient clichés. By simultaneously synthesizing divergent linguistic layers (often playing between Yiddish and Hebrew) and restoring to ancient constructions and metaphorical expressions their original literal meanings, he succeeded not only in approximating the vibrancy of Yiddish writing but also in humanizing the exalted language. In giving contemporary Hebrew fiction a language, he also produced its uniqueness within modern European writing. Precisely because the resulting style hovered between mimetic representation and canonical allusion, Mendele's fiction, for all its social critique, never became quite realistic. Consequently, Mendele manufactured a fictional form distinct from the related traditions of European naturalism and realism, from which it was also derived.

Like many other writers of his time, Mendele expressed profound disillusion with the failed aspirations of the Haskalah. In temperament a rationalist, Mendele desired the evolution of Jewish society beyond its disfigurement, when it would take on the contours of a more rational existence. But his experience of European Jewish life did not encourage confidence in such possibilities of gradual development and amelioration. In direct contradistinction to the dominant assumptions of the Haskalah, he saw that the conditions of Jewish life in Europe demanded immediate social and intellectual revolution. Therefore, what began for him as social satire, which depicted the lives of Jews in Lithuania—in the Pale of Settlement—as well as in the big city of Odessa, eventually evolved into a literature of the grotesque, which depicted reality as essentially and irreparably deformed. Mendele was less concerned with the symptoms of Jewish communal dysfunction, that is, with those social manifestations that might be thought amenable to social reform, than with the inherent disease of diaspora existence itself—a disease which Mendele insisted on diagnosing with unswerving accuracy, and with no small measure of pain and compassion.

Thus, for example, listening to the "great noise and shouting hubbub and wailing" of his fellow *beggarsburghers,* the narrator of the short story "Burned Out" ["Hanisrafim"; also published in English as "Victims of the Fire"] can respond to the catastrophe of a Jewish community laid to waste by fire with both contempt and sorrow. "Scatter, beggars!" he chastises them ("gently," we are told); "why are you bunched together, crowded, fighting, squabbling, and annoying each other? You're only harming yourselves" (pp. 20–21). But while Mendele is thus haranguing them, "one wretched child, a weak, frail boy" lays his head on Mendele's knees and goes to sleep. Mendele will not permit the parents of this wretched child to disturb his slumbers by removing him.

Therefore, Mendele's entire presentation of the *beggarsburghers* as "that great horde of men and women, children and suckling babes, all of them with their clothes torn, barefoot, hungry and thirsty, their faces as sooty as the bottom of a pot" (p. 18), and his tirade against their folly and greed, has to be understood as taking place with the child sleeping on his knee. Though it may be impossible to identify the precise register of the following statement, the possibility of the sincerity of its grief is not to be dismissed out of hand. "My heart cried out to the Lord," he tells us. "'Oh you heavens, . . . how afflicted are the Jews'" (p. 23).

This feature of pathos joined to bitter satire achieves searing power in Mendele's most sophisticated and affecting work, *The Book of Beggars* [*Sefer haqabtsanim*]. (The Yiddish original, *Fishke der Krumer,* appeared in 1888; Mendele's own Hebrew version was published between 1909 and 1912. The English translation appears in the volume *Fishke the Lame.*) The novel is a complex set of narratives within narratives; Mendele's own framing of it makes way for the narrative interventions of (among others) his interlocutor Reb Alter, also a traveling peddler, and, finally, and most important, Fishke the Lame, whose story constitutes the major subject of the book. The novel is wit, humor, and social grotesquerie raised to the power of tragic knowledge, never surrendering the comic note that saves the narrative (let alone the human condition it describes) from excessive self-pity.

For example, in one of the opening scenes, when Reb Mendele and Reb Alter first run into each other, the two Jews are presented as ridiculous mirrors of each other and of the split that each one of them embodies between their religious and their pagan tendencies. It is a Jewish fast-day, and Mendele (likely Alter, too) is hard at work deliberating between his spiritual and his physical desires. Both of them are driving their wagons attired in their prayer shawls and phylacteries when they stop to chat and argue in the middle of the road. The scene is nothing if not a parody of Jews caught, almost literally, between the secular and the sacred. But it is parody in the grip of something much more sinister and dire that significantly recasts the text's social critique of the Jews:

> Anyhow the while Alter's fuming so, and generally working himself up . . . a couple of cartloads of heathen yokelry come along the road. . . . Well, now, obviously they are sort of riled at seeing a pair of wagons blocking the road; so now they're also shouting at us to clear the way and let 'em pass. But when they pull up close, and see the two of us standing there, cowled in our prayershawls like that, with big scripboxes on both our heads and all the rest, well that's when they get kind of abusive and disrespectful on a sudden; and start into raggin' us, don't you know. . . . Well naturally both me and Alter hastened to comply. And don't you know but a couple towheaded bucks from amongst that rowdy crowd was good enough to climb down from off their carts and bear a hand. Which was kind of nice of them, when you only think of it. . . . With their

pair of "Esau's kin" (as 'twere) givin' us a hand, it was a different story altogether . . . because these lads really did have the knack; for pushing, I mean, . . . Anyway the moment the road was clear, the whole gang of country clowns went their ways. . . . Though they were still laughing uproariously, and ragging us 'bout being all "doll up" . . . and looking like we was priests! . . . while hollering insults at us, along the lines of "*Here piggy, piggy, piggy.*" . . . Now, this didn't seem to trouble Alter very much . . . but did too bother me. . . . And I addressed a prayer to the Almighty in the style much favored of our womenfolk, as it seemed to suit my mood. (*Tales of Mendele,* pp. 24–26)

The rest of the book, with its raw and unrelenting depiction of Jewish depravity, cannot but be read against the larger world of threat and victimization within which the East European Jewish experience occurs (at one point Mendele will have one of his *peoth*—earlocks—cut off by a gentile policeman). This theme predominates in a text such as "Shem and Japeth in the Train."

Still, the central narrative of *The Book of Beggars* does not concern Jewish-gentile relations. It deals, rather, with the self-contained universe of Jewish thieves and beggars, who come to constitute a microcosm of the Jewish community in its most desperate and depraved outlines. There are the "*Infantry, or your Foot-paupers . . . and the Cavalry, or your Horse-drawn paupers . . . the Wild-folk, or Paupers-of-the-field . . . your Paupers-in-ordinary, or Beggars-simple . . . Holy-service paupers . . . Torah-and-Devotions paupers,*" and so on and so forth. In short, among "*all Jewry's Paupery*" begging is an "art," and "genuine articles" like Fishke, who is lame, and his wife, who is blind, are particularly valuable property within the community (ibid., pp. 148–171). Within this world of violence and abuse, two of the characters—Fishke and the young hunchback girl, Beyla, who is the victim of abandonment and sexual abuse—discover each other and fall in love. However, they are cruelly separated when the beggar caravan moves on, taking Beyla with them and leaving Fishke trussed up and abandoned to die, until he is discovered by Reb Alter to whom (along with Mendele) he narrates his tale.

But the satire exceeds even its depiction of the beggars. For in a shocking turn of plot, which almost unbearably tightens the screw of the text's social critique and produces the deep gravity of its ethical engagement, it emerges that the father who abandoned Beyla's mother, who in turn abandoned her, is none other than Reb Alter himself. The wretched of Mendele's earth are indeed social victims. But their victimizers include apparently upright citizens who are no less deformed than their victims. Although at the end of the text Reb Alter takes it upon himself to find and save his daughter, it is by no means certain that rescue is the name of Mendele's game, even if humor continues to mitigate the despair:

In a trice my Alter vaulted out of the wagon onto the ground and was climbing into his cart. And taking leave of us at a distance, he'd got his thills turned round and had whipped up his mare, and set out on his way. For a time Fishke and I silently followed his progress from behind. I looked up at the sky again, where moon and stars followed their appointed paths, though the aspect they bore was different from the one they had before—haughty they looked so away up high, and so far, so very far from our paltry, earthbound selves. It saddened. No happy thought that. . . .

I gee-upped my "eagle" (so-called in coachman's lingo), teching him up with my whip . . . and at a rather late hour my cart jarred over the pitted, dark streets of Glupsk, the clop of hooves and rattle of heel, and the chinking of collar bell, all seemingly drumming up the clamoring call of the town crier by night: "*Oyez! O-yez! a-here b-eee a fresh pair of Jewish gents made their way to Glupsk!*" (Ibid., pp. 297–298)

As in *Fishke the Lame,* Mendele's characters represent mentalities rather than personalities. He is concerned not with individual Jews but rather with forms of Jewish behavior which were not self-determined but were rather produced by external social conditions. The characters are static and cartoon-like, drawn from a fairly conventional inventory of social stereotypes and possessing few distinctive qualities or psychological verisimilitude. For the most part, they are debased, petty wheeler-dealers, as ridiculous as they are repulsive, who are governed by economic and social forces beyond their control. Provincials without any sense of historical or geographical proportion who reduce universal concepts to their own size, they are, for all their pettiness and greed, also wretched misfits, floundering around helplessly in a cruel and inexplicable world, pathetic victims of impersonal circumstance. And as much as the narrator who narrates their story despises them, he also feels pity and compassion for them. The stories produce considerable humor alongside their social critique.

In a good many of his stories and novels, including *The Book of Beggars,* "Shem and Japheth in the Train," "The Time of the Earthquake" ["Biymei hara'ash"], the opening of *In Those Days* [*Bayamim haheim*], *The Travels of Benjamin III* [*Masa'ot Binyamin hashlishi*], and the conclusion of "The Wishing Ring" ["Be'emek habkhah," literally: "In the Valley of Tears"], this narrator of the tale is none other than "Mendele" himself, the ordinary, work-a-day-world sort of Jew, close to his people and much like them. Mendele, however, as we have seen, is also somewhat detached, possessing a broader vision. As partially implicated, partially objective witness, he is capable of judgment and satirical interpretation, but also of compassion and warmth. The narrator's wry comments reframe the narrative, taking the sting out of many of its excruciatingly painful climaxes.

Taking on both a socially pragmatic and a metaphysically expansive program for his writings, and blending together various literary genres and conventions of world literature with stylistic elements and symbols derived from Jewish tradition, Mendele produced a wholly original literary text. Essentially, he incorporated four complementary literary traditions, two of them Jewish, two of them deriving from the literatures of Europe. One of the Jewish forms that Mendele adapted was the sentimental Yiddish tale, which was mere trivial melodrama. The other was the novel of the Haskalah, which, in his youth, he had himself helped to fashion. The dominant feature of pseudo-romantic Haskalah fiction had been its ideological component, in particular the portrayal of the conflict between the Enlightenment and its opponents, to which all other features of the text, including the story's love interest, were subordinated.

The European influences that Mendele absorbed were not only sharply differentiated from their Jewish counterparts but themselves represented diverse traditions. These included, on the one hand, Russian social satire, as practiced by such figures as Gogol and Saltykov-Shchedrin and, on the other, a variety of diverse European genres, made accessible to him in Russian translation, including the sentimental novel (Samuel Richardson's *Pamela*), the picaresque (Richard Fielding's *Tom Jones*), the bildungsroman (Charles Dickens's *David Copperfield* and *Oliver Twist*), and the novel of social pathos (Victor Hugo's *The Hunchback of Notre Dame*). To some degree Yiddish sentimentality and melodrama corresponded to the Anglo-French tradition, and Haskalah-inspired social satires to the Russian tradition, producing doublings and discrepancies between and among the various influences on his work. The Jewish forms were of lesser artistic quality than the European models. Nonetheless, they blended with their European counterparts to create rich artistic tensions.

The Travels of Benjamin III (published in Hebrew in the periodical *Hapardes* [*The Orchard*] in 1896), for example, is a parody of a picaresque novel. The two protagonists, Benjamin and Senderl, are homegrown versions of Cervantes' Don Quixote and Sancho Panza, a pair of static characters who wander from place to place—"Idletown" ("Batalon"), "Darktown" ("Zalmonah"), "Foolstown" ("Kessalon")—their fortunes always remaining unaltered. Ostensibly, they are looking for the legendary "ten lost tribes of Israel." In actual fact, they are only fleeing their wives. The two characters lack the adventurous spirit which animates the true traveler, and their escapades only succeed in delivering them to a military jail. It is possible that the story conceals a political-satiric motive and that Mendele intended his story to poke fun at the Hibbat Zion movement. A contemporary, anachronistic reading, which misses the satirical distortion of the text, will also likely miss these further dimensions of Mendele's biting wit.

"The Wishing Ring," which appeared in *Hashiloah* [*The Shiloah*] in 1897, is sentimental fiction. Its first Yiddish version was entitled "Vinshfingerl," and its message was that the Haskalah was a magic ring which could lead the story's children from the valley of their tears into the light of day. As in all sentimental novels, the plot is based on an unconvincing intrigue. The main characters are Hershele, Moishele, and Baileh, poor children of the Pale of Settlement, who find themselves in the menacing city, which almost destroys them. Baileh is abducted by pimps, Moishele by kidnappers for the Czar's army, and Hershele, too, faces grave dangers. Jewish society is depicted, at least in part, as a criminal gang, preying upon its own children. Through a very contrived plot, the children are saved by some well-meaning *maskilim*. But their rescue later turns out to be illusory. After Hershele leaves the Pale of Settlement and becomes a *maskil* himself, the girl Baileh is violated by gentile rioters, and the Haskalah-type solution, with which the early Yiddish version concluded, is changed in a pathos-laden epilogue. This is the most doleful of Mendele's stories. It escapes cloying sentimentality only because of ironic and mocking digressions that break the otherwise causal narrative.

Mendele's last novella, written from the start in Hebrew, was the autobiographical *In Those Days*. More than any other of his writings it heralded a new era in Hebrew fiction. It is in fact a kind of mournful pseudo-autobiography, in which the author contemplates with sadness and humor his lost childhood and the vanishing world of the Jewish village. This may be one of the first stories of self-awareness in Hebrew fiction. Here idyllic and nostalgic qualities overcome satire and the grotesque. The old narrator observes his young self and contemplates his own writings and the meaning of his life. The impact of this text on the coming generations, on Berkowitz, Barash, Agnon, Hazaz, and Bialik (in such stories as "After-growth" ["Safiah"] and "The Offended Trumpet" ["Hahatsots-rah nitbayshah"]), was perhaps even greater than that of Mendele's major works.

* * *

In a letter to his friend Menashe Margolis, which he included as a foreword to *Fishke der Krumer*, Mendele described his tragicomic vision of the Jewish diaspora in this way:

> Sad is my song in the chorus of Jewish literature. In my writing the Jew is shown as he is, through and through—a Jew who, even when he hums a cheerful song, sounds from afar as if he were weeping, as if there were grief in it. His singing always has an air of Lamentations about it. When he laughs, tears course from his eyes. He may wish to rejoice a little, but a bitter sigh breaks from his breast, as though a great cry of *oy vay* is always on his tongue. (p. 5, 1888 edition)

Though the Jew as he is will, in the literature of Eretz Yisrael, come to meet stiff competition from the image of the Jew as he (or she) might be, nonetheless, the attempt to define that Jew and depict his or her essential consciousness continues to characterize one major trajectory of modern Hebrew literature. The Jew will emerge differently in different writers and be drawn through a range of aesthetic conventions in accordance with a variety of social and cultural agendas. But for the writers of Hebrew romantic fiction, as for the writers of social and psychological realism, the interpretive lens of literature focuses on the same individual who occupies the first of the modern Hebrew writers, Mendele Mokher Seforim. It is to the writers of Hebrew romanticism that we now turn.

3

HEBREW LITERARY ROMANTICISM
RELIGION, MYTH, AND THE
WESTERNIZATION OF HEBREW LITERATURE

Although Mendele and his younger contemporaries, such as David Frisch-mann, I. L. Peretz, M. Y. Berdyczewski, and M. Z. Feierberg, all covered the same social ground, namely, the Jewish shtetl, they not only evoked different aspects of this variegated world, but they did so in radically different ways. The younger writers were not persuaded either by the tradition of the Haskalah or the formulated language of Mendele, with its syntactical symmetries and intertextual allusions. They formed the vanguard of a literary revolution that revamped Hebrew fiction.

In the early days of the two main Jewish national movements in Eastern Europe—the Bund and Hibbat Zion—Hebrew literature, like its counterparts in Europe, bore heavy traces of the romantic movement. In fact, romantic elements continued to characterize Hebrew writing even after romanticism in other European literatures had begun to yield to newer literary currents. Thus, Hebrew romantic fiction was a mixture of traditions, old and modern. Frischmann and Berdyczewski followed both the original romantic style (as represented by Alexander Dumas, Lord Byron, Alexander Pushkin, Hans Christian Andersen) and its modern manifestations (notably, the symbolism of Maurice Maeterlinck and Anatole France). Their writings took on many of the features of European romanticism: poetic-picturesque diction, replete with symbols and myths; the image of the poet as the bearer of the suffering of the world; and a longing for the innocence and perfection of a distant past. The protagonists are moved by romantic weltschmerz. They embrace the universal human condition through sympathy for the weak and a sense of cosmic loneliness and estrangement. In addition, they emphasize distinctively national themes. They also celebrate the great rebel who resists social convention, such as, for example, the Nietzsche-inspired Promethean heroes of Berdyczewski, who revolt against both God and humankind. Frischmann even translated *Thus Spoke Zarathustra* into Hebrew.

Also in keeping with their romanticism, many of the writers' motifs were derived from folklore—not, as in the European literatures, medieval epic romance or peasant lore or local legends, but specifically Jewish myths and stories. Peretz and Berdyczewski even collected such folk tales and songs, while Feierberg frequently used them in his writings. Among other kinds of writings, Frischmann and Peretz produced *feuilletons,* works of popular fiction catering to public tastes.

The four writers did not form a literary group. There was intense rivalry between Peretz and Frischmann, and Feierberg criticized Berdyczewski. But Berdyczewski considered Feierberg an ally and was close to both Peretz and Frischmann. Frischmann and Peretz started out in the footsteps of the *maskilim.* They later published their stories in the popular *sifrei agorah* anthologies of Ben-Avigdor, which were supposed to be the organ of the new "Hebrew naturalism." Though some of Berdyczewski's stories actually resembled those of Ben-Avigdor and his coterie, most of Frischmann's and Peretz's work amounted to little more than sentimental depictions of everyday life. The romantics (Peretz, for example) later criticized Ben-Avigdor, whose literary populism, they argued, made nonsense of his claim that he was writing realistic fiction. If Mendele and others wrote something like novels, Frischmann, Peretz, Berdyczewski, and Feierberg produced those introverted fictional forms that Northrop Frye had designated *romance* and *confession,* in which external reality is a projection of the perceiving self (romance) and in which that self articulates and reveals its inner world (confession).

DAVID FRISCHMANN

As critic, translator, and editor, Frischmann seemed to his contemporaries nothing less than the revolutionary pioneer who would deliver Hebrew literature from the abyss of Jewish self-enclosure to the safe shores of European civilization. Born near Lodz in 1859 and raised there at a time when the city stood at the crossroads of Jewish, Polish, and German culture, Frischmann was educated in Breslau, Germany, which became his spiritual homeland. At the height of his career, between 1918 and 1921, he edited the literary quarterly *Hatkufah* [*The Epoch*]. During this period he also translated various writers into Hebrew, among them Oscar Wilde, Rabindranath Tagore, Byron, Anatole France, F. Schumacher, Andersen, Spielhagen, Pushkin, Ibsen, the Brothers Grimm, and Nietzsche. These

translations introduced a generation of Jewish readers to Western literature and "gentile" culture. As editor of the weekly *Hador* [*The Generation*], 1901–1904, Frischmann cultivated the idea of art for art's sake. His
motto, taken from Goethe, was: "By means of the good we gradually give
rise to right feeling and taste for the good." Of this emphasis on beauty
and good taste Frischmann became his generation's leading arbiter. He
was one of the first Western European critics of Hebrew literature, which,
before his appearance, had been dominated by Russian influences.

Thus, Frischmann occupies a unique and significant position in Hebrew literary history, even though he did not himself produce a distinguished canon of literary texts. His fiction, which he began publishing
along with reviews, poems, and translations at an early age, was Haskalah-
inspired, imitative, and of mediocre literary quality, with little social significance. He also wrote pathos-laden stories resembling the would-be
naturalistic tales written by the socially engaged but ungifted positivists
led by Ben-Avigdor. Even though these stories dealt with real issues, such
as the disintegration of the community, the isolation of the older generation, and anti-Semitism, nevertheless they inclined toward the fabulous
and were marred by romantic yearnings for worldly happiness. If anything, his fiction served merely as a transition between the writings of the
Haskalah and the new literature.

The one exception by which Frischmann did achieve some sort of
distinction was his collection of stories entitled *In the Desert* [*Bamidbar*]
(1923). Set during the time of the Israelites' wanderings in the desert
between Egypt and the Promised Land, these stories revolve around the
conflicts between the people and their priests. In *In the Desert* Frischmann
manages what elsewhere eludes him: the transition from the social tale to
the romance, from depictions of everyday life to flights of imagination.
Some critics interpreted these tales as timely moral fables, upholding love
as opposed to religious law, defending the poor and downtrodden against
the rigidity of social convention, and supporting the rebel against the re-
pressive patriarchs and priests. However, the conflicts in all these stories
are so highly colored by the fabulous and by quasi-biblical language, exotic mythical desert backdrops, and exaggerated characterizations that the
stories do not achieve any straightforward level of referentiality that might
make them into contemporary moral parables. Instead, they maintain an
exotic, emotive quality, constructed out of ancient rites, magic, archaic
laws, and folk motifs: "And in those wondrous days the heavens were a
thousandfold newer and bluer than they are now, and the earth was a
thousand times thousandfold fresher and greener than it is now, and love
also was a thousand-thousand times thousandfold stronger and more im-
passioned than love is in our time" ("Dances" ["Meholot"]). Death-in-
love (*liebestod* in German) and similar elements recall the European ro-

mantic tradition, as in the story "The Brazen Serpent" ["Nahash hane-hoshet"], where the men of the tribe of Dodanim must avoid loving women or risk death. The hero, Dishon ben Keturah, who does fall in love with a woman, perishes before his mother can cure him with the aid of the brazen serpent.

For Frischmann the Hebrew Bible was the nation's pre-history and its heritage. By reassessing myths of older and later sources (the role of the priests, the ancient laws, the magician-rabbis of Prague, and so on), he attempted to effect changes in the present. At the same time, by transposing contemporary issues onto the archaic world, he sought to revivify, revitalize, and reclaim that world for a contemporary audience. In interpreting the biblical text anti-traditionally, Frischmann followed the Haskalah, thus linking his writings to those of Berdyczewski and, later on, Tchernichowski. He also followed the tradition of the Haskalah in using unadapted biblical diction. For this reason, he made no contribution to the actual language of Hebrew fiction, even though, by avoiding the formulation of Mendele and others, he helped usher in the opposition to it.

I. L. PERETZ

Like Frischmann, I. L. Peretz was educated, cosmopolitan, and yet deeply rooted in the world of East European Jewry. He was brought up in his native Zamosc, where he learned German, Russian, and Polish as well as the usual Yiddish and Hebrew. He traveled for a while, and in 1878 returned and began to practice law. In 1889 he settled permanently in Warsaw, where he became a central figure on the Yiddish and Hebrew literary scene. Like Frischmann, he engaged in a variety of literary activities, producing plays, criticism, essays, *feuilletons,* and poetry, as well as fiction. Also like Frischmann, he began his career in Hebrew literature as a talented practitioner of the Haskalah tradition. Eventually he matured into a master of the sentimental commonplace story.

Peretz began his literary career in 1874 by publishing poetry in Polish. By 1875 he was writing fiction in Hebrew and Yiddish, becoming increasingly identified with Yiddish after 1888. Indeed, although his fiction won him a fairly central place in Hebrew literature, his major impact was on the Yiddish literary tradition, with which, as one of the spiritual fathers of the Bund, he was ideologically identified. This bilingualism of his literary output was decisive for the role he was to play in Hebrew literature. While there is probably no way to prove a direct correlation between the themes and structures of a particular work and the language in which those themes and structures are expressed, still and all the distinctive stylistic qualities of the two languages could not but have affected the works produced in them. In this contest between Yiddish and Hebrew as the vehicles of Peretz's prose, canonical Hebrew could provide no match for colorful Yiddish expressions strongly rooted in folk speech. In order to achieve in Hebrew the comic effect that was achieved through a few brief strokes of his Yiddish pen, Peretz had to burden his dialogues with lengthy background descriptions and superfluous characterizations.

Peretz's chief contribution to Hebrew literature was not in terms of the excellence of his own Hebrew prose style, but, rather, in the wealth of structures which he introduced into both Hebrew and Yiddish literature. So profoundly was Peretz influenced by European literature that he was accused of merely imitating other writers. Nonetheless, his immersion in the European tradition was to enrich the inventory of both Yiddish and Hebrew fictional forms. There is, for example, not a single short story form which cannot be found in his oeuvre. He also developed the epistolary novel and the travel tale. The epistolary form, which reveals Peretz's resemblance to his great contemporary Sholem Aleichem, allowed the narrator-protagonist to depict his own situation in his own words while providing more oblique or indirect glimpses into the lives of the other characters. "The Woman Mrs. Hannah" ["Ha'ishah marat Hanah"], which was published in Hebrew in the periodical *Hatsfirah* [*The Siren*] in 1896 and in Yiddish in the *Collected Works* in 1901, is a sophisticated example of this form. It consists of nine letters of different family members to Hannah and the beginning of a letter from Hannah to her husband. The form objectifies the heroine's abandonment by all the people around her. At the same time it serves to illuminate her from several different perspectives. The series of letters concludes with one more external vantage point: that of the "editor" of the letters. "This unfinished letter," he writes, "was among the other letters, hereby transcribed from the spoken language, which were found among the clothes of the woman Hannah, who has lost her mind." The travel tale was another form Peretz used skillfully. As a government official taking the census of the various communities, the narrator in a work such as *Travel Sketches* [*Tsiyurei masa'*] was permitted to describe, as an unimplicated observer, various facets of life in the Pale of Settlement.

Peretz's narrative techniques were also sophisticated and varied. He was fond of using patterns of repetition that depended either on drawing parallels or projecting opposites. In "Three Gifts" ["Shalosh matanot"], for instance, three tales are set within a frame narrative. In each of the subsidiary tales a soul goes down to earth to look for evidences of redemptive human action. Each time, it finds a Jewish victim of gentile aggression who prefers religious values to life itself. These values achieve material form in the objects which the soul then proceeds to bring back to heaven (a handful of the earth, signifying the love of Eretz Yisrael; a pin, designating modesty of dress and demeanor; and a blood-stained thread from a yarmulke, evidencing religious conviction). Here, as in other of his moral parables, the parallel motifs and repeating serial structure give the three-fold story a powerful unity of ethical signification.

Another, related, structure that Peretz also used to good effect was antithesis and paradox: two persons reacting in opposite ways to equivalent situations. Generally, one of the characters appears to behave well, but in reality turns out to have done wrong, while the other enacts the reverse process. Peretz gave these stories of antithesis and paradox sharp ironic endings and moral climaxes, the virtuous person receiving his or her reward by some contrivance or miracle (cf. "The Pledge" ["Hapiqadon"]).

Peretz also played with narrative voice. An important structural device that he utilized was that of the bystander-narrator, a young child, for example, whose naive testimony casts an ironic light on the story. There was also the straightforward storyteller, who could be both an ironic interpreter of reality and its faithful chronicler. The storyteller's awareness of his audience often mitigates the narrative's pathos and creates fertile ambiguities. In fact, Peretz's major strength lay not so much in the situations he depicted or in his plots but in his dialogues—those that he conducted through his narrators with his readers, and those that took place among his protagonists.

Most of his protagonists are simple folk, such as Reb Johanan the Waterman, who, able to smell the difference between a true rabbinical scholar and a bogus one, stands as the antithesis of the airy intellectual type that was beginning to haunt not only Jewish literature but Jewish reality as well. For the most part, Peretz was more interested in general human conditions than in the individual. Even in those stories which initially appear to be "psychological," he directs the reader's attention away from the protagonist's emotions to the predicaments which produce those feelings. As Brenner once pointed out, Peretz was much more interested in staging brilliant juxtapositions and in presenting dramatic situations than in exploring the human soul (see Brenner's *Collected Works II*).

Although his readers tend to think of him primarily in terms of his Hasidic and folk tales, I. L. Peretz's corpus contains many other kinds of writing. Indeed, focusing only on his folk writings consigns a large part of his oeuvre to oblivion and unduly emphasizes the neo-romantic aspects of his work. Such a focus also distorts this neo-romanticism, since it allows readers to overlook his more "revolutionary" *feuilletons* and comical and grotesque tales, which subscribe to a different romantic tradition. Peretz's affiliation with romanticism is, indeed, a major feature of his writing. But it is often best evidenced by some of his lesser stories, many of them no more than impressionistic sketches that are rich in local color, others evoking the tragic roles played by individuals who seem to bear the world's sorrows on their frail shoulders (e.g., "Four Gems" ["Arba‘ ’avanim tovot"]). Focused on these and other themes of sadness, the tales and sketches are not memorable pieces; their synthesis of traditional Jewish materials and symbolism produces largely artificial effects. Yet they are infused with a subtle irony that redeems them as literary works. In many ways, Peretz's most interesting stories are his comic pieces, many of them in the nature of jests that constitute neither satire nor subtle irony, but a kind of expanded practical joke with a touch of implied social criticism mixed in. Nor are his talents as a *feuilletonist* to be dismissed. These were displayed in the *Yomtov Bletlach* [*Holy Day Pages*], a journal ostensibly devoted to the Jewish holidays, but in reality a seditious periodical that cleverly circumvented public censorship.

Peretz's romanticism constituted an important element in his social agenda. As a supporter of the Bund, Peretz expressed his affiliation with Jewish socialism through his biting social criticism. Peretz focused on the habits and customs which ruined the Jewish family (e.g., "A Virgin Marries" ["Betulah niseit"]) or discriminated against women ("The Woman Mrs. Hannah") or drove them to prostitution ("Sinful Blood" ["Dam hote’"]). He explored the stresses and abuses of human relationships in provincial society ("Pictures from Chaos" ["Tmunot me‘olam hatohu"]), the laziness of the Jewish community ("The Sabbath Goy" ["Hagoy shel shabat"]), and the community's mistreatment of the poor and the sick ("The Kaddish" ["Haqadish"]).

He also expressed his socialist sympathies through the social pathos of his stories. If his comic fiction exposed the absurdity of the dominant forces in Jewish or in human society at large, the tales of pathos aroused the reader's compassion by vividly depicting the state of its victims. As in the sentimental commonplace tales, Peretz mixed Haskalah plots and characters with a romantic quest for social change, producing melodramas that were more sentimental than romantic. While many stories of social critique had been written since the Haskalah in both Hebrew and Yiddish, Peretz's stories mark an important stage in the evolution of Hebrew literature because of their clear socialist sympathies.

A case in point is the later fiction, for which Peretz is primarily remembered and which is often considered no more than folk story or Hasidic tale. Such designations do not convey the complexity or depth of the author's achievement in these stories, in which he dealt in a different way with many of the same subjects he had already tackled in his sentimental fictions of the ordinary and everyday. Insofar as these works express the author's commitment to the common people, as opposed to those of privilege, and to those who are warm of heart and feeling (the Hasidim), as opposed to the legalistic and cerebral *mitnagdim* (as in "Bonche the Silent"

["Bonchei shtoq"], where a poor simple man is celebrated over respectable citizens and scholars), the Hasidic tales add an important mystical and folk element to the tradition of Hebrew romanticism.

Indeed, Peretz's attitude toward the pietism of Hasidism was primarily social in orientation. For him Hasidism was a social, ethical movement that in its essence expressed the religious needs of ordinary people and thereby celebrated a spiritual proletariat. The most complex of the folk tales or Hasidic stories were built upon moral opposites and had double plots (e.g., "Lowered Eyes" ["'Einayim mushpalot"]). They drew the obvious moral that genuine devotion, inner purity, simple needs, and love of humanity are the highest human values and that such values are to be found among ordinary Jews and in Hasidic society. "Lowered Eyes," for example, concerns two sisters. The younger falls in love with a non-Jewish landowner, but is married off instead to a Jew. Though her family considers her now redeemed, she persists in dreaming of her lover and is thus damned, her soul going to hell when she dies. The older sister, on the other hand, is abducted by non-Jewish noblemen and though her body is defiled her soul remains pure. Even though the community perceives her as fallen and buries her outside the Jewish cemetery, her soul, in the end, arrives in heaven.

In the stories' evocation of miracles and moral justice, and in their dedication to the simple folk and the rule of innocence, Peretz was a romantic symbolist who created uniquely Jewish fiction with a strong social message. Although at times Peretz's impressive structural innovations did more harm than good, his experiments with form sometimes coming at the expense of artistic authenticity, nonetheless his writing achieves cogency and power through the diversity of its modes and methodologies. And despite its lack of artistic success, the fiction marked the breakthrough of romanticism into the Hebrew literary tradition.

M. Y. BERDYCZEWSKI

Like Frischmann and Peretz, Micha Yosef Berdyczewski, too, began his career in the fold of the Haskalah and the sentimental commonplace stories of Ben-Avigdor and his school. His first story, "Quotation Marks" ["Gershayim"], appeared in 1890. Berdyczewski was unquestionably the most important romantic writer in modern Hebrew literature; no other writer was as influential in his day as he was. While the critics and writers who followed Mendele's formulation treated Berdyczewski with reserve, the younger generation regarded him as their stylistic and spiritual leader. Indeed, his impact extended as far as such later writers as Amos Oz. It may even be the case that his influence was even greater on subsequent authors than on his contemporaries.

Nonetheless, his contemporary influence was powerful, and the opposition fierce. The leading proponent of formulation, H. N. Bialik,
refused to publish Berdyczewski's *Summer and Winter* [*Kayitz vehoref*].
Even though he admitted that "there is a spark of a Jewish painter in this
man," still, he maintained, his "technique is ramshackle, and the corrupt
language degrades it" (from a letter to A. S. Gutmann, known as S. Ben-
Zion, in Bialik, *Letters*). Even more powerfully, perhaps, than Frischmann's and Peretz's praise of him, this kind of ambivalent, threatened
response of older critics such as Bialik served to establish Berdyczewski as
a trailblazer in Hebrew literature. As the writer who liberated the fiction
from its commitment to depict the ordinary and everyday in realistic
dimensions and who released it from Mendele's stylistic influence, Berdyczewski was to Brenner and other writers of Brenner's generation the
author who first gave voice to their contemporary concerns.

Berdyczewski redefined the preoccupation of Hebrew literature from
general Jewish issues (as prescribed by Berdyczewski's contemporary Asher Ginsburg [Ahad Haam]) to the subject of the individual. He gave that
individual his new identity: the torn and divided Jewish intellectual. And
he produced an anti-formulaic alternative to the style of Mendele and
Bialik. His followers were especially affected by his early works: *Two Camps*
[*Mahanayim*, which also appeared in English as *Dodgeball*], *Nonsense* [*Orva
parah*], and "Beyond the River" ["Me'ever lanahar"].

Like many of his contemporaries and successors, Berdyczewski did
not confine himself to a single literary language or a single activity. He
engaged in research and literary criticism and was a notable compiler and
interpreter of folk tales, some of which appeared in German before they
were published in Hebrew (such as *Der Born Juda's*). This placed him in
the forefront not only of Hebrew fiction but of Hebrew nonfiction as
well. Berdyczewski was born on August 19, 1865 in Medzibezh to a Hasidic rabbinical family; his writings wove together the tradition of German
romanticism (notably the writings of Schopenhauer and Nietzsche) and
the fantastic elements of Hasidism. He was the first Hebrew writer to
produce his own historiography of the Jews. Seeking to change the accepted view of Jewish history and tradition, he argued that an overly rational Jewish spirit had caused the dispersal and exile. Only by a thorough
spiritual upheaval, which would turn the people back toward nature, beauty, and the sword, could Jewish mentality be transformed, and, with it,
Jewish history. In his view, the disfigurement of the Jewish people could
only be cured by a fundamental change in the people's view of itself, which
meant also separating national and religious identity. To that end, his com-
pilation of myths and legends, *Mimekor Yisrael: Classical Jewish Folktales*
[*Mimekor Yisra'el*; literally: from the source of Israel], was intended to
demonstrate how Jewish culture had once been quite different from the

ways in which it was usually portrayed and the ways in which it had subsequently come to be distorted. Here, as in his stories, Berdyczewski put before his reading public many pagan and mythical fables from ancient Hebrew sources. These, in his view, expressed the archaic mysticism of the Jewish collective unconscious. By reintroducing these ancient materials, he intended to justify his call for a spiritual revolution.

Brenner's appreciation of Berdyczewski as the greatest Hebrew writer serves even today as a useful introduction to Berdyczewski's literary oeuvre. His writings, Brenner argued, expressed the author's emotions directly. Intensely charged subjects were overtly expressed in symbols, and there was no false pretense of objectivity. Confessional in format and written in a broken, elliptical, impressionist style, the fiction did not, like the works of Mendele or Ben-Zion, seek either to directly represent reality or to judge it. Rather, it endeavored to express the subjective, existential position of the author or protagonist. In contrast to Mendele, who saw the world as entire and solid and who, correspondingly, created fully formed character types, Berdyczewski perceived society as in a state of flux and flow. For this reason, Berdyczewski eschewed the purist rules of formulation. Rather, as Brenner observed, he fashioned his own linguistic rules to serve his artistic needs.

And yet, despite his revolt against Jewish tradition, in his articles and essays, as in his fiction, he remained deeply rooted in it. He plumbed its depths and drew upon its myths to construct a conduit between observed reality and a hidden mythical universe. The romantic assumptions informing this interest in legend and myth are reflected throughout his fiction, which everywhere sought to introduce into daily Jewish usage mythical figures and situations and archaic motifs. Because of his investment in the mythic and unconscious, he objected to the "mimetic" style as practiced by Mendele and Bialik. Although he proclaimed the individual to be the important subject of Hebrew literature, he was also conscious of and committed to the idea that the individual is bound to environment and cultural heritage.

Thus, for example, the narrator-protagonist of the short story "Beyond the River," from the collection *Without Hope* [*Bli tiqvot* (1899)], embodies disdain, even contempt, for the unenlightened religious mentality of his community, which, in his view, shuts it off from the world of beauty and nature. Yet he feels for that community and its traditions inexpressible, heart-rending tenderness. Indeed, he feels for the "wife of [his] bosom" a passion, both erotic and emotional, that seems impossible in the context of religious law and observance. Yet this passion exists, and is sanctioned by the community. It comes to stand for nothing less than a passion within Judaism itself:

On Saturday evening, when the whole congregation gathered in the house of the Lord for evening prayers, each man absorbed in his own world while his lips whispered to the Lord of the sabbath and the profane, my heart would carry me far away and I would stand there bewildered and amazed.

Sometimes I pitied my people and felt sorry for them, and was angry with their misguided teachers, who did not know the difference between darkness and light. But why did the children of Israel not break their bonds, once and for all? Why did they not open the windows? Why did they bar them? . . .

At noon, in the midday quiet, I sit on the soft divan in my father-in-law's house, and the beautiful girl, the wife of my bosom, sits beside me, sewing. She looks at me and I am far away, from her, from her father's house and her native land. . . . But I love the moon, the stars, the night and its sadness. . . .

Through the windows we can see the flames of the Sabbath candles in the neighboring houses. They move me inexplicably. At such a moment I am filled with warmth. My wife stands beside me, whispering in my ear. Tears of love fill my eyes, tears of joy. (*Without Hope,* pp. 30–31)

Shot through with ambivalence and self-contradiction, this struggle between the individual and his community is above all a private, personal experience. Quintessentially a European writer, imbued with the intellectual currents of turn-of-the-century German philosophy, Berdyczewski brings romantic individualism to bear upon his Jewish inheritance. He does not do this frivolously, in order to discard or discredit his past. Rather he attempts to portray the excruciating agony of an individual torn between two loves.

Berdyczewski does not reject God or the Jewish past. Rather, he rejects the inflexibility of the religious and scholarly leaders of the people, who refuse to deliver them into their proper freedom and who thus imprison and violate their souls. The story ends with an irresolvable contortion of love, hatred, and prayer to the Jewish God:

I hate these people, them and their houses, their religious schools and their books. I cannot forgive, shall never forgive those fanatics, who barred my way. Down there, in the darkness, lives an innocent soul, my beloved. Tears filled my eyes. I look at those old houses filled to the brim with all those books, beliefs and ideas, which were my stumbling-blocks, which reared up in front of us both.

"O Lord God, to whom vengeance belongest! O God, to whom vengeance belongest!" I fell down and wept. (*Without Hope,* p. 39)

Although at the end of the story the protagonist abandons his community and is, as in the English title of the volume, "without hope," nonetheless the story itself, preserving an image of Judaism behind and beyond its contemporary stuntedness, embodies the idea of an enlightened Judaism that is able to both conserve the past and enlighten the present and the future.

"Beyond the River" is essentially a portrait of a Jewish soul in torment. In later writings plot elements increased and the anecdotal-descriptive and confessional elements diminished. At the same time, the mythical elements also began to achieve greater prominence and the settings became reflections of myths and primordial archetypes. In one long novel, *Miriam: A Novel about Life in Two Townships* [*Miriyam*], and in three novellas, *Thou Shalt Build a House* [*Bayit tivneh*], *The People of the Street* [*Garei rehov*], and *The Secret Place of Thunder*, he used epic elements. These were his best writings. Here the motifs and tendencies of his earlier writings and other of his distinctive features—the solitary individual, the anecdotal depiction of the village, the tragic consequences of hubris, and the infusion of mythical elements in a realistic setting—achieve full realization.

A prominent recurring feature of Berdyczewski's fiction is genealogical continuity, in which the fate of the individual is determined by the community. Human stories begin not with the individual but with their ancestors, who predetermine the destinies of the next generation. *Four Generations* [*'Arba'a dorot*] is typical of these genealogical stories. In this case, the consequences of sin pass from the head of the family, Nathan-Neta, a man who "prayed like a storm," "like a man uprooting trees," to the child, Reuvele-Mazik (meaning, "little Reuven the pest"), who "ran in the fields with the children of the goyim" (*Collected Works* [*Kol kitvei*], p. 180). The story suggests that the fate of a family or a community is inescapable. If it is not manifested in the first generation, it will be realized in the last. Similarly, in the plots in *The House of Koresh* [*Beit Koresh*], *The Enmity* [*Ha'eivah*], *The People of the Street, The Secret Place of Thunder*, and *Miriam*, the race experiences progressive debilitation and decline.

What is diminished is not the family's moral fiber but its energy. This degeneration usually begins with the collapse of the powerful paterfamilias (e.g., Shlomo the Red in *The Secret Place of Thunder*) and ends with the final failure of his feeble sons and grandsons. Especially significant in this genealogical pattern is the text's interpretation of the relations between the sexes. Family and society pair off men and women in arbitrary and ill-matched couples with disastrous results. In most cases, a remarkable woman finds herself tied to an unsuitable husband, and the imbalance between the two of them destroys them both.

Although Berdyczewski manages to raise fundamental psychological and metaphysical questions about his fictional personae, he never fully realizes them as characters. He tells us a great deal about them. But the depiction of their lived experience, both internal and external, remains meager. Furthermore, by interpolating elements from Canaanite and biblical mythology into the social chronicle of his stories, Berdyczewski endows his personae with archetypal dimensions, transforming them into timeless representations of the human spirit. The relation of father to son, for example, is primordially powerful (for example, as between Abraham and his father Terah in *Miriam* or between David and his son Adonijah in *The Secret Place of Thunder*). Therefore, what Berdyczewski's genealogical patterns tend toward is less the realistic depiction of a family history than a more abstract mythological point about genetic fortunes, including his own. Ghosts of the past populate the present, forcing themselves upon it and determining its course.

Similar patterns characterize what might be called his stories of fate. Like other of his fictions, "Klonimos and Naomi" ["Klonimus veNe'omi"] is also based on a genealogical motif. Its atmosphere is romantic. The characters move in a strange world in which weird and wonderful things can happen. Indeed, the two protagonists are both in the bloom of youth. Yet they are controlled by a suffocating spiritual and biological inheritance, which gradually causes them to lose their humanity and their love. On the surface, "Klonimos and Naomi" is a social tale. It illustrates the conflict between human drives and social conventions (a common theme in its time). But the mythic quality of the tale is decisive. Behind social forces, erotic desire and a metaphysical search for answers obsess and destroy human beings.

Berdyczewski used two kinds of narrators: the confessional narrator and the chronicler. The first addresses the reader directly, offering personal remembrances and revelations that expose the implacable powers of human destiny in which the various characters are trapped. The fragmentary style—a multitude of paragraphs and broken sentences—conveys a romantic Young Werther–like agonizing and a longing for unattainable love. By contrast, the chronicler narrative (for example, the full-scale novel *Miriam*), by seeming to document the lives of Jewish communities and personalities, provides otherwise imaginative depictions with a quality of authenticity. Few writers succeeded so well as Berdyczewski in making the mythical-imaginary world seem real. The confessional form was later taken up by both Feierberg and Brenner, while Barash and Agnon inherited the technique of the chronicler-narrator.

Berdyczewski's personae are extremely varied, but his treatment of them was uneven. At times he saw their comical side, at other times only the pathetic. His weaknesses as a writer are most vividly revealed in his depictions of erotic relations, which remain unconvincing. The great majority of his characters are Eastern European students in Western European university cities, where their intellectuality, loneliness, and ineptitude make them seem trivial and ridiculous. They are the archetypes of the "uprooted" protagonists (*hatlushim*) who would come to populate Hebrew fiction in the early twentieth century. The polar opposites of these impotent scholars are Berdyczewski's Promethean rebels, who arise from time to time in the Jewish village, especially among its more privileged families. They resist destiny and come to tragic ends; they shatter their societies, rebel against God by raising the banner of a great ideal in defiance of divine prohibition, and taste the fruits of erotic love.

In these stories, the influence of Nietzsche is clearly discernible, as is the myth of the hero as exemplified in Wagner's operas and in various historical-heroic-tragic novels. The philosophical position they put forward imagines erotic sin and the violation of taboos to be manifestations of the freedom of the human spirit, which rises up against divine dictates in order to transform the world. This is the idea expressed in the novel *The Secret Place of Thunder* in the description of the sexual encounter between the father Shlomo and his daughter-in-law Shoshana during which, we are told, "suddenly the world shook. Two mountains broke away and crashed together. The life in the bowels of the earth cried out. Echo called out to thunder, abyss to abyss. The laws of nature were overturned, lightning flashed and broke. The constellations changed places."

Berdyczewski's inheritors, such as Shoffman and Gnessin and their contemporaries, would psychologically flesh out his characters and themes, using the techniques of introspective representation developed by Russian psychological novelists such as Dostoyevsky. But it was Berdyczewksi who provided the linguistic psychological model of the Hebrew literature subject and character that the later writers would inherit and revise.

MORDECHAI ZEEV (E. M. S.) FEIERBERG

Much of the fiction of Berdyczewski's followers, notably Brenner and Agnon, engaged the aesthetic forms he had created. So did the writing of the fourth of the romantic writers, E. M. S. Feierberg. Even though Feierberg resisted Berdyczewski ideologically (in the name of Ahad Haam, who criticized Berdyczewski coolly and thoroughly), attacking him publicly in "An Open Letter to Berdyczewski" (in the journal *Luah Ahiasaf* [*Achiasaf Notice Board*, 1900]), artistically and emotionally he was closer to Berdyczewski than to any of his other literary compeers. Berdyczewski, for his part, was lavish in his praise for Feierberg's writing, which in his view demonstrated imagination and sensitivity to change and expressed the "divided heart" and weltschmerz characteristic of romanticism.

Typically romantic in style as well as content, Feierberg appeared at the end of the period of Hebrew romanticism, after Frischmann, Peretz, and Berdyczewski, when Bialik and Ahad Haam were the new luminaries on the Hebrew literary scene. His life and death were themselves a romantic tale. He was born in 1874 in the village of Hilsk in Volhynia, Russia, moved to Volynsk Novgorod, and died there in 1899 at the age of twenty-five of consumption. Because Feierberg's education, unlike that of Frischmann, Peretz, and Berdyczewski, was principally Hebraic, he was less influenced by European literature, and his writings, with their many ancient motifs, strongly evidence his roots in Jewish tradition. For this reason, despite the differences between them, Feierberg enjoyed the qualified support of Bialik and Ahad Haam, both of whom influenced his writing.

Feierberg's output, which consisted of some short stories and one longish novella, began to appear in the 1890s in the journals *Hatsfirah, Hashiloah,* and *Luah Ahiasaf.* His stories depicted the progress from traditional religious education to the Haskalah, which, like Berdyczewski, he presented more as an assault against the pilgrim than as a spiritual journey. Nor did he describe this journey from religion to secularism objectively, from some external perspective. Rather, again like Berdyczewski, he portrayed it as the inner conflict of individuals torn between loyalty to their heritage and a longing for a different, romantically defined world of beauty and nature.

In a very short and touching story entitled "The Calf" ["Ha'egel"], Feierberg presents this divided self through the unpremeditated, nonideological innocence of a child, restless, as children are wont to be, with the rigors of Torah learning and anxious to be out with "those spinning sunbeams that twirled through the window with the fondest of ease" (p. 41). The focus of the child's excitement and passion for the world of nature is a newly born calf who, no sooner has he befriended it, is scheduled to be slaughtered. Through the most natural, unaffected thoughts of a child, Feierberg presents the timeless paradoxes of religious belief. At the same time, and also like Berdyczewski, he associates genuine Jewish faith with romantic childlike innocence and not with the community, with its institutional insistence and emotional disregard:

> I knew that the calf would not, could not be slaughtered, yet my heart pounded within me. I knew that God would think of something . . . the angels would come to its rescue . . . the knife would explode or its throat turn to marble. . . . [T]here was no other way out. My mother was adamant—but a miracle was bound to take place. . . . The calf was so pretty, and I had promised so much to the alms box. . . . My heart pounded. There were tears in my eyes. I was bursting with emotion. My thoughts raced out of control. It was too much to make sense of. Even

> the rabbi wouldn't know. . . . [N]o, I wouldn't even ask him. He would
> just laugh at me like my mother and call me a fool. . . .
>   They slaughtered the calf. (p. 44)

Strongly reminiscent of Berdyczewski's confessional style, Feierberg's protagonists, here and elsewhere, are torn, not by erotic desires, but by spiritual turmoil—as in the novella *Whither?* [*Le'an?*], which appeared in *Hashiloah*. Even though Feierberg cast the novella in the third person, thereby creating a distance between the narrator and the author, nonetheless *Whither?* is very clearly autobiographical and was perceived as such by the next generation of writers. It is also a novella of paradoxes. Rich in traditional materials, it depicts the rejection of tradition in the search for true faith. A national creed, which is deeply emotional and visionary rather than intellectual (as in Ahad Haam), replaces religious conviction in these writings. Feierberg's strength lay in conveying this visionary, picturesque, and symbolic quality of his vision, as in the opening passages of the novella, which recall both the Book of Job and *Faust*. Also relevant in this context is his description later on of one of the characters, Nachman. Nachman's sin of extinguishing a candle on Yom Kippur comes to symbolize the Jew's final and absolute break with tradition. The fiery vision of the opening, which is repeated in the description of the protagonist's growing unbelief as "a conflagration bursting from below," and many other poetic-symbolic images borrowed from Jewish tradition, lend an apocalyptic quality (recalling the Revelation of St. John) to the protagonist's visions.

* * *

The four romantic writers—Frischmann, Peretz, Berdyczewski, and Feierberg—can be described as the progenitors of twentieth-century Hebrew fiction. It is not possible to ignore the influence of Mendele on the continuing development of Hebrew literature. Nonetheless, it was the four romantic writers who forged the tradition's relationship to Western literature and revolutionized the form of the Hebrew text. Without them there would not have been Brenner, Shoffman, Gnessin, Baron, and Steinberg. Later authors, too, such as Bistritski and Vogel, continued to evidence their influence. It was this influence, together with that of the Russian novel and short story, which determined the path of Hebrew fiction in this century.

4

HEBREW LITERARY REALISM
FROM THE NEW PATH TO LOCAL COLOR FICTION

The naturalistic aspects of Mendele's writings, as expressed in his presentation (sometimes satiric, sometimes sentimental) of the social behavior of the simple folk, persisted contemporaneously with the romantic movement (Frischmann, Peretz, Berdyczewski, and Feierberg) in a secondary, less literarily significant, movement, which critics have dubbed the New Path. Although the New Path writers actually represented the final phase of the Haskalah, they, like Mendele, Frischmann, and Peretz, rejected aspects of its literary agenda. Under the leadership of Abraham Laib Ben-Avigdor, they were influenced by the Russian positivists (notably Dimitri Ivanovich Pisarev), who regarded literature as a determinant in historical process and who therefore demanded that it assume its proper role in the social struggle.

Guided by this assumption, the New Path positivists strove to produce a literature that would educate the masses. This social literary agenda led to the production of *sifrei agorah,* which, in Ben-Avigdor's words, were to be "penny books for the people, small booklets which would attract buyers even among this tight-fisted public, the Hebrew readers" (*Leah,* p. 1). For this reason, even though the New Path authors themselves produced no literature of note, they did promote the publication of Hebrew literary texts. They also paved the way for the group of writers that would contribute more significantly to the production of Hebrew literature—the regional local color realists who were born in the 1870s and 1880s in Europe. These included Haim Nahman Bialik, S. Ben-Zion, A. A. Kabak, Y. D. Berkowitz, and Asher Barash. Yaacov Rabinowitz and Shlomo Zemach were also closely affiliated with the local color realists.

The collective biography of this group of writers tells a story of European wanderings and eventual settlement in Palestine. And just as the lives of the writers were directed by shared social-historical forces, so too were their choices of subject matter, critical perspective, and fictional structure shaped by a common lived experience. They matured during the period between the 1881 pogroms and the First World War. They came of age, in other words, at a time when the Jewish world of Eastern Europe was disintegrating. Many of the themes that preoccupied these writers, therefore, had to do with transformations in Jewish society, such as the decline of religion and traditional Jewish education; changes in the use of language; migration and urbanization; and the growing presence of Jews in various social movements.

Naturalistic in form and content, the local color realists, like the New Path writers, repeatedly drew the reader's attention to the social and extra-literary contexts that would imbue their writing with ethical meaning. At the same time, however, they immersed themselves wholly in their fictional worlds. Straightforward storytellers of the ordinary and the everyday, they attempted to depict their worlds with vibrancy and authenticity. They expressed themselves with emotional immediacy rather than through intellectual distance.

In this endeavor, the writers were widely eclectic. They brought forward a multitude of different kinds of protagonists, backgrounds, and settings, which, for the most part, they rendered with meticulous accuracy. At the same time, however, the local color realist writers evaded rendering that world in its full concreteness or in precise mimetic detail. Stylistically, they remained faithful to formulation (indeed, Bialik was one of its perfecters). They did not seek to create the illusion of reality through the rendition of folk speech. Rather, by resisting larger-than-life narratives of extraordinary or heroic figures, they depicted ordinary human beings going through the ordinary course of human affairs. By stressing the dominance of social context over private motivation, they also tended to create protagonists who were not psychologically complex; rather, they served to illustrate their context. The first generation of realists were sincere in their desire to meet the challenges of realist fiction that were set by Mendele; nonetheless, the changes they wrought were at best superficial. Although they were to some degree significant as a transitional phenomenon, this group was not the principal inheritor of Mendele's literary realism.

H. N. BIALIK, STORYTELLER

As the editor of *Hashiloah*, Haim Nahman Bialik exerted broad influence on his contemporaries and as a writer of essays as well as poetry and fiction he served as something of an arbiter of literary taste whose approval everyone sought. Although many contemporary critics preferred his poetry to his prose, which they felt was purely imitative of Mendele's work, Bialik's symbolic realism abounds with human and artistic vitality. Unlike Mendele, Bialik creates a broadly based intertextual allusiveness in his writing that is only superficially realistic and is in fact rich in metaphoric imagery. Indeed, much of Bialik's strength lies in his seamless blending of the real with the symbolic. For example, the short story "From Behind the Fence" ["Me'ahorei hagader"] ostensibly concerns an erotic relationship between a Jewish boy and a gentile girl. Yet, without in any way violating the story's realism, the story uses images such as the Garden of Eden and the Tree of Knowledge to create a parallel symbolic plane of reference. Similarly, by embedding the narrative in the story "Aftergrowth" within the complexity and distance of the adult protagonist's relationship to his past, Bialik transforms what could have been one more trite story about the Jewish family and the *heder* into a powerfully symbolic tale of mature psychological anguish and its relationship to the experiences of childhood. Like many of his stories, "Aftergrowth," which was published in three installments (in *Hashiloah*, 1908/1909; *Masu'ot* [*Beacons*, 1919]; and *Ha'olam* [*The World*, 1923]), has many counterparts in Bialik's poetry and essays. But whereas his poetry is often preoccupied with death and loneliness, the stories are full of vitality. What was suppressed in his poetry (e.g., in "The Dead in the Desert" ["Metei midbar"]) is realized in the fiction.

While Bialik himself defined his art through reference to its context, it is his language that reveals his full powers as an expressive artist. More skillfully than any of his contemporaries, Bialik blended Jewish traditions with European culture, bringing the binary dialectic of Hebrew literature to its sharpest fruition. Although his fiction was not his highest achievement, it nevertheless towers above the work of his peers. Such brilliance and power do not recur again in Hebrew literature until Agnon.

S. BEN-ZION AND A. A. KABAK

The writer who was more attached than any of his contemporaries to the expression of the ordinary and everyday was S. Ben-Zion. He was at his most creative when he lived in the Hebrew milieu of Odessa, where he taught for some years in a modern *heder* before moving to Palestine in 1905. Ben-Zion was a transitional figure. He was a follower of Mendele, Yehuda Steinberg, and the authors of local color regional fiction. He was also a contemporary of the "uprooted" writers, whom we shall meet in a moment. The main objective of his fiction was to depict the realities of

Jewish society, both its solid bases in tradition and its contemporary decline. The social background of his fiction, in other words, was not merely its setting, but its central theme. His oeuvre includes both stories from the Haskalah, which deal with the communal world and its typical folk, and those from modern literature, which treat the alienation, dislocation, and loneliness of the individual. In structure and in style these stories resemble those of Mendele. Ben-Zion's main literary contribution was a short bildungsroman called *A Shattered Soul* [*Nefesh retsutsah*]. A novel of protest by an individual who has rejected the community that destroyed his childhood, it describes the destructive power of traditional Jewish education.

A. A. Kabak was the one Lithuanian among the regional realists. After wandering about Russia, Europe, and Turkey, he settled in Palestine in 1921. Through expansive plots that chronicle Jewish social life, his novels paint broad epic pictures, covering a wide geographical terrain. He wrote trilogies and tetralogies. He also produced several collections of stories as well as literary criticism and translations of European works. He described himself as an admirer of the French realists (Flaubert, Maupassant, Anatole France), and was ferocious in his attacks on the non-realists.

Kabak set greater store by the depiction of social reality than by the aesthetic and emotional features of his work. He constructed social models that were intended to enlighten his readers in Zionist history. His characteristic protagonist is the uprooted visionary who, having become disillusioned with his ideals, goes in search of messianic salvation. These male protagonists have their female counterparts, who are victims of historical events or of their lovers' social delusions. His style does not assume the balanced, orderly forms of Mendele, Ben-Zion, or Bialik. Rather, in its fragmented and emotional style it resembles the work of Feierberg.

As in French realism, Kabak's characters were meant to represent the spirit of the age. For this reason he was less concerned with engaging Jewish tradition than with depicting the existing social world. He was, in certain ways, a late exponent of the social novel of the Haskalah, though he refined it and gave it greater depth, as for example, in his last trilogy, *History of One Family* [*Toldot mishpaha 'ahat*], which was probably his most ambitious undertaking in the social realist mode. *History of One Family* is an extended historical novel which takes place during the mid- to late nineteenth century in several different cities: Minsk and Kovno in *The Empty Space* [*Bahalal harek*, 1943], Warsaw and Kovno in *In the Shadow of the Gallows* [*Betsel 'eitz hatliyah*, 1944], and, in the last volume, *A Story without Heroes* [*Sipur bli giborim*, 1945], Odessa. The volumes of the trilogy are held together by the complex interrelations among several families, whose two main protagonists, Yossel Yanover and Haim Lapuner, are at the center of the ideologically driven dramatic action. The objective of the trilogy was to bring the central character to Eretz Yisrael. To that end, it uses documentary materials and attempts to be as accurate and authentic as possible. Kabak intended to continue the story even further and create a large-scale Zionist epic, but he died before the realization of this goal.

His most important novel, however, which vividly evidences the influence of the French historical romance on his writing, is *The Narrow Path: The Man of Nazareth* [*Bamish'ol hatsar,* 1937]. In this novel, Kabak depicts a visionary Jesus, seeking to save the world through suffering and rejecting the various national movements of his day (namely, the Zealots, the Pharisees, and the Sadducees). The book stresses the importance of human salvation even in the fateful period of nation-building. According to Kabak, Jesus was motivated primarily by his own human aspirations. It was his disciples who turned him into a myth. Opposing Jesus is Judas Iscariot, the visionary who resolves to sacrifice himself in order to demolish the myth which has enveloped Jesus. Judas doubts the possibilities of salvation. Therefore, Kabak hints, his agony may have been even greater than that of Jesus. Both Jesus and Judas are depicted less as historical figures than as personifications of opposite tendencies and desires, like Hormuz and Ahriman, the god of light and the god of darkness.

By and large Kabak was less interested in the lives and struggles of individuals and more concerned with the social context in which his protagonists operated. His social novels were followed by works in a similar vein by native writers, such as Zarchi, Bar-Yosef, and even Shamir, who are closer to him than it might at first appear. In the 1960s Yigal Mossinsohn returned to the subject of Jesus and Judas in his novel *Judas* [*Yehudah 'Ish-Krayot*], once again casting them in the context of nationalist issues.

Y. D. BERKOWITZ

The writings of Yitzhak Dov Berkowitz illustrate the complexity and originality that regional realism could achieve. So strongly influenced by the Russian realist Anton Chekhov that some of his plots and characters seem mere imitations of those of his more famous counterpart, Berkowitz was considered by Bialik to be the most talented of the new generation of writers. For his part, Berkowitz regarded Bialik as his spiritual father, and, like Bialik, he described contemporary desolation and uprootedness. Although stylistically Berkowitz remained close to formulation, both thematically and in terms of subject matter, structure, and characterization, he was less like Mendele and Bialik than like Brenner, Gnessin, and Shoffman. He wrote differently in Hebrew and Yiddish, but his best achievements were his short stories in Hebrew, collections of which he began to publish in 1910.

Berkowitz wandered about Europe for several years, and in 1914 went with his father-in-law, Sholem Aleichem, to the United States, where he remained until 1928. He then migrated to Palestine, where he lived until his death in 1967. His most productive years were in Eastern Europe, from 1903, when he published his first story, "The Eve of Yom Kippur" ["Be'erev Yom Kipur"] in *Hatsofeh* [*The Scout*], until 1914, when he left Eastern Europe. His short stories, most of which were written between 1903 and 1906, were generally constructed around a single character, with a close-knit plot and narrow bounds of time and space. Typically the story opens with a protagonist in normal everyday circumstances who then passes into crisis or conflict and arrives at a condition of inexorable wretchedness. The story "Cut Off" ["Karet," meaning "severed"], for example, deals with an old woman who emigrates from Eastern Europe to the United States to live with her prosperous assimilated son and his family. Despite their best efforts to accommodate her, including putting in facilities so that she can prepare her own kosher food, there is no comfort for her in the new world, no peace. The story concludes as follows: "His old mother was sitting on the book chest, looking smaller and more bent than ever, clutching her shaking head and weeping feebly, bereft of hope and comfort, like a tiny abandoned orphan, forsaken by God and man" ("Cut Off," p. 202).

In another short story, "Uprooted" ["Talush"], a son of poor parents, whose successful professional career has elevated his social position, also finds himself, like the old woman in "Cut Off," outside the community of his peers. Dr. Vinnik cannot adjust to the prosperous class in which he now finds himself. Yet he is equally cut off from his humble background. A meeting with his family during his brother's illness and death highlights his double isolation. A Chekhovian tale, "Uprooted" delineates the increasing loneliness that finally leaves individuals solitary and helpless in the midst of their lives, despairing of the possibility of revival and recovery. For Berkowitz, this isolation, of old people stricken by misfortune, of children and of individuals torn from their natural setting, ethnic or social, and set adrift in an alien environment, has less to do with personal temperament than with social conditions: class difference, poverty, family breakups, intergenerational conflict, migration, translocation, and immigration.

Berkowitz wrote two novels, but his attempts to break out of the limitations of the short story form did not quite succeed. Even in his memoirs, in which he described his childhood and the writers he had known (including his father-in-law Sholem Aleichem) and his first years in Palestine in the late 1920s and early 1930s, he remained an illustrator of commonplace experience. As a short story writer he had no true heirs among the later Hebrew writers, though his novels did exert some influence on several of the Third Aliyah authors and even on a few later ones.

ASHER BARASH

Asher Barash's writings reveal the influence of the German and Scandinavian impressionist and neo-romantic writers, such as Adalbert Stifter, Knut Hamsun, and Bjornsterne Bjornson, as well as of the Hebrew realists themselves. Barash attempted elegiac depictions of everyday life. In style he followed Mendele, but unlike Mendele he made no effort toward satirical distortion. His main concern was to expose social crises and upheavals as they were.

Born in Lopatin, near Brodi, in 1889, Barash spent some time in Lvov, emigrating to Palestine in 1914, before the outbreak of the First World War. He became one of the founders of the new Hebrew literary establishment in Palestine. Together with Yaacov Rabinowitz he founded the periodical *Heidim,* which became a significant platform for Hebrew literature in the 1920s. Like the more romantic Berdyczewski, Barash also sought to bring out hidden drives and passions. In some of his short stories, and more markedly in the novellas *Rudorfer's Episodes [Pirkei Rudorfer,* 1928] and *Pictures from a Brewery [Tmunot mibeit mivshal hasheikhar],* primordial instincts clash with more moderating rational and social forces. Usually set in rural society, close to "Mother Earth," Barash's writings present passionate protagonists who are not crude primitives, but are rather noble, if uneducated, people who confront the crises in their lives with inner grandeur and dignity. Tragedy is imposed on Barash's characters from without, in the economic and social crises they encounter in the Galician villages where they reside and in the changes, upheavals, and sufferings experienced by both Jews and gentiles. Much of the strength of the fiction derives from its loose weave. Moral and social message are left significantly understated, and the foci shift among different characters and episodic subplots.

In his most important work, the novella *Pictures from a Brewery* (published in its entirety in 1929), Barash skillfully balances the epic, fragmentary, and dramatic elements of his style. The story follows the career of a commercial enterprise, its transfer from the hands of the Aberdam family to new lease-holders, and the economic and social consequences of that change. The Aberdams had treated the enterprise as a moral trust and sought to put its profit to pious usage. The new lease-holders are newly bourgeois. They lack moral restraint and exploit the reduced circumstances of the Polish landowner in order to drive the Aberdams out. The crisis that overwhelms the Aberdam family epitomizes the deeper upheaval in the status of the religious scholar in Jewish society, namely the loss of his privilege as a learned individual who does not need some other commercially productive employment in order to survive and be recognized as a valuable member of the community.

For the most part, the world depicted in this novel is driven by external social and economic forces that largely determine the fate of the characters. However, the process of disintegration is not wholly decided from without. Beneath the surface of this world are other mysterious forces, which are hinted at by ominous dreams. They, too, bring calamity in their wake. Events do not rush forward toward catharsis. On the contrary, the tragedy remains suspended. The central plot advances through seemingly separate episodes whose interconnectedness is only gradually revealed as the relationship between the subplots and the central theme slowly comes into focus. Faced with destructive forces, this society has attempted, quite futilely, to retreat into an imaginary idyllic experience. In *Pictures from a Brewery* Barash gave new and original form to older motifs in Hebrew literature, so that, while he is not exactly a pioneer of the new literary era, he is also not a mere follower of his predecessors in the tradition.

***

The local color realists were still on the scene when another, more rigorous school of realist writers made its appearance, the two literary groups coexisting and mutually influencing each other. This second group, psychological realists headed by Yosef Haim Brenner, also interacted with another contemporaneous movement, which had its own relationship to the conventions of literary realism: the "genrists," that is, the writers of what Brenner labeled the Eretz Yisrael genre. Indeed, these settlement novels, which began to be written during the Second Aliyah and continued on the scene until after the creation of the State, simply replaced the fiction of the East European shtetl and the diaspora experience as the major vehicles of regional realism. Although its literary quality was not the highest, the settlement novel, as we shall see, made a major contribution to the development of realism in Hebrew fiction. Before returning to the local realist tradition, begun in the shtetls and taken up later on the farms and settlements of Eretz Yisrael as genre fiction, I turn to the anti-genrists who occupied the literary scene at the same time as both literary schools. These are the psychological realists Brenner, Nomberg, Gnessin, Shoffman, Steinberg, and Baron.

5

PSYCHOLOGICAL REALISM AND THE POETICS OF DISENCHANTMENT
LITERATURE *DE PROFUNDIS*

Unlike their contemporaries, the regional realists—Y. H. Brenner, H. D. Nomberg, U. N. Gnessin, G. Shoffman, Yaacov Steinberg, and Devorah Baron—did not follow in the footsteps of Mendele's social realism. Their chief spokesperson and representative, Brenner, put their collective case as follows: "When I turn to the vestiges of culture in our literature I see the cup of despair filled to the brim, and its song in the mouth of the few remaining stragglers. . . . For despair too is a value in life and needs its poets" (*Collected Works,* II, pp. 215–216; first published in *Hame'orer* [*The Awakener*] in 1906). Despair features prominently in Brenner's fiction as well as in his essays. The protagonist in *Nerves* ['*Atsabim,* 1911] describes his relocation to Palestine in the following way, without irony (we are told) and "with a peculiar sort of earnestness":

> Here we live in self-imposed poverty. A village barely twenty-five years old . . . and lived in by whom? . . . [T]he sad thing about it . . . is what our treetops see, or should I say foresee, right around them. Let's say they can forget the great cities. Let's say they can't even see them and needn't compare them with our pitiful Jewish village. They still can't help noticing their surroundings. And I tell you, my heart goes out to them . . . my heart goes out to anything that is forced to put forth branches before it has time to strike root. (pp. 32–33)

Protagonists such as this, or such as the character Fliegelman in H. D Nomberg's "Excerpts from the Life of Fliegelman" ["Kta'im mehayei Fliegelman"], which was first published in Hebrew in *Hazman* [*The Time*] in 1903 and in *Sifrut* [*Literature*] in 1905, later appearing in Yiddish as

"Fliegelman, Das Yiddishe Vort" in 1905, were typical of the personalities created by the psychological realists. Like the inept *maskil* of "Fliegelman," they escape from the real world of socio-political engagement into the barrenness of metaphysical speculation. The expression of the inwardness and social isolation of the protagonists primarily took the form of short stories and sketches. Shoffman, Baron, and Nomberg wrote nothing else, though Brenner and Gnessin also attempted to write short novels and novellas. Almost all of the works were confessional: anatomies of souls, rather than narratives with external social referents.

The helplessness, sexual inadequacies, and emotional inhibitions of the characters reflected not only their own existential and social rootlessness within the fictional world, but that of their authors as well. Aimless, rootless, and disaffected, the characters mirror the writers' extreme mental anguish, the severe disenchantment with Hebrew culture and literature that afflicted Brenner and the others and that provoked sharp rebuttal among their contemporaries, such as S. Niger:

> They philosophize about themselves, they are their own Inquisitors. They cut into their living flesh and take apart their own souls, dissecting them as the corpse of a suicide is dissected. They are forever poised above their own heads with the cold steel scalpel of self-analysis ready in their hands, like an avenger's sword resting on their necks. (*Vegen Yiddishe Shreiber,* p. 91)

Responding to the writers' pervasive sense of despair, which so penetrated their consciousness that they regarded even the emerging Hebrew literature as evidence of decline and disintegration, another critic, Baal Mahshavot (Eliashiv), described them in a term borrowed from Russian literature as "from under the cellar"—*de profundis.*

Of the same generation and background as the local color realists (Bialik, Kabak, Berkowitz, and Barash), the practitioners of psychological realism also wandered throughout Jewish Europe, congregating in the various centers of Jewish cultural activity (such as Puchep, Homel, Lvov, Warsaw, London; though, significantly, not Odessa). Eventually they settled in Palestine, where they affiliated with literary circles in Jaffa and Jerusalem. Their periodicals reflected the peripatetic nature of their experience. Journals such as *Hame'orer, Revivim, Shalekhet* [*Falling Leaves*], *Snunit* [*Swallow*], *Nisyonot* [*Experiments*], *Gvulot* [*Borders*], *Hapo'el Hatza'ir* and *Ha'adamah* [*The Earth*] accompanied them on their journeys and served as their common platform. As a group, the writers edited and criticized each other's writings, supported each other in times of trouble, and helped each other bewail their collective double disenfranchisement: the absence of a reading public and the cultural vacuum in which they wrote.

On their way to writing Hebrew fiction, they absorbed a variety of literary influences: the Russian authors Anton Chekhov and Fyodor Dostoyevsky (Brenner's Hebrew translation of *Crime and Punishment* was published in Warsaw in 1924); the Scandinavians, Jacobsen and Hamsun; the German-Austrian neo-romantics Arthur Schnitzler and Peter Altenberg; the Germans, naturalist Gerhard Hauptmann and the philosopher Friedrich Nietzsche; and the Belgian symbolist Maurice Maeterlinck. Above all, they incorporated the divergent literary tendencies of their predecessors in romanticism and realism. Berdyczewski was their revered mentor, whose forms and style they emulated. Eschewing formulation, they broke up stylized phrases and sanctioned vulgarisms (Brenner, Rabinowitz) and unbalanced syntax (Steinberg, Brenner, Gnessin, Nomberg). More important than the commonalities that linked these writers was their great diversity of style and expression, which introduced powerful new models in the Hebrew literary tradition.

Y. H. BRENNER

The foremost writer of his time, Yosef Haim Brenner dominated the scene not only as author, but also as editor, critic, translator, and above all, as literary personality. He was to his contemporaries what Mendele and Bialik were to theirs. Indeed, it could be said that the impact of his personality was even greater than his literary production. His compeers regarded him as a secular servant of God, a martyr who bore upon his shoulders the burdens of Judaic humanism. At times this admiration for his person overwhelmed his value as a literary figure.

Brenner edited some of the main Hebrew periodicals in Europe and in Eretz Yisrael. He was the sole editor of *Hame'orer* and *Revivim*. He co-edited *Ha'adamah, Hapo'el Hatza'ir,* and several other publications, whose contributors were the founding fathers of modern Hebrew and Israeli literature. Brenner laid down the principles of a new literary project which called for concrete social involvement, abhorred abstract ideologies, and demanded simplicity of expression, rejecting all the ornamentation and frills of an art-for-art's-sake aesthetic.

Brenner turned his back on the Jewish past, considering it a useless distraction from the cultural work at hand. Jewish existence in the diaspora, he maintained, was mere parasitism. Only a life of labor could redeem Jewish society. In this Brenner tended toward what might be called "Jewish anti-Semitism," as Yehezkel Kaufmann has rightly noted (*Goleh,* pp. 405–417). These convictions also animated his literary criticism. It was not Judaism that, in Brenner's view, should preoccupy the society and its literature. Rather, the subject was, as Brenner put it in an essay in *Heid hazman* [*Time's Echo*] in 1912: "What are we Jews to do? How should we live? How do we stop being parasites in every sense of the word? How do we achieve the conditions in which a decent life may be lived? How do we stop being children of the ghetto?"

Brenner demanded an authentic literature that would not vie to displace reality but instead would reveal its true contours. In its satiric elements and in its tendencies toward distortion, Brenner's writing evidences the influence of Mendele, even though Brenner opposed the aestheticism of formulation. In the abjectness of their suffering, his characters and communities—like the fathers in *In the Winter* [*Bahoref*] and *Around the Point* [*Misaviv lanequdah*]; the English Jews in *Beyond the Border* [*Me'ever ligvulin*]; and the Jerusalemites in *Breakdown and Bereavement* [*Shkhol vekishalon*]—also recall Berdyczewski and Feierberg; while the sadomasochistic quality of the characters' relationships and the conflict between metaphysical and erotic elements in the text put one in mind of Dostoyevsky. In time he outgrew these various influences and, in a kind of constructive betrayal of his literary predecessors, he began to produce distinctly original literary fictions.

Obeying the dictates of his own critical maxims, according to which writers must reflect the surrounding social world and use their own experience as raw material, much of Brenner's writing follows the contours of his own life. Having spent his early years in his native town in the Ukraine, he attended the Puchep yeshivah before moving to Homel, where he joined the Jewish labor movement, the Bund. His first story, "A Slice of Bread" ["Pat lehem"], appeared in *Hamelitz* in 1900. He spent that year in Bialistok and Warsaw, until he was conscripted into the Russian army in 1901. He remained in the army until 1904 and escaped when the Russo-Japanese War broke out, making his way to London with the help of friends. In 1908 he moved to Lvov and the following year migrated to Palestine. The intense literary activity of the previous five years continued in Eretz Yisrael, until his murder by Arabs in Jaffa in 1921.

These biographical dimensions of his experience directly inform his writings. Thus, for example, the stories in *Between Water and Water* [*Bein mayim lemayim*, 1910] and *From Here and There* [*Mikan umikan*, 1911] depict life in Palestine before the First World War. The narrator-protagonist of *From Here and There*, for example, is one of the editors of a fictional periodical entitled *Hamahreshah* [*The Plough*], which strongly evokes the journal Brenner himself was editing at the time, *Hapo'el hatza'ir* [*The Young Worker*]. His later writings, too, *Breakdown and Bereavement* (1920), *The Way Out* [*Hamotsa'*], and *From the Beginning* [*Mehathalah*], closely followed his own career, in particular his experiences as an agricultural laborer and a high school teacher.

Through the integration of his writing and his own life story, Brenner sought to create a fictional mode that would be largely independent of imagination and responsible to the quotidian world. But critics attacked him for this strategy, accusing him of writing mere romans à clef in which all the characters were simply contemporary historical figures in disguise. These literary critics who denigrated Brenner's approach did not understand the depths of his aesthetic enterprise, in particular the difficulties of creating a literary technique commensurate with his aesthetic beliefs. Highly stylized writing, such as Agnon's, that created a closed world transported the reader into an illusory existence that was convincing by virtue of its very divergence from reality. The rigid "authenticity" Brenner demanded, which sought to bring art closer to reality, required the writer to persuade and enchant the reader without betraying any signs of artifice and style. This is not to say that artifice and style do not exist in Brenner's writings. The non-fictitious fiction Brenner sought to create required all the devices of fiction to achieve verisimilitude, and indeed Brenner's subversion of the tradition of high art is full of rhetorical devices. But the anti-artistic intention of Brenner's aesthetic required extreme subtlety and skill in its manipulation and use of artistic conventions. Brenner's technique gave rise to nothing less than a new art form, one that is often extremely difficult to isolate and define, as the misguided responses of many of his critics reveal.

Take, for example, the novella *Nerves*. A narrative within a narrative, the primary story concerns the narrator's "companion—an ordinary-looking man of about thirty with a set of strong sloping shoulders and a coarse-featured, acne-studded face, who because he was ill had not gone to work this September day, the heat of which was worse than midsummer's" (p. 32). The companion's story perfectly embodies Brenner's famous statement that "it is possible, it is quite possible, that here it is impossible to live, but here we must remain. . . . [T]here is no other place" (*From Here and There*, 1955). It also provides the logic informing Brenner's poetics of despair, which the protagonist (the companion) introduces even before he has begun to tell his story:

> Here more than anywhere (do you think that on our way back we might rest for a while on that little hill?) . . . [H]ere of all places, where our ruin, the ruin of our people is most obvious . . . here I've had some of the best days of my life. . . . If only they didn't blather so much back there about the sweet land of our fathers! I'm sure that's why new arrivals in this place are always so depressed. . . . [I]t's like waking from a dream. (*Nerves*, p. 33)

What precedes this rude awakening from the dream of a promised land (which nonetheless contains some of the best days of his life) is a nightmare of human deprivation and misery: poverty, starvation, illness, and death. Driven by his own idealism to journey to Eretz Yisrael, the protagonist experiences both his own intense physical and mental suffering and the suffering of other Jewish refugees with no place else to go. He records their abuse, not only at the hands of anti-Semites, but also by unscrupulous Jews who profit by the misery of their brethren. What begins as a story of immigration becomes a cry of anguish against an inexplicable universe of good and evil:

> This is not, the storyteller hastens to insist, good and evil simply in relation to me or the effect it had on me, or on that wreck of a woman with her five children who was the symbol of Jewish homelessness and misfortune. . . . What I mean is . . . good and evil, and all that they imply, in themselves. . . . Good and evil as two different worlds, two essences . . . with an infinite abyss between them. Good lord, how infinite it was. And how tragic human life was, how hard, how hard it was to live! (Ibid., p. 49)

In the kind of Manichean universe Brenner depicts, even national solutions and promises of redemption cannot suffice.

Of course, the protagonist may be crazy, hallucinatory as the result of his illness. Thus the story returns at the end to the narrator and the following distressing, but perhaps also reassuring, resumption of everyday life: "It must be the malaria," says the innkeeper, "and to think that people like him want to be pioneers."

> While the innkeeper's wife set the supper table the talk went from malaria to other current diseases. Some neighbors dropped in to chat and changed the subject to the opening of new shops and the question of bank credit. . . . The innkeeper's daughter, who was finishing the last grade of the local school, sat studying French beyond the oilcloth at the far end of the table. They talked, yawned, drank coffee, and ate pickled herring just as they always had done. (Ibid., p. 58)

Whether one is to take this as confirmation of the protagonist's despair or whether it suggests the viability of the new nation on the protagonist's own terms of the ordinary and everyday is left for the reader to decide.

As in the above story, Brenner typically confined his narrators to convincingly narrow viewpoints, as befits real witnesses. He used this strategy in both the autobiographical pieces and in the confessional monologues. This technique was accompanied, again as in the above text, by a deliberate blurring of the stories' frames: repetitions, time gaps, frequent transitions from story to story or event to event, and personal revelations, by which the author-narrator interrupts the narrative to interject a personal critique (in the above example, everything, the narrator and protagonist both agree, is a consequence of Jewish "nerves"). Brenner called his own literary construction "the movement of the soul," highlighting the fact that the plots were not in themselves dramatic and did not resolve mysteries or complications. On the contrary, his stories usually described the wanderings of characters who believe that by changing places they might change their fortunes, only to discover that that is not the case. The typical Brenner denouement does not resolve the hero's inner predicament.

Reminiscent of Berdyczewski's characters, many of Brenner's wandering souls are disaffected and alienated individuals who, after acquiring an education and leaving the Pale of Settlement, move either to the big city or to Palestine. They long for erotic experience, ideological answers, and social recognition. Invariably they are frustrated in their desires. There is much self-irony in these representations of the protagonist-narrators, who Brenner depicted as little more than miserable insects. Nonetheless, he preferred these anti-heroes, gnawed by their disenchantment and suicidal tendencies, to the more romanticized and heroic figures of other fictional genres. Not associated with any particular social ideology, not lauding even Zionism, Brenner believed only in personal truths. He valued the individual who, Job-like, voluntarily endures life's struggles, makes of his heap of ugly miseries a home, and, reed-like, bends in the storms of human vicissitude (cf. *Breakdown and Bereavement*). Though most of his heroes fail to achieve their goals, their strivings become an existential value in themselves. This commitment to the existential moral life is as much discernible in his diaspora novels, like *In the Winter* and *One Year* [*Shanah 'ahat*] as in his Israeli ones, like *From Here and There* and *Breakdown and Bereavement*.

Breakdown and Bereavement is his most important novel. The protagonist Yehezkel Heifetz is the classic Brenner hero: a neurotic individual who tries to become a *halutz* (pioneer) but whose tendencies toward moroseness and despair are only exacerbated by his experiences in Palestine. Almost as soon as the story has begun, Heifetz, suffering both physical and psychological maladies (his "rupture," i.e., hernia, serves as a symbol for both), escapes from physical labor in the country to the house of his Orthodox relatives in Jerusalem, only to wind up in a mental institution for several months, where he experiences weird sexual delusions. Eventually he falls in love with his beautiful cousin Miriam, only to have his love returned by her less desirable sister Esther. Like other Brenner protagonists, Heifetz discovers that his life has arrived at a harrowing dead end. Indeed, the worlds of Jerusalem, Jaffa, and Tiberias depicted in the novel are filled with ideologically and religiously motivated immigrants, uprooted from their familiar environments and unable to find satisfaction, or even proper employment, in a community that everywhere disappoints and defeats them. The following describes the protagonist at the end of the novel:

And he had no illusions about the fact that he was beaten. In every way. A beaten man. Not just by the inevitable death that was yet to come, but by the other, the potentially living side of him too, which had never been able to express itself, though it had gone on existing inside him. He had never had the feeling of being fully alive. Something essential was lacking, something that could never be made good. Alack, alack! And it was useless, too, to comfort himself with the thought that he still had other qualities with which he could also serve. No, he would never be "a priest of God most high," never experience the call to rise to such empyrean peaks. Not for him to minister augustly to the destitute father . . . or to the soldier . . . or to the defenseless prisoner . . . or to the poor, debilitated bachelor . . . or to the mother. . . . A man who was not in the best of shape himself, who hovered between light and darkness . . . such a man had better refrain from brave words, had better not chant any hymns. . . . And yet wasn't it true that there had been many hours of light in his life all the same? Perhaps there had been nothing actual or tangible about them, nothing that could be grasped or put into words. There was no satisfactory way of explaining them. And yet they had existed: they had been flooded with light and warmth and sun! (*Breakdown*, pp. 297–298)

Breakdown and Bereavement embodied many of Brenner's complex literary concepts and social messages. Brenner opens with a foreword claiming that the protagonist's "notes" were found by the author, who put them together into a literary testament to the life of Yehezkel; he presents a quasi-autobiographical narrative of the story of a part migrant, part pioneer Job, whose life in Palestine culminates in loss and bereavement, even if there is "no place else."

Like his thematic structures, Brenner's language is carefully crafted, responding thematically and linguistically to the new language environment of Eretz Yisrael, as in the following passage from *Nerves:*

A bareheaded adolescent girl stepped out of one of the houses in the colony and crossed the narrow street, humming to a popular Arab melody the words of a Hebrew "folk song" written by a poet in Europe. . . . From a courtyard opposite a voice that could have been either a man's or a woman's shouted in a mixture of Arabic and Yiddish through the night air: *"Rukh, rukh min hon! S'tezikh tsugetsheppet?"* (p. 52)

Brenner preferred flexible "natural" diction, for which he virtually invented a colloquial speech sprinkled with English, Yiddish, Arabic, and Russian words. He opened the Hebrew language to foreign vulgarisms, incursions of words and phrases from outside standard Hebrew vocabulary. At the same time, he took liberties with the forms and rules of grammar and syntax. In contrast to Mendele, who attempted to find suitable Hebrew substitutes for Yiddish phrases, Brenner (as in the above example) tended to transcribe the Yiddish directly into the text. This not only introduced new forms into the language, but, like the use of Aramaic, it helped to diminish excessive pathos and to produce irony instead by breaking up the linguistic homogeneity.

Brenner's heirs, the writers of the Third Aliyah, more or less followed in his footsteps, an author such as Haim Hazaz adopting Brenner's critical principles even while reverting stylistically to formulation. On the other hand, the writers of *Dor Ba'aretz* (the native generation), that is, those who were born in Eretz Yisrael, invented a Brenner of their own, in whose name they threw themselves into social issues and criticism (e.g., S. Yizhar) and concerned themselves with the "ugly Israeli," forever struggling with his pettiness and failures (Pinhas Sadeh). If Brenner and his contemporaries grew up in the shadow of Mendele and Berdyczewski, the following generations stood in the shadow of Brenner, the great rebel who had blazed new trails in the form and content of Hebrew literature.

G. SHOFFMAN

Unlike Gnessin and Brenner, Gershon Shoffman produced no literary theory or school of his own. Although he was an important writer who attempted literary forms no one else even thought of trying, he did not play a significant part in the development of Hebrew literature. He was one of its most Westernized contributors, having been nurtured on sources similar to Brenner's, and in his early years he tended to follow the example of Chekhov. He came under the influence of Austro-German literature during his time in Lvov (1904) and Vienna (1913), and during his subsequent lengthy stay near Gratz. The Viennese impressionists, notably Peter Altenberg, became the dominant influence on his writing. Indeed, Shoffman had more in common with fin de siècle Vienna than with the Russian tradition on which most of his contemporaries had cut their teeth.

Shoffman began to write when he was nineteen, and his first stories were published in 1902. They met with mixed critical reaction, perhaps because his writing, like Gnessin's, did not directly represent social reality, but presented the world impressionistically and through sketches. Subjectivity dominates Shoffman's poetics throughout. As he himself put it in an essay entitled "You Win!" ["Nitsahtini"], he preferred writing that is essentially confessional, rejecting literature that hides intimate experience behind ornamentation and rhetoric. Yet for all their subjective impressionism, his vignettes create a sense of an objective, felt reality. It was this immediacy of sensual touch, be it of the landscape or a woman, which distinguished his poetics. The short story "Hanya," for example, narrates the protagonist's life in five separate episodes, from her birth in the country to her death in an urban brothel. The moral thrust of the narrative is clear, so much so that the separate sketches verge on being morality tales. Yet the story's structure, in particular the looseness of the plot, invites the reader to reflect personally and privately on the contrast between country and city, thus emphasizing affective feeling over social critique.

Shoffman was a child of his age, and his experiences and wanderings are reflected in his writings just as Brenner's are in his. The background of his early fiction is the Jewish village in Russia. In another group of stories he makes use of his military service. Later, Vienna became the main backdrop of his writing. His relocation to Palestine caused profound upheaval in his personal life, and thereby in his literary life. Before his immigration Shoffman's protagonists were almost invariably typical *de profundis* types. They are highly ambivalent and self-divided. They long for the sensuous and the erotic, but they recoil from direct human contact. Conscious of the physical menace of their environment, they (like the eponymous protagonist of the story "Yonah") flee in terror as soon as they are exposed to such experience. For Shoffman, Eretz Yisrael represented a safe haven from impending catastrophe, thus making him closer in some ways to Berkowitz and other writers of the Third Aliyah (e.g., Aharon Ever-Hadani, Shlomo Reichenstein) than to his contemporaries and literary comrades of the Second Aliyah (e.g., Brenner, Agnon, Reuveni).

Above all, Shoffman sought to evade life's contradictions. He strung together individual leitmotifs to produce an image of life in its ironic wholeness. Isolated episodes extrapolated from a full life story highlight a human predicament or its ironic recurrence. For Shoffman, human strivings always come up against a more potent reality that made it impossible to achieve heroic objectives. Even when aspiration seemed to have been realized, it soon dissolved again and grim reality once again achieved dominion. Thus, the visionary who persists in clinging to his illusions, and with whom the reader is made to sympathize, is continuously disenchanted. In portraying this view of reality, Shoffman was less interested in the diversity and richness of human experience than in its expressive, emotional aspects. He sought to discover through his immediate observations the underlying laws that fleeting events delineated. Portraying an idea was more important for him than producing authenticity of social portraiture, and, for this reason, his writing tended toward the didactic rather than the purely descriptive.

U. N. GNESSIN

Although he was one of Brenner's closest friends, Uri Nissan Gnessin disagreed with Brenner on literary matters, in particular about the social role of art. Unlike Brenner, who demanded socially conscious literature,

Gnessin refused to preach or to guide. Like many of his generation, he was influenced by Berdyczewski and Chekhov (among others), but, beginning with his novella *Sideways* [*Hatsidah*] in 1905, he developed an aesthetic that went beyond the atmospheric realism of a writer like Chekhov. Through what came to be known in literary criticism as stream of consciousness, Gnessin presented the external world through the interior emotional processes of the characters. Though he could not have read the major European practitioners of stream-of-consciousness fiction—James Joyce, Virginia Woolf, or Marcel Proust—he was influenced by the same social and literary developments as those writers. Throughout the European bourgeoisie, including Jewish society, individual isolation and the breakdown of religious tradition demanded, and were given, literary voice.

Revitalizing the tradition of social realism was one possibility for all these writers. Only a few of them, however, took up the challenge and tried, as Gnessin did, to achieve what he called "the verbalization of the soul's blurry shadows." The responses of Hebrew critics to Gnessin's stylistic innovations, which emerged only after he had written a few fairly conventional stories, were mixed. Though Bialik and others objected to his break with formulation and to the linguistic contortions that seemed to them to characterize his writing, his novellas *Sideways* and *Meanwhile* [*Beinatayim*], published by Nissyonot Publishing House [Experiments] in London in 1906, were hailed by many as among the most original Hebrew fictions ever to be written.

The stylistic and structural revolution embodied by *Sideways* was also exhibited in the figure of its protagonist, Nahum Hegzer. A scholar of Hebrew literature and a tutor, Hegzer is no tragicomic schlemiel, incapable of introspection and interaction with his world. Rather, he is an individual of genuine intellectual gifts and deep sensibility. Yet he is incapable of committing himself to life. He retreats from human relations, yielding to an unremitting sense of his own impotence and alienation. Early in the novella, he throws himself into life with all the exaggerated melodramatic (but deep) passion of a young man:

> And so when one day long slender cobwebs spiraled down through the air and yellow leaves dropped from the trees and littered the paths in the parks, Hegzer trampled on them with a joyous burst of energy unleashed. He stood straighter now, his chest more expanded and his face more alert. In another week or two the skies would cloud over; the wind would howl; windowpanes and tin roofs would rattle once more in gloom: Hurrah! His mood would be defiant then; his mind free of fetters; his heart brimful; his work crowded with satisfying new discoveries. . . . Yes, a week or two would bring black nights pierced by a few quivering streetlights, torrents of rain, mud up to the ankles . . . but that dear, pleasant house would be warm and well lit. Beneath its spread of red

velvet the couch would be spacious and soft; the lively eyes of the three
pretty sisters would glow with a tender light. (p. 9)

Gradually, however, his own failure of nerve and the casual disregard of
others for his existence defeat his youthful energy:

> What was he doing here? He stood reeling beneath the memory of Car-
> mel's smug smile, of Hanna Heler's arms pinned behind her, of the bois-
> terous laugh of Manya's tutor as he held them. . . . He felt that he was
> going to choke. Something hummed in his ears and he could hardly see.
> Dazedly he laid the glass on the chair and stumbled toward the door.
> . . . His temples throbbed and his heart went on pounding as he walked
> down the street to the end of the town and continued beyond it. He
> ambled slowly now, staring with melancholy detachment at the long
> endless railroad track that stretched flatly out before him, quite faint and
> desolate in the heart of the day. (p. 27)

Nahum is not unlike characters created by Nomberg, Shoffman, and Brenner. Nonetheless, he, like other of Gnessin's protagonists, has greater self-
awareness. Taken out of their specific Jewish milieu, these characters become, like Nahum, radically detached, tragically divided within themselves,
and ultimately incapable of interpersonal relations. Hegzer is not merely
uprooted (*talush*). He is a creative person incapable of creativity, a lover
who cannot love, a human being who is incapable of living.

A major theme for Gnessin is this struggle between the will to live and
a longing for death, the death wish gradually triumphing as the human
being, who can no longer believe in social and metaphysical consolations,
comes to confront the one over-riding fact of his existence: his mortality.
This is vividly expressed in the thoughts of Ephraim, the protagonist of *By*
[*'Etsel*] (1912), when he faces the woman who loves him: "Oh to be
really immobile, like that oil-press beam. Insensible to thought and impervious to feeling, too dull and stupid to take in any impression. . . . To be
dead!" It is this experience, in which thanatos overcomes the libido and
the individual prefers death to life, that Gnessin introduces into Hebrew
literature.

In most of the novellas the plots and interpersonal relationships are
easy to follow and serve to structure the writing, but the meanings of
the texts far exceed the story lines. In fact, the plots are usually petty
melodramas revolving around disappointed love (three end in suicide).
These plots, however, with their situations of detachment, alienation, and
depression, primarily function to provide a medium for the exploration of
the inner emotional lives of the characters. From story to story, internal
psychological processes become progressively farther removed from the
external plot, till they achieve thematic centrality in their own right.

These inner plot lines are constituted through techniques that varied from one novella to the next. In later stories such as *By*, intricate arrays of repeating motifs are spread across the entire story, filling the inner monologues, the landscape descriptions, sometimes even the elliptical dialogues, such that they begin to convey meanings independent of the dramatic action. Sometimes these motifs serve to create an atmosphere (e.g., the yellow color and the azure smoke in *Meanwhile, Before* [*Beterem*], and others) or spatial unity distinct from the dramatic developments and independent of the temporal dimensions of the story. Stream of consciousness in Gnessin's fiction depends on these networks of motifs which attempt directly to project the consciousness of the characters.

Also distinguishing Gnessin's work were its stylistic features, like the use of the cyclic-pendant sentence: "Opposite, behind the long range of mountains at the back of the solitary hospital, its wide courtyard and scattered buildings, which had come down from the top of the horizontal mountain and were surrounded by a single long low fence along the river's other bank, arranged as on a map, from behind those mountains the moon rose, already blue and pure" (*By*, p. 240). The interiorization of the observed object by means of vivid impressionistic adjectival language and the imposition upon the outer world of the individual's ephemeral existence, arresting the flow of time, characterize Gnessin's later fiction:

> There were gleams. But these frozen gleams which broke through and turned the surrounding area into marble recalled other gleams and another moon. The heart filled with sadness. Sadness, because it was already plain that the fruitful days of childhood would not return and the blooming flowers of the heart had withered and would never again bloom! And these trees with their dreamy boughs, which once spoke eloquently to the yearning soul, they no longer said anything—no, nothing. It is all finished, brothers! An ice-cold vice has reached and gripped the heart and the watches of the night send forth sententious winds, which rattle like a black box: For all his ways are judgment. . . And that is a judgment, merciful Jews! (*By*, p. 240)

Although Gnessin did not leave a massive oeuvre, his legacy is one of the most important in Hebrew literature. In his own generation Jacob Steinberg and Elisheva Bikhovski were most closely identified with his aesthetic innovations; Halkin, Steinman, Horowitz, and Bistritski also bore traces of his influence. S. Yizhar, in his 1938 *Ephraim Returns to Alfalfa* [*'Ephraim hozer la'aspeset*], names his own protagonist after Gnessin's Ephraim in *By*.

YAACOV STEINBERG

Like many of his contemporaries, Yaacov Steinberg, poet, novelist, essayist, and playwright, was also a borderline realist. Born Balaya Tserkov,

Ukraine, 1887, his writing reflected Jewish life both in the Ukraine and in Eretz Yisrael. However, he also sought to exceed literal mimesis. Even while dealing with concrete realities, his realism was refined and enhanced by his expressive language and rich poetic diction. A talented poet as well as fiction writer, Steinberg created, through metaphorical and linguistically complex language, a multifaceted world that collapsed the distance between external reality and the subjective experience of that reality. Methodologically, the stories alternate between direct mimetic representation and emotive-poetic evocation. They fluctuate between the reality depicted and the intellectual and emotional impact of that reality on a perceiving consciousness. This alternation, as we have seen, also characterized the writings of Shoffman. Unlike Shoffman, however, Steinberg retained a coherent plot structure, with the consequence that Steinberg's fiction sustains a more comprehensive social commentary than Shoffman's.

His first stories, like those of Berkowitz, appeared in *Hatsofeh* in 1903–1904. After settling in Palestine in 1914, his writing flourished. Most of his stories were of medium length (like the stories of Brenner and Gnessin); a few were very short (like those of Berkowitz). His distinctive place in the tradition of Hebrew psychological realism can be assessed by comparing his stories with those of Berkowitz. In Berkowitz's fiction, the main thrust of the story lies on the plane of concrete reality. In Steinberg's work, the impact is achieved indirectly through the meticulous depiction of inward processes. Steinberg does not describe emotions directly. Rather, he represents them symbolically. In this way he was able to transport the reader into the interior lives of his characters without evoking the excessive pathos that lurks in explicit emotional melodrama. Steinberg's protagonists are typical of his generation. Like Berkowitz and Brenner, he too looked to social motivation, and his protagonists strongly reflect class distinctions. Members of the poorer classes, they are afraid to act, not believing that they are entitled to a political say. Yet they are driven, primarily by sexual passions and primal energies, to rebel. Among the most powerful and complex aspects of his work are his descriptions of erotic situations, in which human beings are compelled to strive for self-realization, or, by contrast, in which men seek to dominate women and rob them of their independent selfhood.

Most of the stories do not end in catharsis or in erotic conquests, but in crises of defeat. Unlike Berdyczewski's characters, who are crushed only after they revolt, Steinberg's protagonists are defeated even before they begin by a failure of nerve and will. Most of his stories culminate in endings which are neither liberating nor totally depressing. Neither condemning nor condoning the protagonists, the fiction expresses the inevitability of the human predicament as existential fact (cf. "The Rabbi's Daughter" ["Bat harav"], "Amid the Silver Birches" ["Bein livnei hakesef"], and "A Daughter of Israel" ["Bat Yisra'el"]).

"The Blind Girl" ["Ha'iveret," 1922] exemplifies both the structure and theme of the typical Steinberg story. A blind young woman is married off to a man about whose age, appearance, and occupation she knows only the lies that her family has told her. Eventually she discovers that he is a gravedigger. His house stands in the middle of a graveyard, and finally it is he who buries the daughter she bears him. The story centers on the conflict between appearance and reality, death being the central fact that determines human existence. By using a blind protagonist, the author suggests that while the sighted can never penetrate the lie of outward appearance, the blind may come to perceive that happiness is illusory and that impenetrable darkness and death are the only truth. The centrality of death as the definitive human experience appears as well in "The Death of the Old Woman" ["Mot hazkeinah," 1928]. In this work, death is depicted from three different perspectives: that of a boy, his grandfather, and his dying great-grandmother. In evoking the aura of decadence which had infused the writings of novelists and poets at the turn of the century, he more than any other writer resembles Gnessin.

DEVORAH BARON

The writings of Devorah Baron also oscillate between the tradition of everyday local color realism and the alternative forms that broke away from it. Some critics see her stories as basically realistic reflections of life in the Jewish communities in Lithuania. Others stress the ways in which she used these materials for new creative ends. Seeking to conjure an idea of reality rather than to elaborate it in all its detail, she is similar in form and style to Shoffman and Steinberg.

The similarities between her own life experience and that of her contemporaries are manifest in her writings and letters. Like many of them, she also made the journey from village to city to Palestine (in 1911). Also like them, she was influenced, stylistically, by Chekhov and Maupassant and, in terms of subject matter and the use of irony, by Flaubert, whose *Madame Bovary* she translated into Hebrew. She began to publish stories in 1903; her first collection was published in 1927.

Her range of subjects was rather limited, and her special quality rests in the portrayal of her protagonists. These were not the culturally or socially uprooted individuals of Berkowitz and Kabak. Nor were they the helpless heroes of Brenner, Gnessin, Nomberg, and Shoffman. Rather, her protagonists, most of whom are women, are victims of their life circumstances. Baron depicted the oppression of women in a male-dominated society; she could well be regarded as the first feminist writer in Hebrew literature.

Brenner and Shoffman both cast their protagonist-narrators in a satirical, uncomplimentary light. Not so Devorah Baron. Her characters are doomed from the start, but through no fault of their own. The author, therefore, directs her irony not at the defeated individuals, but at the cruel fate that overwhelms them. She treats her protagonists warmly and with love, reserving her contempt for their enemies and for their inimical fate. Her compassion is reflected through her narrators, who, writing in an autobiographical mode, serve as witnesses—sometimes passive, sometimes active—to the unfolding events. At times the stories appear to be fragments of a single novel, with the same characters reappearing in its different installments.

Baron's plots often record the trajectory of a protagonist's life from an "idyllic" point of departure to an "anti-idyllic" ending. Being orphaned is the pivotal event in the lives of many of her female characters. This theme recurs in the stories about the autobiographical figure of the rabbi's daughter, as in "Depth" ["Metsulah"], "Summer House" ["Beit qayitz"] and "Wild Duck" ["Bar'avaz"] (Baron herself was a rabbi's daughter), as well as in other stories about defenseless women (e.g., "Henikh," "Fradel," "A Thorny Path" ["Derekh qotsim"], "Sunbeams" ["Shavririm"], "As a Fallen Leaf" ["Ke'aleh nidaf"], and "Shifra"). In some of her stories, the heroine's trials and tribulations culminate in unmitigated disaster. In others, the protagonist manages to escape ultimate catastrophe and achieve some deliverance, albeit minimal (e.g., "Family" ["Mishpahah"], "A Thorny Path," and "Fradel").

In "Sunbeams," for example, the heroine, Haya-Frumah, lives the typical life of an orphan, "roam[ing] about in her peasant smock, her faded hair tangled and unkempt, her face devoid of a single endearing feature" (p. 86). Eventually she marries a widower who, "impressed by her strength," takes her to his "neglected" home to keep house for him: "[T]he dankness inside her soon permeated her whole being, filling her with the dark desolation of a long-forgotten dungeon. It was not that her husband was unkind to her: most of the time he was too busy even to acknowledge her presence" (pp. 88–89). But, even in the midst of her misery and despair, Haya-Frumah finds consolation in the beauty of things. Even before her marriage, "she preferred to be alone with the inanimate objects at the far edge of the yard or in a corner of the kitchen; for the kettle she was polishing would send back a kindly gleam, and the firewood she kindled in the stove would respond with a gay, dancing flame" (p. 87). Eventually, her husband purchases a "milch cow," through whom Haya-Frumah comes to experience "a sense of release, as though the warmth of the sun and the freshness of the spring breezes were dispelling the long-accumulated dankness inside her. And when one evening, as she sat alone in the doorway of the cowshed, the cow turned to her and affectionately licked her hand with its rough tongue, she—who had never known laughter—felt as though her inner being were pervaded by a broad smile, and the dark dungeon was suddenly filled with dancing sunbeams" (p. 90). "Sunbeams" ends in the death of the protagonist, but not before her husband himself has died and Haya-Frumah has built up for herself a flourishing cottage industry. This enables her not only to become self-supporting but to become charitable as well: "As she sank down into slumber, she felt as though she were becoming enveloped in the golden haze of an unseen sunrise. This radiance that dawned on her . . . awaits all those who have been refined and burnished by suffering in this world" (p. 93). In representing the world at large through minor, emotionally laden, episodes such as the one above, Baron resembles no one so much as Berdyczewski.

Style and textual harmony constitute Baron's major strengths as a writer. She often uses biblical allusions, not, as in the tradition of the formulation, for purely formal reasons, but in order to draw direct analogies between past and present. Baron also employs biblical similes. In "Small Things" ["Qtanot"] (from the 1933 collection of the same name), for example, the rabbi's young wife is compared to Jepthah's daughter; in "Summer House" the old merchant Barukh Bren is likened to Saul, who fell in with a band of prophets; and, in "Fradel," Fradel is equated with Jacob's rejected wife Leah. These biblical similes are woven into tales of a Lithuanian Jewish village to endow the anti-heroes with mythical depth. They enlarge the provincial settings, simultaneously revitalizing the ancient texts and producing in the present a larger-than-life historical-national or archetypal dimension.

Although Devorah Baron did not leave any direct literary heirs, there are clear affinities between her and Elisheva Bikhovski and Leah Goldberg. Although not a central figure in the history of Hebrew literature, she occupies an important place in the tradition.

* * *

The writers of Hebrew psychological realism did not so much seek to portray a particular reality as to depict the inner dimensions of the people who were shaped by and had an impact on that reality. Methodologically, they present certain problems of literary-historical definition. To separate them into those that followed or revived formulation versus those that opposed it obscures the way in which, in both groups, the focus was on a particular relation to mimetic representation as a tool of psychological analysis. As a group, the writers tended to use less stylized verbal expression, in this way deviating from classical formulation and attempting to produce literary forms freed from the restraints of ancient Hebrew sources. Poetical symbolism, complex sentence structure (evidencing the influence of Western models), and psychological exploration took the place of classical allusion, such as had characterized Mendele and his successors. Intricate sentences (Gnessin, Steinberg), and the attempt to approximate spoken language (Brenner), substituted for rhythmically and rhetorically balanced sentences. In this, they followed Berdyczewski and Feierberg rather than Mendele and Bialik.

Like other writers of Hebrew literature, these authors also emigrated to Palestine, and the transition was reflected in their writings. Some (Shoffman and Berkowitz) attempted to adjust to the new reality, which came to dominate their distinctive styles. Others (Brenner, Baron, Steinberg) adapted the reality to their particular fictional personae and forms. The latter group became the founders of the new literature of Eretz Yisrael, while the former set the terms for a school of genre writing; "Eretz Yisrael genre" was the term Brenner used to describe that domestic fiction which sought (like local color realism in Europe) to evoke the ethos of the place. But although the European shtetl had a long history on which the Jewish writer might draw, the Eretz Yisrael genrists, driven by their ideological convictions, sought to depict the pioneering community in Eretz Yisrael, not only as the ordinary and everyday world of the Jews, but as an already fully established society with its own mores and norms.

The writers of Hebrew literary romanticism and realism (of both the local color and psychological varieties) represent an end to the painful history of a literature without a country and without a spoken language. Once Hebrew literature arrived in Eretz Yisrael, the conditions of its production were utterly transformed. The language lifted up off the pages of the written text to become the language of everyday speech, and the writers began to write for a public that not only spoke Hebrew but for whom Hebrew, as a language and a literature both, was a part of their everyday existence. Thus the literature that had been born and raised in the confines of cultural ghettoes took root in new, more natural, soil, and it flourished in marvelous and largely unforeseen ways.

6

GENRE AND ANTI-GENRE
WILL ALL HOPES BE FULFILLED?

Here in our beloved ancestors' land
All our hopes will be fulfilled
Here we shall live and shall create
A life of radiance, a life of liberty
Here will the abode of the spirit be . . .

—From a song of the Second Aliyah

At the end of the nineteenth century and the beginning of the twentieth, Palestine was an insignificant spot on the map of Jewish and Hebraic culture. Gradually, however, it began to replace the centers of the diaspora. The idea that Eretz Yisrael could be a cultural as well as a material haven for Jews first emerged at the beginning of the century, when the immigrants of the Second Aliyah began to create a linguistic and social culture there. Nonetheless, the new literature started to take shape only after the First World War.

From the beginning of the century, relations between Eretz Yisrael and the diaspora preoccupied both the literature and the criticism. Many feared that the emergent culture would merely constitute a continuation or repetition of the provinciality of the Eastern European communities. Dominating Hebrew fiction was this tension between the expectation, on the one hand, that Zionist settlement would change Jewish fate and bring about a revolution in the very nature of the people and, on the other, the worry that it would do nothing of the sort. Although by and large the writers viewed the new reality optimistically, the literature conveyed such contradictory expressions as the euphoria of Meir Wilkansky and the despair and disenchantment of writers such as Yosef Haim Brenner and Aharon Reuveni.

The growth of the literary center in Palestine was naturally affected by demographic fluctuations in the Jewish community. In 1855 there were about 10,500 Jews in the country. The pogroms in Russia in 1881, which came to be known as "desert storms," prompted a new wave of immigration of about 1,500 per year. By 1898 there were already about 50,000 Jews in Palestine, and by 1907, at the start of the Second Aliyah, some 75,000. When the First World War broke out there were 85,000 Jews in the country, but the war caused their numbers to dwindle to 65,000. Then in 1922 immigration began again in the form of the Third Aliyah, and the Jewish community, known as the Yishuv, once again began to grow. By 1930 there were about 165,000 Jews in Palestine.

These demographic changes might not have been significant had they not coincided with the decline of the Eastern European Jewish communities. Still and all, until the Second World War the new center in Eretz Israel remained closely affiliated with the cultural centers of Eastern Europe, depending on them for material and other assistance. Hebrew periodicals in Palestine looked for subscribers in Europe and the United States. Their editors called upon the Hebrew writers in the diaspora to help them raise funds. Moreover, the writers of Eretz Yisrael still addressed themselves to a diaspora readership. When they wrote about local affairs, such as the life of the Yishuv or the local Arabs, they felt that they were providing exotic reading matter for non-resident readers. But as the old Hebrew periodicals in Eastern Europe such as *Hashiloah* (1896–1927) closed down, leaving no successors in Europe or America, literary life began to concentrate itself in Palestine.

The new periodicals which began to appear in Eretz Yisrael reflected the emergent literary life. Although a periodical like *Moledet* [*Homeland*] continued to address the needs and interests of overseas as well as of local readers, for the most part the journals turned inward to report on and speak to the local scene. The first such publication to be motivated by the call to establish a cultural homeland in the country was *Ha'omer* [*The Swath*], which appeared in the early days of the Second Aliyah, in 1907–1908. Distinctly innovative among Jewish journals, *Ha'omer* insisted on publishing literary materials that reflected the place and its environment. The appearance in 1908 of *Hapo'el hatza'ir* gave fresh impetus to the local literature. Edited by Yosef Aharonowitz, it was an organ of the Second Aliyah movement. Its early issues typically included stories by M. Wilkansky, Moshe Smilansky (whose pseudonym was Hawajah Moussa), Nehama Pukhachewsky, and others, which not only described the country in positive, even idealized, terms (for the most part), but also served as virtual propaganda in the Yishuv's relations with the diaspora.

In its early stages, in the late nineteenth century, Hebrew literature in Palestine resembled that of the Haskalah. Here too was a hodgepodge of traditions and influences taken from diverse sources, literary and otherwise. Like the writers of the Haskalah, these writers also shaped their characters and plots to serve didactic moral purposes. Their early works included travel notes, documentary stories, and extracts from the press of the Old Yishuv. Much as the early Haskalah writers in the diaspora had done (Abraham Mapu and Peretz Smolenskin, for example) the early Hebrew writers in Eretz Yisrael either depicted the country as a reflection of its legendary ideal form or directed fierce attacks against the local obscurantists who belonged to the Old Yishuv. But whereas diaspora literature had produced some impressive works by the end of the century, the literature of Eretz Yisrael failed to get beyond the cumbersome conventions of the Haskalah and the tendentious narrative of social critique.

The work of the next group of Eretz Yisrael writers corresponds to late-nineteenth- and early-twentieth-century realism and is characterized by an ideologically directed plot, a melodramatic presentation of social issues, and a less inflated, more natural, language. Its main difference from its diaspora counterpart was that it presented the Jew not as an exile among the goyim but in a homeland set in a different non-Jewish environment, namely the Arab Middle East. Whereas the protagonists of the villages of Europe were peddlers, shopkeepers, and artisans contending with gentile landowners and policemen, in Palestine good Jewish farmers, pioneers, laborers, and watchmen of the Third Aliyah clashed with bad exploitative farmers of the First Aliyah and with hostile Arabs.

Most of the writers of Eretz Yisrael were self-conscious about their lack of familiarity with the new environment. For this reason they were sometimes carried away by their passion for the land that finally enabled them to feel that, like other writers of national literatures, they too had native geographical roots. For them, the pioneering experience was a form of religious redemption. Their writings did not so much mirror the surrounding reality as express a naive enthusiasm for it. For the most part, these writers ignored the objective conditions of their world, creating instead a sort of dreamland. Eretz Yisrael writers, notably Moshe Smilansky, Yosef Luidor, and Meir Wilkanksy produced a literature that not only confirmed the values and ideals of pioneering Zionism but, in a way, invented them. So powerfully persuasive were these writers, both the Jews living in Eretz Yisrael and those living in the diaspora, that one might say of their perceptions of the homeland that the influence of life on their literature was less important than the influence of their literature on life.

As we have already seen, not all the writers responded with the same youthful enthusiasm. The fiction of Brenner and others vigorously resisted this ideologizing and idealization both in life and literature: "They were all, after all," Brenner writes of the pioneers in *Breakdown and Bereavement*,

> neurasthenics, cosmic worriers, who bore the world's burden on their shoulders and judged everything in terms of the group. If one of them traveled abroad, for example, he had not simply gone someplace else, but had "given up" and "betrayed the ideal"; if someone stood guard in a vineyard he was not just a lookout, but "a watchman in the fatherland"; if the cook burned the food in the inn—and when did she not burn it? and who really cared, anyway, except that it was something to talk about?—she was an execrable cook, of course, but she was also "an irresponsible woman with no sense of duty to her comrades." (p. 15)

Brenner formalized his position in an extremely influential inaugural editorial entitled "The Eretz Israel Genre and Its Artifacts" (1911), which appeared in the last periodical he edited, *Ha'adamah* (1920–1923). Brenner called for a realistic literature that would in no way attempt to fabricate or alter the truth. Life and literature, he asserted, were more important than any set of ideological assumptions. Therefore, the literature must not idealize the life. Rather, it must (like his own fiction) mirror it, however painful or perplexing it was. In defining the new literature this way, Brenner was specifically attacking the newly emerging "genre writing," which he felt was ideological and tendentious; literature that was excessively devoted to imported artistic models and indulged in a compromising aestheticism. "Genre" referred to those depictions of Eretz Yisrael that, rather than grappling with the realities of dislocation and culture-building, imagined the new Jewish world of Palestine as a fully formed society that was already realizing the dreams and aspirations of the Jewish people. Brenner resisted this idealization vigorously, maintaining the same guidelines for literary critics as he did for the writers. He rejected criticism that depended on alien theories and that lacked insight into the realities of everyday life in the Yishuv.

Brenner was not alone in reacting this way to genre fiction. At first the immigrants of the Second Aliyah believed, in the words of an early Zionist anthem, that "in the beloved ancestral land / all hopes shall be fulfilled." But many were disappointed. Up to ninety percent returned to Europe. The tension between the physical, psychological, and emotional demands of Zionist immigration and the limited capacities of the immigrants to make the necessary adjustments produced the complexity of the new literary corpus. A good many came to believe, like Brenner, that Eretz Yisrael had not changed the people, who remained foreigners in their ancient homeland. Continuing in the tradition of the psychological realists, they wrote what we might call, following Brenner's terminology, "anti-genre" literature.

Despite Brenner's low opinion of them, the handful of Second Aliyah immigrants who remained in Eretz Yisrael laid the foundations for the future of the culture. These were the individuals who had established most of the literary organs that produced a new readership and, just as important, determined the primacy of Hebrew as the language of the emergent culture. A powerful force in the consolidation of the new literature was the gradual disappearance, during the period of the Second Aliyah, of bilingualism. Hebrew began to take the place of Yiddish, and the ancient sacred tongue became the vernacular language. Non-literary Hebrew infused the literature with new vitality.

Language, however, was only one of the elements of settlement which greased the gears of creative process. The genre writers turned history into myth, making literature out of the national birthing itself. This birthing included "the conquest of labor" (meaning the creation of a Hebrew laboring class); the settlement in the Galilee (in preference to the established farming communities in the center of the country, whose residents were unwilling to employ the Jewish pioneers); the establishment of Sejera (an agricultural college in the Galilee, where the first collective farm was established) and of the *moshav* (farming village) Ein Ganim; the founding of Hashomer (The Watchman), an association of guards for the Jewish settlements, in 1909; and even the efforts to produce a Hebrew press. Over Brenner's objections, genre fiction, with its pseudo- or idealized realism and elevated language, its simplistic characterization, and its documentary or melodramatic plotting, would continue to dominate Hebrew fiction until at least the 1950s. The indomitable pioneers and fighters of genre fiction would coexist, however, in diametrical opposition to another set of characters: the half-crazed and suicidal figures who were more like storm-driven souls lost in a new world than bold new settlers seeking to build the land and be rebuilt by it.

In both genre and anti-genre literature, a new geographical and psychological landscape took hold. Wintry scenes of timbered houses and birch trees gave way to the hot dry land, wedged between the desert and the sea. In place of the villages and cities of Europe appeared agricultural *moshavot* (farming communities), communes, and the Levantine town. These new locations were populated with equally original personae: Middle Eastern Jews, members of the Old Yishuv, Arabs, and Jewish farmers and guards. The native-born Jew, who had never before been a figure in Hebrew literature, emerges as a heroic protagonist in the fiction of Barzilai-Eisenstadt, Luidor, Reuveni, Arieli-Orloff, and Smilansky, who also featured the pioneer-laborer as the leader of his people.

A number of literary styles influence the emerging literature. The genre literature of the early period, up to and including the Third Aliyah, was still very much a product of the Haskalah and the realist school of the earlier generation of Hebrew writers. In the style of Hebrew literature as far back as the 1890s, it remained positivistic, setting utility above beauty. The stylistic influences of Mendele were still very much in evidence in the language of Agnon and Shami. At the same time, the influence of Brenner increased, directly affecting such different authors as Agnon, Reuveni, Kimhi, and Arieli-Orloff. It blended with the influence of Berdyczewski to produce the sober romanticism that infused the writings of the anti-genrists. As in the past, there was also the influence of non-Jewish writing. The immigrants from Russia brought with them the works of Dostoyevsky and Chekhov. Brenner, who himself translated *Crime and Punishment,* also translated several of the plays of Gerhard Hauptmann, while some of the Scandinavian neo-romantics, such as Bjornson, Jacobsen, and Hamsun, were also at this time being translated into Hebrew.

Genre versus anti-genre is only one way of classifying this generation of Hebrew texts. One can also speak in terms of (a) regional fiction that emphasized the link between the community and the soil (Smilansky, Hurgin, Zemach, and Reuveni); (b) pioneering stories that dealt with the conflict between the pioneering settlers and the local inhabitants (Smilansky and Burla); (c) documentary fiction that recorded the heroism of individuals (notably Wilkansky); (d) immigrant stories that depicted the alienation of the new immigrants (Brenner, Rabinowitz, Kimhi, and Agnon); (e) quasi-romantic legends (Arieli-Orloff and Agnon); and (f) exotic tales that depicted for their readers a heretofore unknown world (Smilansky, Shami, Burla, and Hurgin). In all of these groupings, however, the essential tension between genre and anti-genre continues to characterize the writers.

MOSHE SMILANSKY, YOSEF LUIDOR, MEIR WILKANKSY

Moshe Smilansky was the most notable author of this generation and an outstanding representative of genre writing. He was one of the leaders of the First Aliyah, most of whom settled in *moshavot* and wrote about the lives of the newcomers. Their values were clear-cut and unequivocal: The settler was fundamentally good and whoever opposed him, or impeded settlement, was bad. Although the Arabs were variously viewed as wretched and pathetic, remarkable and heroic (they occasionally even appeared as idealized, romantic-exotic sons of the land whom the settlers might emulate), insofar as they opposed the pioneers, they were depicted as the enemy. This insistence on a set of values determined the artistic quality of the fiction. Simple, at times archaic, in style, the fiction proceeded through polarized characterizations, melodrama, and an overstated, heavy-handed, not always convincing plot.

Smilansky's protagonists were simple, innocent pioneers, resisting equally the forces of nature and the local inhabitants. The author made no attempt to examine their inner lives, only to record their outward actions. A typical protagonist is the eponymous hero of the story "Hawaja Nazar" (1910), a pioneer who exemplified the new values which Berdyczewski, following Nietzsche, had called for earlier. The hero, who is called "Hawaja" ("Mister") by his Arab friends, is a half-Jew from Russia who becomes a Zionist after reading the Bible in Russian. He is admired by the Arabs, makes love to Bedouin women, and meets his end when he jumps into the river Jordan, which he had always dreamed of and which he wishes, through his suicide, to prove to be as much a river as the Volga. This character becomes the archetype of the New Hebrew Man, who in various guises haunts Hebrew literature until the 1950s, if not later.

This was exactly the kind of idealized fictionalizing that Brenner opposed. Yet, despite Brenner's protests, the later writers of the Second Aliyah, such as Wilkansky, Luidor, and Burla, and several authors of the Third Aliyah as well, followed in Smilansky's footsteps. They glorified the pioneers, set the pioneering enterprise above personal issues, and constructed their narratives to serve Zionist efforts abroad. Even if, in reality, expectation and aspiration had not yet been translated into everyday reality, they were depicted as if they were. To this end, much of the fiction based itself on documentary material drawn from the chronicles of the times.

While the psychological realists, such as Gnessin, Berkowitz, Shoffman, and Brenner, portrayed the alienated and disaffected, Yosef Luidor (who was murdered with Brenner in Jaffa in 1921) created figures such as Yehuda the orchard watchman ("The Hebrew" [Haʿivri], Berlin 1912) and Yoash ("Yoash," published in *Hashiloah,* Odessa 1912), indomitable, native-born men who speak only Hebrew and know no other homeland. While Gnessin sought to plumb the agonies of the human soul, Meir Wilkansky detailed the working days of the immigrants, working shoulder to shoulder digging wells and competing with Arab laborers. Wilkansky's stories evidenced the collective effort, on the parts of its ordinary citizens as much as of its writers, to sanctify everyday life. His elevated diction, poetic to the point of worshipfulness, was intended to invest agrarian labor with a spiritual quality. Such elevated style was employed by the Second Aliyah writers in order to produce an emotionally charged relationship to commonplace matters such as the plough, the furrow, physical labor, malaria, and sweat. The heroes of Wilkansky and Luidor were fructifying the ancestral land. Even if all their hopes were not to be fulfilled, at least they were living their aspirations in reality, not only in their dreams.

YITZHAK SHAMI, YEHUDAH BURLA, YAACOV HURGIN

In contrast to the innocent enthusiasm of immigrant writers such as Smilansky, Luidor, and Wilkansky, the native-born genrists, who grew up under Ottoman rule, expressed a different naiveté. Two of them, Yitzhak Shami and Yehudah Burla, who belonged to the old Sephardic community, began to write in the first decade of the century. Yaacov Hurgin, who was younger, began to publish in the early 1920s. Burla, Shami, and Hurgin all attended the teachers' college Ezra in Jerusalem and were employed as schoolteachers. They were close friends, exchanging letters and helping each other to publish their writings. Because they were rooted in the country and enjoyed a direct relationship with Arab Middle Eastern culture, for them Eretz Yisrael was not the beloved promised land. It was simply the country of their birth, where they had to make their way and deal with people and societies about which diaspora Jewry knew absolutely nothing: the Eastern Jewish community, the Arab and Turkish communities, and the old Ashkenazi Yishuv (which Hurgin, in particular, depicted).

Despite the fact that for them Eretz Yisrael and its inhabitants were not exotic, as they appeared to the immigrants to be, nonetheless these writers were greatly influenced by the literature of the Second Aliyah, which opened a window not only on European culture but also on pioneering Zionism itself. This affected their writing, both artistically and (especially in the case of Burla) ideologically. The influence was manifested primarily in the formal structures of their fiction, which were essentially modern and Western (the novel, the short story, and the novella). In other aspects of style and in the psychological motivation of the characters the works reflected the surrounding Arabic culture in which the writers had grown up.

Yitzhak Shami is the most original and grounded of these writers. Resisting genre, he wrote little, his total output consisting of several short stories and one long novella, *The Vengeance of the Fathers* [*Nikmat ha 'avot*]. *The Vengeance of the Fathers,* which was his major work, is one of the most important works in Hebrew literature. It first appeared in book form in 1927 in Jerusalem. At the heart of the story—which, according to the author, was based on events that happened at the beginning of the century—is the age-old rivalry between the Arab inhabitants of two cities, Nablus and Hebron. During the annual pilgrimage to the shrine of Nebi Moussa (the prophet Moses), the Arab leader of Nablus, driven by pride and ambition, murders the equally vain and conceited leader of Hebron, after which he is subject not only to the laws of blood-vengeance on the part of the Hebronites, but also to divine retribution itself: In murdering his antagonist, Nimmer Abu Il-Shawarab violates the basic code of conduct which regulates pilgrimage. The protagonist is finally destroyed, not by any of his human enemies, but by the ghosts of the patriarchs themselves, who appear to him in his exile in Egypt and to whom he finally surrenders his being at the Tomb of the Patriarchs in Hebron.

Although Shami was the first native-born writer to successfully harness the literary traditions imported by the Second Aliyah writers to the themes and motifs of his time and place, he (unlike his contemporary Burla) did not attempt to express Zionist ideology in his fiction. Just as German-Jewish or Jewish-American authors wrote in their native languages, so too did this Arab-Jewish writer write in Hebrew. In diction and style he kept to the tradition of Mendele and his followers, yet a strong infusion of Arabisms marked the distinct locality of his composition. The world Shami depicted—his own community and the surrounding Arab society— and his seemingly straightforward subjects are, in fact, rescued from reductiveness by the richness and intricacy of his language.

Thus, *The Vengeance of the Fathers* achieves its power not through the writer's romanticization of a world which, though not exotic for him, would likely seem so to any of his foreign readers; rather it is a consequence of Shami's rather meticulous realistic rendering of this world. This is not to deny the density of popular beliefs and folkloric resonances integrated into the tale by its Arab narrator but to bring into relief the depth of religious, political, and psychological motivation that produces the dramatic action. From the beginning of the novella, its protagonist, Nimmer Abu Il-Shawarab, is presented as embodying the paradox of religious conviction:

> Nimmer Abu Il-Shawarab was the only man in Nablus who scrupulously observed the customs of the fathers. A courageous and generous man, devoted since childhood to the prophets and the saints, on the upkeep of whose tombs he had spent much of his gold. The treasurers of the mosques could tell many stories of his generosity and charity. All the young men of Nablus would have responded to his call, despite his hot temper and reputation as a proud, angry man who insisted on obedience and brooked no opposition. His excitability and stubbornness often got him into serious conflicts and unpleasant situations, from which he managed to extricate himself only with the help of police officers who were among his many devoted friends, and of his family's connections with the authorities in Nablus and Jerusalem. (*The Vengeance of the Fathers,* p. 65)

This is at once a story of religious belief and of socio-political, religious power. In the style of classic naturalistic fiction, the pilgrims, including their leaders, are described throughout the story in terms of their animal

qualities. But whereas the throngs emerge as unthinking brutes, their leaders project a vitality and drive that turns out to be even more dangerous
and compromising in the end:

> The entire valley, from Abu Il-Shawarab's house to the square mosque
> of Nebi Youssef, was covered by thin wisps of mist which rose from the
> many rivulets hiding among the tall bushes and grasses. From afar the
> valley looked as if it were part of the fertile slopes of Mount Gerizim
> bejeweled with glittering spring flowers on which pearls of dew trembled
> in the fresh spring breeze. Now it was filled with many-colored *keffiyehs,*
> headbands, and *abbayehs,* as masses of heads mingled and separated,
> covering the ground like swarms of mosquitoes over a river. Their noise
> and din, their snorting camels, whinnying horses, braying donkeys, and
> screaming children filled the air of the valley with a prolonged cacoph-
> ony. (Ibid., p. 76)

If the masses are like mosquitoes, and "locusts," and "sheep" (p. 82), Abu
Il-Shawarab is an extension of his horse, which is as "aware of his own
importance and splendor" as is his rider: "[P]roudly raising his head, he
shook his ears, as if to show the other horses the red silk scarf tied around
his forehead. . . . He dilated his nostrils, threw up his head, shook his
mane, stamped his hooves several times, and waggled his ankles to let the
sunlight fall on his horseshoes of polished steel that gleamed like silver"
(p. 83). "Lithe as a cat," "glowing, radiant, with sunbeams dancing on his
sword blade and flag" (p. 86), Abu Il-Shawarab lets this animal power
deliver him to violation and sin. The unleashed forces of nature, this novel
suggests, are, like the powers of the divine, not so easily controlled by
mere mortals. At the end of the story, Abu Il-Shawarab dies—a sacrifice to
the "vengeance of the Fathers," where these "Fathers" are not human
beings (the ancestors or descendants of the man he murdered), but the
patriarchs themselves. The world that Shami depicts is uniquely Middle
Eastern in its concepts of honor and fate. Shami's protagonists do not
(like their European counterparts) resist fate but accept it, alleviating
themselves of all responsibility for their situation. Thus, it is the protagonist's withdrawal into a hashish-induced haze that ultimately produces his act of repentance. Although Shami did not innovate much by
way of literary forms, his themes, style, and structure, and, above all, his
insights into national and private psychologies, ensure his position in the
Hebrew literary canon.

Despite the fact that he was Shami's contemporary and good friend,
in many ways Yehudah Burla more closely resembles the writers of the
Second Aliyah and the Zionist and labor movements. Although he also
incorporated elements of his Middle Eastern background, his fiction, in
its naiveté and simplistic characterization, constitutes a variety of genre

fiction. Many of his native-born Middle Eastern protagonists eventually wind up on that ideal embodiment of the new ideology, the kibbutz. Burla was at his best when he created unexpected dramatic narratives that were rich in Middle Eastern ambience. Most of his work took the form of novels, some picaresque, such as *The Adventures of Akavia* [*Alilot ʿAkavia*, 1939], and some romantic melodrama, such as *His Hated Wife* [*ʾIshto hasnuʾah*], published in installments in *Hatekufah*, 1922–1923. He specialized in intricate plots, in which psychological motivation and characterization were secondary to the effects of tension and catharsis, fear and pity. The less ideological his plots, the better they succeeded as literary works.

The critics did not praise Burla's style, even though it did have a certain distinctiveness. Whereas his Second Aliyah contemporaries fashioned non-existent Hebrew-speaking protagonists to represent Yiddish speakers, Burla's Hebrew speakers stood for people who in real life spoke Arabic and Ladino. Their discourse is infused with phrases and sayings from those other languages, as in *The Adventures of Akavia*. By including ritualistic and folkloric terminologies, as well as through deliberate syntactical deformations of the writing (reminiscent of Gnessin), he produced an epic romance about an eponymous hero's search for the secret of his life and for universal salvation. This hero aids the poor, rescues the unfortunate, and battles against the forces of evil. Like all heroes, he is driven by an overwhelming passion. He fights for his beloved Anahit, who leaves him; marries an ordinary woman, Viduga; and later falls in love with the romantic Diamanti. After his immigration to Jerusalem he becomes the Jewish hero who protects his community from an Arab attack. He is, in the final analysis, a tragic figure with unrealizable romantic aspirations.

Although Burla tried to endow his hero with a philosophical dimension, converting him into a minor Job or Faust whose protests seem to have cosmic significance, as a philosophical text the novel is not very convincing. As romance, however, it has its attractions. In an age of non-heroes, his heroic figures and their exploits appealed to the young immigrants who were eager to read about adventures that matched the intensities of their fantasies about the Arab Middle East.

The final member of this triumvirate of native-born writers, Yaacov Hurgin, served as an intermediary figure between those who joined ranks with the Second Aliyah and those who became affiliated with the Third Aliyah (native born writers such as Yehoshua Bar-Yosef and the *Dor Baʾaretz* writers, such as S. Yizhar and Moshe Shamir, who began publishing in the late 1930s). In his themes, albeit not in his style, Hurgin belonged to the anti-genre writers. Like Shami and Reuveni, and unlike the young immigrants, he did not depict the Old Yishuv as homogeneous, but as vital and multifaceted, even somewhat grotesque. But, whereas Agnon and Reuveni described the Old Yishuv as pitted against the newcomers, he described it from within, producing his protagonist from within the local scene.

In a way, without ever distorting the country's physical reality, he succeeded in constructing a native Eretz Yisrael diaspora community. In contradistinction to both genre and anti-genre, for most of his protagonists Eretz Yisrael is not the Promised Land. Jews and Arabs leave the country and come back to it in much the same way as the characters of Brenner and Agnon move in and out of Eastern Europe. His protagonists, Jews and Arabs alike, are attached to the place not by ideology but by habit and circumstance. Hurgin's best stories are those which take place in this familiar environment of the Old Yishuv, both the Sephardi community (as in "At Uncle Raful's House" ["Beveit hadod Raful"] and "Eliyahu the Butcher" ["Eliyahu haqatsav"]) and its Ashkenazi, Arab, Turkish, and Armenian neighbors (as in "Professor Leonardo," "Munira," and *In the Mountains of Ephraim* [*Bein harei 'Ephraim*]). Indeed, his canvas stretched from Jewish and Arab Jaffa to Jerusalem and Tiberias and the mountains of Ephraim—wherever Arabs and Jews resided.

The society that Hurgin depicts is characterized by the rigidity of its social norms, especially concerning love, marriage, and old age. Anyone who violates communal practice is ejected. For the most part Hurgin's stories shed comic and pathetic light on characters who either overdo their adherence to convention or deliberately flout it. His most grotesque story of married life is *Eliyahu the Butcher,* which deals with the intrigues and complex interactions of a traditional Sephardic family. The story proceeds through exaggerations and grotesque oppositions, which produce the book's comic effect. The patriarch of the family, Eliyahu, stands in stark contrast to a number of the book's characters: Rivkeh, his wife; his son Yaacov; his father; his young daughter Rahelina; and his prosperous and overpowering relative, the merchant Gino. The basis for all of Eliyahu's relationships to these members of his family is some manner of commercial exchange. While during the week Eliyahu intimidates all of his neighbors, on weekends he wins his right to sex with his wife by providing her with the weekly housekeeping expenses, attending to the children's needs, and visiting his wife's Uncle Gino. This web of love, sexual avarice, and commercial exchange prevails in his relationships with his children and father as well.

Hurgin also wrote more serious studies in this vein, including several stories about passion, in which the relations between the sexes are determined by the dominant forces of their respective societies, be they Sephardi, Ashkenazi, or Arab. These presumably diverse ethnic societies differ only in the intensities of the repressions they impose, and, therefore, in the nature of the eruption, which is directly proportional to the degree of communal control. One of the more interesting stories in this category is the novella *In the Mountains of Ephraim,* in which the Jewish anti-hero, incapable of overcoming social convention, unintentionally victimizes a young Arab woman, Zain, with whom he has defied the taboos on love relations between Jews and Arabs.

Old age fascinated Hurgin, and there is an absurd aspect to the pathos of the stories in which his elderly protagonists face death. One of his best stories in this vein is Professor Leonardo, which describes the isolation and pretension of a lonely eccentric in a little Jewish community in Palestine, reminiscent of one of Berdyczewski's and Shoffman's comic-pathetic characters. An aging pantaloon trying desperately to play the role of the romantic lover, he is in reality not Professor Leonardo, a European professor of music, but poor old Leibele, who lives with his sick mother. Dressing and speaking as he imagines a figure like a Professor Leonardo would, he tries to win a place in the stifling provincialism of the town.

The story is farce, making fun of both the impostor and the people around him, since neither one can tell the difference between the reality and the fake. Underlying the story and the narrator's personality is the duality of the intellectual as hungry animal, the romantic man as fool, and the musician as beggar. The story concludes pathetically, when the protagonist throws off his disguise and rips off the strings of his violin. At the end of illusion is loneliness once again, and Hurgin exposes the absurdity of a man who adopts a noble posture for trivial purposes.

Hurgin was an important link in the chain that leads from the early writers who emulated the literature of the Haskalah, through the first immigrants who were unable to strike viable roots in the country, to the integrated native-born authors. The minor dramas in his stories do not deal with the lives of uprooted newcomers who are at loose ends but with members of the settled population in their normal environment. He therefore saw no need to describe the surroundings as such or to present them in an exotic light in order to appeal to overseas readers. To him, the locale and the life of its people were the natural materials of his literary creation.

LEV ARIEH ARIELI-ORLOFF, DOV KIMHI, AHARON REUVENI

The anti-genrists, whose undisputed spiritual leader was Brenner, and whose writing did not, therefore, conform to the idealized model that Brenner opposed, included Aharon Reuveni, Lev Arieh Arieli-Orloff, Shmuel Yosef Agnon, Dov Kimhi, and Z. Schatz (who was killed with Brenner in Jaffa in 1921). Although Brenner regarded Agnon, Reuveni, and Arieli-Orloff as equals and although their contemporaries had not yet distinguished Agnon from the others or paid him any special attention, nonetheless Agnon is so extraordinary and accomplished and so central to the canon of Hebrew literature that he will be dealt with separately in the next chapter.

While Brenner was still strongly influenced by the Russian writers, most notably Dostoyevsky, the younger anti-genrists had been exposed to Scandinavian impressionism. In the beginning, they avoided all depiction of "context," deliberately ignoring the surrounding society and concentrating instead on the inner emotional world of the individual. In time, however, they achieved more balance, most of them undergoing several stylistic transformations. The similar biographical profile of these immigrant authors gave rise to a uniformity of themes. The circumstances in which their protagonists find themselves are quite unlike those described by Smilansky and Luidor. Not only does Eretz Yisrael treat them inhospitably but they are themselves highly ambivalent about the heroic self-sacrifice that is demanded of them. Therefore, while these protagonists are by no means identical to one another, they do share certain distinctive characteristics. Most of them are weak and insecure. Fully self-aware, they are incapable of true love relationships, and they fail at every undertaking. With the notable exception of Agnon and his personae, they resemble Brenner's anti-heroes, and like their authors, they have little interest in Judaism and its traditions.

The biography of L. A. Arieli-Orloff parallels that of ninety percent of the Second Aliyah immigrants who tried to settle in Eretz Yisrael and left. He arrived in 1909 to become one of the leading figures of the literature of the Second Aliyah. Brenner often mentioned him together with Agnon and in one article described the two as the rightful heirs of Gnessin and Shoffman. But in 1923 Arieli-Orloff moved to the United States. Thereafter his literary voice grew weaker, until it finally faded altogether. He lost touch with his readership and evidently also with his literary spark. All that remained, as he put it in one of his letters, was sadness and the knowledge that memories are more real than reality. The relocation of the Hebrew literary center to Palestine and the failure of the most prosperous diaspora communities to produce another spelled the downfall of this gifted writer, as it did for others. Although he migrated from a backward province to the developed world, as a Hebrew writer he left a literary hothouse for a desert.

Arieli-Orloffs's significance is mainly illustrative. His writing underwent the gamut of changes which the literature of the Second Aliyah experienced, from fantastic impressionism to psychological realism. The influence of Brenner and of the Scandinavian writers is evident in his work.

His style resembles Reuveni's plain, unpretentious language and occasionally he slips into something like formulation and the Bialik tradition. His realistic stories are more mature than the impressionistic ones, and at least three of them are artistically sophisticated. The most mature of these realistic stories is the serialized *Wilderness* [*Yeshimon*], the first two parts of which were published in *Ha'adamah* in 1920, and the third in *Dapim* [*Pages*], edited by Kimhi, in Jerusalem in 1922.

The protagonist of this quasi-autobiographical story is a young Jew by name of David Ostrovsky who is conscripted into the Turkish army. Arieli-Orloff's achievement is to depict, in the style of Brenner, Reuveni, and Agnon, the profound isolation of a man alienated by social-psychological circumstances; a Jew among gentiles, a European in the East. Alone among his fellow bondsmen, Ostrovsky undergoes many harrowing experiences that expose his impotence and absurd loneliness, until he finally returns home, only to discover that the woman he loves has married another man.

Of all the anti-genrists, Dov Kimhi was the most Western European, for which feature of his writing Brenner (who Kimhi idolized) most praised him: "You are not popular, hearty, earthy," he wrote to Kimhi in a 1919 letter, "but intelligent, European, modern, somewhat Schnitzlerish." Indeed, his literary education (he produced many translations of German and Scandinavian texts) is sometimes more discernible in his work than is any artistic achievement. His writing may be divided into three categories: impressionist stories in the style of the Austrian neo-romantic school (e.g., *Small Tales* [*Sipurim qtanim*, 1928]; *Epilogue* [*Aharit*], and *The Book of Destruction* [*Sefer haqilyonot*]); an impressionistic novel, *Transitions* [*Ma'avarot*, 1923], which resembles the writing of the later modernist authors of the Third Aliyah, such as Steinmann and Horowitz; and nearly realistic novels with an impressionistic-atmospheric quality (e.g., *On the Seven Seas* ['*Al shiv'ah yamim*, 1934] and *The House of Hefetz* [*Beit Heifetz*, 1951]).

The last of these shows Kimhi at his best. Similar in style to the novels of Knut Hamsun (*Victoria, Pan, Mystery*), *The House of Hefetz* is set in Jerusalem, which is depicted simply as a provincial Middle Eastern town that serves as the background of a family saga. The main protagonist is Dr. Haim Sapir, an incompetent, dislocated new immigrant, who makes the acquaintance of the Hefetz family, dominated by powerful matriarch Nehama Hefetz, who marries her daughters off against their wishes. Sapir marries the wrong sister, while another sister obediently marries a degenerate Jewish-Indian prince. Later she escapes from his family and returns to her mother's house in Jerusalem, where she commits suicide. The novel enacts the familiar conflict between materialistic parentally arranged marriages and romantic love. The most interesting character in the book is the great matriarch herself, who plays god with her daughters' lives—a character which Agnon had depicted earlier in his novel *A Simple Story* [*Sipur pashut*], and which had appeared in various guises in Jewish and non-Jewish family novels before and after these two works.

As a writer, Kimhi by and large failed to achieve literary originality, leaving little mark on his generation or its successors. In a 1920 letter Kimhi took the measure of himself and his generation of authors. "I am a compulsive reader," he wrote; "I read as many as three or four stories a day, and I read everything. Yet in the last few years not a single line from our tidal wave of pages has stuck in my mind. In that case, to use Frischmann's ornamental phrase, an age of dwarfs must eventually produce a giant. And in that case we are merely the fertilizer for the giant who must come. . . . Believe me, nothing but fertilizer." Only Agnon, the "giant who must come," as Kimhi put it, knew how to combine the European heritage with local materials and age-old Jewish tradition.

"What then is to happen?" opens Aharon Reuveni's 1930 novel *Sadness* [*'Itsavon*]. His answer recalls the sobriety of Brenner: "It's good to live in Eretz Israel," says one of the characters, who is trying to make a go of it; "[A]t any rate, it's no worse than elsewhere." This, in a nutshell, is Reuveni's philosophy: a clear-eyed and realistic skepticism, unwilling to apotheosize the country but capable of meeting its challenges.

The writings of Aharon Reuveni (Shimshelevitz) reflected his stormy biography: Born in the Ukraine, he moved to the United States in 1904, returned to Russia, was deported to Siberia, escaped, and wandered about for some time before reaching Eretz Yisrael, which became his home and the locale of most of his fiction. In many ways, he was the Hebrew writer who came closest to turn-of-the-century naturalism. Like the naturalists of Europe, he sought to depict humankind in its raw, naked reality.

Reuveni's place in Hebrew literature rests mainly on his trilogy, which came to be known by the title *Unto Jerusalem* [*'Ad Yerushalayim*] after it appeared in a single volume in 1954. Its three parts—*In the Beginning Was Confusion* [*Bereishit hamevukhah*], *The Last Boats* [*Ha'oniyot ha'aharonot*], and *Devastation* [*Shamot*], each published separately in the 1920s—stand alone as separate novels; the unifying feature that links them rests in the overall atmosphere rather than in the dramatic structure. This is an atmosphere of stifling dullness, which the writer depicts through unrelenting irony. His plots are full of minor characters who fall victim to social pressure and are thrown into trivial, insignificant crises. The setting (mainly Jerusalem) is also depicted as meager, affording little in the way of material opportunity or cultural life. In the first two parts the plot is fairly monotonous, moved largely by impersonal forces—the First World War, the political authorities, the Turks. The characters are for the most part ideologically motivated immigrants who have come from Eastern Europe to Jerusalem, some of them willingly, some not, where they mix with the local inhabitants, to whom the place is merely one more Jewish community among many. The newcomers' idealism crumbles before their eyes. Most of them wish to leave. A few cling on.

Only in the third part of the trilogy does a real plot develop that reveals relationships among fully realized individuals. In *Devastation* the protagonist Meir Funk is admirable but tragic, struggling to make for himself a meaningful existence in Eretz Yisrael. His life becomes entwined with that of the Wattstein family, in whose house he lodges and into which he marries. It is also the story of the decline of a Jerusalemite family as the Great War exposes it to new currents blowing through the world. Contrary to the reader's expectations, the city Reuveni's novel depicts is not a spiritual place, as it is in genre fiction. Rather, Jerusalem is an earthly city, and very cruel. In the course of the novel, the head of the family dies and, in order to provide for the family, one of the daughters becomes a prostitute, with her mother's tacit compliance. The son, who served in the Ottoman army and was subjected to homosexual abuse, becomes a pimp. An idealistic pioneer, Funk marries the most innocent daughter but is conscripted into the Ottoman army and is killed during the war.

It is in this part of the trilogy that everything undergoes its ultimate deterioration into corruption and horror. But it is also at this stage that Meir Funk discovers his own resources for self-survival, and even though he dies, the book constitutes something of an affirmation and renewal of hope in the birth of his child. In Reuveni's novel, the future of Jewish survival in its ancient homeland is delivered from genre's insistence on idealism and ideology as the twin conditions of life and literature in Eretz Yisrael. That future is brought instead to the place where a reasoned acceptance of life and people, in all of their vicissitudes, greatness and pettiness, ugliness and beauty, misery and triumph, can come to assure the emergence of the new culture.

* * *

Like Funk, the protagonists of the anti-genre fiction of Arieli-Orloff, Kimhi, and Reuveni did not espouse lofty ideologies; nor did they reside in prettified settings. While their counterparts in genre fiction saw in every action another step toward the fulfillment of the hopes they had brought with them, these characters struggled with the question of why they should even remain in Eretz Yisrael. And they resolved to remain and tackle the hostile reality, even if it did not bring about the promised "life of radiance, life of liberty." It was this uncompromising honesty of the fiction, as demanded by Brenner, which made the works believable and established their place in Hebrew literature.

Of course, there is no absolute line dividing the genrists from the anti-genrists. Shami and Hurgin were not strictly genre writers, just as Kimhi, and even Reuveni were not always free of aspects of genre writing. The two trends continued their dialectical pull on Hebrew fiction from the 1920s until the 1970s. However, in time, the division becomes less distinct, and when it comes to the later literature, the terms genre and anti-genre become inadequate to define the literary forms that emerge.

7

THE CROSSROADS; OR, IS THIS THE ABODE OF THE SPIRIT?

S. Y. AGNON

All the achievements of Hebrew literature that preceded S. Y. Agnon culminated in his work. Agnon took the literary conventions that had been handed down from Mendele and Berdyczewski and innovated by Brenner and Shoffman, and, blending them with traditional Jewish and European themes and structures, he created a new Hebrew fiction. During the years of his creative life, from the Second Aliyah to the 1970s, the Jewish people experienced overwhelming historical upheaval. Though Agnon himself stated that the times were greater than the capacity of the literature to express them, nonetheless he himself succeeded in reflecting the enormity of the cultural transformation.

Born Shmuel Yosef Czaczkes on July 17, 1888, in Buczacz, Poland, Agnon emigrated to Palestine in 1908, left again in 1912 to spend twelve years in Germany, and returned in 1924 to settle in Jerusalem. In 1966 he received the Nobel Prize for Literature. He died in 1970. Like certain other writers, he created for himself a national-symbolic autobiography. He claimed as his birthdate the 9th of Av, the date on which, according to tradition, the temple was destroyed and the Messiah was to be born. And he cited as the day of his arrival in Israel and the anniversary of his first published Hebrew poem the 33rd day of the Omer, a day of rebellion and joy in the middle of the weeks of mourning between Passover and Shavuoth. His name itself derived from his fiction: "'Agunot" ("Forsaken Wives") is the title of the first story he published in Eretz Yisrael, in *Ha'omer* in 1908. Aptly enough, it is a story of eternal chasms: between lover and beloved, man and his soul, religion and everyday life, and Eretz Yisrael and the diaspora.

The stories and poems which he published in Yiddish and Hebrew before his arrival in Eretz Yisrael were of no significance. It was his arrival in Eretz Yisrael and the publication of "Forsaken Wives" and "And the Crooked Shall Become Straight" ["Vehayah he'akov lemishor," 1912] that established his place at the forefront of Hebrew literature and constituted the major turning point in his life. Brenner hailed "Forsaken Wives" with enthusiasm, and the two writers became close friends. Spiritually, Agnon belonged to the world of the Second Aliyah and, as he himself acknowledged, he was influenced by its leading figures, Brenner in particular. A Zionist who did not accept Zionist ideology uncritically, in an essay from the collection *From Myself to Myself* [*Me'atsmi 'el'atsmi*, 1976] Agnon acknowledged his debts and identified his own position as follows:

> Brenner taught me that young Jews have no place in the world except the Land of Israel. Though he spoke accusingly of the land and complained about its inhabitants, warning several of his friends not to come to "Palestina," in life he kept the commandment of dwelling in the land, and he died for the land. He also taught us to behave with modesty and humility and not to make the heavens ring with our small deeds. And if we look upon our comrades of the Second Aliyah we see that the better part of them learned from him. And those few who departed somewhat from his system did not stray far afield.
>
> Rupin taught us not to expect great things but to do whatever was in our power. Our great Rabbi [Kook] of blessed memory taught us the truth about the Land of Israel, that working the land was holy service. And Berl Katzenelson taught us all of those things. (p. 140)

For Agnon, the primary issue to be resolved in Eretz Yisrael, which did not, for the most part, preoccupy his contemporaries, was whether this would be the abode of the spirit; that is, whether it would be possible to achieve in Eretz Yisrael spiritual as well as material liberation. This is the question that circulates throughout his writings, in "Forsaken Wives," *Yesteryear* [*Tmol shilshom*, 1945], "Tehillah" (1950), "Edo and Enam" ["'Ido ve'Einam," 1950], and "Covering the Blood" ["Kisuy hadam," 1975].

The uniqueness of Agnon's position vis-à-vis contemporary politics and Jewish tradition is revealed in his blending of the forms of both genre and anti-genre. Like the genrists he accepted the ideological values of the Second Aliyah and evaluated his protagonists accordingly. For example, he celebrated the kibbutz as the new society's highest social achievement. But like the anti-genrists, his work did not dramatize the realization of the values he expounded. Even though Agnon's protagonists believe that the kibbutz will be the place of human perfectibility, they do not themselves live in *kevutzot* ("groups"—the early name of the kibbutzim).

Thus, while he remained faithful to the values of the Second Aliyah throughout his life, he diverged from the various forms of its fictional representations. From early in his career, there is a certain stylistic and atmospheric resemblance between his work and the impressionistic fiction of Arieli-Orloff and Kimhi. In the stories he published during the period of the Second Aliyah ("Miriam's Well" ["Be᾿erah shel Miriyam," 1909]; "Tishre," 1911) and in later writings which deal with that period (*Yesteryear* and "Betrothed" ["Shvuʿat᾿emunim," 1943]), his immigrant protagonists remain unillustrious and uncelebrated, like those of Reuveni and Brenner. More than many of his literary companions, Agnon realized that the heroes of the Second Aliyah were mostly failed dreamers—little, ordinary folk who had taken on more than they could manage.

Agnon's creative roots extend deeper than early-twentieth-century Eretz Yisrael, reaching back into his native town of Buczacz, the shtetl of his writings. The representation of his native village hovers poignantly and powerfully between his early memories of it and his later experience of the town; in the 1930s he revisited it in its post-War decline. The world of Buczacz is present in several of his works: from one of his first novellas, "And the Crooked Shall Become Straight" (1912) ("a tale about a man by name Menashe Haim, an inhabitant of the blessed community of Buczacz, who lost all his property and the poverty, God preserve us, drove him out of his mind") to the novel *A Guest for the Night* [*᾿Oreah natah lalun*, 1939], which was based on his later visit there. Something between a real place and a symbol, Agnon's Buczacz inherits a tradition of such representations in Jewish literature in the works of Mendele, Berdyczewski, Peretz, and Sholem Aleichem. It is invested with nostalgic pathos, but it is also an object of satire and burlesque. Like Sholem Aleichem, Agnon depicts the shtetl as a lost world, a city of the dead. But for Agnon there is no tolerant humor in this portrayal, only the macabre-grotesque realization of the slow demise of a world.

Agnon's major cultural resource was Jewish tradition itself, which underlies such stories as "Forsaken Wives" and "And the Crooked Shall Become Straight." In "Forsaken Wives," for example, Agnon used such primary materials as Jewish mysticism and the various responses to it, and it is possible to trace the roots of the story in the traditional canon. Nonetheless, his attitude toward religious tradition was at best ambivalent. He secularized and even desecrated hallowed texts, positioning them in absurd, even grotesque, juxtaposition to modern life or presenting ancient perspectives from unconventional and compromising points of view. In *Yesteryear,* for example, the creation of the world is presented in the Midrashic language of *Bereshith Rabbah* (a Midrashic commentary on Genesis) by a dog, aptly named Balak, who brings to the description a canine point of view.

In other words, in taking on traditional materials Agnon was not, or not merely, reaffirming old values and beliefs. Rather he was exposing and perhaps even setting himself in opposition to the mindset for which they stood. Sometimes his revisionism had a decisive secular purpose, as, for example, when Agnon appropriated traditional diction and even borrowed whole forms from the religious sources (the letter, the responsum, the sermon, the anecdote, and the parable) in order to make a story of failed love suggestive of historical, mythical, or psychological processes. Agnon's ideal reader was one who recognized the canonical material and thus perceived the socio-historical, political, and theological commentary of the text.

As familiar as he was with Jewish tradition, Agnon was equally well-versed in European culture. His writing thrived on the dialectical tension between the two that was already enriching the new Hebrew literature. When he desacralized canonical sources by combining them with modern European forms, Agnon underlined his relationship to his heritage by underscoring his difference from it. Like other anti-genre writers of his time, he was influenced in his early years by the Scandinavian neo-romantics, such as Jens Peter Jacobsen, Bjornstjerne Bjornson and especially Knut Hamsun (he even translated Bjornson's story "Dust" into Hebrew from a Yiddish translation in 1913). In his letters he also mentions the influences of Flaubert (which are discernable throughout his work), Gottfried Keller, and August Strindberg. During his sojourn in Germany, the Scandinavian influences waned and he came closer to the moderate controlled realism of Keller and Flaubert, and perhaps also of Thomas Mann.

After 1932 Agnon began to publish surrealist stories such as *The Book of Deeds* [*Sefer hama'asim*]. These stories have been compared with those of Kafka. Yet, Agnon's departure from realism was due to his own inner development as a writer, not to any external influence. There are also definitive differences between Kafka and Agnon, who, in fact, rejected the comparisons with Kafka. Kafka depicted a world out of time and place wherein the unreal becomes real. Agnon took recognizable times and places and defamiliarized and distorted them. The former deprived reality of its verisimilitude, the latter gave verisimilitude to the unreal. Agnon and Kafka were indeed almost opposites. In this sense, Agnon more resembles Gogol than Kafka.

In addition to traditional Jewish sources and European literature, the legacy of modern Hebrew fiction also influenced Agnon's work. Even though stylistically he took on the imperatives of Mendele and Bialik, from early on he used motifs from the literary romanticism of Peretz, Frischmann, and Berdyczewski. These he combined with the social materials of the commonplace tradition. His protagonists wandered about in a hybrid world constructed of the real and the fantastic and were as rootless and helpless as those of Brenner, Gnessin, and Shoffman. As he matured, Agnon tended more and more toward the strictly disciplined classical formulation of Mendele and Bialik, which acted as a barrier against the excesses of passion and emotion to which his neo-romanticism had inclined him. The contrast between the balanced perspectives of his technical formal style and the romantic subject matter he chose produced the author's characteristic irony. Agnon regarded traditional literature as an artistic ideal; by returning to its classical values he hoped to avoid what he perceived as the excessive intensities of the new literature. He wanted to display the sights rather than be excited by them, to evoke emotion rather than be swept away by it. He did not articulate this aspect of his literary aesthetic in the form of theoretical criticism. Rather, it emerges as implicit within the fiction itself.

Agnon's method of repeatedly rewriting his stories until he was satisfied with them makes it possible to follow his development from a pseudo-realist, through his neo-romantic phase, to the uniquely Agnonian style that, from 1912 on (after his stay in Germany), characterizes his work. "Tishre" (1911) evolved into "A Hill of Sand" ["Givʻat hahol," 1920]; "Miriam's Well" (1909) reappears in *The Tale of the Scribe* [*Agadat hasofer,* 1929]; "Nights" ["Leilot," 1913] is discernible in *Yesteryear* (1945), "The Broken Dish" ["Hapinkah hashvurah"] (1906 in Yiddish, and later in Hebrew), "The Dream of Yaacov Nahum" ["Halomo shel Yaʻaqov Nahum"], and later in "Orphan and Widow" ["Yatom veʼalmanah," 1923].

These short stories and novellas also reveal the treasury of forms and traditions that he commanded. Beginning with the years in Germany, he published psychological love stories in the style of European realism (e.g., "A Hill of Sand," "Ovadia the Cripple" ["ʻOvadiah baʻal mum," 1921], "The Doctor's Divorce" ["Harofeʼ vegrushato," 1941], "In the Prime of Her Life" ["Bidmi yameyah"], "Metamorphosis" ["Panim aherot," 1933], and "Fahrenheim" ["Farenheim"]) alongside stories that made extensive use of traditional Jewish materials in their symbolic renderings of their subjects (e.g., "Orphan and Widow"). He made frequent use of comic observation, from social satire (as in "With Our Youth and with Our Aged" ["Bineʻareinu uveziqneinu," 1920]) through the *feuilleton* (as in "On Taxes" ["ʼAl hamisim," 1950] and the rest of *Chapters of the Book of the State* [*Pirkei sefer hamedinah*]) to the Rabelaisian manner ("Pisces" ["Mazal dagim"]). Many stories are comic anecdotes bordering on the grotesque (e.g., "Upon the Death of the Tzaddik" ["ʻIm ptirat hatsadiq"], "The Frogs" ["Hatsfardeʻim"], and "Pisces"). His most interesting stories combine realism with symbolism (e.g., "Betrothed," "Covering the Blood"). He made artistic use of primary popular forms, such as folk tales and legends about saints (e.g., *Gadiel, the Wonder Child* [*Ma 'aseh berabi Gadi'el hatinoq*, 1920] and "The Pipe of My Departed Grandfather" ["Miqtarto shel zqeini 'alav hashalom," 1941]) and about historical figures (e.g., *Nice Stories about R. Israel Baal Shem-Tov* [*Sipurim na''im shel rabi Yisra'el ba'al shem-tov*]) alongside ballad-like and sad tales ("Atonement" ["Kipurim"] and "The Dead Child" ["Hayaldah ha-meitah"]). He wrote family chronicles (*The Beams of Our House* [*Korot beiteinu*, 1979]); historical works ("The Father of the Ox" ["Avi hashor"]); the posthumously published chapters of the collection *A City and the Fullness Thereof* [*Ir umlo'ah*, 1973]; novellas in the style of homiletic literature with a hint of modernity ("And the Crooked Shall Become Straight," "The Tale of the Scribe"); and others with a markedly surrealistic form and subject matter ("Edo and Enam," *The Book of Deeds*, "The Overcoat" ["Hamalbush"], "Forevermore" ["'Ad'olam"], "Footstool and Throne" ["Hadom vekise'"]). Some of the rather gothic stories (e.g., "The Dance of Death" ["Meholat hamavet," 1919], "The Canopy of Love" ["Hupat dodim," 1922], and "The Lady and the Peddler" ["Ha'adonit vehar-okhel"]) contained a fairly complex modernist core.

Agnon's return to Eretz Yisrael in 1924 did not effect major changes in his writing. Only in the 1930s, when he began to publish *The Book of Deeds*, did he start to produce a different kind of fiction. These are temporally and geographically defamiliarized stories, revealing the insecurity of the religious mind in a modern world. They are not among his most interesting work. Their influence upon the emergent Hebrew fiction in Eretz Yisrael was greater, however, than that of his realistic writings. His major novels also appeared in this period of the 1930s on, and it is on these works that I wish to dwell: *The Bridal Canopy* [*Hakhnasat kalah*, 1931], *A Simple Story* (1935), *A Guest for the Night* (1939) and *Yesteryear* (chapters of the novel appeared in the 1930s; the complete novel only appeared in book form in 1945). He went on writing fiction in various modes until the 1960s. After his death several collections were published that included some material that had appeared before (if only in part); holographic manuscripts; his final novels, *Shira* (1971), chapters of which had been previously published, and *In Mr. Lublin's Shop* [*Behanuto shel mar Lublin*, 1974]; plus a number of additional volumes.

The Bridal Canopy, a short version of which appeared in 1920, was Agnon's first novel. It tells the story of "a Hasid with neither food nor a living" who, at his rabbi's behest, goes about collecting money to marry off his three daughters. In many ways, it is a conventional pietistic tale. However, it also incorporates features of the European literary tradition—in this case, the picaresque novel—in which the protagonist's wanderings expose hidden aspects of the society. (Don Quixote had entered Jewish literature through Mendele's *The Travels of Benjamin III.*) *The Bridal Canopy* is a comic Quixotic saga of Jewish faith, with Reb Yudel as the Quixotic dreamer and Reb Neta the coachman as the down-to-earth Sancho. It is set in Jewish Galicia and pays ironic homage to the figure of the "great believer" who has passed from this world.

The story begins with poverty and sexual barrenness. "Once there was a Hasid who was greatly poor and oppressed with poverty, may the All-merciful preserve us, and he used to sit and study Torah and pray, far from worldly matters." The plot, which brings the characters to wealth and sexual fertility, the hero's knowledge of the Torah and his faith remaining intact, is based on a comedy of errors. Reb Yudel manages to find a groom for his daughter because the future in-laws are certain he is none other than the wealthy Reb Yudel Nathansohn. The logic of the plot might well have led to comic catastrophe, but Reb Yudel's daughter, with the help of Rabbi Zerah, a rooster, discovers the treasure that makes Reb Yudel a rich man without in any way compromising his religious dedication. The story concludes with the two Reb Yudels, who are homonymous in name but antonymic in their social positions, fused into a single character, such that Reb Yudel's Torah becomes (as in the words of a Yiddish lullaby) the "best merchandise" in town: "How fine and sweet was the sitting of the fathers-in-law together, both the real father-in-law and Reb Yudel Nathansohn, the supposed father-in-law. And when folk stood behind them and called out, Long life to you, Reb Yudel, both of the Reb Yudels would turn their heads around together and reply, Long life, long life" (p. 369). In a kind of fertility festival of eating and drinking, matter and spirit and poverty and wealth are married together; and Jewish faith, which depends upon the power of the believer, is restored and renewed.

A Simple Story is a more psychological novel than *The Bridal Canopy*, closer to the fiction of such early-twentieth-century writers as Knut Hamsun and Thomas Mann (*The Buddenbrooks*). Yet it also achieves a suprarealistic, mythical depth. The plot revolves around the conflict between the desires of the individual and the constraints of the bourgeois family. Blume Nacht, a poor relation employed by the protagonist Hershl's mother, unleashes repressed forces in Hershl, who, like most of Agnon's protagonists, has no internal resources for resolving the conflict between personal wishes and social expectations. The family tries to domesticate Hershl by marrying him to another woman, Minna Ziemlich, but the repression only leads to eruption. Hershl goes mad, and the scene of his madness is the novel's climax. He is delivered to Dr. Langsam's sanatorium, where his emotions are blunted and "cured"; thus he is enabled to resume his place in society. He makes no further efforts to remediate his situation but adjusts his personality to the world's demands and expectations.

Although this at first appears to be a trivial, clichéd story about frustrated love, nonetheless it achieves mythical depth through an array of symbolic motifs that construct an autonomous, secondary subtext. Irrational forces, which can only be represented in poetic language, act upon the hero's soul and determine its course. Hershl and Blume become mere incarnations of superhuman forces, Hershl reincarnating Eros, Blume becoming the eternal beloved who cannot be possessed in this world: "[Hershl] sat lazily on a wooden bench with his feet barely grazing the ground, half listening to the snatches of voices that drifted from the village. Some peasant girls were singing a song about a mermaid who married a prince. What did the prince do when he realized that his bride was half fish? The village girls were far, far off, and their voices barely reached him." In the construction of Agnon's story, Blume is that mermaid, Hershl the prince. But the fairy tale is never realized. So typical a bourgeois social novel that it can almost be described in Marxist terms, *A Simple Story* is also a Jewishly configured archetype of the defeat of desire by the world of familial and communal restraint.

The novel *A Guest for the Night,* which was published a few months before the outbreak of the Second World War, in 1939, exemplifies Agnon's art at its most accomplished. It is both a chronicle of the disintegrating Jewish village between the two world wars and a portrait of the artist contending with those historical circumstances. Although in previous writings Agnon had sought to distance art from reality, in this book he set out, Brenner-like, to create a non-fictitious fiction, albeit in his own distinctive style. What might have been no more than an ordinary tale of travel, incorporating autobiographical materials and proving the legitimacy of the narrator-author's worldview, becomes, under Agnon's guiding genius, a collection of contending testimonies. The narrator-protagonist's presentation of the collectivity of refugee stories transforms not the refugees' view of the world, but his own perspective.

Destiny plays an over-riding role in *A Guest for the Night.* Each individual person faces his or her own fate privately and personally. Nonetheless, a stern and terrible decree threatens them all, and there is, the narrator discovers, no way of reversing history or rolling back the wheel of fate. This is not, for Agnon, simply a socio-historical truth. Rather, it is a profoundly spiritual fact about the workings of a largely inexplicable and terrifyingly painful world, in which there is precisely no way to know truth from non-truth:

> I do not remember whether I was awake or dreaming. But I remember
> that at that moment I was standing in a forest clearing, wrapped in my

prayer shawl and crowned with my tefillin, when the child Raphael, Daniel Bach's son, came up with a satchel under his arm. "Who brought you here, my son?" said I. "Today I have become bar mitzvah," said he, "and I am going to the Beit Midrash." I was overcome with pity for this pitiful child, because he was docked of both his hands and could not put on tefillin. He gazed at me with his beautiful eyes and said, "Daddy promised to make me rubber hands." "Your Daddy is an honest man," said I, "and if he has made a promise he will keep it. Perhaps you know why your father saw fit to ask me about Schutzling." Said Raphael, "Daddy has gone to war and I can't ask him."

"Between ourselves, Raphael," said I to him, "I suspect that your sister Erela is a communist. Doesn't she mock your father?" "Oh, no," said Raphael, "she cried over him, because he can't find his arm." I asked him, "What does it mean, 'he cannot find his arm'?" "He lost his arm," said Raphael. "If so" said I, "where does he put on his tefillin?" "Don't worry about that," said Raphael, "those for the head he puts on his head, and those for the hand he puts on someone else's arm." "Where does he find someone else's arm?" said I. "He found a soldier's arm in the trench," replied Raphael. "Do you think he can meet his obligations with that one's arm? Isn't it written that the dead are free? When a man becomes dead, he is exempt from religious precepts, and anyone who is exempt from a precept cannot exempt anyone else." "I don't know," he replied. "You don't know," said I, "so why did you pretend you knew?" "Until you asked me I knew" replied Raphael, "once you asked me I forgot." "From now on," said I, "I will not ask. Go my son, go." (p. 383)

The dream proceeds as something like a normal conversation between the narrator and a child. But its content, in which fragments of reality from elsewhere in the story appear in disjointed and distorted form, produces a strangely grotesque portrait of an illogical, incomprehensible nonconversation between two unequal and mismatched participants. In this unreal world, horror (missing hands and arms) is a trivial, everyday occurrence, and the political and the spiritual know no separation from each other. On the allegorical level, the text suggests that, amputated and crippled, the members of the community can no longer perform their spiritual obligations, except (perhaps) through forms so grotesque as to raise questions as to whether they are in any way fulfillments of the commandments. It may be better, the passage suggests, not to ask questions than to point out the hideous paradoxes of religious faith in a devastated world.

The narrator of the novel had returned to his native city in order to rebuild his faith, and be rebuilt by it. But this is not to be. In one episode in the text, he reopens the old Beit Midrash (house of study), only to lose the key; and though he makes a new key, he cannot attract any of the town's folk. It is only when he returns to Eretz Yisrael that he finds the lost key. What the narrator discovers, then, is that he cannot resuscitate the glory of the past. And more: He comes to realize that the physical and material suffering of the people requires more immediate remediation. In that process of remediation, he is himself responsible to act.

In *A Guest for the Night* the synthesis of Hebrew and European elements achieves a kind of formal perfection. Formerly subsidiary and marginal components move to the center; parallelisms, digressions, and concealed subtexts control the text, and the ostensible plot is rendered secondary to other features of the work, which produces an emphasis on overall textual meaning rather than on the immediate drama of events. This innovative kaleidoscoping of literary conventions was not simply the product of Agnon's personal development as a writer. It also represented a response to the changed condition of the Jews in the period preceding the Holocaust. The world which the narrator discovers on his return to his native Shebush (Buczacz) is one in which the urgent need for concrete, material aid overwhelms any notion of a distanced, nostalgic, art-for-art's-sake aesthetic. An ironic quality had always been part of Agnon's presentation of the artist-observer's standpoint; it now becomes a crucial thematic issue. The aesthetic of impartiality by which the artist, revisiting his native town, might objectively appraise its devastation comes to appear immoral, because it distances itself from the genuine agony that has overtaken the town. Thus in this pre-Holocaust novel Agnon tackled, brilliantly and prophetically, the issue of art and the Holocaust.

In *Yesteryear* Agnon returned to the period of the Second Aliyah. Although it features Agnon's characteristic deviations from realistic representation, this is essentially a social and psychological novel, laden with documentary materials. The novel describes the failure of the newcomer Yitzhak Kummer, who is still profoundly bound up with his past and his native town, to become a part of the Second Aliyah. The novel's settings —Jaffa, the embryonic Tel Aviv, Jerusalem, and Ein Ganim—serve as metaphors for the protagonist's psychological and social struggles. In the tug-of-war that pulls him apart, Jaffa is a secular city of immigration and Jerusalem is the city of religious return. His to-ing and fro-ing between the two centers is mirrored in his indecision with regard to the two women in his life, the flighty Sonia, who lives in Jaffa, and Shifrah, his intended, who lives in Jerusalem.

Yitzhak is the sacrificial victim of the eternal split between exile and redemption and between Judaism and Zionism. Like the patriarch himself, he is bound for sacrifice, but God does not provide a substitute for him. Bitten by a mad dog which itself symbolizes the split in Yitzhak, he dies, and only after his funeral does the drought that has been ravaging the land dissipate: "When we went out we saw the land smiling with buds and blossoms. From one end to the other the shepherds came with their flocks, and from the moist earth rose the sound of the sheep, and the birds of the heavens answered them. Great joy was in the world. Never was such joy seen" (p. 606). Unlike the heroes of a Greek tragedy, Yitzhak is an innocent victim who will never attain self-awareness or knowledge of his guilt. The anti-hero is destroyed, but the society is reborn.

After transcending the tradition of realism in *A Guest for the Night* and *Yesteryear,* Agnon returned to it in *Shira,* a family novel in the manner of *Madame Bovary, Anna Karenina,* and the Forsythe Saga. The novel began to appear in print in the late 1940s, but was published in its entirety only after his death in 1971. As in other such novels, the subject is the decline of a family; that is to say, the dissolution of the reassuring idyll of order and stability that the family represents:

> Once again the patterns of life were arranged without excessive incident.
> Gabi was growing nicely. He was like his little sister: just as she did not
> annoy her mother very much, so too he does not annoy his mother very
> much, and it goes without saying not his father. And it is well that he
> does not disturb his father, who must prepare his lectures for the winter
> season and ought not give his attention to extraneous matters. (p. 522)

Set against this discipline of the ordinary is the world of the erotic and decadent. The main protagonist, the intellectual Dr. Manfred Herbst, is torn between the routine security of the family and the wonderful but dreadful adventures outside its confines, which are symbolized in the character of the midwife Shira. Increasingly, the relationship with Shira is made to seem fantastic and demonic, such that, even after she has disappeared from the real events of the story, her soul continues to haunt the protagonist. When Herbst can no longer call on her in his waking hours, he visits her in his dreams. The loss of Shira, who occasions Herbst's emotional and spiritual awakening, causes the gradual dissolution of the entire pattern, on the level of both plot and structure. It is as if author, as well as protagonist, were in the grip of a muse who, when she departs, takes their powers of creativity with her. The fragmentariness of *Shira* is even more marked in *In Mr. Lublin's Shop,* the other posthumously published novel, which concerns the loneliness and isolation of an East European Jew in Germany during the First World War.

Although it is possible to trace the stylistic and thematic development of Agnon's writing, his work is best treated synchronously. From early on in his career he produced a rich literary entity, integrating the various influences at work on him and forcefully combining, often in productive tension, stylistic and thematic features. Agnon's fiction incorporates a multiplicity of fictional forms in intricate linguistic variations. It deals intimately and comfortably with a complex population of diverse classes and communities in Eastern Europe, Germany, and Eretz Yisrael, chronologically spread across an expanse of time from the beginning of the nineteenth century to the middle of the twentieth.

The perception of time and space in Agnon's fiction moves through a variety of perspectives. At times, the view is from within; at other times, it projects a disorienting double vision, the uprooted observer in a new world perceiving that world both from within and from outside and from afar, as in "Forsaken Wives," "And the Crooked Shall Become Straight," and *In Mr. Lublin's Shop*. Such contrapuntal vision is also achieved through geographical, temporal, and psychological mirrorings and dislocations. Thus the protagonist of *Yesteryear* observes Jaffa from the viewpoint of his father's house and Jerusalem from the viewpoint of Jaffa, also viewing the ancient city from the ironic standpoint of the present, a strategy similar to that of *A City and the Fullness Thereof,* which offers an ironized view of Buczacz as its past glory is put in contemporary perspective.

The uniqueness of his literary style is what unifies his work throughout his career. Like the formulation of Mendele, his diction is rooted in the treasury of age-old Hebrew culture and its symmetrical linguistic patterns, principally expressed through analogies and rhythmic sentence structures. However, unlike other writers of such formulated language, Agnon's aim in juxtaposing disconsonant linguistic layers was not to produce comedy. Rather, he endeavored to hint at ancient sources and deeper symbolic meanings. Simultaneously incorporating numerous, diverse, linguistic layers, from the Bible through the Talmud and from the pietistic literature to Jewish liturgy and religious booklets, he permitted observation to dominate emotion and produced a certain remote irony. In *The Tale of the Scribe* he says of the writer (a scribe of sacred scrolls) what might also be said of Agnon himself: that before approaching his work he must "pause like a man who stands in a pool of icy water on a snowy day." Not only did Agnon make no attempt to produce a "living language," but, stylizing and aestheticizing his language, he assiduously avoided the partiality and bias of realistic, documentary fiction, such as characterized, for example, a writer like Brenner.

Every one of Agnon's texts is carefully crafted to regulate the balance between the plot development and the comprehensive overview, such that the work's meaning predominates over the drama of sequential discovery. As his writing progressed, this dominance of pattern over plot becomes even more pronounced. In early works such as "Forsaken Wives" and "And the Crooked Shall Become Straight" the plots are tighter and more coherent. By the end of the 1930s (from *A Guest for the Night* on) structural analogies and symmetries begin to take over, and in the writings of the 1950s (*Thus Far* ['*Ad henah*], 1952) and in such posthumous works as

In Mr. Lublin's Shop and "Covering the Blood," plot yields even more to the prominence of the controlling authorial perspective. In the novella *Thus Far,* plot emerges only through the delicate coherence of very subtle parallels among parts of the story.

Again and again Agnon's plots reflect the power of fate. The protagonist discovers himself or herself in a predicament demanding resolution, resolves the crisis, and is punished for it. In most cases the predicament is itself insoluble, so that, while it seems as though the protagonists are being penalized for making wrong choices, they are, in fact, only realizing their victimization at the dictates of a cruel destiny. Plots involving insoluble crisis, resolution, and punishment generally involve immigrants in their new country (as in "And the Crooked Shall Become Straight," *The Bridal Canopy, In the Heart of the Seas* [*Bilvav hayamim,* 1935], *Thus Far, Yesteryear* and *A Guest for the Night*) or individuals alienated by their own surroundings (as in *The Banished One* [*Hanidah*], *A Simple Story, Shira,* and "Edo and Enam"). Sometimes the two conditions are combined, as in *Yesteryear.* These plots unfold in various emotional registers, from the tragic-pathetic to the comic-farcical, and they traverse diverse social arenas.

Agnon sometimes amplified the sequential plot by means of parallelisms, which linked characters, linguistic features, motifs, and events (as in *A Guest for the Night,* for example). He also juxtaposed contemporary drama and ancient texts. In some of his non-realistic stories, such as "The Overcoat," the plot can only be accessed by deciphering the subtext, which derives from traditional Jewish sources. Some of the interpretive decoding is intratextual. Even though each of Agnon's fictions stands by itself, nonetheless, they also constitute parts of a coherent, inter-referential canon. A good example of such cross-reference within Agnon's work is the character Kraindl Charny (meaning: the black crownlet), the heroine of "And the Crooked Shall Become Straight," who is mentioned in the story "With Our Youth and With Our Aged": "On the way I met a friend of mine by name of Hoffmann. Mr. Hoffmann was the son of the abandoned wife Kraindl Charny" (p. 314). In order to understand this statement the reader needs to know the circumstances of Kraindl's son's birth. Such cross-referencing carries meanings from one text to another, making for brief digressions from the sequential plot, which draw into one work the resonances and significations of another work.

Oftentimes Agnon breaks the sequentialities of ordinary plot through the construction of secondary plots that come to occupy disproportionate significance in the work as a whole. Sometimes the parallel plots and structures reinforce each other, adding depth to the overview they collectively produce (in *A Guest for the Night,* for example). At other times, the links among the subsidiary elements, or between them and the main story, are purely mechanical. Lacking compelling logic or coherence, they border on the absurd, even the grotesque. In extreme cases, the multiple digressions and parallels produce a non-coherent, almost post-modern, tale (*Thus Far* and *In Mr. Lublin's Shop* are examples).

It is more difficult to generalize about Agnon's personae than about his style. The gamut of characters spans four or five generations and crosses ideological and social divides. It includes penitents, Hasidim, unbelievers, Zionists, assimilated Jews, Orthodox fanatics, the affluent and the impoverished, ignoramuses and scholars, great rabbis, conventional stereotypes such as the femme fatale and the pedant, and real historical persons, such as Brenner. Nonetheless, despite this diversity, the typical Agnon protagonist tends toward passivity; he is incapable of objective analysis, stuck at a cross-roads, perplexed about how to proceed. When the characters do act, they are naive and their actions are ironized, as in the cases of the eponymous heroine of "Tehillah," or Reb Yudel in *The Bridal Canopy*. In many ways, the typical Agnon protagonist recalls those of the psychological realists, who are similarly overwhelmed and defeated by insoluble existential, social, and religious conflicts. Unlike Brenner's and Gnessin's characters, however, Agnon's are not portrayed from within. Nor do they expose themselves confessionally by means of interior monologues or stream of consciousness. Their states of mind are revealed only by their external actions and behavior. In characterizing his personae Agnon used a variety of techniques, from such relatively simplistic devices as symbolic names or nicknames (generally in Yiddish or German: Blume Nacht, Fahrenheim, Hartmann, Yitzhak Kummer, Ben-Uri—this latter a reference to Bezalel Ben Uri, the architect of the Holy Tent in the desert) to intricate patterns of character doubling, in which synonymous and antithetical characters broaden each other's significance and add dimensions to the text. Because Agnon did not create straightforwardly realistic characters and because he did not engage in character analysis as such, his cast of characters demands the reader's active interpretation.

Agnon's novels are clearly set in their time and place: Galicia in the early nineteenth century and between the two world wars, the Jewish village in the early twentieth century, Germany during the First World War, and Eretz Yisrael during the Second Aliyah, in the 1930s and 1940s. Yet despite this feature of their historicity, which places them in the category of social novels, they all reach beyond their time and place. Though his finest work is to be found in his three novels, Agnon also published many novellas (e.g., "Betrothed," *The Banished One*, "In The Prime of Her Life") and collections of short fiction: realistic (*At the Handles of the Lock* ['*Al kapot haman'ul*]), legendary (*Of Such and Such* ['*Eilu va'eilu*]), and surrealistic (*The Book of Deeds*). His stories also appeared in other collections such as *Thus Far, The Fire and the Trees* [*Ha 'eish veha 'eitsim*], and *A City and the Fullness Thereof.* After 1910, when Ernst Muller translated "Forsaken Wives" into German, Agnon's work began to appear in other languages. In time, his work appeared in most European languages, as well as in Chinese, Esperanto, Hindi, Mongolian, Persian, Turkish, Japanese, and Arabic. Max Strauss's German translation of "And the Crooked Shall Become Straight" ("Und das Krumme wurde gerade," 1918), drew many young German Jews to Agnon. Some of his stories, such as *The Tale of the Scribe* [*Die Erzühlung vom Toraschreiber*], even appeared in German translation before their publication in Hebrew.

* * *

For the most part, the writers who wrote in Eretz Yisrael between the two world wars and those who were born in the country (*Dor Ba' aretz*) steered clear of Agnon. Agnon represented a formidable literary precursor, not easy to assimilate and almost impossible to surpass. The next generation, however, in their escape from the demanding realism of the generation of their fathers, discovered in Agnon's anti-mimetic aesthetic a way to redirect the tradition of Hebrew fiction. The encounter of *Dor Hamedinah* (the State Generation) with the genius of Agnon led to the recovery of the rich cultural sphere that he represented. In enabling writers such as Yehuda Amichai, David Shahar, Pinhas Sadeh, A. B. Yehoshua, Amos Oz, Yitzhak Orpaz, and Aharon Appelfeld to discard the shackles of realistic convention, Agnon's influence was a blessing. However, it also presented barriers to creativity that not all of his inheritors were able to surmount. To emulate Agnon did not in the least guarantee that one would reach the heart of his achievement. That achievement remains a permanent fixture in the constellation of Hebrew literature: a guiding, even if daunting, light.

8

TO BUILD AND BE REBUILT
HOMELAND ART AND THE THIRD ALIYAH

> We came to this country to build and to be
> rebuilt.
> —Song of the Third Aliyah

As the First World War drew to an end, the Jews of Europe experienced a series of great upheavals. The October Revolution in Russia led to a decline in Jewish communal life; anti-Semitism flared up in the course of civil war; and the Petelyura pogroms raged in the Ukraine. At the same time, the new immigration quotas in the United States stemmed the tide of migration there. The 1917 Balfour Declaration, expressing the British government's support for the creation of a Jewish national home in Palestine, coupled with the rise of small nation-states in the former Austro-Hungarian empire, led to increased interest in the Zionist movement and to new waves of immigration to Palestine. There were three main waves of *aliyah* during the decades of the 1920s and 1930s: the pioneering Third Aliyah (1919–1923); the Fourth Aliyah (1924–1926), which consisted mostly of middle-class Polish Jews whose subsistence had been wrecked by the policies of Polish Premier Grabski; and finally, beginning in 1932, the so-called Fifth Aliyah, largely from Germany.

Simultaneous with these developments, conditions in Eretz Yisrael also began to change. During this period the Jewish population seesawed between immigration and emigration; hordes of people came to settle and then left again. Relations between Jews and Arabs were increasingly tense, periodically erupting in bloody riots, and relations between the Jewish community and the British authorities were at best uneasy. The high hopes with which the Zionist leadership had greeted the British Mandate of Palestine were dashed. Cooperation alternated with confrontation, especially with regard to restrictions on Jewish immigration and land purchases.

IDEOLOGY AND LITERATURE

The main experience that Hebrew literature sought to express during this period was that of *aliyah,* meaning not only the literal experience of immigration, but also the ideological dimensions of the commitment to settling the land. Although the agrarian sector of the new community never constituted more than twenty percent of the population, its ethos and imagery occupied a central place in the collective consciousness of the place. In many ways, the literature of the Third Aliyah resembled that of its predecessor, except that whereas the literature of the Second Aliyah was predominantly anti-genre, that of the Third Aliyah revived and re-vivified genre writing. This return to genre was primarily expressed through the choice of subject matter rather than through the style of writing.

Of all the materials available in Eretz Yisrael during the period of the British Mandate (1920–1948), the genrists chose only those that suited their ideological objectives. Placing themselves between irreconcilable op-positions, they charted the course of the pioneering ideal and plotted it with clear-cut moral lucidity. The writers, in other words, were occupied by the tension between the ideal of pioneering labor itself and the pursuit of ordinary life. The agricultural was set against the urban; the *halutz* (pioneer) against the merchant; the worker against the landowner; the Jew against the Arab, and so on. Just as the Zionist mythology of Jewish settlement had clearly defined heroes and enemies and unambiguous goals, so also did its fiction. It dealt with the "conquest of the land" by means of agricultural employment and the struggle against disease, hu-man weakness, and political threat. Purportedly realistic, the fiction did not attempt a critique of the Zionist paradigm (as had the anti-genrists of the Second Aliyah). Rather it tried to serve the requirements of the ideal and advance its cause, heeding the call of the spiritual leader of the Second Aliyah, Aharon David Gordon, for a new breed of laborer-writer, who would write a "labor literature" expressive of the contact with nature and the cultivation of the land.

Although a few writers tackled the national conflict between Jews and Arabs and the triangular confrontation during the mandate among Jews, Arabs, and the British, hardly any dared to describe real social relations between these groups. They ignored, for example, such phenomena as the "deviationists" and the so-called Grabski migration of bankrupt Jews from Poland, who did not fit the contours of the Zionist story. Instead, they concentrated on the agricultural settlements, which received a larger share of the literature than did the cities, the Valley of Jezreel looming larger than Tel Aviv. What Brenner, Agnon, and Reuveni had envisioned as possibility, the next generation treated as an already established reality.

Most of the writers of the Third Aliyah were born in Eastern Europe (Russia, Poland, Lithuania, Bessarabia) around the turn of the century. They settled in Palestine in the 1920s and 1930s. Among the writers who came from Galicia, Poland, were Yehudah Yaari, David Maletz, and Israel Zarchi. From greater Russia came Ever-Hadani (Aharon Feldman), Yitzhak Shenhar, Yosef Aricha, and Zvi Rudnik Arad. From Bessarabia, Transylvania, and Hungary came S. Hillel and Avigdor Hameiri (Feuerstein). The one writer who was a native of Eretz Yisrael, Yehoshua Bar-Yosef, spent the years 1916 to 1930 in Transylvania. The biographies of the more modern writers such as Haim Hazaz and Nathan Bistritski (who will be treated in Chapter 9) followed the same pattern.

The shared features of their life stories highlight the common ideological choices these writers made when they immigrated to Eretz Yisrael. Many of them were associated with the labor movement and they all sought to express the dual values of *aliyah* and labor, out of which they constructed nothing less than a mythology. Two figures symbolized the cultural and material pioneering venture they would celebrate: Y. H. Brenner and A. D. Gordon, who invented the term "the religion of labor." Many of the writers incorporated these figures into their writings. They set themselves the task of writing a literature committed to the depiction of the real and the true, in which the working man and the intellectual, culture and cultivation, formed a consolidated identity and a single purpose. Nor were these subjects and values relevant only to their art. They were also the precepts by which they conducted their own lives. Most of them did not become professional writers and they shunned the usual occupations of their predecessors, namely, teaching, translating, and editing.

Thus, in the beginning most of them were themselves pioneer-laborers. Only later did they turn to the more traditional literary occupations. Ideology was not the only factor that prevented their immediate professionalization as writers. The conditions for professional authorship did not yet exist in the country. The writers themselves faced multiple problems of adjustment to a new social and cultural environment. Still and all, it was the literature itself which had to mount the harder effort to establish itself in a largely inhospitable cultural environment. Hebrew literature during this period was still dependent on the diaspora for the bulk of its readership and its material resources, as well as for its artistic and linguistic motivation. Its very language had been shaped by a former generation, and its literary criteria were established outside the country.

This close interrelation with the diaspora and the reliance of the new community on the larger Jewish world were frequent subjects of both public and private exchange. The question was whether a locale as small as Eretz Yisrael (the population of which ranged from 83,000 in 1922 to 400,000 in 1936) could even create a cultural world for itself, let alone become a spiritual center for diaspora Jewry. How viable could this literature be, with its roots in the landscape and in the values of the labor movement, when its readership was so limited and its cultural and material survival still depended on the diaspora? While various writers emphasized these limitations and the narrowness of its scope, others, such as A. Zioni, argued that it was nonetheless the mandate of the creative writers in Israel to work "intensively and qualitatively and to create a corner of solid, stable Hebrew culture" ("Culture of Labor," *Heidim* 4, no. 1 [1925], p. 26).

This conviction informed the thinking of leading literary figures as they began to organize periodicals and publishing houses in Eretz Yisrael in the 1920s and 1930s. The other centers of Hebrew literature—in Russia, Germany, America, France, England, and Poland—had already began their rapid decline. Bolshevik Russia outlawed Hebrew literature in the 1920s. Assimilation produced similar consequences in France, England, and the United States. The German center was moribund even before the rise of Nazism, while the Polish community produced little of merit. In the face of this widespread decline in Hebrew literature, writers were drawn to Eretz Yisrael, where one by one they joined the existing literary establishments or created new ones.

This produced an extremely lively literary scene. Short-lived periodicals served as arenas for stormy literary disputes. The publications, their editors, their policies, and their explicit and unspoken worldviews all testified to social and artistic ferment. One of the central arguments revolved around the question of whether Hebrew literature was to be national or tribal; that is, whether it was to be a Jewish literature rooted in the people's tradition and history or a native, national literature born in the new locale. The dispute was manifested in the attitudes toward the two Jewish languages. Some looked with equal favor on both Hebrew and Yiddish. Others heatedly campaigned for Hebrew. Another aspect of the same debate was the argument between those who preferred traditional formulaic diction, accent, and style as against those who opted for the emerging modern language and its neologisms. Similarly, some remained faithful to the old Eastern European literature and the familiar Western models, while others sought to open the doors to the contemporary currents and literary schools of Western Europe. The camps formed around key figures and organizations: Haim Nahman Bialik versus Eliezer Steinmann and Avraham Shlonsky; the Writers' Association versus outside groups; established publishing houses versus the new ones.

There were several literary periodicals in those years. *Heidim* (1922–1929), under the editorship of two of the younger Second Aliyah authors, Asher Barash and Yaacov Rabinowitz, successfully provided an open platform for all the camps, although it took no bold risks. The more marginal periodical *Sadan* [*Anvil*, 1924–1926], edited by the poet Uri Zvi Greenberg, was more adventurous. It voiced avid objections to the importation of the exiled diaspora character to Eretz Yisrael. It demanded complete change and renewal. It also sought a clean break with the poetics of Bialik's generation.

The arrival of Haim Nahman Bialik from Berlin in 1924 led to many changes in the literary establishment. His arrival coincided with that of Eliezer Steinmann, a former Hebrew Communist, who was appointed editor of *Ktuvim* [*Texts*]. This periodical, which began to appear in 1926, was meant to be the organ of the Writers' Association, but it attracted many oppositional figures. The following year it broke away from the Association, splitting the literary community in two. In 1929 the Association began to publish its own weekly, *M'oznayim* [*Scales*], which was edited mainly by Bialik's contemporaries (the first editor was Y. D. Berkowitz). *Ktuvim* continued to be edited by Steinmann, along with Avraham Shlonsky.

The rivalry between these two publications was partly about prestige and sales, but it also constituted a serious cultural debate. The *Ktuvim* camp was characterized by its Western European orientation, native Eretz Yisrael manner, innovative neologistic language, argumentative brashness, and modernist style that resembled post-Revolutionary Russian formalism and futurism. By contrast, *M'oznayim* oriented itself toward Eastern Europe and traditional Judaism. Its writing style was more conservative and conventional. Eager to discard the heavy burden of traditional obligation, *Ktuvim* had to enter into direct battle with Bialik and his colleagues, who they regarded as obstacles to European modernism (as represented by such movements as expressionism and Dada). In a way, *Ktuvim* set itself the task of creating an urban literary response to the country's prevailing anti-urban ideology. It attempted to produce a Western European–style periodical in a society that had turned its back on Europe. There were several other marginal periodicals, some of them supporting extreme right-wing nationalism, and others taking more moderate, middle-of-the-road political positions. One of the latter was *Gilyonot* [*Print-sheets*, 1933–1954], edited by Yitzhak Lamdan, which was politically engaged but nonpartisan and rather traditional in its literary and critical tone.

The prolonged antagonism between *Moznayim* and *Ktuvim* (and later its successor *Turim* [*Columns*], 1933–1939) enlivened Hebrew literature, especially the poetry, throughout the 1930s. The war of the journals had less effect on the fiction, which tended to respond to the hopes and aspirations expressed by the kibbutz movement periodical *Gilbo'a* (1926). It was *Gilbo'a* that called for a homeland literature (*Heimatliteratur*), a song of labor depicting the life of the agricultural settlers.

The publishing houses also contributed to determining the course of the new Eretz Yisraeli literature. The kibbutz movements (*Ha'artzi* and *Hame'uhad*) and the Labor Federation each set up their own publishing houses in the late 1930s and early 1940s, with the consequence that the cultural scene was tilted toward the labor movement, the writers associated with that camp coming to occupy center stage. After Bialik's death in 1934 the balance of power between the literary camps shifted, and the *Ktuvim-Turim* group was transformed from a group of rebels into an establishment, which brought up a whole new generation of writers and poets, gradually marginalizing the official Writers' Association and its entourage. In the 1940s the influence of the political forces in the community intensified, with the result that there were fewer genuine literary disputes.

The artistic currents represented by the periodicals and publishing houses, as defined by their authoritative figures and shaped by socio-political events, provided the milieu in which literary creativity occurred. As in earlier periods, literary criticism concerned itself with the relationship between literature and life, between the production of fiction and the needs and goals of the new society. Critics such as Yaacov Fichman and Yaacov Rabinowitz concurred with Brenner that life in Eretz Yisrael was not yet sufficiently crystallized to produce mature literature. Rabinowitz, on the other hand, objected to fiction that purported to represent reality when it was in fact inventing, ornamenting, and prettifying it. For Rabinowitz it was the encounter between foreign models and the as yet unformed and emerging reality that would produce new cultural forms. The writer, therefore, ought, in Rabinowitz's view, to depict the contrast between the expectations of the newcomers and the chaos which confronted them upon their arrival. This did not mean producing some sort of narrow realism. It meant not affirming social norms but confronting and exposing them. Some Second Aliyah writers, such as Reuveni, Agnon, and Kimhi, met this critical demand. Most, however, did not. Rabinowitz's ideas met with little positive response between the two world wars, although something of what he proposes may be found in the writings of Yehoshua Bar-Yosef and Yitzhak Shenhar.

Other critics, such as Shlomo Zemach, thought that art must help facilitate the process of social crystallization that seemed lacking in the country. Rather than contend hopelessly with existing models that were inappropriate to the new reality, the artist, these critics maintained, had to produce the art form ideally suited to the new society's cultural needs. This required depicting the culture as if it already existed to give readers a social model to adopt. This is the literary-critical approach that predominated: the call for the fiction to adapt itself to the new environment of the Middle East and to serve as a mouthpiece for the pioneering enterprise. Recalling genre fiction and Russian positivism, the literary form that would dominate the next fifty years of Hebrew fiction conformed to the expectation that the literature would embody the ideology of labor Zionism.

Of course there were exceptions and modifications to this aesthetics of genre. There were those who argued that since Hebrew literature expressed nothing less than a revolution (albeit a Zionist revolution), it ought to express its subject in a revolutionary way in style as well as in content. Uri Zvi Greenberg, who rejected literary realism, was the foremost proponent of this approach. He was joined by a few other writers who were also influenced by European expressionism. The impact of expressionism on Hebrew literature was noticeable above all in the poetry, but the prose of Nathan Bistritski and Haim Hazaz also evidenced its influence. Quantitatively speaking, expressionism made few inroads into Hebrew fiction. It is nevertheless significant, if only as an interesting antithesis to the dominant socialist realism. Similarly, there was the call (represented by Eliezer Steinmann), for a universalist, anti–local color fiction that would transcend the limitations of time and place. Steinmann, Shlonsky, and their colleagues of the *Ktuvim-Turim* group opposed the solipsism that threatened to make of Eretz Yisrael one more Jewish ghetto. They demanded that the forms of the local literature conform to those of Western culture.

Despite these countercurrents, the literature followed the lead of the Second Aliyah authors of genre, producing a local, nationalistic literature that featured the new Hebrew warrior who was as forceful in his relations with women as he was in his fighting with the Arabs—a perfect antithesis to the stereotype of the hapless and helpless failures of Brenner's *Breakdown and Bereavement,* Agnon's *Yesteryear,* and Reuveni's *Unto Jerusalem.* The favorite embodiment of the native Israeli was the figure of the *shomer,* the guard or guardian, taken from the reality and the mythology of Eretz Yisrael. There is also the *halutz,* whose attachment to the land withstands even the lure of wealth and women and who defeats his diaspora-like impulses to wander and make money. The novels of Yosef Aricha (e.g., *Bread and Vision* [*Lehem vehazon*]) and Israel Zarchi (e.g., his first novel *Youth* [*'Alumim,* 1933] and the two historical settlement novels, *A Land Unsown* [*'Eretz lo zru'ah,* 1946] and *The Village of Silwan* [*Kfar Hashiloah,* published posthumously in 1948]) are full of these types of New Hebrews. Another figure was that of the common peasant, who embodies primal, natural forces and is glorious because he produces bread from the soil, the very antithesis of the stereotypical Jewish scholar. What Berdyczewski depicted as a superhuman, mythical possibility (e.g., Red Shlomo in *The Secret Place of Thunder*) became a real human being, no longer exceptional, but ordinary, the local inhabitant of the land of Israel. Although the interwar anti-hero still appeared in the writing of those who followed the dictates of the anti-genrists (namely, Shenhar and Yaari), for the most part he was rejected and marginalized by the new fiction.

The Second Aliyah had made Hebrew into the spoken language of Eretz Yisrael, but the interwar literature did not integrate the changes that had occurred in the language. The dominant style of that generation was still that of formulation. Some of the writers adopted the popular rhetorical style of editorials, essays, and speeches of the dominant (i.e., Zionist) elite. The idea was to persuade the reader emotionally, by overcoming his or her resistance. Rhetorical excess suited the ideological bent of the stories. Others, who also ignored the spoken language, nonetheless sought to renovate the written language. Writers such as Eliezer Steinmann, Yaacov Horowitz, and Menashe Levin produced all kinds of alternatives to traditional phraseology and archaic speech patterns. The neologism was the banner of their revolt against stylistic conservatism. It was no less elitist than the formulated style and just as oblivious to the spoken language. Nonetheless, it proceeded on the premise that not life but literature and language were the creative media. This approach, which corresponded with the desire to produce a universalist literature, was especially noticeable in the poetry of the *Ktuvim-Turim* group and in the modernist fiction that was written. However, it also made some inroads into genre fiction, where it produced a curious combination of new literary style and conventional social message. The logic controlling this synthesis was that just as the reality of the new place was elevating or, at least, was worth elevating, so also must it be presented in elevated and elevating language and not, as in Brenner's writings, through the language of everyday discourse.

Elements of vernacular speech did, of course, creep into the prose. The process had begun even earlier, in the first decades of the century, with the writings of Burla and Shami, who used Ladino and Arabic to define the difference between written and spoken language. But Hebrew fiction still suffered from the appearance of having been translated, as if the written language were only a representation of some other, oral, language. Some Ashkenazi writers, such as Yitzhak Shenhar and Yosef Aricha, tried to reproduce the vernacular of the Eastern Jews and the Arabs, but in none of these experiments was there an attempt to transform the spoken vernacular into a new literary language. Later, the writers of the War of Independence would institutionalize their spoken language and make it the language of the native-born elite (the sabras). Some vernacular usage entered into the writing of an older writer such as Yehoshua Bar-Yosef, but neither he nor any of his generation could penetrate to the organic, literary aspects of these forms. They could only mimic them, with the consequence that their dialogues read like importations into the story and not as natural continuations of it. In other words, vernacular language functioned in these texts primarily as quotations from reality. And, indeed, quoting from reality was a major goal of the literature in all of its aspects; the basic socio-historical, political reality that interwar Hebrew fiction sought to represent was settlement itself.

In the introduction to his 1934 novel *Produce* [*Tnuvah*], Avigdor Hameiri expressed the commitment which defined not only his work, but the writings of his entire generation:

> The author is well aware of his responsibility in writing this novel, which seeks to depict the period of pioneering mass movement intoxicated with political liberation, which has grown into the liberation of man from his own exile. It is difficult to put an epic work before a public, when most of the readers are its protagonists, and most of those, its former protagonists. But should anyone accuse the author of excessive idealization, he would be told, "I am sorry that you seemed finer to me then than you are today. In my mirror was depicted your stature of yesterday."

In this school of thought, literature, which seems at first glance to exaggerate the virtues of reality, emerges as an accurate and inspirational reflection of reality. This literary style produced melodramatic novels with strong documentary and ideological elements. Often the works followed historical developments. Non-literary markers from the chronicles of the settlement movement verified their authenticity. Generally, these were stories of young men and women, utterly devoted to the collectivity of the community, whose falling in love added romantic, legendary dimensions to the story. And just as legends are realized only in fabulous circumstances, so the pairing of the two protagonists proceeded under magical circumstances, while the dream of settlement turned into reality.

The semi-documentary *Hashomer* (*The Guard*) novels are one of the foremost examples of this fictional aesthetic, although from an artistic point of view they are minor, even trivial, works. The books were produced for popular consumption; their protagonists were Jewish heroes of the Wild West, or, more precisely, the Wild East, who performed their heroic feats in the name of Zionism and the Holy Land. Like all nationalist fictions, these texts combined imaginary adventures with historical acts of bravery to produce heroic nationalistic myths. Most remarkable, perhaps, about this body of fiction was that, while it was being written for the masses, it did not actually reach them. The socio-literary role it aimed to fulfill was instead provided in Eretz Yisrael by foreign fiction, read either in translation or in the original.

Another brand of popular trivial (and trivializing) fiction was the propagandistic literature directed at the local Palestinian/Jewish readership. This set of texts depicted the Old Yishuv in terms of poverty, social disintegration, and emotional repression (e.g., in the stories of Yehoshua Bar-Yosef). Sinners (such as Berdyczewski's promethean Red Shlomo in *The Secret Place of Thunder*) were no longer seen as heroes but as destructive enemies. In this second type of minor fiction, there was usually visible intrigue and covert (or overt) ideology, combined with various extra-literary hints which rarely referred to a recognizable external reality.

The more serious novels of the period were of two kinds. The first dealt with Zionist ideology rather than with its realization in Eretz Yisrael. Usually these novels were based on activities in the diaspora and were centered on a group of young revolutionaries. Sometimes the emphasis was on social revolution generally, sometimes on Zionism itself. In either case, ideological decisions went hand in hand with erotic choices, and in between negotiating the plot, the text expounded ideology. A typical example of this is S. Hillel's *Under the Sky of Bessarabia* [*Tahat shmei Besarabiya,* 1942], which is set against the background of the October Revolution. Another, and weightier, example of such ideologically driven fiction is the documentary novel of ideas, which depicted the realization of ideological presuppositions in Eretz Yisrael. These writings, which we will now discuss, included Avigdor Hameiri's war stories and Israel Zarchi's historical settlement novels (*A Land Unsown* and *The Village of Silwan*).

ZARCHI, HAMEIRI, YAARI, SHENHAR, AND BAR-YOSEF

Israel Zarchi is the quintessential writer of his generation. His entire oeuvre takes its materials and themes from historical circumstances (immigration, adaptation, settlement) and is based on the values of labor Zionism. His fiction encompassed the principal literary expressions of his time: from trivializing fiction with its ideologically inspired intrigues (exemplified by his early short stories and novellas—*Youth*, "Barefoot Days" ["Yamim yeheifim, 1935"], "Petroleum Flows to the Mediterranean" ["Haneft zorem layam hatikhon, 1936"], and "Mount Scopus" ["Har Hatsofim, 1940"]) through small-scale vignettes of life on the social margins, to quasi-documentary novels of settlement. His later novella, *Guest House* [*Malon 'orhim,* 1943], which dealt with the problems of German Jewish immigrants, showed greater originality.

Zarchi did not use any new techniques when he wrote *Guest House,* but he organized his materials cleverly, chose appropriate characters, and conveyed a more complex message than he had done before. The story revolves around a group of protagonists who come to Palestine not for Zionistic reasons but simply to find refuge. The action takes place in a Jerusalem hotel established by the German-born Mrs. Nathan, who is intent upon carrying on the old German way of life. She accepts only guests from the same background as her own, and she imposes German table manners and mores on them. Eventually the hotel comes to represent an extension of her personality and of the world she left behind. For the characters in this book, we come to realize, the mental adjustments to this miniature Europe in the Middle East are far more tormenting than any physical acclimation. Some of the characters try to adapt themselves to the new reality. Others cannot. One couple, a former judge and his wife, commit suicide because they are unable to live an obsolete life as misfits in a new, inhospitable society.

Like the Second Aliyah anti-genrists (Brenner and Agnon), Zarchi did not construct idealized characters. Rather he portrayed conflict and indecision. In this way he was able, as in genre fiction, to affirm the basic values of *aliyah* and resettlement. At the same time, like the anti-genrists, he produced a valid critique of the contemporary society. His last two settlement novels are more typical of the straight genre fiction of his contemporaries, such as Maletz. *A Land Unsown* is an adulatory chronicle of the young Bilu immigrants in the First Aliyah; *The Village of Silwan* a documentary novel concerning the hardships of the Yemenite immigration during the First World War and the 1920s in the village of Silwan (the biblical Shiloah). It was only in a very few of his works, such as *Guest House,* that he demonstrated how genre writing might also achieve aesthetic distinction.

Another writer (older than Zarchi but of a similar background) who was fairly successful in his choice of materials and their organization was Avigdor Hameiri. Hameiri was one of the more colorful figures in interwar Hebrew literature—a poet, songwriter, and director of a satirical theater. Through his periodical *Hamahar* [*Tomorrow,* 1927–1931] he was a thorn in the side of the literary establishment; he was detested by the leaders of the establishment. Despite their objections, however, Hameiri was not to be ignored.

Hameiri is remembered chiefly for two documentary-memoir novels, which effectively depicted the experiences of a Jewish officer in the Austro-Hungarian army, first in the battlefields of the First World War (*The Great Madness* [*Hashiga'on hagadol,* 1929]) and later in captivity (*Lower Hell* [*Begeheinom shel matah,* 1932]). These novels appeared not long after similar stories, with similar messages, were published in the former Habsburg Empire and in Germany (e.g., "Man is Good," 1917, "The Citizen," 1924, and especially "Karl and Anna," in 1927, by Leonard Frank [1882–1961]; *All Quiet on the Western Front* in 1929 by Erich Maria Remarque [1897–1970]; and *Sergeant Grisha* in 1927 by Arnold Zweig).

Although Hameiri's attitude toward the war participated in this international pacifism, his anti-war thesis was specifically Jewish. For him, the world was divided not only into enemies and friends, but also into Jews and non-Jews. While acknowledging that he felt close affinities with certain non-Jews, he refused to close his eyes to the existence of international anti-Semitism. Jewish solidarity across national borders that functioned in defiance of this anti-Semitism was a major subject of the text. To bring this aspect of Jewish fraternal and mutual support into focus, he drew on the experience of his own captivity. Something of a Bohemian and a rebel, Hameiri abandoned the autobiographical angle, with its unique take on contemporary Jewish history, when he wrote the stereotypical ideological settlement novel *Produce.*

Although Yehudah Yaari was closer to the Brenner-Agnon tradition than any of his contemporaries, he followed the outlines of their vision naively and simplistically, in no way absorbing the complexities of their critical views. Whereas Brenner was sarcastic and Agnon venomously ironic, Yaari appealed to empathy and sentimental pathos. He used the elevated pathos-laden language of his generation without any self-irony. As a result, his protagonists seem hopelessly naive, as do his themes. Like his mentors, and unlike most of the novelists of his generation, Yaari tended to depict the pioneer as a young anti-hero. Yet when his protagonists failed to meet the challenges set them, Yaari did not rail against them, or even against the ideals of labor Zionism. Rather he faulted the circumstances which made the ideals so difficult to achieve.

These features characterize Yaari's two principal novels, the autobiographical *When the Candle Was Burning* [*Ke'or yahel,* 1937] and *A Root upon Water* [*Shoresh alei mayim,* 1950]. Having arrived in Palestine in 1920 as part of the Third Aliyah, Yaari participated in the founding of Kibbutz Beit Alpha, but left it for Jerusalem in 1926. Immigration, the kibbutz, and the migration from commune to city provide the three major events of the novel. As one of the protagonists, Shaul, puts the central question of *When the Candle Was Burning:* "Why have we come here . . . to suffer together? Why do we live together, work together? . . . What is the idea that unites us?" (p. 151). Although the narrator-witness immediately answers these musings, the very fact that they are posed suggests the degree to which Yaari, like Brenner before him, did not accept uncritically the values of Zionist settlement. Still and all, for Yaari the national experience is transparently religious: "A man who cleaves to the soil, the spirit of God rests upon him. He who unites with the soil of his homeland unites with the whole world. Unites with God. How I envy you, you simple men of the soil. We have been orphaned of our soil, our homeland was a homeland of the heart, and so our world darkened, and our God wept for us, and we were oppressed. . . . Eretz Yisrael . . . Homeland . . . The soil. . . . This is our return—to the world, to God" (Ibid., p. 112).

There are some who consider Yitzhak Shenhar the outstanding writer of the Third Aliyah. He was certainly typical of its socialization processes, starting out as a railway and agricultural laborer before becoming a professional writer in 1931. His best work was produced in the 1930s and 1940s, when he published both short fiction and two long novellas, *Chapters of a Novel* [*Pirkei roman,* 1960] and *One of a Thousand* [*'Ehad me'elef,* 1947]. In his choice of themes Shenhar closely resembled antigenrists such as Brenner and Reuveni. In structure and style, however, he clung, Berkowitz-like, to formulation. Many of his stories recall the didacticism of genre, even when the work as a whole is anti-genrist. Thematically and structurally, Shenhar was one of the most literary writers of his generation, having been heavily influenced by European literature, in particular the work of Chekhov. Where others set out to document their portraits of the age, he sought to stylize that picture.

Although he used many of the same materials as Zarchi and Yaari, he emphasized different elements of the inventory and used different techniques to portray those themes. For the most part, he wrote stories about the collective, in which he showed greater interest in the atmosphere of the commune than in the lives of the individuals that composed it. His ideological stories are synecdochal-historical. They use a particular detail, or series of details, to depict a central event in the life of the society and of the Zionist enterprise. These synecdoches, which are not fully developed, are intended as symbols. Characteristically, the stories deal with immigration, with the conflict between Jews and Arabs, and with Jews of the Middle East. In his best fiction, such as *One of a Thousand,* he tried to dramatize what he regarded as the principal polarity in the Jewish community of Eretz Yisrael in the 1920s and 1930s—the differences between the immigrant and the native:

> Ehrich felt that his face was turning green, like those wretched plants in their clay pots. Who says, he asked himself, that the class divisions in this country are employers, workers, and the in-between people? It's a lie. The three classes here are the sabras, the new immigrants, and the refugees. Right here, on this little balcony, are the three classes in miniature, and only a deaf man can fail to hear the fanfares of battle. A mental class war. And here, too, woe to the loser, woe! (pp. 274–275)

In stories like "Country Town" ["Prazon," 1960], the failure of the immigrants to adapt produces anxiety and guilt.

By turning his attention away from the city centers to the provinces, Shenhar produced some of the country's best fiction dealing with the uprooted isolated newcomer in the new homeland. Immigrants are doubly alienated, since they live in communities which are themselves isolated. This condition of isolation is reflected by the very landscape: "the houses [standing] far apart . . . as if the life in them never flowed together but slipped in between and away, out of sight, like those omnibuses laden with tourists."

Shenhar's strength lay in his ability to connect the epic past of his protagonists (in the diaspora) with their present deprivation and desolation. Moving back from the time of the narration to earlier moments enabled him to put present circumstances in the context of past realities, as in his depiction of Havah in "Country Town," who projects upon Eretz Yisrael the loneliness and barrenness she feels having left her native city of Warsaw. Havah views the local society not only as deeply divided; screened by its workaday routine from facing the abyss, it also seems to her largely unconscious of its internal fracture. She detests this new society. By mindlessly adapting itself to the new environment, it has forfeited the richness of mental conflict, which, in her view, produces human complexity and meaning. Although the author does not himself endorse his protagonist's point of view, he does, by presenting her musings on the subject, offer it as alternate perspective, a kind of gap in the ideational wall of Zionism. This ability to illuminate social situations from a variety of angles, to juxtapose opposites, and to expose false unities, characterized much of Shenhar's work (*One of a Thousand*, "Hovevei Zion Street" ["Rehov Hovevei Tsiyon," 1960], and "'Ere Summer" ["Beterem qayitz," 1960]).

Unlike his contemporaries, Yehoshua Bar-Yosef, who was born in Safed in 1912, did not experience the crises of immigration that formed the subject matter of his contemporaries. During the First World War, when he was four years old, his mother fled with him to Transylvania, and even though his years in the diaspora also left their mark, he never forgot his early childhood in Safed. Consequently, Bar-Yosef's writing primarily reflected the conflicts between traditional and Orthodox religion and secular society. Indeed, the beginning of his literary career coincides with his own break with traditional orthodoxy. His first publication, "The Voices of Bridegroom and Bride" ["Qol hatan veqol kalah"] (in the newspaper *Davar*, 1936), is a heretic's description of a young religious couple's innocent sexual awakening. From that time on the critics regarded him as the writer who had broken out of the ghetto to express the instinctual drives of those liberated from religious orthodoxy. In this regard, he was the heir of the Haskalah and the literature of Revival (e.g., Bialik and Berdyczewski) more than the successor to the authors of the Second Aliyah or a contemporary of the Hebrew writers of the interwar years.

Of the Second Aliyah writers he was closest to Reuveni, depicting, like him, the forces of sensuality that clashed with the Old Yishuv milieu. With their themes of sexual desire and repression, Bar-Yosef's novels tend toward naturalism. And while they are no more stylistically innovative than the works of his contemporaries, by concentrating on aspects of the human experience that the pioneering writers viewed as marginal but which he, as a once-Orthodox Jew experienced as central, they do succeed in evoking the tensions between tradition and revolt, desire and conventionality, and the preservation and violation of the social fabric.

In his most notable novel, *Enchanted City* [*'Ir qsumah*, 1949–1951], Bar-Yosef achieved an even broader sweep. Not content to propose only social and psychological (naturalistic) reasons for the text's dramatic developments, he wrote a mystical tale set in old Safed, which has a legacy of supernatural and kabbalistic associations. This three-part novel (published between 1949 and 1951, appearing in full in 1958) is a family saga. It spans several generations between the mid-nineteenth and the early twentieth centuries, each volume focusing on a single generation. As in most family chronicles, the process is one of decline. Erotic tensions between the couples—which are depicted with Bar-Yosef's customary naturalism—confront forces of madness and death, which consistently come to bear upon and erode the lives of the second and third generations of protagonists. A dual structure of dramatic and epic patterning doubly represented by events and as imminent within the landscape itself produces the trilogy's vibrant tension. Cycles of nature and daily existence assert the continuity of generation, while natural and historical disruptions defy that continuity. These include the earthquake in Safed, the Druze uprising in the north, epidemics of diphtheria and typhus, and finally the landslide at Har Meiron during the celebrations for Lag Ba'omer, the holiday thirty-three days after Passover when Bar Kochbah's rebellion against the Romans is commemorated. In this way Safed comes to symbolize a perennial archetypical tension between life and death. In contrast to the permanence of its landscape, its population is always in a state of flux. The family chronicle itself serves as a synecdoche for the social and cosmic processes experienced by the place. The decline of traditional Safed in the imminent advent of a new era (Zionism) can clearly be read between the lines.

Also set in Safed, this time at the height of its flowering in the sixteenth century, when it was the center of the kabbalistic movement, Bar-Yosef's second Safed novel, *Tabernacle of Peace* [*Sukat shalom*, 1958], made freer use of historical materials than *Enchanted City*. The protagonists are historical figures, the novel's title signifying a group of mystical seekers of salvation whose collective experience becomes a substitute for universal messianism. Yet, despite its historical specificity, the book's real subject was the Zionist present, which it tried to represent in ways that went beyond both documented history and the dramatic intrigues of power and sex. It dealt with exile and the corruption of redemption, as redemption becomes a mere instrument of human purposes. As one character in the novel says to another: "You yourself fear the redemption which you are supposedly trying to bring about by force. You too are afraid of the tedium which will grip you at the sight of sinless people" (p. 307).

Although he did not quite succeed in his objectives, what Bar-Yosef tried to do in this novel was expose the distance between messianic vision and human limitation. In moving from the familiar territory of the decline of traditional society in Eretz Yisrael, Bar Yosef pointed the way for Haim Hazaz and some of the other younger writers, also natives of Eretz Yisrael and the State of Israel, who would tackle similar issues in different ways. Such writers as Yigal Mossinsohn, Aharon Megged, and Dan Ben-Amotz took up Bar Yosef's anti-establishment position and utterly transformed it.

The writers of the interwar generation went on writing after the establishment of the State of Israel in 1948, but the changes brought about by statehood did not favor them. They had wielded some influence over the upcoming generation of writers, and had even been influenced in return, but they did not have the means to contend with the new social context. In the 1940s the settlement novel had already begun to take on some critical new features. There was not yet a full-blown critical theory of the settlement novel. There was only the occasional deviation from its form, which stopped short of radical revision. Nonetheless, the settlement novel began to develop from a documentary-ideological affirmation of existing reality toward creative writing that would confront and contend with discrepancies between expectation and reality (e.g., the novels of Amos Oz and Yonat and Alexander Sened). Novels such as Yehudah Yaari's *When the Candle Was Burning*, Nathan Bistritski's *Days and Nights* [*Yamim veleilot*, 1927], S. Yizhar's *Ephraim Returns to Alphafa* (1938), and David Maletz's *Young Hearts* [*Ma'agalot*, literally: "cycles," 1945] were hardly unequivocal paeans of praise for kibbutz life.

Indeed, in *Young Hearts* Maletz produced something of an exposé of Kibbutz Ein Harod in the Jezreel valley. The protagonist Menahem is an outsider who is unable to fit into kibbutz society, while his wife has an affair with the glorious warrior type, not a member of the kibbutz itself but of Hashomer. Maletz also exposed some of the ideological disputes in the kibbutz, and some of the disputants in the novel were identifiable prototypes. The book created a great stir in kibbutz society, which treated it as though it were a documentary, or at least a roman à clef, rather than a work of fiction. And because it did not conform to the idealized model of the kibbutz, and even ventured to criticize it, the book was rejected by many of its readers.

Future writers such as Amos Oz and Yitzhak Ben-Ner, who appeared on the literary scene only in the 1960s, would continue elements of the interwar tradition, such as the settlement novel, in order to radically revise them. Similarly, the ideological-Zionist novel would become utterly transformed in the hands of authors such as Pinhas Sadeh and Yehuda Amichai. The trivial novel, too, experienced a revisionary revival: Yigal Mossinsohn and Dan Ben-Amotz, among others, picking up where a previous generation left off.

* * *

Because the interwar fiction of the Third Aliyah was not particularly original in either its subject matter or its formal qualities, it did not achieve the canonical status of the writings of the Second Aliyah and their contemporaries who arrived from the diaspora (Agnon, Brenner, Berkowitz, Shoffman). Nonetheless, this fiction was popular with the settlers and pioneers, who sought to discover in it idealized portraits of themselves. It also left its mark on the ensuing literary generations. Indeed, the next generation of writers (Yizhar, Shamir, Megged), who seemed to be the devoted acolytes of the modern fathers of Hebrew literature (Brenner, Agnon, and Gnessin), themselves remained faithful to the social and literary values of the would-be realistic-programmatic literature of the interwar generation. Despite its lack of artistic merit, such literature played a major role in shaping the literary and cultural consciousness of Eretz Yisrael.

Nor did the interwar generation of writers intend to accomplish more than this. "A future generation will come which will be unable to ignore us in discussing the literature of Eretz Yisrael," wrote Zarchi to Aricha in 1945; "for we found it in its early infancy and left it big and growing fast. And we should be content with the conviction and the sense that we served the people and the country faithfully and to the best of our ability—and did nothing else." The writers, in other words, did not aspire to greatness. They did not delude themselves about the quality of their writings. Their fiction was, in their own view of it, local and quite provincial, but for them this native or homeland art (*Heimatliteratur*) was enough.

9

HEBREW LITERARY MODERNISM
JEWISH FICTION AND THE INTERNATIONAL SCENE

By and large the authors of Hebrew literary modernism did not grow up in Eretz Yisrael. Some of them, like Reuven Wallenrod, David Vogel, and Ephraim Lisitzky, never settled there. Others did not even use specifically Jewish or Eretz Yisraeli materials; their novels read like Hebrew versions of German, American, or Russian novels. Jewish elements played no more significant a role in the writings of authors like Vogel and Wallenrod than they did in the works of such German-Jewish novelists as Arthur Schnitzler, Josef Roth, or Jacob Wassermann or Jewish-American authors like Abraham Cahan, Ludwig Lewisohn, Saul Bellow, or Bernard Malamud. Their novels and novellas were populated with non-Jewish protagonists, and they presented a way of life which was typically recognizably American or Austrian.

Diverting the gaze of Hebrew literature from its rustic little corner in the Middle East to the setting in which most of world Jewry lived, namely the big city, writers like Steinmann, Vogel, Wallenrod, and Halkin followed in the footsteps of the great Western writers. Just as Alfred Döblin portrayed Berlin, and James Joyce evoked Dublin, so Steinmann depicted Odessa; Vogel, Vienna; Lisitzky, Boston; Wallenrod, New York; and Elisheva Bikhovski (known simply as "Elisheva"), Moscow. Influenced by August Strindberg and such books as Otto Weininger's book *Sex and Character* [*Geschlecht und Charakter*, 1903], these writers were also heavily Freudian; the struggle with sexual repression dominates the fiction of Steinmann, Vogel, Horowitz, and Halkin, among others. Of course, relations between the sexes is an old literary subject. But the representation of these relations as out-and-out warfare, with the repeated return to childhood memories and the extensive use of sexual symbols, attested to the new Freudian turn of the literature.

Although the non–Eretz Yisrael writers were connected in diverse ways to the Hebrew literary tradition, especially as exemplified in the anti-genrists like Brenner, Gnessin, Barash, and Berkowitz, in giving themselves over to outside influences they broke with its essential lines of development. Although they were radical innovators in comparison with writers of local settlement fiction, in terms of European literature they were mere imitators of the leading modes of literary composition. The one modernist writer who remained faithful to the particular habitat of the Jews—namely, the shtetl and the communities in Eretz Yisrael—was Haim Hazaz.

Even the modernists could not ignore the major upheavals taking place in the interwar Jewish world. Most of them wrote about immigration and about the processes of socialization that the immigrants experienced in their new countries. Such experiences of uprooting and reintegration were at the heart of the writings of Hazaz, Steinmann, Wallenrod, and Vogel, who for the most part depicted the big cities of new Jewish life as man-eating monsters, not in the least hospitable to their new inhabitants. The typical protagonists of these modernist writers resembled the rootless, disaffected anti-heroes of Berdyczewski, Brenner, Gnessin, and Reuveni. The modernist writers, however, portrayed these characters differently. Halkin, for example, wrote stream-of-consciousness fiction, dominated by interior monologues and confessions; Steinmann and Horowitz made extensive use of expository prose, inserting lengthy expositions of theoretical ideas into their texts. While the settlement novels of Eretz Yisrael combined documentary-historical materials with intrigue and ideology, modernist fiction made little use of such elements. The modernists (Bistritski, Vogel, Wallenrod, Elisheva, and Leah Goldberg, among them) favored analysis over plot. They dissected and explicated rather than simply narrated events. And they retarded plot development by means of landscape descriptions, psychological digressions, and character confessions. In general, European modernism reduced the role of the omniscient narrator, and used multiple viewpoints, indirect speech, and interior monologues. The new Jewish modernism, however, both within Eretz Yisrael and outside it, expanded the narrator's authority. Although this tendency characterized much of this fiction, the only writer who put the approach to good literary use was Hazaz.

The contrast between modernist and other Eretz Yisrael fiction was present also in the modernists' different approach to language. In terms of the stylistic polarities that had heretofore dominated Hebrew writing—formulation or pseudo-formulation versus neologism—the modernists took up several positions: Steinmann, Horowitz, and Levin tended toward neologisms; Vogel, Elisheva, Wallenrod, and Goldberg adopted Brenner's brand of mimetic representation and Shoffman's lyricism; Halkin took on Gnessin's emotive stream of consciousness; and Hazaz and Bistritski developed their own brand of expressionism.

While each of the modernists distinguished himself or herself from the others, nonetheless they tended toward certain groupings. There were the universalists, led by Eliezer Steinmann; the expressionists (Hazaz); and the impressionists (Elisheva, Vogel, and Goldberg). In general, their objective was to directly oppose the dominant literary tendencies of their generation. In this ideology of revolt, Eliezer Steinmann, Menashe Levin, and Yaacov Horowitz combined opposition to the literary establishment with a struggle for personal self-realization. Their rebellion, however, lacked a social theory. Therefore it often seemed more like the petty ambitions of youth to upset parental authority than a mature aesthetic theory.

ELIEZER STEINMANN, YAACOV HOROWITZ, MENASHE LEVIN

The chief spokesperson for Hebrew literary modernism was Eliezer Steinmann, a former Communist revolutionary who emigrated to Eretz Yisrael in 1924. Unlike most of the other new arrivals, Steinmann did not change his fictional subject but, with the conviction that it was better to write about life in the diaspora than to write Eretz Yisrael genre fiction, he continued to present characters floundering in a rather generalized, geographically unspecified urban setting. Because he believed that the quality of fiction is measured by its ability to portray the individual, he admired Gnessin above all the anti-genrists. In contrast to Gnessin's genuine and singular individuals, however, his own characters tended toward generalized abstractions, more suitable to treatment in essays than in fiction.

Steinmann tried to shake up the socio-cultural environment by producing a kind of anti-novel. Even in his early stories he was innovative; more than any of his predecessors, he accentuated the unreal and the fantastic. After the novel *Esther Hayot* (1923), whose protagonist was a kind of Jewish Emma Bovary, the authorial presence grew more and more prominent, increasingly inclined to explicate rather than observe. Interpretation and commentary displaced plot and characterization. There were more and more references to Freudian motives, and his late stories were confessional narratives dominated by an essayist-lyrical element. His narrative style was characterized by literary self-consciousness and self-reflexivity. This investigation of the literariness of the fictional text was conducted through a repetitive dialogue with the reader, the narrator serving as a mediator between the fictional and the quotidian worlds. Steinmann's plots subscribed to the pattern which Sheldon Sacks (*Fiction and the Shape of Belief*) has termed "apologue": tales constructed so as to convey a specific authorial idea.

The essayist quality of Steinmann's works is much in evidence in one of his principal novels, *Couples* [*Zugot,* 1930]. This is also a poetic novel. It combines melodramatic intrigue, in the form of two love triangles, with a series of sophisticated aphorisms and authorial commentaries that run throughout. The book issued something of a challenge to the realism of the period. Whereas specified time and place and externally observed personae who experienced real-life events dominated the settlement novel, in Steinmann's novels there is no Zionist plotting. Furthermore, his personified abstractions move around in indistinct surroundings. Settlement novel protagonists acted on the basis of social, historical, and ideological considerations. Steinmann's characters are driven by Freudian impulses, which produce nothing more than trivial encounters between the sexes.

In style Steinmann's fiction recalls what Herbert Read has called "the poetics of wit." Verbal juggling, clever phrasing, and flirting with the reader emerge as more significant to the novel than plot or characterization. From *Couples* on, there is an extreme tendency toward neologism, which Steinmann considered the appropriate modernist response to conservatism's attachment to classical phraseology. In a sense, his witticisms and essayist moralistic propensities brought him closer to the late-nineteenth-century Haskalah writers than to his immediate predecessors or contemporaries, thus exposing how, underneath all the modernist theory and psychoanalytical influence, this new literature also rested on the foundations of prior Hebrew literary production.

His work met with mixed reactions. He was regarded more as symbol of literary revolution than as a truly revolutionary artist, and many critics pointed out the ordinariness and heavy-handedness of his creative writing. Although his influence on his contemporaries can be glimpsed in the prose fiction of Horowitz and Levin and in the criticism and poetry of Shlonsky, the younger generation of writers took little note of him.

Yaacov Horowitz served from the mid-1920s on as a standard-bearer of the modernist revolution. Horowitz was also the most urban of the Eretz Yisrael writers, allied in spirit with the Viennese fin de siècle writers such as Schnitzler, Zweig, Josef Roth, and Altenberg; Viennese impressionism (with its poetical essayist romanticism); and the rootlessness of Hebrew novelists such as Brenner, Shoffman, and Gnessin. Like Steinmann (and Shlonsky), wit and the clever phrase mattered more to Horowitz than any other aspect of his work. Indeed, the centrality of poetry in the new Hebrew fiction is evident in Horowitz's writing, which used many of the devices of witty verse.

Like many of Agnon's protagonists, Horowitz's characters are dropouts from kibbutz society who end up in the city, joining the bohemian working milieu of Little Tel Aviv. Although the building of the country as such did not interest Horowitz, it served as a background for the inner conflicts of his protagonists, who are skeptical about Zionist liberation and the blessings of the earth. However, for all their apparent difference from genre fiction, including the absence of real historical and social materials, Horowitz's novels posit essentially the same social and moral contrasts as genre fiction did.

In many of his stories what matters is atmosphere and idea, all other elements of the fiction being reduced to insignificance. Even when he tried to develop his characters more fully they remained representatives of ideas rather than convincing personae. For example, the characters in *Shining Light* [*'Or zarua'*, 1929] are more embodiments of religious ideas than participants in a melodrama. In the absence of social materials, events seem to happen in a void, even though the novel makes use of historical and social materials. The novel is based on real events (the expulsion of the Jews from Spain in the late fifteenth century). It deals with genuine intercommunal relations. Nonetheless, it remains universalist and transhistorical. The story is told from several viewpoints, describing the expulsion as seen by the Jewish physician Don Abram Bonafios, his daughter Pamela, the Christian ship captain who falls in love with her, the monk Father Vicenzi, and a Moslem dervish. Even though the end brings together individuals of different religious factions, the denouement, as in other of his novels, brings disillusionment. The romantic heroes are disenchanted with the world. They are betrayed by friends and lovers.

The pivotal theme in much of Horowitz's fiction is the conflict between the sexes. Most of the plots are stereotypically melodramatic (one woman and two or more men). They lack psychological depth or the full realization of the relationships. Digressions from the melodrama take the form of ironic commentaries by the narrator, who poses romantic polarities: purity versus bourgeois defilement, comradeship in contrast to a woman's love, longing for youth and a pure spiritual self as opposed to urban anxiety and descent into the quagmire of materialism.

At the core of almost everything that he wrote, from the poetic short stories to the novels (historical and otherwise) to the novellas, is a deep attachment to the abstract values of the Zionist youth movement (similar to that of the genrists). Horowitz's modern man longs to escape from petty bourgeois reality into the dreamy visionary world of the eternal adolescent, as in the novella *A World that Still Stands* [*'Olam shelo nehrav 'adayin*, 1950]. But whereas the genre writers portrayed the world as though the romantic ambitions of the Zionist youth movement had already been fulfilled, Horowitz's protagonists fail to prosper and mature;

they persist in following an ineffable vision that transcends the frontiers of Eretz Yisrael. In effect, Horowitz sought to depict the impact of the Zionist revolution on the life of the individual in rebellion against the bourgeois world. Although Horowitz's contemporaries were divided in their opinion of him, younger and older critics of the 1950s and 1960s revalued his position as the link between early modernism and later writers of *Dor Hamedinah* such as Yehoshua, Oz, and Amichai, who echo but little of his faith in the Zionist revolution.

One last and extremely pronounced expression of the anti-genrist revolt of the Steinmann-Horowitz-Shlonsky group (which had by this time broken up) was the novella by Menashe Levin, *One Hundred Nights in Old Jaffa* [*Me'ah leilot beyafo ha'atiqah,* 1938]. The book met with sharp criticism, perhaps because it lacked any social or moral message. Based on brilliant futuristic constructs, one of the purposes of which was the parodic delegitimization of the traditional novel, its form was its message.

HAIM HAZAZ, NATHAN BISTRITSKI

The modernist-expressionist writers such as Haim Hazaz and Nathan Bistritski viewed the historical events which overtook the Jewish world as nothing less than apocalyptic. For them, the October Revolution and Zionism were two sides of a single coin. The Old World was crumbling and truth might just yet arise from the new earth. For these writers, then, social transformation was nothing less than an ecstatic experience, rich in metaphysical implication. It was an experience that genre literature was inadequate to convey. Yaacov Horowitz, who himself started out as an expressionist, defined it in the following words:

> Hebrew creativity here, on our own land, needs dynamite to match the earthly labors on the sands and rocks. Only the creative man who sets things ablaze and causes the spirit to effervesce madly will be capable of smashing the windows in our thick literary walls. ("Opposite the Furnace of Creation," *Sadan* [1925], p. 22)

If the outstanding expressionist poet was Uri Zvi Greenberg, his prose equivalent was Hazaz. Along with Bistritski, he founded in Hebrew fiction an ecstatic, expressionist tradition which has never disappeared, even if its continuation and evolution are less obvious than the heritage of, say, Agnon. The life and work of Hazaz were marked by two experiences. The first was the Russian Revolution, the second, his sojourn in 1921 in Istanbul in the company of Jewish pioneers. From the publication of his first story in 1924, he linked his literary message with the existential issues of Jewish life, thus following faithfully in the tradition which began in the Haskalah, climaxed in Mendele, and was perpetuated by Brenner. The fate of the Jewish people, whether determined by external forces or by the people's own nature, preoccupied Hazaz in everything he wrote. This is true from his stories of the Russian Revolution and of Jewish *halutzim* fleeing from Russia through his nostalgic portraits of the Old World before or just after the Revolution to tales about the waves of immigration to Eretz Yisrael. The novellas *Horizon* [*'Ofeq natui*, 1958] and *The Gallows* [*Beqolar'ehad*, 1963] dealt, respectively, with the settlement in the Lachish region and the underground struggle against British rule. Finally, he dealt with life in Israel after the establishment of the State. Unlike many of his contemporaries, Hazaz sought neither to affirm nor to reject conventional Zionist-Jewish models. Rather, he attempted to explore and come to terms with these models, treating socio-historical materials as subsidiary to the complexities of ideology.

Typically, therefore, Hazaz constructed series of antitheses: exile versus redemption, religious traditionalism versus secularism, petty bourgeois life versus revolution, Eretz Yisrael as reality versus Eretz Yisrael as utopia, rootlessness versus rootedness, and pragmatism versus spiritual aspiration. In particular, Hazaz alternately criticized and adulated exile and liberation, the two definitive poles of the Zionist revolution, this particular dialectic informing both plots and dialogue. Some of Hazaz's characters argue that Eretz Yisrael means the end of a civilization, namely that of the diaspora. Others (in the *halutzim* stories of the 1930s, notably in "The Sermon" ["Hadrashah"]) reject the diaspora outright, asserting that the end to exile will cure the ills of the people, not only in the diaspora but also in the land of their liberation. In yet another story ("Drabkin") Hazaz warned that Eretz Yisrael itself could become another kind of exile.

In the short story "Rahamim" ["Rahamim," 1933], for example, Hazaz creates a conversation between a "dejected, despairing" individual, "lean as a pole" and "sickly looking," who has all sorts of "recriminations and accusations . . . against the labor Federation and Zionism" with a happy-go-lucky "Kurd from Zacho" named Rahamim. Rahamim, whose name means "pity," is a "short fellow with thick black eyebrows, beard like a thicket, his face bright as a copper pot and his chest uncommonly virile and broad . . . dressed in rags and tatters," who has two wives and unending faith in the divine. The diametrical opposition presented through the two men and their discourse externalizes the divide within the major protagonist himself, Menashke Bezprozvani, who, as much as he "wished to torture himself, to cry out aloud and rebel and remonstrate against the whole state of affairs . . . possessed a great love for the land and a great love of the Hebrew language, a strong, deeply irrational, obstinate love that went past all theories and views, and led beyond all personal advantage" (pp. 94–95). The story ends without resolution, projecting the protagonist's divided self both onto the landscape and back into his earlier memories, where, bathed in natural beauty and nostalgia, they take on ameliorating qualities:

> Menashke Bezprozvani sat himself down on a stone. He looked up at the Mountains of Moab—desolate in their blue, indistinct outline—as though they had been swallowed by the sky or, perhaps, as though the sky had been swallowed by them. Before his eyes stood the likeness of the porter with his smile; his spirits rising within him, his thoughts divided, he sighed, almost tearful, then began to hum to himself the words of the song which the children had been accustomed to sing at Kfar Gileadi in those days of hardship and hunger:

> In Kfar Gileadi, in the upper court,
> Next to the runnel, within the big butt
> There's never a drop of water. (p. 101)

In accordance with the dominant moral standard in literature (and in life) since the beginning of the twentieth century, for Hazaz, as for others, actions mattered more than intentions. Most of Hazaz's work yielded to the pressure for literature to be ideological. His fiction assumed the form of a story framing an ideological discussion, with the plots serving as little more than pegs on which to hang ideas. These stories were presented either in the form of monologues or dialogues, as in the above story or in "The Sermon." Narrative continuity mattered little, and the contents of the digressions were far more important than the events of the plot. Like Brenner, Agnon, Shenhar, Bar-Yosef, and others, Hazaz measured his protagonists by the standards of labor Zionism. Like them, he ended up preferring the Zionist enterprise to messianic visions, even though the Zionist reality might cost the lives of its fighters (as in the novella *The Gallows*).

The novella *The Gates of Bronze* [*Daltot hanehoshet*, 1956, revised 1965] provides a late example of his revolutionary stories. Its protagonists belong to two different generations. The older generation, represented by Reb Simha, rejects the Revolution out of hand. The younger generation seeks to realize itself through radical activism. Three male characters (Pribisker, who upholds tradition; Polishuk, a Bolshevik communist; and Soroka, a pro-Zionist anarchist committed to human liberty) fight over one woman (Reb Simha's daughter Letse). Yet the plot is driven by an impersonal force, namely, the Revolution itself, which advances or impedes the relationships between the characters. Multifaceted discussions among the characters punctuate the story. Each of the characters interprets events in his or her own way, not really engaging the others in debate but rather proceeding autonomously, from within their own arguments. Indeed, the characters emerge as something of an atomized chorus whose vocalizations comically reveal the immutability of each position. All the elements of the novella serve a single purpose. They call for unceasing revolution in order to defeat the tendency of those in power to become established and power-hungry. Exchanging the authority of religion for Bolshevism, for example, does not produce liberation, and Soroka, who supposedly represents the idea of liberty, is incapable of achieving it.

As with the character Soroka, in Hazaz's fiction characters generally stand for social groups or some other aspect of the external world (religious, spiritual, communal, or moral). Like Mendele, Hazaz described his personae from outside. He took no interest in their inner worlds. He never hinted at what is unseen by his protagonists or the reader or revealed all mysteries, either general or individual. Nor is the range of his characters particularly broad. The recurring protagonist, from *Revolutionary Chapters* [*Pirqei mahapekhah*, 1926] through *Bell and Pomegranate* [*Pa'amon verimon*, 1974], is the same figure of the visionary revolutionary, absurdly possessed of a single idea, incapable of adapting to changing circumstances. In general, this weak, pathetic, disaffiliated visionary is paired or juxtaposed with a more self-confident character, such as the communist who has no doubts concerning the revolution, or the man of action who resists the other's utopian visions. Nor is the visionary a popular character: Society resents the truth that the revolutionary presumes to fling in its face.

Such polarizations as run throughout Hazaz's writing had also served Brenner, Agnon, Reuveni, and Shenhar. But Hazaz further developed their complexities, as he did the figure of the grotesque, which he inherited from Mendele. These qualities are exemplified more in his Yemenite novels than in his more Eurocentric fiction. In his only two novels, *Mori Said* [*Hayoshevet baganim*, literally meaning "she who dwells in the gardens," 1944] and *Yaish* (a four-part novel, 1947–1952), Hazaz turned to the world of Yemenite Jewry. The former is the better crafted of the two; in it his essayist methodology achieves genuine richness.

Of all his writings, *Mori Said* most closely recalls Mendele. The central figure, Mori Said, represents an entire community and embodies all its characteristics: "Mori Said," we are told, "is like everybody else." This sociological design affects every element in the novel, which revolves around two families: that of Mori Said (his son Tzion and his granddaughter Rumiah), and that of Mori Alfaqaah. The tensions between the generations (fathers, sons, grandchildren) fuel the plot, which deals with the social conflicts that erupt in a community that finds itself in a new country in unfamiliar circumstances. The story is about the failure of a man obsessed with a single idea. It is about the collapse of the family and the loss of paternal authority.

Although the materials of the novel, taken almost entirely from the life, language, and folklore of the Yemenite Jewish community, give the novel an appearance of verisimilitude, its central artistic element, as in much of Hazaz's fiction, is grotesque parody. This is rendered, for example, in the dialogue between Mori Said and Mori Alfaqaah, in which they dream of the longed-for Messiah and redemption. To the naive and wonder-struck Mori Alfaqaah, who serves as something of a Sancho Panza to the visionary Mori Said, such expectation seems reasonable. But Mori Said's visions are messianic madness. They bear no relation to the surrounding reality. Mori Said becomes more and more marginalized. From a simple prophet of consolation, he turns into a prophet of wrath, who plants himself beside the Wailing Wall and announces that he will not budge until the Messiah comes. The savior does not come, and Mori Said dies a madman. To intensify the book's message about the dangers of single-minded messianism, Tzion, his son, exploits his father's beliefs to his own materialistic ends. In this book, too, revolutionary ideas are shown to be incapable of accommodating real social conditions.

The failure of Hazaz's characters to achieve humanness in their own right amounts to a kind of dehumanization, a feature which is intensified by the formal quality of the writing, with its series of paired ideological opposites. The protagonists are more like bizarre caricatures than normal human beings. In this Hazaz followed the example of Mendele, adding Yemenite grotesques to the repertoire of Eastern European grotesques. Indeed, Hazaz's great originality emerges from the contrast between his Mendele-inspired forms of composition and the personae he depicts: rebels, visionaries, and unanchored intellectuals who belong more to the tradition of Brenner than Mendele. What saves the stories from being simplistic, despite their unexceptional foundations and their lack of psychological depth, is the expressive force achieved by this unlikely pairing of pathetic grotesque and intellectual disenchantment.

In this enhancement of the literary subject, Hazaz's aesthetic success was further assisted by his careful adaptation of Mendele's formulated style. Unlike Agnon, who had perfected formulation to the point of excessive equilibrium, Hazaz intensified it until it suggested inner contrasts and oppositions that reflected the dichotomies that were the text's subjects. It is this quality of intensification—on the level of both theme and structure—that most distinguishes Hazaz's art, especially in the original versions of the works. In the 1968 revised edition of his work, Hazaz attempted to dilute some of this intensification. It was as if he wished to forgo his expressionist distinction and return like a penitent to the more purist Mendele fold.

Essentially authoritative—directing, pointing, and assessing—the writing does not claim to be objective. Rather it assigns values according to the author's artistic and ideological standards. The language of its intensity, however, is expressive rather than mimetic, emotive rather than referential. It uses the devices of poetry, taking far-reaching liberties with the language and creating a largely autonomous linguistic universe of an exotic or even grotesque and absurd nature. This tendency of the fictional world to split off from its referential reality is conveyed within the stories themselves, in the doers who do not talk but do and the talkers who do not act but converse. Moreover, the world of the talkers is often more fantastic than real, the word-drunk heroes coming to represent an unreal experience. Better than any of his contemporaries, Hazaz knew how to overcome the limitations of the documentary, melodramatic, and ideological mode through extremities of distortion and the intensification of grotesque disjunctions.

Hazaz was also affected by European literary traditions, and many parallels (though not necessarily through influence) may be found between his stories of the Revolution and those of Isaac Babel (who grew up under similar circumstances), and between his stories and his play *At the End of Days* [*Bekeits hayamim*] and the plays and stories of F. Wedekind, G. Kayser, and E. Toller. He in turn had a profound effect on the next generation of writers, the so-called Native Generation. S. Yizhar, for example, followed Hazaz in matters of material, though not in style. Moshe Shamir and Aharon Megged adopted his style, but not his subjects. A kind of latter-day expressionism appeared in the work of younger writers such as Pinhas Sadeh and Yehuda Amichai. Although in style, materials, and themes they were quite different from Hazaz, they too sought to convert personal biography into a mythical substrate. Traces of influence may also be found in the writing of Amos Oz and Yoram Kaniuk, who also tend toward expressionist modes. The work of writers like Yehoshua Kenaz and Aharon Appelfeld can be seen as a reaction to the elevated style of which Hazaz was one of the foremost practitioners.

Stylization, intensification, the view of the individual as a representative of a group, a tendency toward the grotesque—these features also characterized the writings of Nathan Bistritski. Soon after he arrived in Eretz Yisrael in 1920 Bistritski joined the Bitaniya group, a commune of young *halutzim,* members of the Zionist leftist Hashomer Hatzair (The Young Guard) youth movement, who worked during the early days of the Third Aliyah in an agricultural settlement in the Lower Galilee and later founded the kibbutz Beit Alpha. Bistritski edited an anthology of their personal reminiscences and memoirs, which blended together to form something of a communal diary entitled *Our Community* [*Kehiliyateinu*] (ongoing, from 1922). In 1927 he published his novel *Days and Nights,* a fictionalized narrative which made extensive use of several months in Bitaniya, where he took part in communal discussions and held many private conversations with the kibbutz members. In addition to this unusual novel, he wrote plays and nonfiction, all markedly expressionist in manner.

Unlike Hazaz and Horowitz, Bistritski wrote chiefly about the pioneering settlement. Even though he used documentary materials and even hinted at prototypes, his characteristic style of distortion and use of the grotesque produced something quite different from the typical genre fiction on the subject. Because *Days and Nights* was so thoroughgoingly honest an attempt to depict the complexities of the relations between the individual and the community, it met with a mixed response and became the focus of widespread discussion of kibbutz society and its values. Nonetheless, everyone granted the originality of Bistritski's presentation. Bistritski made no effort to depict things as they were. Rather he sought to bring out their unconscious aspects, their root causes.

Days and Nights is structured, however obscurely, by two basic patterns. The first is the ostensible plot. This is the story of the writer Binyamin Mogelyansky, his immigration to Eretz Yisrael, the decision to join Givʿat Ariʾeh (a fictional commune, based on Bitaniya), and his eventual return to his beloved Miriam. Toward the end of the novel we find the protagonist living in isolation in an Arab town, attempting to record his experiences on the commune, the written record of which had been burned by the members.

The second pattern, wherein lies the heart of the book (Parts Two and Three and some chapters in Part Four), depicts the commune of Givʿat Ariʾeh. Although they seem to enjoy a communal existence, in reality each of the many characters, who pour out in lengthy confessions their past lives and relationships to the present, leads a painfully solitary life. Each one of them carries burdensome memories. Each longs for the partitions between them to fall, for the walls of the isolated suffering self to dissolve. But nothing can bring this about, not the communal life or Zionism or the external threats of the enemy. Only on rare occasions, under the rhetorical sway of the leader, during an orgiastic dance, or in the confessional communal anthology, do the interpersonal barriers fall. At such moments the commune comes to resemble a latter-day Hasidic congregation, with the leader (the Tzaddik), Alexander Tzuri, binding up the disparate parts with his (secular) confessional sermons, like Jesus preaching to his disciples. Tzuri's speeches sometimes resemble Freudian essays, with the interpretation of dreams serving as a substitute for religion and art.

By all the accepted standards, kibbutz society was supposed to be an instrument of Zionist settlement as well as a gem of social justice. Bistritski's novel exposes how the communal enterprise constituted a variety of psychotherapeutic intervention, wherein small confessions were poured out in larger communal enterprises and human beings were thus cleansed of their sins. Since the collapse of the religious congregation, whose commandments, rituals, and ceremonies had in the past saved the individual from himself, loneliness had become the sin afflicting the modern Jew. Community was to serve as a new religion, its commandments the practical objectives of labor Zionism.

The core themes of the novel—communion, disaffiliation, loneliness—well suited expressionist exposition. In place of plot there are myths, rituals, and ceremonies. Colorful and intricately composed outcries of personal pain substitute for concrete characterization. Born of the Brenner tradition, and, like the fiction of Hazaz, expressionist in its mode of exposition, it sought to bridge the documentary-ideological settlement genre novel and the expressionist cry of the individual in the midst of the Zionist revolution. For this alone, the novel, despite its doubtful literary value, deserves to be remembered. Indeed, Bistritski's influence may have been greater than was at first imagined, especially in terms of his dominant theme: the paradoxical relationship between the individual and the commune. Both Yizhar and Oz, for example, were deeply aware of this paradox, though their characters, unlike those of Bistritski, do not find release in the group therapy of confession and the intoxication of dance.

ELISHEVA BIKHOVSKI, DAVID VOGEL, LEAH GOLDBERG

At the same time that Hebrew modernism tackled the bread-and-butter subjects of the Hebrew tradition—the shtetl, the uprooted Jew, the crisis of migration—other Hebrew modernists explored the subjects of non-Jewish modernist writing, namely, the city, bohemianism, and relationships between Jews and gentiles. Indeed, the fiction and to a certain extent the poetry of Elisheva Bikhovski, David Vogel, and Leah Goldberg were more closely related to early-twentieth-century Russian and German literature than to the Hebrew writings of their contemporaries.

Touching on Jewish subjects only tangentially, these writers remain on the fringes of Hebrew literature, maintaining closer links to literary traditions other than that of Brenner, Shoffman, or Gnessin: Elisheva and Goldberg to Chekhov, Biely, and the Freudian novels of the 1920s; Vogel to turn-of-the-century Viennese writers such as Schnitzler, Zweig, or Roth. Inevitably, their Hebrew language steered clear of formulation. Since their protagonists were not supposed to be speaking Hebrew or Yiddish but Russian or German, of which the written Hebrew was merely a translation, they did not cultivate neologisms. Indeed, because their protagonists and narrators did not belong to an organic Jewish context, the fiction itself seems like something of a transplanted reality, as if these were in fact translated texts rather than original compositions.

All three writers were better known for their poetry than for their prose, so it is not at all surprising that their fiction was much more lyrical than any discussed so far. The epic quality of their work derived from the various delaying tactics they used, such as descriptive digressions and close attention to setting, which were more intense than the dramatic element. Lyricism was produced in the detailing of the thoughts and actions of the protagonists, the affective quality of the language dominating other aspects and producing an emotionally charged pictorial texture. Far more important than the dramatic significance of the plot, or the description of the environment, was the fiction's heightened emotionality. Elisheva Bikhovski (born Zhirkova) was a Russian Christian by birth. Initially she wrote poetry in Russian, translating Hebrew literature into Russian as well. From 1920 on she published poems and stories in Hebrew under the name Elisheva. Her impressionistic novel *Alleys* [*Simta 'ot*, 1929] dealt with gentile and Jewish bohemian intellectuals and emphasized especially the changing sexual mores of the times.

Leah Goldberg, who was born in Koenigsberg in 1911, came to Eretz Yisrael in 1935 and remained there until her death in Jerusalem in 1970. Her chief contribution to Hebrew literature is her poetry, but she also wrote fine children's stories, plays, literary essays, and theater criticism. Prose fiction was not her principal mode of expression and aside from some sketches and stories, she produced only two significant works of prose: *Encounter with a Poet* [*Pgishah 'im meshorer,* 1952], a portrait of the poet Avraham Ben-Yitzhak, and a psychological novella, *And He Is the Light* [*Vehu ha 'or,* 1946].

And He Is the Light is a rather complex novella which develops simultaneously on several levels. Ostensibly, it is the story of the return of a young woman, Nora Krieger, from Germany to her birthplace in Eastern Europe. Her arrival and departure expose a sharp opposition between Europe and the town. Nora loathes the small provincial village and feels closer, emotionally and culturally, to Europe, though she fears it and clings to her native ground. This central tension produces several others, such as her loathing of the petty bourgeois existence as opposed to the bohemian life of Berlin, and assimilation versus her Zionist aspirations, which seem to Nora to provide a way out of the dead end she feels trapped in.

The plot begins and ends with a riddle, the solution to which is, from the outset, known to Nora but withheld from the reader. In the course of the novel it is revealed that Nora's father has been institutionalized in an insane asylum. Although Nora always seems to be covering up the truth about him, she is actually searching for him. She lives with the threat, articulated by several of the book's characters, that madness hangs over her like a sword and that she is fated to follow in her father's footsteps. Her flight from the town, therefore, enacts her flight from her father, while her return home traces the opposite impulse, which finally overtakes her and determines her fate. Nora desires escape: "To go for many days with the caravans, to suffer great hunger and thirst, to arrive exhausted, famished and weakened at a place no one has known, and there to discover new life, new plants, songs and dances, which the world knows nothing of" (*And He Is the Light,* p. 135). Her destiny is disaster. Falling in love with her father's friend Erin, who has also recently returned to the town, Nora discovers that her lover is not her father's substitute but his double. Erin is also a victim of mental illness.

The most important of the three writers was David Vogel. He moved from Russia to Vienna to Paris, but he always thought of himself as belonging to Hapsburg culture; he even attempted to write a novel in German, and he wanted his other works to appear in German translation. He had spent some of his early years wandering about Russia before reaching Vienna in 1912. In 1917 he began to publish, and although he came to Eretz Yisrael in 1929 he was unable to settle there. He spent most of his remaining years in Paris. Although he was alone and without connections, he felt that he belonged in Europe and that his basic identity was that of a European Jew. It was as a European Jew that he died, deported in 1944 to a German concentration camp, from which he did not return.

Vogel was above all an expressionist poet, influenced by the Austrian poet Georg Trakl. His first book of poems, *Before the Dark Gate* [*Lifnei hasha'ar ha'afel*], appeared in 1923 (an extended edition, edited by the poet and scholar Dan Pagis, was published in 1966). He also wrote fiction. His first novella, *In the Sanatorium* [*Beveit hamarpe'*], appeared in 1928, and his principal novel, *Married Life* [*Hayei nisu'im*], was published between 1929 and 1930 (it was reissued in 1986 and has since been translated into many European languages). *Facing the Sea* [*Nokhah hayam*] was published in 1934 and reissued in 1974.

As a Hebrew writer Vogel regarded himself as a follower of Brenner and Gnessin, whom he praised highly in his public speeches, rejecting the prose writings of Steinmann at the same time. Powerfully influenced by the decadent atmosphere of Vienna before and after the First World War, by the anti-Semitism and sexism of Otto Weininger's *Sex and Character,* and by the work of Sigmund Freud, Vogel evidences in particular the impact of the writers Schnitzler, Altenberg, Rilke, Thomas and Heinrich Mann, and Joseph Roth, among others. For example, his early novella *In the Sanatorium* blended his own personal stay in a sanatorium for tuberculosis with literary representations of the same experience, such as Mann's

Magic Mountain and Hamsun's *The Last Chapter*. Unlike his predecessors, however, he did not depict the world of the sanatorium as a microcosm.

Like the Viennese impressionists, Vogel was fascinated by the pull of eros and death, which seemed to evidence a world beyond our ordinary, everyday existence. Like the late-nineteenth-century authors, he used irony to expose concealed desires and motivations, such as the petty bourgeois fantasies that drove his society. His doomed protagonists deny the truth of their mortality, vainly clinging to their unreal lives. Lacking a clear structure or a firm plot, and more atmospheric than concrete, *In the Sanatorium* bore little resemblance to the romantic-dramatic novellas of Kleist or Schnitzler and may have been primarily a practice run for his more accomplished *Married Life*.

Married Life is an Austrian-Viennese novel that happened to be written in Hebrew. It might even be said that Roth's *Job, The Story of a Simple Man* (1930) is more Jewish in its subject matter and theme than *Married Life*. Three cultural currents shaped this novel: the novel of the metropolis; the world of alienation and disaffection, which, as portrayed by Brenner, had its own origins in Russian literature (notably in Dostoyevsky); and Viennese decadence, as embodied in writings of Schnitzler (his novellas *Dying, Flowers, Lieutenant Gustel*, and *Miss Else;* and his novel *Therese*). Schnitzler's main themes—love and betrayal, death and suicide—also appeared in the fiction of Altenberg, Zweig, and Roth, all of whom, like Vogel himself, depicted the perverse pleasure to be achieved in the experiences of pain and decline.

Like many other literary wanderers who made for themselves a sort of home in the city's cafés, beer halls, and boulevards, Vogel's protagonist in *Married Life* loses himself in the labyrinths of Vienna. His feelings for the city, which are an intimate part of his life, are as ambivalent as his feelings for his wife, who tempts him with her lighthearted love-making, yet terrifies and chills him too. The erotic urban experience is communicated to the reader through long series of impressionist passages, whose impact lies not so much in the writer's meticulous descriptions of real sites as in the complexity of their evocations:

> It was a warm spring evening. A soft fresh hush fell from the darkening, patchy sky. The almost empty streets appeared swept clean. The big city was falling asleep in the orangey electric light. From time to time, at growing intervals, it was pierced by trams like sudden nightmare awakenings. Carrying few passengers, they ran more noisily, more hurriedly. A faraway train sounded a long, somewhat muffled, hoot. The imagination flickered with images of long journeys through a dark night, breathing unheard, and alien cities with millions of inhabitants. (p. 34)

By the end of the novel, ambivalence gives way to sheer terror and hatred for both women and the city, as the raw aspects of the urban experience invade and take over his mind.

The novel develops along two tracks. One follows the protagonist's peripatetic motions: Gordweil leaves his rented room and wanders about the streets of Vienna, stopping at cafés or otherwise ambling aimlessly about. The cyclical nature of this pattern gives the novel a kind of urban anti-picaresque quality. The hero is not a rogue who wanders across social classes and worlds, beguiling both men and women. Rather, he is the very opposite: a dull, pathetic anti-hero, a victim of urbanism, haunted by his own fears as much as by his wife. This other track slowly constructs the tragic dimensions of the tale of the urban anti-hero. Increasingly the environment comes to oppress and isolate him until he has no avenue of escape except to commit a crime.

The novel is primarily introspective; not only is it told from Gordweil's viewpoint, but for the most part it takes place in his mind. The protagonist makes no attempt to achieve an overall understanding of his life or to illuminate the story as a whole. The one dominant fact of his life, which exists almost as an independent entity, is his pain. This is the suffering of a man who fears the world and himself, in particular his own irrational drives and desires. This is not just a battle of the sexes (as in the work of Strindberg, Heinrich Mann, or Otto Weininger). Rather *Married Life* depicts the private internal hell of urban man. Nor is the novel without a Jewish message. Gordweil's initial error stems from his falling in love with a cruel manipulative woman, Thea von Tuko, whom he eventually resolves to murder. Depictions of sado-masochist relationships between an anti-hero and a femme fatale were not new. Heinrich Mann's famous novel *Professor Unrath* (published in 1905) dealt with just such a relationship that took place across class lines (a professor and a dancer). In Vogel's book, however, a racial aspect is added: Gordweil is Jewish, Thea a Christian aristocrat. Although the love-hate relationship between the Jewish intelligentsia and the Christian aristocracy is not the central issue in the book (which is what distinguishes Vogel's *Married Life* from the major tradition of Hebrew novels), nonetheless it does feature as an element of the book's social critique. When all is said and done, Gordweil is an object of the eroding social mores of Austrian society after the Great War.

Even more distinguished than *Married Life* is Vogel's novella *Facing the Sea*, which was published in 1934 (reissued in 1974). Set in the Riviera with a cast of characters who are only minimalistically and obliquely identified as Jewish, if that (the male protagonist, Barth, refers to another woman as having "*shiksa* taste"—p. 220), this is a European story which is only incidentally written in Hebrew. Its style is unrelated to Hebrew sources, and the subject matter has nothing to do with the mainstream preoccupations of Hebrew literature. Like *Married Life,* it exhibits a close relationship to Viennese impressionism. In the manner of Freud, it explores the hidden sexual urges of men and women, which erupt when people are separated from the constraints of their familiar social worlds and released into the world of nature and lower-class sensuality. Adolf and Gina Barth, an overly wealthy, self-indulgent Viennese couple, arrive for their summer vacation. The husband meets a French girl, Marcelle, and the wife a primitive Italian man, Cici. By the time their vacation ends, they are each transformed and their marriage is at an end.

In placing its action in a resort town, *Facing the Sea* is hardly unique (cf. Mann's *Death in Venice*). What distinguishes Vogel's novella from other similar works is the way in which the erotic atmosphere emerges as more interesting and complex than the sexual encounter itself and extends into the relationships of the characters to the natural world itself. The erotic passion the characters come to feel is not life-affirming: After two night-time swims, Barth and Marcelle wind up seriously ill with fever. Nor does it complement or complete their lives. Instead, it empties their lives of passion as well as of meaning: "Gina didn't understand a thing. She only sensed her body burning, as if touched by fever. And Cici's scalding, biting kisses on her hands, on her bare arms, on her neck, on her face. In these kisses was the stomping of a mad, murderous animal. Had she wanted to protest, she would not have been able. And had he wanted to kill her, she would not have protested. . . . [Her body] seemed strange to her . . . this body of hers was different now, incomprehensible. . . . It aroused fear and nausea in her" (pp. 251, 253). By giving themselves over to desire, Gina and Barth kill desire and, in a way, themselves:

> Who was to blame? Soon the train would come and she would journey from here, never to return. . . . Gina would pass through all of these jumbled stations during the night, and the train would distance her further and further. It would not be difficult to climb on a train such as this one afternoon, and pass through days and nights and garbled stops to reach her—but nevertheless you will never board and never arrive. From now on you have no emotional possibility of doing so. He set his eyes on her and saw that she was quite pale, and veiled in sadness. . . . The train lurched forward. Gina leaned out the open window and waved her handkerchief. For a long while, she could distinguish his figure, standing still, like a lifeless post, head tilted slightly, holding his hat high and motionless. (p. 268)

Artistically, the strength of the novella lies not in its plot or in the tangled relations of Barth-Marcelle and Gina-Cici, but in the overall atmosphere, with its detailed descriptions of the landscape and the special intermingling of interior and outdoor spaces. Although in *Married Life* setting and atmosphere were subsidiary, in *Facing the Sea* they move center stage, where their symbolic power overshadows the social minutiae of the story. The sea is "a shimmering carpet of silver . . . waves glittered like sequins . . . [wandering] from the horizon to stroke the shore with light, muffled slaps. The scene, rendered in the moon's gossamer light, seemed unreal" (pp. 228–229). And, indeed, nature and the human know no boundaries:

> The waves of the warm melody spilled over the balcony into the darkness of the night, which was furrowed with light breezes, like a man's breath, and into the breadth of the sleepy sea. A hidden tremor stirred in the hearts of the listeners . . . Gina leaned against the balcony railing. She looked at the deserted midnight street and beyond, toward the sea that heaved silently, interwoven with night into one great heaviness. There arose in her a slight sadness, not without a touch of pleasantness. . . . With their backs to the sea, they sat and gazed at the darkened houses opposite and were filled with the nocturnal sense of loss. Far away a few sharp dog barks hammered into the night like nails, then stopped. Only behind them the sea went on panting dully, endlessly. (pp. 240–242)

Set against the vast beauty and power of the sea, human beings are mere details, their primal urges faint inexplicit echoes of a cosmic sensuality they are doomed never to experience.

In order to produce Hebrew fiction about German speakers Vogel created new literary constructions, translating literally from German and Yiddish ("Man is not a swine, order there must be!") and ignoring the normative rules of the language. His novels, therefore, although they did not follow the path of other interwar Hebrew fiction, constitute an important moment in Hebrew literary history. They represent a kind of transition between Hebrew fiction written for Hebrew readers and German fiction written for German Jewish readers who had not entirely lost touch with Jewish culture. We might go so far as to say that Vogel produced an "anti–Eretz Yisrael" fiction, written as though Eretz Yisrael did not exist and as though the diaspora, despite the existence there of anti-Semitism, was where Jews had to conduct their lives. Vogel did not share the anxieties of those who viewed assimilation and intermarriage as major existential issues, as did most Hebrew writers in America, for example. Having produced in *Facing the Sea* one of the most truly outstanding works of Hebrew fiction, Vogel may be considered the second most important nonmainstream writer in the tradition (after Gnessin).

Since the Hebrew reading public in the 1930s and 1940s identified strongly with contemporary Zionist ideology, it did not look favorably on the fiction of Bikhovski, Goldberg, and Vogel. Consequently, this fiction remained marginal until the 1960s and 1970s, when public tastes changed. Vogel in particular experienced a special revival at that time. In their impressionistic lyricism three writers can be said to continue the tradition of Goldberg, Elisheva, and Vogel—Amalia Kahana-Carmon, Shulamith Hareven, and Yehudit Hendel. This may be less a matter of direct influence than family resemblance, literary tradition proceeding not only through obvious genetic connections, but through a continuity of literary expectations and conditions.

ARIELI-ORLOFF, R. WALLENROD, S. HALKIN, AND A. A. LISITZKY

Perhaps the dominant note struck by Hebrew literary expression in the United States was the isolation of the author who was writing in a cultural void. This feeling only intensified over the years. If, at the beginning of the century, Hebrew fiction was a minor but significant phenomenon, accompanying into birth a flourishing Yiddish literature and a burgeoning tradition of Jewish-American writing in English, Hebrew literature as well as Yiddish literature all but vanished in America after the creation of the State of Israel. Although this decline of Hebrew literature (and of traditional Jewish culture) in the United States stood in inverse ratio to the growth of the Jewish community there, it did reflect the new realities of American Jewish life. The number of Jews had swelled in the United States from 275,000 in 1880 to over five million in 1955; but it was precisely their prosperity, economic and social as well as numerical, that signaled the end of their cultural distinction. Gabriel Preil was probably the last Hebrew poet in America.

For the most part, American Jewish writers of Hebrew, Yiddish, and English fiction wrote about the same subject: the immigrant experience, with its long journey from the shtetl through the sweatshops to the successes of capitalistic ventures (e.g., Henry Roth's *Call It Sleep*, 1934, and Abraham Cahan's *The Rise of David Levinsky*, 1917). Many of these immigrant success stories used comical or pathetic anecdotes from the real-life experience of American Jewry, which were constructed in such a way as to direct attention away from the pseudo-documentary significance of the text to the plot. Many such social-paradigmatic stories were written by H. A. Friedland and B. Isaacs.

So autobiographical as to border on personal journals, these texts were, for the most part, written in a familiar realistic manner, as if readers were expected to recognize this world as their own and to emulate the experience of the characters. Insofar as these texts were directed to an Eretz Yisrael readership, they were intended to present a non-resident population with the American model of immigration, which also stood in direct opposition to the life of the shtetl. In Friedland's fiction, for example, there is a constant distinction being drawn between the old religious model of Jewish life and the new secular mode of Jewish existence in the United States. For Friedland a major issue to be addressed was the cost of integration and success, which often occurred at the expense of tradition and were thus accompanied by spiritual loss and emptiness. American Jewish fiction in all three languages presented the paradox of Jewish life in America. It simultaneously glorified the American experience and expressed traditional anti-assimilationist values.

Like its wandering brethren throughout the world, Hebrew literature in the United States had to adapt to new conditions. The models and anti-models of the East European shtetl were irrelevant. Furthermore, the writers knew that if they did not change their materials, they would lose the next generation of readers, who had little interest in the language and culture of their parents' generation. Although it became increasingly evident that the appeal of the surrounding culture and the genuine possibilities of assimilation it afforded invalidated the need for a segregated Hebrew-language culture, nonetheless the Hebrew writers remained committed to the idea that, so long as the Jewish people existed, wherever they existed, its cultural identity had to be preserved. Involved at one time or another in their careers with the teaching of Hebrew, the writers established the image of the teacher-writer as a basic motif in their fiction.

Hebrew fiction in the United States resembled the realistic literature written in Eretz Yisrael. And, just as the Eretz Yisraeli fiction produced no new literary forms or models, neither did its American counterpart, which clung to the pseudo-realist tradition of Ben-Avigdor. Brenner's fragmentation, Gnessin's stream of consciousness, Steinberg's and Shoffman's intricate impressionism, and the stylized ironies of Agnon had no effect on the American Hebrew writer (with the exception of Shimon Halkin, who, as we shall see, is the exception who proves the rule). Thus, despite the fact that between the turn of the century and the 1940s there was tremendous literary ferment in the United States, the Hebrew writers remained largely static and prosaic. They did not immerse themselves in the vital current of realistic literature in the United States, which included such writers as William Dean Howells, Stephen Crane, Jack London, and Theodore Dreiser. Nor did they respond to the profound interwar experimentations in subject and form which characterized the output of the realist-naturalists, such as Sherwood Anderson, Sinclair Lewis, John Dos Passos, Thomas Wolfe, and John Steinbeck, or the writers of the "lost generation"—Ernest Hemingway, William Faulkner, and F. Scott Fitzgerald.

Cut off from the major developments transforming Hebrew literature in Eretz Israel and impervious to domestic American influences, Hebrew writing in the United States achieved no great literary feats, produced almost no formal or stylistic innovations, and made virtually no impact on the younger generation of writers. Insofar as the writers in Eretz Yisrael were influenced by outside Hebrew writing, it was that of Eastern Europe. Nevertheless, three authors who spent most of their creative lives in the United States did contribute to the Hebrew literary canon: Ephraim A. Lisitzky, Reuven Wallenrod, and Shimon Halkin.

A poet as well as a novelist, Lisitzky is one of the founding fathers of Hebrew writing in America. His single novel, *In the Grip of Cross Currents* [*'Eleh toldot 'adam*, literally: "this is man's history," 1949], is an ecstatic, quasi-autobiographical confession in the Berdyczewski-Brenner tradition about the narrator's immigration to the United States and his wanderings in North America. Although its materials are fairly typical of such novels, its overall structure, in particular its use of narrative digressions to interrupt the sociological character of the text, is such that it constitutes one of the best and most original autobiographical fictions in Hebrew literature. Addressed to a Zionist readership in Eretz Yisrael, the text amounts to something of an apology; the narrator attempts to justify his decision to remain in the United States and to lay Hebrew roots in what from a Hebrew viewpoint was a cultural void.

Reuven Wallenrod was a writer whose subjects, though not his design, were typical of American genre fiction. Wallenrod came to Palestine in 1920 with the Third Aliyah, but left again in 1923 and moved to America. In some ways Wallenrod's writing recalls that of the lost generation of American writers. Wallenrod, as Yeshayahu Rabinowitz once put it, "wants only to peer into this or that soul, to listen to its sad murmur, and to describe that soul and that murmur." In terms of its subjects and themes, Wallenrod's writing partakes of the Eastern European tradition of the unrooted and disenchanted. In its formal aspects, it bears affinities with Hebrew impressionism (Shoffman, Barash). He perceived the world as a sequence of poetic impressions that constituted a perpetual and inspired present.

Wallenrod published two collections of short stories and novellas, *On the Third Floor* [*Badyotah hashlishit*, 1939], and *Amid the Walls of New York* [*Bein homot Nyu York*, 1952]; two long novellas, *Dusk in the Catskills* [*Ki Panah Hayom*, literally: "because the day turned," 1946] and *A Failing Generation* [*Be'ein dor*, 1953]; and a travel book, *Roads and a Way* [*Drakhim vederekh*, 1951]. For the most part, Wallenrod's materials were urban. He dealt with generational conflict (e.g., *Like Olive Seedlings* [*Kishtilei zeitim*]), Jews in small-town America, the relations of the sexes in bourgeois Jewish society, and interactions between post-Holocaust newcomers and the older immigrant community (*The Four Rooms in Williamsburg* [*Be'arba'at hahadarim shebe Wilyamsberg*]).

The story which best sums up Wallenrod's subjects and artistic qualities is "In the Shadow of the Walls" ["Betsel hahomot"], in *Amid the Walls of New York,* which is the longest and the most complex of the short novellas, resembling naturalist American literature, in particular Theodore Dreiser's 1925 novel of social downfall, *An American Tragedy.* The pattern is intricate. It combines urban-naturalist melodrama (including a beggar's confession) with the paradigmatic tale of departure and return. Having rebelled against his father and lost his identity, the protagonist attempts to forge a new self. But no longer able to go back to being a Jew, nor yet a gentile, the hero becomes an anonymous particle in an amorphous mass, a beggar who lacks economic, social, or familial grounding. Although his break with the father is justified, nonetheless the total loss of identity is the penalty he pays for discarding tradition.

Dusk in the Catskills is set in a hotel in the Catskills in upstate New York run by a Jewish couple as a holiday resort for the New York Jewish intelligentsia, mainly Yiddish writers. The crisis and decline of this society and the relationships between the immigrant fathers and the native-born sons are exposed in this resort novel, in which the guests share their personal experiences with the landlords and with one another and mourn the decline and fall of Jewish culture in America. The story takes place during the Second World War. It is enriched with delicate psychological insight into the irrevocable process of assimilation. *A Failing Generation* is a typical immigrant story, describing the transition from the shtetl to New York. The fictional situations Wallenrod depicted were projections of his own situation as a Jew among gentiles and as a universalist intellectual among traditional Jews. Even though subsequent Hebrew literature continues to rest on the neo-realist, quasi-impressionist mode used by Wallenrod, whose writings rival those of Vogel and Goldberg, he made no impact on his own or later generations.

Of all the American Hebrew writers, Shimon Halkin (a poet, essayist, and novelist) was by far the most talented and successful. Like most of the others, he was born in Eastern Europe. And like them, he too had difficulties adapting to life in America. He spent the years 1932–1939 in Palestine, went back to the United States, and returned to what had by then become the State of Israel in 1949. There he took up the post of professor of Hebrew literature at the Hebrew University in Jerusalem. His *Modern Hebrew Literature: Trends and Values* was published in 1950 (in English). A literary critic and translator as well as a writer of fiction, he was above all a poet, highly lauded by the literary establishments in both Israel and America.

As a writer of fiction, his work most closely resembles that of the literary generation immediately succeeding Bialik. Completely unlike anything produced by his contemporaries in America, Europe, or Eretz Yisrael,

Yehiel Hahagri (1928) bears the traces of Feierberg, Berdyczewski, and Gnessin. It is a highly intellectual, richly suggestive, if somewhat curious mixture of religious-mystical confession and eroticism. Nonetheless, it is *Crisis* [*'Ad mashber*] (an early version was written in 1929, the revised edition published in 1945) that is Halkin's consummate achievement and one of the most important Hebrew novels written in the interwar years. In *Crisis*, as in *Yehiel Hahagri*, Halkin created a typical uprooted character, whom he depicted with great empathy and poetical lyricism. Here, however, he moved away from the manner of Berdyczewski and closer to Gnessin, even blending Hebrew with American and European modernism (Marcel Proust, Thomas Wolfe, and Virginia Woolf).

Like the novels of Steinmann and Vogel, and unlike the novels of most of their contemporaries, *Crisis* is an urban story. It deals, stream-of-consciousness style, with the problems of the isolated Jewish intellectual in metropolitan New York and with two generations of immigrants: the fathers, Professor Poller and Laiser Luskin, who seek new meanings for old alienations, and the children, Tolly and Elsie Luskin, Lena Poller, and Leon Ekst, who find themselves in crisis, searching for a way out. Its climax coincides with the stock market crash of 1929 (the book was originally titled *Winter 1929* and was intended to be part of a trilogy, which was never completed). But this is only an external marker of the inner processes that the novel wishes to examine. At once a panoramic view of its society and an inward-looking psychological portrait, *Crisis* is reminiscent of Proust's *Remembrance of Things Past*.

Fragmentary in its plot, with multiple streams of consciousness and characters reacting in individual and idiosyncratic ways to forces that appear to be independent of social causation, the novel exerts pressure on the reader to discern the tangential links between social behavior and private existential matters like identity and erotic desire. Halkin tried to overcome the atomizing effects of his technique by means of such unifying devices as the social and psychological connections between the principal personalities, who are, in various ways, familial and otherwise, related to each other. (Elsie Luskin, for example, Laiser's daughter, is the eternal fiancée of Leon Ekst, the story's third pivot.) Far more interesting than the interactions between the characters are the various personalities themselves, which come replete with private personal histories, sensitivities, and responses.

The chapter that casts its shadow over the entire book is an ironic ode to New York, particularly Jewish New York. Stylistically and structurally different from the rest of the novel, this essay-like chapter, entitled "Inside New York," tries to explain the young people's profound spiritual attachment to the city, so unlike the purely material attachment of their parents. This intense attachment is problematic for the young people, who, seduced by the city's charms, lose their primary identities in their desire to define themselves in relation to the city.

A skillful poet, Halkin was well able to meet the challenges of stream-of-consciousness writing, and, indeed he contributed to expanding and enriching the genre. His diction tended toward epic images, which crystallized into independent pictures, recollections or reflections that constituted microtexts within a trans-temporal, trans-spatial associative web. Constructed of long, intricate sentences and images, the text diverts the reader's attention from actual events to the protagonists' imaginations and inner desires. Because Halkin developed and concretized his images throughout, the novel, despite its fragmentary and expositional form, emerges as vivid and complete. Shimon Halkin was probably the only Hebrew writer of his generation to so completely realize urban alienation. Nonetheless, even though Halkin made a special contribution to Hebrew literature, and not only in the United States, and while *Crisis* might have opened new options to Hebrew fiction, his work remained marginal and made no impact on the younger generation.

YITZHAK OREN

In form and subject matter, the work of Yitzhak Oren is liable to confuse the historical researcher, so perfectly positioned is he as a transition between generations. A contemporary of the Native Generation, beginning to publish concurrently with Moshe Shamir, S. Yizhar, and others in 1946, he is also a successor to Horowitz and Levin, and, in part, a precursor of the 1960s and 1970s authors such as Yehoshua, Kaniuk, and Orpaz. His first book, *Somewhere* [*'Ei sham*], appeared in 1950, and his first novel, *Behind the Lines* [*Ba'oref*], in 1953.

Resisting the realism of his contemporaries, Yitzhak Oren wrote surrealistic fiction. His materials form collages, assembled and disassembled at the author's whim. He has little regard for the Aristotelian rules of unity and enjoys shocking the bourgeois reader with his unexpected postmodernist hybrid genres, mixing realism, universalism, essayist commentary, detective fiction, and the fantastic picaresque. The principal and guiding theme in his work is the discrepancy between the narrowly circumscribed natural world, in which human beings experience their limited and dwarfish existences locked in time and place, and the infinite possibilities of the universe of dream and imagination (including the worlds of science and literature). In the 1950s, when this literature began to appear, fantastic fiction which blended imaginative journeys, intertextual parody, and picaresque adventure was too advanced for its readership.

Subsequent changes in society and in its literary sensibilities created a new acceptance for his work. Nonetheless, Oren remained on the fringes of Hebrew fiction.

* * *

Modernist Hebrew fiction between and around the two world wars, beginning with the Freudian experiments of Steinmann and culminating in Yitzhak Oren's post-modernism, produced a stylistically and thematically diversified set of texts. To be fully appreciated, Hebrew literary modernism must be juxtaposed with the writing of Agnon and observed in its interaction with the impressionist works of Shoffman, Steinberg, and Devorah Baron. It also maintained a constant dialogue with the writing of Gnessin and Brenner. Unlike most realistic writers, the modernists preserved a close relationship with the poetry of their time, especially that of Greenberg and Shlonsky, and they never severed their important ties with the literatures of Europe.

Because each writer absorbed and responded to these influences differently, Hebrew literary modernism is far from homogeneous. Furthermore, it is difficult to determine the extent to which modernism affected the later development of Hebrew literature. In the late 1950s, the writers seemed to look to other progenitors, allying themselves with, and differentiating themselves from, such figures as Gnessin and Agnon. These writers also turned to such Western models as Kafka, Camus, Faulkner, and Woolf, in some cases preferring the influence of these non-Hebrew writers. This is not to say that parallels cannot be drawn between the modernist fiction of the interwar years and the writing of the 1960s; the meanderings, retracings, and departures constitute the complex path of literary history.

10

LITERARY REALISM, 1940–1980
TRANSFORMATIONS OF A GENRE
AND THE STRUGGLE FOR A NATIONAL NARRATIVE

Around us the tempest rises
But our heads will not be bent
Always at your command
This is us, the Palmah

—THE HYMN OF THE PALMAH COMMANDO TROOPS

From the beginning of the century until the 1940s Hebrew literature in Eretz Yisrael was largely an imported product. Most of the writers had arrived there from Eastern Europe, or by a roundabout route after years in Western Europe or America. Only later did native writers, the children of the immigrants of the earlier waves of *aliyah,* begin to take their places on the literary scene. We might date this process with the publication in 1938 of S. Yizhar's first story, "Ephraim Returns to Alfalfa." Born in 1916 in Rehovoth into a family of farmers and writers from the First Aliyah (his father actually arrived with the Second Aliyah), Yizhar was to come to symbolize his generation of writers, which included Yigal Mossinsohn, Moshe Shamir, Hanoch Bartov, Aharon Megged, and Natan Shaham. His writing concluded the intermediate generation of Hebrew literature—that of Shenhar, Hameiri, and others—and paved the way for a new start. Like Agnon, he stood at a crossroads where the different paths of previous generations converged and new ones began.

The first literary generation of native-born writers began to publish in the 1930s and came into its own in the 1940s and early 1950s. Dubbed the "Palmah Generation" (after an army corps to which few of the authors actually belonged), or Dor Ba'aretz (the Native Generation, after an anthology of the same name which was published in 1958), its difference from the previous generation of writers is easily discernable. The earlier generation consisted mostly of individuals who were educated in two or more languages. They had firsthand familiarity with European literatures and some degree of involvement with Jewish tradition. In contrast, the native-born authors were raised on Hebrew, in which language they read both original and translated works of literature. Born toward the end of the First World War and in the 1920s, they came to maturity during the years of the British Mandate. The historical landmarks of their lives were the Holocaust, the War of Independence, and the establishment of the State in 1948.

What is more difficult to define is the difference between the first and second native generations. This second native generation, most of whom were born in the 1930s, was labeled Dor Hamedinah (the State Generation), or the New Wave. They appeared on the literary scene in the mid-1950s and early 1960s, when their predecessors were still very much active contributors to Israeli culture. This group, which includes such figures as Yehuda Amichai, Pinhas Sadeh, Amalia Kahana-Carmon, A. B. Yehoshua, Amos Oz, Aharon Appelfeld, Yaakov Shabtai, and Yehoshua Kenaz (among others, whose names will emerge in the following chapters), has been associated by some with a more surrealistic or fantastic than a realistic fictional style. A close examination of the two generations, however, reveals that binary opposites do not distinguish the one group from the other. Their interrelation is fairly complex, and although the earlier group influenced the later (if only by arousing opposition), the younger also influenced the older. Indeed, many of the native-born and young immigrant writers of the second generation belong chronologically to the first.

It is this interaction between the first two generations of native-born writers that I wish to examine in this chapter, as the two groups struggle, with their materials and with each other, to produce a national literature. To some degree, my reason for examining the two generations simultaneously is simply to emphasize the vibrancy and diversity of literary production in the years immediately preceding and following statehood. The two native generations of Hebrew writers, Dor Ba'aretz and Dor Hamedinah, however their writings divide along generational and non-generational lines and however the individual writers distinguish themselves from one another within formal and thematic groupings, do share a set of historical, cultural, and social backgrounds. These become, in their fiction, grounds for common assumptions, including shared resistance to features of their common reality. They also become the bases for dissension from and competition with each other.

These features of the communal project as it comes to be expressed in the writings of extremely different, oftentimes immensely talented, individual authors come into particularly clear view if one examines, as I intend to do in this chapter, the writers' relations to a single tradition of literary representation, namely the social realist tradition put in place by the Native Generation (Dor Ba'aretz), most prominently by Yizhar, Shamir, and Megged. Social realism is a slippery concept at best. It variously and sometimes simultaneously refers to a form of mimetic representation and to a philosophy of the relationship of literature to life, namely, the responsibility of the text to accurately reflect the socio-political reality it depicts.

For Yizhar, Shamir, Megged, and other writers of Dor Ba'aretz, social realism built on prior modes and models of Hebrew fiction. More important, perhaps, it answered to the immediate necessities and challenges of nation- and culture-building. Although many of the writers of Dor Hamedinah chose to depart from social realism by opting for non-mimetic modes of representation and by subverting both the basic metaplot of Zionist history and the requirements that that plot seemed to impose for mimetic social realist representation, nonetheless, what emerges as one examines post-1948 fiction is that the social realist tradition continued to characterize much Hebrew literary production. However, what did occur was that the coexistence of Dor Hamedinah and Dor Ba'aretz produced radical transformations, in that social realism as the literary form, like the story it was intended to tell, strained against the limits of the genre. This exposed both what was problematic in social realist fiction and what genuine needs and cultural objectives it could and could not achieve. It also produced variations on a theme and transformations of a literary genre such that, at times, it is not quite clear whether a work still fits within the rubric of social realism (either aesthetically or politically defined) or whether it has already wrenched loose into some more non-realist or post-realist form, as has often been associated with the writers of the New Wave. Literary texts rarely fit neatly into genre categories. Hebrew literary texts are no exception to this rule. Still, from the 1940s through the 1970s, social realism played an important role—perhaps the dominant role—in the creation of the national literature.

The reasons for this certainly have to do with the fact that the literary problem with which native-born Israeli writers of both generations grappled was the same problem that had confronted earlier generations of Hebrew writers: how to separate the powerful political and historical context of their lives from the demands of literary fiction. To pose the question in the terms of Brenner's famous essay on genre, how was a small country, full of monumental and life-transforming upheavals, to produce fictional creations whose association with real-life figures would be "entirely fortuitous"? How was one to create a literature of the commonplace in a society which had not yet achieved commonplace existence? Writers did not seem to need to apply imagination to the real: Reality itself seemed so rich and wondrous. The points of departure in most of the writings of Yizhar, Shamir, and Megged, as well as of Haim Gouri, Hanoch Bartov, Shlomo Nitzan, and others, were those same shared historical experiences that had from the beginning characterized one trajectory of Hebrew writing.

The generation that had arrived with the Second or Third Aliyot had laid down essential values and underlying rules of conduct, which their sons, for the most part, inherited without a murmur. These offspring of the founding fathers, most of them born in the 1920s, identified strongly with the pioneering elite of the labor movement. This was more than casual ideological commitment. The movement formed every aspect of their being. Whether or not they obeyed its imperatives in their personal lives, they idealized the transition from city to country, the return to nature, the youth movement, and the Spartan life. Turning away from religious tradition and other institutions of diaspora existence, Dor Ba'aretz sought to merge with the people of the region, such as Bedouins. Where once Yiddish expressions had punctuated the fiction, now it was infused with Arabic words and phrases.

The portrait of the young sabra emerged as a central feature of their fiction. Although the sabras were not, of course, a homogeneous mass, their self-image was a consistent blend of naive romantic idealism and a desire to convert vision into reality. Based on an unequivocal love for the land, their idealism and desire for self-sacrifice were products of their Zionist upbringing at home, in school, and in the youth movements. The sabras willingly took it upon themselves to fulfill the dreams of their fathers, whether or not those ambitions suited their individual personalities. The prototype of the idealistic, self-sacrificing sabra was Uri, the protagonist of Moshe Shamir's 1947 novel *He Walked through the Fields* [*Hu halakh basadot*]. The youthful commander, who places national duty before love for his immigrant girlfriend, who functions well despite the disintegration of his parental home, and who is killed in the attempt to save his comrades because of an error made by another immigrant, enchanted the critics as well as the reading public. He was perceived as emblematic of a new model of Jew who reversed many of the attributes of the previous generation's religious scholars and disaffected intellectuals. Characters cast in his image appeared in many Hebrew texts. In combination with oppositional figures, they served to mark the binary dichotomy of collectivism versus individuality. In the stage adaptation of the book, Uri matched the popular image of the Israeli, in fact and fiction both: a shock of wild hair, the distinctive *kova'tembel* (a typical Israeli hat), heavy boots, short trousers, and a blue or khaki shirt. Although many writers tried to shake off Shamir's Uri and create alternative protagonists, he continued, and continues today, to haunt Israeli literature.

The existential crisis of the nation's writers occurred not during the Second World War or during the War of Independence, but afterward. The transition from a voluntary community founded on the ideals of pioneering fighters to an established state whose leading figures were government officials, politicians, and the newly rich dismayed the soldiers and writers returning from the battlefields. The shattering of their great hopes became the central experience and main subject of the post-1948 writing. Pre-State Eretz Yisrael had constituted a largely homogeneous community, which discouraged dissent and deviance from the norm. The waves of immigrants who flooded the country after independence brought social groups who met neither the norms nor expectations of the native-born populations. The original community soon became a minority in the State it had created. Nostalgia for the intimate society before the war, coupled with serious reappraisal of the new reality, began to dominate the fiction, both implicitly and explicitly, between the 1950s and 1970s. One marked response to disillusion, which preceded the entry of this subject into the major literary productions of the time, was the satirical newspaper column. These columns began to appear regularly from the end of the 1940s; they ranged in tone from the humorous to the sarcastic, offering illustrative samplings reflective of the absurd discrepancies separating the imagined ideal from the new reality. Two kinds of satirical observation in particular influenced the more serious fiction. The first (for example, Haim Heffer and Dan Ben-Amotz's *A Bag of Fibs* [*Yalqut hakzavim*]) parodied nostalgia for the Old Yishuv, as expressed in stories celebrating the men of the pre-State Palmah. The second more iconoclastic type of satire trashed the slogans and beliefs that once sustained the community but that now seemed hollow; for example, the satirical column "Uzi & Co." ["Uzi veshut"] of Benjamin Tammuz and Amos Kenan.

The satirical writing of Ephraim Kishon also contributed to the slaughtering of some of the Israeli establishment's sacred cows. Measuring Israeli society by rational Central European yardsticks, he exposed a great deal of bureaucratic corruption and human stupidity. In his satirical newspaper columns he created a number of regular characters that he subsequently transferred into his plays and films. The satirical model provided the basis for the fiction of a variety of authors, such as Aharon Megged, Benjamin Tammuz, Yitzhak Orpaz, Yoram Kaniuk, and Yitzhak Ben-Ner, who attempted to represent their generation's disappointment and disillusionment. Their curious blend of nostalgia for the myth, on the one hand, and, on the other, sober confrontation with the dysfunction of the new reality dominated much of Hebrew literature for thirty-five years.

Not only were the Dor Ba'aretz writers dominated in their early years by inherited ideals, they also submitted in matters of aesthetic judgment to the older generation of Shlonsky, Alterman, and others. During the 1940s and early 1950s the literary establishment and its principal media were controlled by a predominantly leftist-Zionist establishment that was staunchly pro-USSR. All the literary platforms, publishing houses, and presses bore the imprint of Russian social realism. The decline of the leftist hegemony after the split in Mapam (the United Workers' Party) in the early 1950s and the concomitant disintegration of ideological consensus and rise of individualism loosened the grip of literary realism on Israeli writing. This development was certainly one of the main external factors which led to the slow disintegration of ideological consensus, the rise of individualistic tendencies in poetry and fiction, and the decline of social realistic fiction after the mid-1950s.

Many of the native-born writers began their careers in the newspapers of the youth movements and most of them continued under the patronage of poet, translator, and editor Avraham Shlonsky in the magazines he controlled— 'Itim [Times] and 'Orlogin [Clock]. Shlonsky filled the role Bialik had filled at the beginning of the century in Odessa and in the 1920s in Tel Aviv. In the 1940s Shlonsky was the supreme authority in all literary matters and was adored by the younger writers who he patronized. Even when the younger generation began to publish periodicals of their own in 1942, they contained no hint of rebellion. Haim Glickstein, the editor of one such periodical, Daf hadash [New Page, 1947], declared that his was a generation of "continuators and completers." Many of the early works of the young writers—for example, Shamir's He Walked through the Fields and With His Own Hands [Bemo yadav: pirqei 'Eliq, 1951]; Aharon Megged's Hedvah and I [Hedvah ve'ani, 1954]; and Yonat and Alexander Sened's Land without Shadow ['Adamah lelo tsel, 1950]— were in line with Glickstein's observation.

THE DOR BA'ARETZ REALISTS: YIZHAR, SHAMIR, MOSSINSOHN, MEGGED, AND SHAHAM

The story of the two generations of native-born writers cohabiting the house of culture-making, mutually constructing and transforming each other and Hebrew literary tradition, is the story of the transformation of a literary genre and the consequent transformation of national narrative that that genre was intended to serve. Before we go on to look at the writers who did, in the 1950s, break ranks with the social realists and produce other forms of literary expression that decidedly subverted the Zionist metaplot, I want to examine in somewhat more detail the five major figures of Hebrew social realism as it was put into place by the Dor Ba'aretz generation: Yizhar, Shamir, Mossinsohn, Megged, and Shaham.

S. Yizhar was the first of his contemporaries to appear on the literary scene. In some ways he typifies his generation. In other ways he stands apart from it. His well-documented, historically accurate stories reflected the standard Zionist narrative. His usual protagonist is a young man of the Jewish elite, and the landscape is almost always the south of the country. Unlike his contemporaries, however, his stories did not go beyond the War of Independence and the establishment of the State. While his contemporaries wrote about the hopeful years immediately preceding 1948 and the disillusion that followed, most of Yizhar's fiction takes place in the 1930s and 1940s. Some of his later stories, collected in 1963 in a volume entitled *Stories of a Plain* [*Sipurei mishor*], even return nostalgically to the 1920s, when Jews and Arabs enjoyed a warmer, more peaceful relationship.

Yizhar differed from his contemporaries primarily in terms of literary style. Critics generally point to Gnessin as a principal influence, whose relationship to Yizhar is made obvious by the fact that Yizhar's first protagonist Ephraim (in the novel *Ephraim Returns to Alfafa*) is named to recall Gnessin's hero Ephraim, in his last novel, *By*. Like Gnessin, Yizhar was a writers' writer. He addressed a select and discerning readership. Yizhar and Gnessin also both used stream-of-consciousness techniques, though, whereas Gnessin's fiction is primarily inner directed and rarely refers to the outer world (which is generally depicted as a projection of the self or as a metaphor for the inner world), Yizhar uses stream of consciousness as a transcript of external reality itself.

Indeed, the most fascinating feature of Yizhar's writing is his application of stream-of-consciousness technique to genre fiction. Like Wilkansky, Smilansky, and Luidor, Yizhar tended to sanctify ordinary life and to ascribe exalted significance to the daily work of the pioneers (for example, digging a well in the story "In the Expanses of the Negev" ["Befa' atei hanegev," 1954], or night watch duty in "A Night without Shots" ["Layla bli yeriyot," 1939]). But he also placed question marks over these pioneering legends by depicting the troubled individual struggling with the monstrous burden of collective myths. More symbolic than naturalistic, Yizhar's writing tended to concern itself less with the feelings of his protagonists than with the world in which they thought and acted. In fact, his writing is remarkable for its detailed, multifaceted observation of the landscape and environs. There is a ceaseless, almost desperate search for signifiers to cover as many phenomena as possible, in order to say everything and to say it correctly. As a result, the landscape often becomes personified and mythologized, symbolic, as in the following passage from "Midnight Convoy" ["Shayarah shel hatsot," 1950], a short story in a collection of the same name:

> Of them all, only Zvialeh lay still, warming his belly on the soft, dusty, scented earth, fragrant with the dust of clay, and he chewed a dusty stalk (with its chalky, not unpleasant, taste recalling some memory of childhood), keeping himself withdrawn from the conversation, and from the business of standing up and everything, going out by himself, slipping away with pleasure, silently escaping to the expanses of the great universe that gradually opened up all around as the sunset became a reality, steadily losing its strangeness and beginning to be grasped and understood. The sheep-like hills. The flat and crumbling ridges. The fervent joy of unlimited expanses. That friable soil, made up entirely of small, pea-like clods which were nothing but fine dust burnt by the sun and wound into a flour of granulose clots, which—if you were to step on it or crumble it in your palm to feel and enjoy its quality, or to put it to your nose to breathe the scent of the granary, the dust of harvest and threshing, the smell of bread and satiation—would disintegrate instantly into dusty powder, dissolved and dispersed. This is what went shooting out from under the wheels in streams of dust, this is what was so easily seduced by every riotous and licentious gust to dance off, capering higher and higher, in wide frolicsome circles, with chaff and thistles, twirling faster and faster like a top in the fields, and then becoming one big living thing in the empty expanses, and falling suddenly into silent, arid hollows, where it died with a minimum of convulsions—this was arable land which a single shower would liquefy into a viscid paste, with a good smell of wet clay, the fragrance of moist soil, renewing youthful loves, and with another shower or two would be all weak, treacherous, swampy mud, with depths here and there, enormous impassable areas into whose mire a world could sink, with unseen swelling udders; sucking and absorbent, the streams in the gullies, and winter over all, and the green of verdant vegetation. (pp. 129–130)

By applying sophisticated literary techniques to the depiction of old scenes and motifs, Yizhar was able simultaneously to revivify and conserve them. He reactivated the attachment to the land that had featured so prominently throughout the literary tradition. Because he reaffirmed old values, the literary establishment was always comfortable with his work.

It scarcely mattered what the stories were about; their language indicated their elite provenance and appeal. Yizhar's protagonists—village-born young men who made possible the Zionist enterprise by settlement and defense, even while dreaming of visionary landscape and imaginary women—were a kind of aristocracy, the knights-errant of Eretz Yisrael. They emerged as such even though Yizhar did not depict extraordinary persons or amazing deeds. In fact, his materials derived from the chronicles of the 1930s and 1940s, and his characters were ordinary people going about their ordinary lives. The stories detail everything from a person's place in the kibbutz rota (in *Ephraim Returns to Alfafa,* for example) to the resistance of a Jewish village against an Arab attack in the story "The Grove on the Hill" ["Hahurshah bagiv'ah," 1947], a convoy to the beleaguered Negev in "Midnight Convoy," and the mistreatment of Arabs during the war in *The Story of Hirbet Hizah* [*Hirbet Hiz'ah*] and "The Prisoner" ["Hashavui," 1949]. What determined the plot of the stories was not human relations or dramatic events, but the length of time between supper and the general meeting that would decide whether or not Ephraim would remain in the alfalfa; or the night spent by the protagonist on watch duty and the memories he recalls in the course of it; or the episodes that take place while a group of men prepare to go into action (*Before Departure* [*Beterem yeitzi'ah*]).

Just as impersonal forces dominated and hung heavy over social realities and its fictionalized reflections, so the interior narratives of the texts did not break out of the ordinariness of events or hint at submerged psychic developments. On the contrary, the interior narrative meticulously repeated everything that was to be observed in the outer world. The protagonists dream about the things that take place before their eyes. They imagine a parallel narrative in which the antagonist serves as an object for comparison.

Nonetheless, there is a lyrical quality to Yizhar's writing, produced largely by his style, which casts a romantic glow on even the most prosaic of his plots and protagonists. This results in an exalted perception of reality that transforms history into legend. Underlying his fiction is a longing for the primeval earth, before the effects of Zionist settlement and its technology. His nostalgia is for the world of almond orchards, horses and carts, and, above all, open spaces. These longings, which in effect reject the achievements of Zionist settlement, permeate his writing. Insofar as there is a pattern of interiority in Yizhar's writing, it has to do with the desire of the protagonists to break out of their mundane existences. But their dreams are invariably shattered by the exigencies of the moment.

Most of Yizhar's protagonists are, like the boys in the story "Habakuk," anonymous representatives of young Israeli manhood. They lack individual histories. They do not fulfill personal destinies. These characters are not well-rounded, nor do they undergo growth and development, not even from story to story. Thus, for example, in the novel *Days of Ziklag* [*Yemei tziqlag*], one character likes poetry, another, music, and a third, archaeology. But all are fundamentally so similar that, without these vocational markers, it is difficult to distinguish their separate streams of consciousness.

Essentially, Yizhar's characters are divided into two types: the introverted and ineffectual pioneer-dreamers who cannot fulfill their designs; and the standard positive pioneers, who are effective but boring. Both types are depicted with mild irony. Admiration is paid the extrovert who steers his own course. Sympathy is expressed for the one who drifts with the current, dreaming of escape but nonetheless obeying the call of history. The opposition between these two types represents the familiar polarity of the individual and the collective, but the conflict takes place less in reality than in the minds of the protagonists. In the final analysis, both types ultimately obey the dictates of the collective. These are individuals who are not psychologically motivated. They are lovers who seem unaware of sex; parentless and siblingless individuals with no hint of the elemental, primitive, unconscious aspect of human life, innocent of lust (a typical example of this is the love of one of the heroes of *Days of Ziklag* for another's girlfriend, whom he has never met). Yizhar's heroes, then, are idealized renderings of youth who are dedicated in their purity to society and the land. Such heroes may fall in love with women, but their greater love is for Mother Earth. Indeed, the landscape is more extensively characterized, and in more erotic terms, than any of his protagonists, and frequently it is their only interlocutor.

Days of Ziklag, which appeared in 1958, was Yizhar's culminating work. His first full-length novel, its length (1,143 pages) set it apart from his previous work, which consisted of long short stories and novellas. Despite its length, it follows a mere seven days in the life of a platoon in a particular outpost, which is supposedly the site of the biblical Ziklag. During these seven days, based on seven actual days in September 1948 when battles raged in the Negev during the week of the Jewish New Year, there are fierce battles between the platoon and the attacking Egyptian forces. Between attacks the soldiers talk among themselves or contemplate the landscape, their lives, and above all the happenings around them in the here and now. Like all of Yizhar's characters, the characters of *Days of Ziklag* oscillate between real emergencies and the landscape. The moment demands of them constant vigilance. The landscape, on the other hand, even though it harbors the enemy, is a site of refuge from the present and from history.

In its principal elements—the character of the protagonist, the attitude toward the landscape, the preference for quasi-documentary over fictional plots, and the stylistic features—Yizhar's writing remained unchanged from its inception to *Stories of a Plain.* For this reason, Yizhar's oeuvre, despite its richness, remains fairly monotonous. Even one of his later works, *Foretellings* [*Miqdamot,* 1992], which uses new materials and juxtapositions, does not represent a substantial change in his style or world-view. Nonetheless, no other Hebrew writer before or after him reached so profoundly to the heart of the physical landscape. Even later, when land-scape description was neglected and other elements took its place, Yizhar's image of the land hung over the writers, who felt they had either to adapt it or suppress it. He became a linguistic and artistic yardstick for such writers as Shamir, Tabib, Megged, Yonat and Alexander Sened, and many others who measured themselves against him.

If Yizhar's heroes were, in his own words, "one poet, trying to walk in step," Moshe Shamir's heroes, more than any of the fictional characters of his contemporaries, personified the New Hebrew Man. While Yizhar's characters are reluctant colonizers and conquerors who would have pre-ferred to live in peace alongside the Arab noble savages rather than fight them, Shamir's characters relish the conquest. Like Yizhar's protagonists they represent a Zionist elite, but whereas for Yizhar this is an aesthetic elite, distinguished by its sensitivity and love for the land, for Shamir the new leadership is a military and political realization of the ideal.

In contrast to the introverted Yizhar, who made no reference to his private life (until two volumes based on memories of his childhood were published in his old age, in 1992 and 1994), Shamir used his personal and social life in order to bolster his Zionist narrative. In his autobiograph-ical writings he described himself as the son of a family whose attachment to Eretz Yisrael and its Jewish community superseded political affiliations. He underscored the family's self-sacrifice, especially the fact that his broth-er, Eliyahu Shamir, was killed in the War of Independence. Born in Safed in 1921 and raised in Tel Aviv, he grew up in the youth movement Hash-omer Hatzaʻir and became one of its leaders, finally joining the kibbutz Mishmar Haʻemek. In his early essays he identified with the Israeli left and expressed a socialist-universalist ideology that supported the Soviet Union. After the Six-Day War in 1967 he left the socialist camp and joined the Zionist right. From an extreme socialist he became an extreme right-winger. His later nationalist stance was actually foreshadowed in his early writing (for example, *Under the Sun* [*Tahat hashemesh*], 1950), but it be-came more explicit in the later historical novels.

Following his political transformation, the national experience—which had been predominant in his life and only scantily concealed by his social-ist-pacifist beliefs—became the principal dynamic of his fiction as well as of his political life (see the trilogy *Above Rubies* [*Rahoq mipninim*], com-prised of *From a Different Yard* [*Yonah mihatser zarah,* 1974], *The Bridal Veil* [*Hinumat kalah,* 1984], and *To the End* [*ʻAd hasof,* 1991]). Like other writers of his generation, who were political journalists and public figures (Yizhar was a member of parliament; Megged, Bartov, and Tammuz served as cultural attachés abroad), Shamir edited various periodicals, wrote political articles, and finally served as a member of parliament. Nonetheless, it was as a writer rather than as a political leader that he tended to conduct his ideological campaigns.

Shamir is often compared with Yizhar, but his readership was much broader. One of the first serious Hebrew novelists whose books, beginning with his first, *He Walked through the Fields,* became best-sellers, his long-standing popularity began to wane during the 1960s, when the expectations of critics and readers began to change and new writers came to occupy center stage. The critics had been divided about his early writings, but most of them regarded *The King of Flesh and Blood* [*Melekh basar vadam,* 1954] as his generation's most solid achievement. Most of Shamir's output took the form of novels, but he also wrote short stories, plays, political essays, and poetry. His style was especially influenced by Mendele, Agnon, and Hazaz and the European, Russian, and American realist tradition.

There are two basic plot patterns in Shamir's fiction, both of which draw on autobiographical sources. One is the story of an immigrant family and its settlement in the country, as described in his autobiographical *Not Far from the Tree* [*Lo rehoqim min ha'eits,* 1983]. The other is the preparation of the younger generation for the "conquest of the Land," as told in *With His Own Hands,* a novel based on the life story of Shamir's brother Elik (Eliyahu), referred to as "Pirkei 'Elik" (The Elik Chronicles). Both narratives are patterned on family chronicles and on the memorial books published by the families and friends of fallen soldiers after the War of Independence. Shamir's heroes are romantic figures, mighty in love and war. Their primary drive is not sexual but militaristic. Indeed, sex is the conqueror's reward; he wins women as well as land, whether he survives to enjoy them or not.

Stylistically, Shamir is more a naturalist than a realist, though he eschews both forms of mimetic writing in refusing to render the natural rhythms of everyday speech. His approach to language was purist and conservative. In this, it reflected the bias of most of his generation for elevated formal language. Nevertheless, he did make use of some nonstandard elements, such as Arabic idioms, which in actual fact punctuated the speech of native Israelis, especially in the Palmah. Especially at the beginning of his career, this produced a marked contrast between the idiomatic language and dialect of the dialogues and the poetical, flowery language of the narration.

In the mid-1950s Shamir moved away from novels dealing with the mores and ideology of 1940s Eretz Yisrael and took up historical subjects. The historical novel had always been a favorite romantic expression of national awareness and pride. Such were the books of Walter Scott for the English and the Scots, Gustav Freitag for the Germans, Alexandre Dumas for the French, and Henryk Sienkiewicz for the Poles. Even Alexei Tolstoy's novel about Peter the Great served this purpose for modern Russia. Many of these books had been translated into Hebrew and were extremely popular with young readers. *The King of Flesh and Blood* came to fill the same function for the nascent Israeli nationalism.

The King of Flesh and Blood is set in the reign of Hasmonean king Alexander Yannai (Jannaeus) in the second and first centuries B.C., when the kingdom of Judea, ravaged from within by the struggle between its two main social-religious factions, also reached the zenith of its territorial expansion and power. Although he made use of historical sources, Shamir was less concerned with historical verisimilitude than with what he regarded as the spirit of the age. This spirit of the age was given a Marxist interpretation. The conflict between the two leading religious movements in Judea, the Pharisees and Sadducees, was presented in socio-economic terms. The Pharisees constitute the masses, the poorer classes who also make up the people's army. The Sadducees are the prosperous and powerful upper class, including the tax collectors and the priests, who rely on mercenaries to do their bidding.

Clearly indebted to the tradition of Sir Walter Scott and the historical plays of Shakespeare, the novel also plays off a familiar biblical motif: the conflict between older and younger brother (Ishmael and Isaac, Esau and Jacob, Joseph and his brothers). This is the pattern in which the younger brother comes to dominate and prevail over the older sibling. In Shamir's novel, the younger Yannai seizes the throne from his older brother Absalom. The relationship between the brothers reflects larger political conflicts. It embodies such time-honored themes as the individual versus the collective and the opposition between, on the one hand, blood ties and social and political activism, and, on the other, passivity and pacifism. Although in Shamir's novel the reversal of the natural order of inheritance enjoys no divine or moral sanction, the author nonetheless affirms it.

The novel's spatial expanses and multitude of personae give it epic force without losing the dramatic tension that derives from personal and social-political conflict. The story is presented through the observer-narrator Absalom. Absalom not only plays an important part in the events, he also stands outside the narrative, providing a final objective interpretation of the events through sections entitled "The Chronicles of King Yannai as written by Absalom, son of Hyrcanos." In order to distinguish these chronicles from the rest of the text, they are printed fully voweled (in general, Hebrew texts, excluding poetic texts, are printed without vowels). At the heart of the novel, however, is Yannai himself, the rejected son who rises by cunning and perseverance to assume the throne. Through his own self-description and through his presentation by the author he emerges as a fully self-conscious yet somewhat Machiavellian personality who is eminently qualified to reign. The author's approval of his protagonist, despite his censure of his criminal acts, produces the rich ambivalence of the text.

Ostensibly, Shamir was decrying the contemporary hero who turned from liberator to conqueror. In fact, he was celebrating the power of a personality which was capable of attracting people, and which, if it manipulated others to his own ends (sometimes ruthlessly), was also capable of generosity. The portrait of Absalom as the antithesis of his brother underscores this feature of the text. Despite Absalom's humanistic tendencies, which cause him to distance himself from his progressively more cruel brother, and despite his verbal resistance, the older brother is clearly pale and feeble in comparison with his brother, and is no real challenge to Yannai.

The novel describes the struggle between power and strong leadership versus the rights of the many. Some of the passages have a decidedly modern ring to them, as when various characters express nostalgia for the early days of the Hasmonean rule, before its corruption. The message is clear, and its relevance to 1950s Israel obvious. Material (flesh-and-blood) kingship, with its imperialist ambitions and greed, weakens the nation. At the same time, there is no mistaking the author's admiration for Alexander Yannai, whose political shrewdness makes up for his moral failings. For this reason, *The King of Flesh and Blood* is not a novel of disillusionment. Rather it is a self-conscious epic-heroic representation of the War of Independence, in which the author's admiration for the fighters and the nation's leaders is projected onto the Hasmoneans.

In *The King of Flesh and Blood* Shamir fully realized the potential of social realist fiction. None of his contemporaries had ever produced a novel of such great dimensions; nor did Shamir himself ever duplicate his achievement in this novel. Nonetheless, his success with *The King of Flesh and Blood* induced him to write another historical novel, *The Hittite Must Die* [*Kivsat harash,* meaning "the pauper's lamb"; the book also appeared in English under the title *David's Stranger,* 1956], set in the reign of King David in the tenth century B.C. Here the Absalom role is filled by Uriah the Hittite, the Yannai role by King David, described from the viewpoint of Uriah, who records the events. Unlike *The King of Flesh and Blood, The Hittite Must Die* is clearly a novel of disillusionment. In this novel Shamir takes elegiac leave of the romantic hero, who represents the pristine premonarchical past. Shamir's disenchantment, in this case with the ideology of Hashomer Hatza῾ir, which culminated with the movement's break with the Soviet Union and Stalinism, was also expressed in the novel *That You Are Naked* [*Ki῾erom ʾatah,* 1959]. A bildungsroman depicting the maturation of a young man in a youth movement camp in 1939, the book questions whether it is any longer possible to imagine peaceable relations between Arabs and Jews. It concludes that the Jewish state will grow and prosper only through constant conflict and at the cost of many lives. These ideas would reappear in his later novels, published after the 1967 war.

Critics and readers alike regarded Shamir as the preeminent writer of his time, and even with the waning of his popularity, there is no mistaking his contribution to Hebrew fiction. Much of the revolt which took place in the late 1950s was aimed directly against Shamir's work; many of the protagonists of Oz and Yehoshua constitute deliberate refutations of Shamir's Uri and Elik.

Yigal Mossinsohn, who was born in the settlement of Ein Ganim in 1917 and died in Tel Aviv in 1993, was one of the first offspring of the pioneers of the Second Aliyah. Like Shamir, he was raised and lived in a kibbutz, and like most men of his generation he served in pre-independence military organizations and later in the Israeli army. Also like many of his contemporaries, he wrote in a variety of genres. He published numerous children's books as well as melodramatic plays of mass appeal. His commercial success in these genres affected his writing of short stories and novels. Melodrama and simplistic characterization infected his serious writing, and from a promising novelist he became increasingly a purveyor of trivial fiction.

Nonetheless, Mossinsohn distinguished himself from others of his generation by rejecting the idealized image of the labor movement and the kibbutz. His first book, for example, a collection of short stories entitled *Grey as a Sack* [*ʾAforim kasaq,* 1946], dealt with the isolated individual, either on the kibbutz or in confrontation with a hostile Arab or English environment, struggling primarily with his fellow Jews rather than with the enemy at large. Writing in a naturalistic style, Mossinsohn sought to expose what he saw as the unconscious primal drives of the people of the kibbutzim and cooperative settlements. This viewpoint also dominated his controversial novel *Man's Way* [*Derekh gever,* 1953].

Mossinsohn's finest work was the novel *Judas* (1962), which was undoubtedly one of the higher achievements of this generation. The story is told by the protagonist-narrator, Judas Iscariot, who, on the eve of his execution, recalls and tries to make sense of his recent life on the Greek island Grimos and his earlier years in Judea. The intricate plot is something of a hermeneutic code (to use R. Barthes's term). Puzzles reach resolutions only to yield new puzzles, in an endless process of embaffiement. Mossinsohn had always been highly inventive in raveling and unraveling mysteries. In *Judas* he exceeded even his own achievement.

The tension of the story does not derive from the question of how the plot will conclude, since the end is known from the beginning. Rather, the interest derives from the unfolding of the events themselves. The confessional narrator does not reveal everything at once. Indeed, he does not even seem fully aware of the significance of what he knows until the end. What is clear, however, is that the true course of events does not correspond to the story that has been disseminated by Jesus' disciples. What emerges is that the sect that finally came to be known as the Christians started out as part of an anti-Roman underground, led by a man called Barabas, who only seemed to be a thief. Iscariot himself, it turns out, was a member of the Jewish underground and was the leader's close associate. In so narrating New Testament history, the gospels are challenged and a new national (rather than religious) interpretation is put before the reader. Seeking to restore Jesus to Judaism and to liberate him from the Pauline interpretation, Mossinsohn (like A. A. Kabak before him in *The Narrow Path: The Man of Nazareth*) invented a myth to harmonize with contemporary national politics. Although Judas supposedly betrayed Jesus for thirty pieces of silver, in reality he was serving the cause of the people's revolt, carrying out the order of the people's leader Barabas to turn Jesus in to the Romans. Judas's heroism is established by the text when Judas, like Christ, dies on the cross. Thus Judas Iscariot emerges as an underground hero, exiled and utterly dedicated to his cause.

The fiction of Aharon Megged did not address the social and linguistic elite (like that of Yizhar). Nor did he purport to encompass a whole world and express the social experience of the age (like Shamir) or to attack the establishment (like Mossinsohn). Rather, Megged was a storyteller, addressing a general reading public. His novels were short and touched on current affairs. Like others of his contemporaries, he too used various genres, including short stories, novellas, novels, plays, and political essays.

Born in Poland in 1920 and brought to Palestine at the age of five, Megged grew up in an agricultural settlement and later joined a kibbutz. In 1950 he left the kibbutz and settled in Tel Aviv. From an early age he was active in the youth and labor movement. He edited several of its journals and was always closely associated with its literary establishment. His early writings were naively realist Eretz Yisrael stories, extolling the achievements of the Zionist endeavor in a language borrowed from Mendele, Hazaz, Berkowitz, and Agnon. Like his contemporaries Natan Shaham and Hanoch Bartov, however, Megged also sought to exceed the limitations of realist convention by means of intricate techniques involving narrative authority. Thus, like them, he produced melodramatic texts in which action often took the place of psychological insight. Most of his fiction may be described by Edwin Muir's term "novels of character." They are works in which the linear connection between the various elements is more important than the causal link, and most of the personae are two-dimensional and static. They are unchanged by their passage through the fictional space, though in passing through it they are made to reveal its various aspects, if not significance. This is not to denigrate the works in question—some classic authors wrote novels of character. Nonetheless, it is important to distinguish one form of writing from another more dramatic and psychological fictional genre.

As he demonstrated in the social-realist didactic novel *Hedva and I* (1953) and the surrealist novel *Fortunes of a Fool* [*Mikreh haksil,* literally meaning "the case of a fool," 1959], Megged was interested in the figure of the naive idealist from the kibbutz who finds himself at a loss in the city. The central figure of the novel seems to everyone to be a fool, and everyone mistreats him. The author alone recognizes that the fool is wiser than his tormentors. Not surprisingly, in both novels it is a woman who seeks to tempt the man out of his social innocence and away from his ideological paradise. Megged differs from his contemporaries in that he never sought to depict the new Israeli. Rather, his protagonists tend to be products of the old Eretz Yisrael, anti-heroes contending uneasily with new Israeli society, living by obsolete standards and dreaming impossible dreams. This figure was born of nostalgia for the pre-State community which upheld the pristine ideals of the youth movement. The narrator who observes the inept fool, his own contemporary, is himself ironized as an urban individual mourning the loss of his own moral virginity. Beginning with Shlomik, the protagonist of *Hedva and I,* Megged's lost and helpless protagonists reflect the continued powerlessness of his generation, which did not believe in its own ability to seize the reins of power and transform the society that had let it down. All that is left for the author is to dream wistfully about the past or confess his failure.

Another issue which increasingly preoccupied Megged was the self-consciously literary subject of the relationship between fiction and reality. Megged's novels, which had been widely accessible and dealt with popular contemporary issues, had met with mixed responses, even though the themes were generally popular, since they usually affirmed the social consensus. As he refined his craft over the course of his literary life from the 1940s to the 1980s, his work became a reflection of the development of literary tastes in the country. His oeuvre, therefore, illustrates the transition from the stylistic influence of Agnon, Hazaz, and Shlonsky and company, who strove for the highest literary language, to the simpler, freer style of writing that was beginning to predominate. It is not surprising, therefore, that the issue of writing should have emerged as a subject of his fiction, beginning with his most important novel, *The Living on the Dead* [*Hahai 'al hamet*, 1965].

This was the first and best of a series of novels that questioned the capacity of fiction to genuinely represent the world (see also *Evyatar Notebooks* [*Mahbarot Evyatar*, 1973] and *Of Trees and Stones* ['*Al 'eitsim va' a-vanim*, 1974]). *The Living on the Dead* concerns the novelist-narrator, Yonas Rabinowitz, who has been commissioned to write the biography of Davidov, a Third Aliyah hero, and who is researching his subject. Rabinowitz is shown in the course of the novel to be ridiculous in his attempt to comprehend reality through fictionalizing it. On one level, the book is social critique:

> It has become a country of parasites. Everyone is growing rich, but not from work. They make a fortune from the land for which innocent young men shed their blood. They accumulate properties from the Reparations, flourish on the victims' ashes, the foundations of the house are rotting: living on the dead! The entire State. No wonder corruption is spreading from root to branch! (p. 38)

More basically, however, the book addresses the discrepancy between historical events and their narration and the profit to be made in the present by the sacrifices of the past. What Yonas has discovered is that while Davidov did indeed serve the Zionist enterprise, he neglected his family in the process. Such sacrifice, the novel implies, was once justifiable. It no longer is. The novel depicts a society which no longer has any heroes, and which therefore tries to retrieve them from the past. Unable to contend with the present, Yonas cannot even complete his book and is sued for failing to meet his contractual obligation. All he can do is dream about a lost hero and a lost set of values. *The Living on the Dead* is not a perfect novel. Nonetheless, it presents an important subject, and, as a novel-about-a-novel (in the manner of André Gide's *The Counterfeiters*), it introduces into Hebrew fiction a heretofore rarely used genre. In a sense, the book may be viewed as a forerunner of Yaakov Shabtai's *Past Continuous* [*Zikhron dvarim*, 1977], which also examines the virtues and weaknesses of the fanatical fathers, who sacrificed their families on the altar of their beliefs for the new society they sought to build.

In his later work Megged made no more innovations in his themes or forms. Still, he continued to observe various social issues from his own distinctive viewpoint. The novel *Foigelman* (1987) deals with the hopeless attempt by a New Hebrew, Zvi Arbel, a professor of Jewish history, to return to the Old Jew at the same time as the Yiddish poet Foigelman, a

Holocaust survivor, makes vain efforts to strike root in Israel. This is probably Megged's most dramatic and psychological novel, dealing with the complex relationships between the generations, between Israel and the Jewish Diaspora, between Hebrew and Yiddish, between the love of knowledge and the love of life, and between the worldviews of the Jewish fathers versus those of the sons, who emigrate or assimilate.

Various writers (e.g., Shaham, Ben-Ner, Oz, and Ruth Almog) followed Megged in experimenting with narrative authority and the use of non-fictional materials within the work of art. Also, the figure of the naive, incompetent protagonist, who cannot fit in because of his innocence or inability to contend with the new social reality, recurred in the writings of many other authors, (e.g., Nitzan, Frankel, Hendel and Orpaz). In most of them the Zionist narrative succeeds at the expense of the protagonist's failures. Whether or not Megged provided the inspiration for these characters, it is certain that he, more than any other writer, delineated the defeat of a generation of ideals in an unfriendly and far from ideal world.

Natan Shaham, the son of the writer Eliezer Steinmann, was born in Tel Aviv in 1925. Like many members of his generation, he joined a youth movement in his childhood and a kibbutz later on. A faithful spokesperson for Zionist-socialist ideology, he always held various public positions on behalf of his movement. It is not surprising that Shaham was perhaps the most typical heir of the interwar genre writers such as Maletz and Ever-Hadani. Like them, he evaluated and judged his protagonists by the standards of labor Zionism.

The critical response to Shaham was ambivalent. Critics on the left regarded him as their movement's best literary spokesman, but as the intellectual establishment began to turn away from ideological fiction his writings became less favorably received. Unlike Shamir and Yizhar, Shaham never occupied literary center stage, nor did he make an effort to meet the demands of the new generation and its literary forms, as did Megged, Hendel, the Seneds, and Tammuz. The change in his writing stemmed from the transformations in Israeli society from the 1960s on, especially the decline of ideologies in general and of Marxism in particular. His ideological expression became more subtle, less simplistic, as in the novel *First Person Plural* [*Guf rish'on rabim*, 1968], which appeared after several New Wave novels—for example, *Elsewhere, Perhaps* [*Makom 'aher*, 1966] by Amos Oz—had already brought Shaham's kind of material to a general public. In *First Person Plural* Shaham attempted to revitalize social realist fiction by depicting protagonists more complexly and by illuminating social issues (such as individuals and the community in the kibbutz and the problem of German reparations) from divergent points of view.

Shaham's novels are dominated by social materials. His first short story collection dealt with a group of youths in the Palmah during the War of Independence (*Grain and Lead* [*Dagan ve'oferet,* 1948]). So did the later *Always Us* [*Tamid 'anahnu,* 1952]. He went on to depict the pioneers of the Third Aliyah, the sociology of the kibbutz, and the arrival and settlement of Polish-Jewish communists in *The Wisdom of the Poor* [*Hokhmat hamisqein,* 1960] and of German Jewry (in *First Person Plural* and *The Rosendorf Quartet* [*Revi'iyat Rosendorf,* 1987]).

The fictions proceed through binary oppositions, such as between the sensitive intellectual and the tough man of the world, the person who submits to reality and the one who conquers it, the potential or actual artist versus the fighter. Like Megged, Shaham sympathized with softer individuals and criticized the rougher aspects of Israeli culture. Over the years, with the author's growing maturity and the waning influence of ideology and social-realist criticism, these oppositions lost their sharpness, to the artistic benefit of the writing.

Shaham's finest work—in the time frame of the present study—is *The Rosendorf Quartet,* which was highly praised at the time of its publication. It revolves around a number of German-Jewish immigrants in Palestine in the 1930s, their cultural contribution to the place (this was the time when the Philharmonic Orchestra was founded), and their various responses to the country. Its structure recalls the multiple-point-of-view technique he had used earlier in *First Person Plural.* Events are multiply depicted and characters are observed through one another's eyes. One of the characters, Egon Loewenthal, proposes to write the story of the Rosendorf Quartet, which is eventually written by the author. Shaham makes use of various devices to create the impression of non-fictional prose: letters, memoirs, notes, a diary.

The five central characters are united in their shared mentality, origins, and professional affiliations. Although they are taken from the stock of stereotypes and the figures of the commedia dell'arte, they are impressively individualized as each one tells his own story and that of the others. The musicians' continued association gives rise to complicated interrelationships; the fifth member of the group is a woman who is loved by all four men. The members of the group are also divided by their attitudes to Eretz Yisrael. Friedman, the only Zionist among them, feels guilty because by playing music rather than tending the soil he is not carrying out his pioneering ideals. Eva and Loewenthal reject Zionism out of hand, dismissing it as a misguided fantasy: "This attempt to breed a simple-minded young generation who will consent to be cannon fodder for their parents' messianic madness," says Loewenthal, "is doomed to failure. When they have children of their own they will rebel. In the meantime the Arabs, who are not short of lunatics either, will grow stronger and wipe these tender shoots of Jewish hope off the face of the earth" (p. 236). Through Loewenthal, Shaham, without taking sides, exposes the skepticism and fear of the failure of the Zionist enterprise that became a familiar theme in the post-realist fiction of Tammuz, Yehoshua, Shabtai, Oz, and Ruth Almog.

Shaham's characters talk a great deal and are gifted at wordplay. The author's verbal talents make his protagonists into eloquent and sophisticated intellectuals. Consequently, Shaham became, for better or worse, the most sophisticated and intellectual of the realists. The narratives are interspersed with self-interpretative passages, and the narrator often indulges in aphorisms and paradoxes. These word games, which became Shaham's literary trademark, sometimes tended toward an embarrassment of riches. Nonetheless, over the course of his career, Shaham developed from a novelist whose ideology overwhelmed the text with melodrama and intrigue to a writer of readable novels of ideas. The books do not seek to shock or amuse. Simply and straightforwardly they aim to convey a social message, which neither plumbs psychological depths nor rises to metaphysical heights. Although his novels were not innovative in style and form, they were certainly accessible, and as such, part of the essential foundations of Hebrew literature.

CURRENTS OF CHANGE

Even though social realism, and in particular the writings of Yizhar, have persisted as positive influences on the Hebrew literary scene, by the late 1950s the literature began to shake off the constraints of realist conventions and the Shlonsky style. The cultural transformation began with a small group of students in Jerusalem who, in 1952, published a little stenciled magazine, *Likrat* [*Towards*], edited by Binyamin Hrushovsky (Harshav) and Natan Zach. One of the very first to appear without the patronage of any political party, the journal, which was published irregularly until 1954, was a milestone in the development of Hebrew literature in Israel. Shlonsky and his companions had also begun as rebels, but they had become by the 1940s an ideological group which sought to subordinate literature to its beliefs. The *Likrat* group diverted emphasis away from ideology and back to poetics. Its inaugural manifesto called for a shift in the balance between collectivism and individualism. Literature, it declared, should not be created either as an expression of ideology or as part of a collective enterprise. Rather, it should be the product of the individual creator's confrontation with his or her own self and experience. Most of the more established literary periodicals which came after *Likrat*—for example, '*Ogdan* [*Binder*], '*Akhshav* [*Now*], and *Yokhani* (which was the name of a legendary bird)—continued the literary revolution until the mid-1970s, when certain periodicals, such as *Siman kri'ah* [*Exclamation Mark*] and *'Iton 77* [*Paper 77*] to some degree reversed direction, and once again called on the artist to accept collective responsibility for social deterioration.

The demand on the native writer to introduce into fictional reality the New Hebrew personality that the new entity of Eretz Yisrael, and later the State of Israel, had founded was encouraged by social conditions. The native literature came into being at a time when the Jewish community in Palestine was preparing itself for a war of independence. It was struggling against British rule and other forces that sought to destroy it. The literature and the theater of Palestine (which reinforced public tastes by staging many of the novels) prepared the public for the moment of sacrifice. Many stories and novels culminated in the protagonist's sacrificial death, on which the survival of the community seemed to depend. The Zionist readership had fathered an imaginary hero; the community expected the country's writers to complete the process of his birth and give him fictional life. This New Man (the New Hebrew was most often depicted as a man rather than a woman) would enact a certain story of heroic self-sacrifice. Supported primarily by its target readership in the agricultural communities, youth movements, and labor organizations and by critics who made no distinction between life and literature, the writers gave the public what it needed and demanded.

Challenges to this master plot could not help but transform the literature—stylistically as well as thematically. Leftist critics guided by Marxist premises or by Soviet literary criteria (under the influence of Lukacz and Zhdanov) objected to merely accepting the world as given. They continued to demand that the writers obey doctrinal dictates and create protagonists who would advance the cause of the revolution. A more influential, and harsher, reaction against first-generation native realism, however, attacked the premises of ideology altogether. Literary scholar and critic Baruch Kurzweil rejected the New Hebrew fiction because, he argued, a people who do not know their past and who have broken the chain of their social and linguistic heritage are incapable of creating a great literature. Insofar as literature does appear under such conditions, he contended, it must remain artificial and shallow.

Kurzweil's resistance to secular political Zionism as the basis for the nation's literature did much to transform Hebrew literature in the late 1950s and early 1960s. Adopting Kurzweil's judgment, a younger generation of critics and writers applied a different standard for judging the social realism of the 1940s. The generation of *Likrat* and other literary magazines of the day was influenced by the so-called New Criticism of

Anglo-American and German provenance as well as by Russian Formalism, which unequivocally rejected the ideological uses of fiction. The result was a convergence between Kurzweil's revulsion for that sort of fiction—which he couched in aesthetic terms—and the desire of the younger critics for subtler, more complex literary forms and subjects, rich in ambivalence, irony, paradox, and tensions. This altered literary taste and created a new horizon of expectations, ushering in new writers and encouraging others to revise their artistic assumptions. As a result the public began to prefer such writers as Pinhas Sadeh, Aharon Appelfeld, Amalia Kahana-Carmon, Yoram Kaniuk, and A. B. Yehoshua over Shamir, Mossinsohn, Megged, Shaham, and others. Non-realist currents, which had formerly been marginalized, moved to the center. At the same time, while some realists receded into the background, others held their own or, yielding to the new literary atmosphere, altered the style and structure of their writings. Two schools or traditions came to coexist, both ranging across the two native generations. Some of the writers who were born in the 1930s and 1940s became realists. Others who were born in the 1920s never were realists to begin with. And still others who had written social realist fiction changed course midstream.

The literature of the 1940s was not revolutionary. It was not set on changing the existing order but, quite the contrary, it seemed intent upon turning back the wheel of literary revolution and promoting the status quo. Two prominent writers of the 1940s, Mossinsohn and Shamir, began to publish more than a decade after the appearance of Agnon's surrealist and revolutionary *The Book of Deeds*. The modernist fiction of Horowitz and Levin had been around since the 1930s, and Halkin published his novel *Crisis* in 1945. None of these achievements in literary sophistication made an impression on the Dor Ba'aretz writers. Yizhar and Oren were the only native writers in the 1940s whose work in any way resembled such European modernists as Joyce, Woolf, Mann, Kafka, Camus, and Gide. The first generation of native-born Israeli writers was more affected by the expectations of critics on the left, who demanded social-realism, and by the expectations of their readers, who wanted literature to mirror the renascent youth experience in Eretz Yisrael.

For this reason, Russian literature remained a dominant influence. In the pre-State period there had been widespread admiration for the heroic Soviet struggle against the Germans. A good deal of Soviet war literature was early translated into Hebrew, such as Aleksander Bek's *The Highway of Wolokolamsk* and Vundu Vassilyevskaya's *The Rainbow*. These translations affected not only the themes of Hebrew fiction, but, through the stylistic elements of the translations, the language itself. Shlonsky was the leading translator of his time. He and his contemporaries were much given to neologisms and high-flown diction. These left their imprint on the native-born writers. The ideological dimensions of Russian literature were also not unfamiliar to the Hebrew reading public, since many of its features, from its heroic pioneering protagonists to its quasi-documentary plots, already had much in common with the Third Aliyah genre fiction (Arikha, Zarchi, Maletz, and others), on which both the Dor Ba'aretz and Dor Hamedinah writers had grown up. Thus, even the New Wave writers told stories of migration and integration (inherited from the writers of the Second and Third Aliyot) and produced latter-day settlement novels, some of which took on interesting new guises, such as Amos Oz's *Elsewhere, Perhaps* (1966) and *A Perfect Peace* [*Menuhah nekhonah*, 1982] and the Seneds' novel *The Land Inhabited* [*Kvar 'eretz noshevet*, 1981].

At the same time, other features of the Hebrew literary tradition were brought forward. There is no mistaking the line of continuity linking the fiction of Binyamin Tammuz, Yehudit Hendel, Shulamith Hareven, Nisim Aloni, Amalia Kahana-Carmon, Yehoshua Kenaz, Ruth Almog, and Yaakov Shabtai to the impressionist writings of Shoffman, Baron, Steinberg, Vogel, and Goldberg. Berdyczewski too made an impact—though he was not a direct influence—on such writers as Pinhas Sadeh, Yoram Kaniuk, and Amos Oz, while Yizhar's style owes something to Gnessin as well. During the 1960s and 1970s other writers—notably Yaakov Shabtai—returned to Gnessin, either directly or via Yizhar's intermediacy. A writer who left his mark on all the generations and groups was Brenner, who was variously adopted and adapted to current needs. By the late 1950s Agnon was an important element in the revolt of such writers as Yehuda Amichai, David Shahar, Aharon Appelfeld, A. B. Yehoshua, and Yitzhak Orpaz against Shamir, Megged, and Yizhar. These influences within the domestic literary tradition were augmented in the 1960s and 1970s by French existentialist literature, particularly the fiction of Albert Camus (*L'Etranger* was translated into Hebrew in 1964). Also crucial were the works of Kafka, whom many viewed as a European version of Agnon. Kafka affected many different writers, such as Megged, Yehoshua, Orpaz, and Appelfeld. Other translated writers who helped to reshape Israeli fiction were Max Frisch (*Homo Faber* appeared in Hebrew in 1963), Günther Grass (*The Tin Drum*, 1975), and Gabriel Garcia Marquez (*One Hundred Years of Solitude*, 1972). At the same time, Proust, Faulkner, and Woolf were rediscovered.

Furthermore, the fiction of the two native generations influenced each other. The first generation was predominantly affected by Yizhar, who was, as it were, the first among equals. In their early works Shamir and the Seneds followed him in meticulously depicting landscapes and in using elevated language to describe the relations between man and the land.

Yizhar's influence did not end in the 1950s and 1960s but continued to act dialectically upon the writers who began to publish in the mid-1950s. Simultaneously, changes in subject matter and style by the second generation of native-born authors produced changes in the first native generation as well. Poetry, too, impacted on the fiction. If certain poets, such as Shlonsky and Goldberg, chiefly influenced the forms of language, others, such as Natan Alterman and Yonatan Ratosh, affected the contents and worldviews of fictional works.

It is on the level of language that one might have expected the greatest transformations in Hebrew literature. The immigrant authors had not been brought up on Hebrew, and even the native-born writers of the earlier generation, such as Burla and Shami, heard more Ladino or Arabic at home than Hebrew. But the new generation of native writers had grown up speaking Hebrew. It might have been expected that the language, having become vernacular, would stamp its character upon the literature and give rise to a fresh, colloquial style. This was not to be. Indeed, Yizhar was the only author who succeeded in creating a style of his own, made up of all the available linguistic materials of the time, high and low, including slang, neologisms, and archaisms.

Native Hebrew, dubbed "Israeli Hebrew" by philologists such as H. Rozen, drew largely on two sources of innovation: the organic development of the spoken language itself and its interjection of alien linguistic elements from its immigrant populations. The result was a substandard speech with vulgarisms and borrowings from Arabic and Yiddish as well as from German, English, and Russian. The arrival of Jews from the Moslem countries also contributed to breaking up linguistic homogeneity in the pre-State country. Another notable phenomenon was the appearance of graduates of intensive courses of Hebrew language study for newcomers (the most outstanding of these was Aharon Appelfeld). Although the writers struggled mightily to find a language in which to express the new Israeli reality, the pre-State community had, together with patterns of behavior and thought, put into place semiotic groundwork that was hard to displace. Literature could thus employ familiar patterns and allusions deriving from the shared social experience. Some of the works of Shamir and Haim Gouri, for instance, were written in a semiotic code which only their contemporaries could fully understand. To Jews in another continent, or even Israelis of another generation, this code would seem remote and idiosyncratic. Having acquired a modern idiom, Hebrew literature seemed all too quickly to be losing it again; fathers and sons, the immigrants and the native-born, no longer spoke the same language. The writers, therefore, were caught in a linguistic dilemma. They had to decide whether to submit to traditional, non-spoken Hebrew and write, as it were, for the ages, or to imitate colloquial speech and enjoy only a brief, ephemeral existence.

Thus, while the spoken language began to appear in print in the 1950s in the journalistic and satirical columns of such writers as Kenan and Kishon, the fiction was slow to seize the opportunities it afforded. Except in dialogue, spoken Hebrew did not become an integral part of the language of the literary text. It was as if the speech of the protagonists were a quotation from the language of the everyday world, while the text itself came from some other linguistic realm. The native generations drew on two major traditions: the formulated language of classical Hebrew fiction, going back to Mendele, Agnon, and Berkowitz; and the new language of the Steinmann and the Shlonsky group. This new language was influenced by contemporary translations and poetry (Shlonsky, Alterman, and Goldberg), and it tried to replace the fixed idiom with neologisms. But since neither the translations nor the poetry had much to do with the spoken language, the new language did not emerge as a natural, unaffected medium of representation. Indeed, the style violated the mimetic premises of the writers, whose texts represented themselves as realistic renderings of the socio-political world.

In this elevated non-colloquial style, literature and the press proceeded hand in glove. Whereas in most countries the language of newspapers is usually simpler than that of literature, the Hebrew press favored an intensified allusive language rich in biblical and Mishnaic connotations, a rhetorical repetitive rhythm, and figurative imagery. Such pathos-laden elevated language permeated everything from journals for children and youth (which were edited by young writers who would later appear on the adult literary scene) to the daily newspapers. It was probably related to the continuing influence of Russian fiction, changing only in the late 1950s and early 1960s, when the spirit of pathos which dictated it began to vanish and the Israeli readership began to rebel against exalted treatments of common everyday phenomena.

Two prominent examples of this late transformation in the language are the 1970s and 1980s writings of Dan Ben-Amotz and Netivah Ben-Yehudah, both of whom had been members of the Palmah before the War of Independence. The language of Ben-Amotz, who was very much a child of his age, went to extremes in his humorous sketches and popular novels, in which he sought to shock his readers with vulgarities and coarseness. Netivah Ben-Yehudah, whose books began to appear in the 1980s, carried on this process of liberating readers from the linguistic and cultural burden of their forefathers. Her style corresponded to the language that was spoken by the kinds of people she depicted in her novels during the period in question, that is, 1947 to 1949. The reality she describes without pathos appears more genuine precisely because the lower register is more convincing to present-day readers. This lowering of the linguistic register characterized literary production in the 1960s and 1970s, in the poetry of Amichai, for example, in the fiction of Appelfeld, and in some older writers as well. Nonetheless, some writers, like Oz and Kaniuk, persisted in using a highly intensified diction, which suited the inner tension of their subject matter. Others, such as Kahana-Carmon, even intensified their language through poetic constructions more intricate than those used by their predecessors.

OLD JEW, NEW HEBREW

The image of the New Hebrew, such as Moshe Shamir's Elik, represented the fulfillment, in fiction as in life, of the parents' desire that their offspring differ as much as possible from the weak, cowering diaspora Jew that, presumably, the new national enterprise had left behind. The idea of *galuti* (i.e., being in exile or belonging to the diaspora) became the polar opposite of Israeli. The desire to shed the burden of historical Jewish identity and the tormented recognition that this was impossible became the twin preoccupations of literature in the post-1948 period. In the 1940s and 1950s the reading public demanded wholesome Israeli protagonists, severed from Jewish history. And the writers, though they knew well enough that the new Israeli had not been born from the sea, chose, in deference to public needs, to represent the youth of Eretz Yisrael as if it were. Thus Shamir's novel *With His Own Hands* opens with just these words: "Elik was born from the sea. That was what Father used to say when we sat down together for supper on the balcony of the little house on summer evenings." Elik, a son of the soil who sacrifices his life for his homeland, comes very close to the idealized native-born Jew envisioned by Luidor (in his 1912 story "Yoash") and by Moshe Smilansky forty years earlier. Many of the protagonists of Yizhar and his younger followers were variations on this single stereotype. Most of them come from the country. Others arrive there and become attached to the soil and the landscape. Many of them are warriors whose stories are tests of manhood from which they emerge triumphant, whether or not they survive. Most of them are handsome and extroverted, popular and in harmony with their fathers with regard to their missions. They may return to their private lives only after fulfilling those missions, and if they do not return, their deaths validate their lives. Their simple dress and their free use of Arabic suggest a resemblance to the Bedouin, a symbol of freedom and manhood, as well as the values of the labor movement and its affiliated youth organizations. To create such protagonists, the writers had to ignore the genealogy and generational conflict. The fiction, notably Yizhar's, is self-consciously non-Oedipal. Such conflicts as occur take place among and within the protagonists, not between the generations.

From the mid-1950s, as Hebrew fiction began to broaden and diversify its materials and personae, the stereotype began to dissolve. The figure of the *picaro,* for instance, which appeared in Israeli fiction after the War of Independence, marked an awakening from the Israeli dream of social perfection. This *picaro* took two forms: the naive protagonist who becomes a victim of circumstances and the protagonist who knows how to exploit the new corruption to his own advantage (e.g., Benjamin Tammuz's novel, *The Life of Elyakum* [*Hayei 'Elyaqum,* 1965]). The works of Naomi Frankel, Yonat and Alexander Sened, Aharon Appelfeld, Itamar Yaoz-Kest, Dan Tzalka, Yehuda Amichai, Uri Orlev, Amos Oz, Yoram Kaniuk, Shimon Ballas, Sami Michael, and Amnon Shamosh introduced a plethora of social settings and periods, such as German Jewry, Jewish youth in Poland during the Second World War, Holocaust survivors abroad and in Israel, Jews of the Middle East, new immigrants in Israel, and Israelis living abroad. The sociological spectrum broadened considerably and there is scarcely a corner of Israeli or Jewish experience which the writers overlooked—much like the authors of earlier generations, who also drew on the varied populations of the region. This process of looking away from the center of Israeli society to its margins did not evade Israeli social reality. Rather it gradually converted the margins into the new center. The world of the protagonists changed, and the familiar images of the kibbutz, the farming community, and Little Tel Aviv of pioneering times yielded to novel and unexpected pictures (notably in the works of David Shahar, Nisim Aloni, Yaakov Shabtai, Shulamith Hareven, Haim Beer, Yehoshua Kenaz, and Yeshayahu Koren). The writers discovered the rich plurality of Israeli society, so unlike the uniform types who had been "born from the sea" and had for so long occupied social center stage. The model of the ideal non-diaspora Israeli had blurred the differences between the personae and stressed the uniformity of the native hero as a new phenomenon, without antecedents. The new prototype reversed this tendency. It endeavored to demonstrate how native protagonists were the products of a concrete and finite environment. The sabra, the writers insisted, was the offspring of parents who were themselves products of particular environments and periods, and who had passed on their variegated heritage. Taking on new guises, social realism deepened rather than dissolved.

The "rootless" Israeli was an image that began to appear in the late 1960s and came to occupy center stage in the 1970s and 1980s. Although the fiction of the first native generation had attempted to realize the creation of the New Hebrew, changing social circumstances caused the second generation of native-born writers to retrieve an older figure from the subconscious depths of the national psyche. The protagonists of Appelfeld, Yehoshua, Oz, Kahana-Carmon, Almog, Kaniuk, and Orpaz are free-floating characters who are cut off from the land and from the social environment. They recall nothing so much as the disaffected and alienated Jews of the anti-genrists. The loneliness and alienation that the fiction of the 1930s and 1940s had sought to submerge within an idealized portrait of communal comradeship in arms returned to invigorate the fiction with new vitality and potential.

The new uprooted and alienated protagonist called for more complex methods of characterization, which expanded the genre's presentation of its story. The authors used a variety of techniques: confessional monologues, diaries, eruptions of the fantastic. They left gaps in the narrative that demanded more active reading on the part of the reader. These techniques were not especially innovative by comparison with European and American fiction from Kafka to Faulkner, or even with the earlier generations of Hebrew writers, from Gnessin and Brenner to Steinberg and Agnon. What is significant is that the Hebrew literary wheel kept turning, and the fiction returned to the Israeli landscape and the inner torment and disconnection experienced by earlier generations of Jews. This new emerging Hebrew/Israeli was culturally more problematic. He, and she, were also far more interesting. The social complexity made for human complexity, and together they gave rise to characters and situations far more reflective of genuine historical and cultural issues.

Throughout the Western world, literature, from the early decades of the century, had been moving away from realism and toward other, anti-mimetic forms of representation. Writers sacrificed the goals and values implicit in social realism for the heightened individualism and subjectivity of other fictional forms. The realist tradition in Israel had served an important, perhaps inescapable, national function: It had provided an ideological social model for a population which lacked an established social reality. This was essentially the same function of indoctrination and exemplification that realism served in other countries that, from the 1930s on, stuck to the realist mode of writing, such as the socialist and Communist nations of Eastern Europe. For the writer of social realism the artistic problem was how, without discarding the tenets of social realism altogether, to separate, or blend, social manifesto and documentary material, on the one hand, and the unfolding of individual human destinies on the other. In other words, how did one organize a plot taken from social reality to produce a literary work that would stand independent of that reality, perhaps even challenge its basic assumptions?

This was the principal challenge undertaken by Yizhar's *Days of Ziklag*, undoubtedly the most important novel of and about the period. Deeply committed to the historical materials it fictionalizes, the novel achieves aesthetic independence by displacing the documentary material from the plotting onto the consciousness of the characters and onto the landscape itself. Most of the realist writers responded to the problem of history's control over the artistic subject in similar ways. Another way of loosening the constraints of reality was to introduce an unsettling anti-plot. That is, if the earlier fiction had established a kind of standard narrative which evoked fixed expectations in the readers, now authors began to construct plots which would exactly not meet those expectations. The most notable examples of such subversions of the national metaplot were Pinhas Sadeh's *Life as a Parable* [*Hahayim kemashal,* 1958] and Yehuda Amichai's *Not of This Time, Not of This Place* [*Lo me'akhshav lo mikan,* 1963]. These novels paved the way for a new fiction which would either continue to contend with the metaplot (the works of Tammuz, Hendel, Bartov, the Seneds, Oz, Yehoshua, Ben-Ner, Appelfeld, Kaniuk, and Orpaz) or depart from it altogether (e.g., Kahana-Carmon, Kenaz, and Shahar). Other responses to the constraints of social realism were, like Yizhar's, more structural or stylistic. Authors like Yoram Kaniuk (in *Adam Resurrected* [*Adam ben kelev,* 1968] and *The Last Jew* [*Hayehudi ha' aharon,* 1982]) and Yaakov Shabtai (in *Past Continuous*) altered the relationship between the causal-linear plot and digressive, retarding, elements. They stressed memory and retrospection over progress toward objective goals. They also replaced the omniscient author, or hero-narrator—which had been popular in the 1940s—with multiple points of view or monologues (in the stories of Yehoshua and Oz). They perfected the epistolary methods, the memoir, elaborate triptych constructions—separate stories which illuminate one another (Kahana-Carmon)—and applied authorial omniscience to the stream-of-consciousness method (Yaakov Shabtai).

These developments appeared not only in the fiction of the younger writers, who thus retained their connection with the tradition of social realism, but also in some of the writings of authors who had begun publishing in the 1940s. The 1940s were indeed the formative years for the authors of the first native generation, but as they continued to write during the 1960s, 1970s, and 1980s their writing participated in the general loosening of social realist modes. Of course, even when the authors of social realist fiction—Shamir, Shaham, Megged, and others—had been the central defining force of the fiction, realism had never wholly dominated the field. Such writers as Yitzhak Oren, who began to publish in 1946, and Benjamin Tammuz, whose *Sands of Gold* [*Holot hazahav*] appeared in 1950, were not traditional realists, while, as we have seen, the dominant figure of realism, S. Yizhar, himself developed a distinctive technique of exterior stream of consciousness which did not conform to realist conventions.

The Dor Hamedinah writers of the 1950s were no less unified in their literary forms than the Dor Ba'aretz group. Although various symbolist stories began to appear in the early 1950s (Yehoshua's first short story was published in 1957), realism was hardly banished from the literary scene. Indeed, it continued, in various guises, to occupy an important position alongside other schools and trends. At its best, the realist tradition underwent some interesting and innovative changes in the work of authors of this generation, as it had in the hands of the authors of the Dor Ba'aretz generation. Initially A. B. Yehoshua and Yitzhak Orpaz followed Agnon and Kafka, and their early writings were markedly surrealist. In later years, however, both modified their literary styles. This new fiction linked into two other central schools of classical Hebrew literature: the two forms of romance represented by Berdyczewski, Baron, and Steinberg. In one form of romance, the protagonists and the depicted world are projections of self rather than pictures of an independent reality. In the other form (Berdyczewski, for example), literature takes the form of confession or of myth or saga. Three quite dissimilar writers who followed Berdyczewski's style of romance were Pinhas Sadeh, Amos Oz, and Yoram Kaniuk. From the outset, Sadeh and Oz favored confession and myth. They intensified representation, and in this sense they, and Kaniuk, approximated the expressionist tradition of Bistritski and Hazaz. Sadeh, Kaniuk, and Oz restored expressionism to the fiction. Attracted by the remote and faraway, they introduced mythological materials into the Israeli experience.

At the same time, a trend toward lyrical impressionism also grew stronger, which also had as its object the depiction of the socio-political world. Although likely more indebted to English and French writers ranging from Katherine Mansfield to Marguerite Duras than to its precursors in Hebrew fiction, the underlying premise of this impressionism was that the depiction of the emergent reality in Israel required not verisimilitude but the poetical responses of sensitive personalities. The responsive hero or anti-hero, who did not represent the communal consensus but existed on the fringes of the society, replaced the heroic protagonist in the works of Amichai, Sadeh, Oz, and many others. This lyrical-impressionist tradition continues in Hebrew fiction in such authors as Nisim Aloni, Yehoshua Kenaz, Ruth Almog, Haim Beer, Aharon Appelfeld, Amalia Kahana-Carmon, Yehuda Amichai, and many others.

Related to this development, and pulling the literature even farther in the direction of a new kind of social realist agenda, was the increasing importance after the 1950s of memory within Hebrew fiction. The reason for this is fairly plain: growing consciousness of the Holocaust forced native Israelis, who regarded themselves as children of the region who were entirely severed from the experience of the diaspora, to acknowledge their own place in Jewish history. It imposed upon them the awful, and unwanted, burden of historical identity. Indeed, some of the native-born authors discovered that they shared with European-born Jewry the trauma of survival. This was especially the case after the Six-Day War and the Yom Kippur War, when Israeli society, which felt itself immune to the annihilation that had claimed six million Jewish lives during the Second World War, suddenly confronted its own vulnerability.

For this reason, writers who were themselves survivors, like Aharon Appelfeld, Yonat Sened, and Uri Orlev, were not the only ones to begin to write about history and memory; Israeli-born and -raised authors such as Amichai, Kaniuk, Oz, and Ruth Almog also set out to discover the relationship of the past to the here and now. Hebrew fiction in Eretz Yisrael, which began by proclaiming itself born from the sea, returned to its historical origins. It discarded the stalwart, bright-eyed young heroes their fathers had dreamt of in favor of more authentic and complex New Hebrews, who combined the revitalization in Eretz Yisrael with the traditional (exilic) Jewish heritage of their forefathers. Confronting historical memory also entailed formal changes. The writers were pressed to search for appropriate ways to express the inexpressible, especially as the always inexpressible ground of the past was configured in the more terrifyingly inexpressible horror of the Holocaust.

The social realism of the 1940s was a response to turbulence and uncertainty. It developed under conditions of continuous political and social tension. World Jewish history between the 1940s and the early 1980s was a long series of dramas, both great and small. The growth of the Jewish community in Israel from 600,000 to over four million was also profoundly significant. Thus not only did the setting in which Israeli literature operated keep changing, its readership and materials did too, as wave after wave of immigration flooded the country. In such a world of persistent radical transformation, social realist fiction provided a sense of permanence. It gave shape to heroes and positive values in an environment marked by radical transformation. The Zionist myth assured the people that Eretz Yisrael would liberate the Jews from exile and destruction, and that their return would bring about the spiritual and social rebirth of the Jewish people. The ancient prophecy about the dry bones and the messianic vision, which had been given a secular-Zionist interpretation, were inculcated into the younger generation and affected their perception of the historical events. Their application in literature produced the standard narrative, whether the writings faithfully followed its pattern in all its details or deliberately deviated from it or even contended with it. Even the most personal experiences of the protagonists were marked by this underlying pattern. This was more than a mere adherence to a literary plot. The real necessities that determined the plot and its mimetic modes of representation so stamped themselves upon the authors and their readers as to make realism inescapable.

Earlier writers in the tradition—Agnon, Brenner, and to a certain extent Bistritski and Hazaz—had not, like the social realists, evaded the dark side of reality. They depicted the immigrants from the viewpoint of those who failed to carry out the mission they had undertaken—namely, "to build and be rebuilt" in Eretz Yisrael. The writings of the social realists reversed direction and were commensurately impoverished by the deliberate avoidance of the disappointment, frustration, and failure that characterized their world. In the late 1950s the writers began to fathom the shadows that lurked in this idealized portrayal of the Jewish reality and the deep falsification of the world that the literature promoted. The fullest confrontation with this feature of the realist tradition was Yaakov Shabtai's 1977 novel *Past Continuous,* which pulled to the surface many of the presumably banished ghosts of the Zionist narrative.

In the 1940s and 1950s, however, the social realist tradition, represented by such writers as Aharon Megged, Yigal Mossinsohn, Mordekhai Tabib, Natan Shaham, Yehudit Hendel, Shlomo Nitzan, Hanoch Bartov, Benjamin Tammuz, Haim Gouri, and Yonat and Alexander Sened, held sway over both the writers and the reading public. Designed to be favorably received by the readership, the works were fashioned to avoid alienating the ordinary readership (the single exception is Yizhar, who addressed the cultural elite). In line with this program of social reassurance, Israeli realist fiction of the 1940s and 1950s so clearly identified its extra-literary frame of reference that the average reader could respond to the fiction as if it were a transcript of reality.

This was not only what the public desired but what the writers themselves chose to do. Thus, Natan Shaham responded to criticism of his novel by saying: "I am ready to accept any comment regarding the guns, and if necessary move them elsewhere. Literature concerns itself only with the man who faces their fire. Furthermore, it is best to refrain from searching for 'the real personages' behind the characters in the novel. I can tell you the secret in advance: behind all the characters hides the human hero we both met last night, walking along the road" (Preface, *The Gods Are Lazy* [*Ha'elim 'atseilim,* 1949]). Although forced to admit that sometimes he allowed himself to deviate slightly from the strict contours of the real world, Shaham insisted that on the whole he faithfully represented historical events and that his writing conformed to the precepts of socialist realism. Writing under the sway of Marxist social-realist ideals, the authors thus voluntarily tied their writings to their time and place by means of concrete social materials. This fiction often lacked an independent plot structure of its own and relied upon the historical sequence of events to provide it. It was understood that history was more dramatic than any imaginary plot and would serve better in its place.

It should be noted that the use of documentary material was not confined to realist fiction. Other literary schools, such as the surrealists and expressionists, also sometimes made use of it. For example, *The Day of the Countess* [*Yom harozenet*, 1976] by David Shahar referred to the riots of 1936; *The Lover* [*Hame'ahev*, 1981] by A. B. Yehoshua referred to the Yom Kippur War; and in *Black Box* [*Qufsah shhorah*, 1987] Amos Oz discussed the changing intercommunal relations following the political upset of 1977. But whereas the non-realists processed these materials in accordance with their other literary purposes, the realists presented the materials largely undigested, almost as quotations.

EXPANDING THE LIMITS OF GENRE

For the social realist author the challenge of the form was to ease the restrictions on his or her materials and enlarge the temporal and spatial scope and range of characters in the fictional world without jettisoning the purposes of social realism altogether. In other words, the social realist had to deliver the literature beyond the immediate documentary or pseudo-documentary data and yet remain faithful to that material. One way of achieving greater latitude and freedom was to disguise the materials, by, for example, going back in time, as did Moshe Shamir in his novels about the Second Temple period (*The King of Flesh and Blood*) and the reign of King David (*The Hittite Must Die*). Another was to increase the range of the text's concerns. Shamir's novel *Under the Sun* (1950) and Aharon Megged's *Journey in the Month of Av* [*Masa' Be'av*, 1980], for example, sought to exceed the limited compass of the youth movements by examining intergenerational relations as well. These strategies were not intended to subvert the Zionist narrative, but to reflect it in a different way. Insofar as they remained loyal to a particular interpretation of reality, the limitations of realism continued to constrain the authors.

Another limitation from which realist fiction suffered that its original practitioners had not been able to cast off was the narrow range of its human subjects. The Zionist elite ignored social groups that differed from it in religious observance or communal or political affiliation. Only from the 1950s on did writers begin to take an interest in social groups which had lain beyond the social horizon. For example, Hanoch Bartov wrote about new immigrants in his novel *Everyone Had Six Wings* [*Shesh knafayim la'ehad*, 1954], as did Natan Shaham in *The Wisdom of the Poor*, and Yehudit Hendel wrote about the Oriental Jews in *The Street of Steps* [*Rehov hamadregot*, 1955]. At a later period the Zionist standard plot would actually be decried as non-egalitarian because it disregarded diverse communities, such as the Oriental Jews, Holocaust survivors, and others. Writers from all social groups—Ehud Ben-Ezer, Shimon Ballas, Sami Michael, and Shammai Golan—rebelled against the overpowering consensus. The dominant elite, they suggested, had forfeited its right to lead because it had abandoned its avowed values.

Most of these writers did not question the values of the Zionist standard narrative. They only argued that it had been betrayed by its supposed proponents. Indeed, in time, the revolt against the dominant elite led to the adoption of everything it had rejected. The once socially marginalized writers, especially those from the Sephardic community, became the inheritors of the social realist tradition. Their response is absolutely different from that of a writer like A. B. Yehoshua, who, between the 1960s and 1980s, also concerned himself with marginalized figures but focused his rebellion on actually subverting national values. For example, in his novel *The Lover*, two of the characters, Arditi and Naim, prevail over the third, Adam, who represents the normative Zionist consensus. Arditi, who has deserted from the Israeli army and emigrated, is Zionism's renegade. He is a Sephardi who pretends to be an ultra-Orthodox Jew. Naim is a young Arab. Together they express the triumph of once-marginalized elements of the society: Sephardic, Orthodox, and non-Zionist Jews and Israeli Arabs, who succeed the elitist Ashkenazi pioneering warrior heroes of the past.

As the writers of realist fiction began, from the 1950s on, to deal with the two major experiences of Jewish society in modern times—the Holocaust and the War of Independence—both the severe limitations of this literary form and its potential for transformation and adaptation came into view: How, indeed, could one represent, in social realist terms, the inexplicable event of the Holocaust? Two novels of this period which succeeded in tackling the Holocaust and the historical circumstances which led up to it were *Saul and Yohanna* [*Shaul veYohana*, 1957–1961], by Naomi Frankel, and the Seneds' *Between the Dead and the Living* [*Bein hameitim uvein hahayim*, 1958–1964]. Both of these books deal with Jewish youth in Europe. In Frankel's novel the protagonists are the children of an assimilated German-Jewish family. The plot exposes the forces that led to the rise of Nazism, which finally forced the issue of the Jewish identity of the protagonists. Inevitably, given the writer's Marxist-Zionist orientation, the protagonists end up becoming Zionists. The novel aimed at epic breadth, encompassing most of the social classes of Germany and German Jewry in the late 1920s and early 1930s, simultaneously reconstructing the history of the Jewish community back to the eighteenth century. Yohanna's grandfather, despairing of the promise of assimilation when the Nazis come to power, commits suicide. Saul and Yohanna, however, who represent the next generation, stand poised to emigrate to Eretz Yisrael. Through traditional, naturalist, and mimetic means of representation, Frankel composed nothing less than a literary memorial to the soul of German Jewry.

In this respect the novel is very close to Yonat and Alexander Sened's *Between the Dead and the Living*, which also set itself the task of preserving the memory of the Jewish communities lost in the Holocaust. *Between the Dead and the Living* is an epic saga in four parts, which focuses on Jewish youth in Poland during the 1930s and 1940s. The plot proceeds through two parallel stories: the story of a young man who emigrates to Eretz Yisrael and that of the struggle of his classmates for their liberty and identity in Poland. This struggle climaxes in the Warsaw ghetto uprising, in which the young people's socialist Zionist upbringing is brought to the ultimate test and proves valid. Unlike Frankel, the Seneds were not concerned with the social forces that culminated in the Holocaust. Even though the novel makes use of historical-documentary materials, from the facts and events themselves to their actual written transcription by inhabitants of the Ghetto, the powers that produced the Holocaust are treated as unalterable and inevitable givens. They are an irreparable and inexplicable evil that erupts like a natural phenomenon. The book focuses on the ways in which facing up to historical circumstances is the existential test of every individual. The problem for the Jews is not only humiliation or death. Rather, it is how an individual preserves his or her human identity in conditions of extremity.

By implying that, through historical circumstances, however horrible, the Jews of Europe were restored to their identity and national pride and that the events that transpired provided the occasion whereby the immense spiritual and mental powers of Jewish youth were made manifest, both Frankel and the Seneds, paradoxically, produced optimistic novels. Both affirmed the standard Zionist narrative. In both books the survivors finally reach Eretz Yisrael. Indeed, what both these epics suggest is how stories of the Holocaust, rather than detracting from the national image, could become part of the nation-building process.

The War of Independence, which seemed to have rendered the impossible possible, produced similar problems of realistic literary representation. All the political and military commentary in the world could not explain how the Jewish population of Eretz Yisrael, no bigger than an average European city, was able to withstand forces several times larger than itself. Very few writers took on the challenge of representing the war by writing historical epic or saga. Most of them treated the war by describing what they knew best—their limited local immediate environment. Most of them did not link local events to preceding circumstances nor did they attempt to depict the larger historical context of the War of Independence.

Typical of these novels was Shlomo Nitzan's trilogy, *Between Him and Them* [*Beino leveinam*], *Togetherness* [*Tsvat bitsvat*], and *Not Even a Tent Peg* [*Yated la'ohel*], which were published between 1953 and 1960. More perceptive than most War of Independence fiction in its depiction of the relations between the founding fathers and their fighter sons, it records the story of Bikel, a veteran Zionist activist, and his two sons, Shaulik and Ezra. The first, a doughty warrior, fulfills the father's dream of the New Hebrew man. The second lets him down as a man and as a warrior and is killed in the war. In the third and final volume, however, the surviving son is also shown to fail the test of new manhood. Although the novel depicts the war from a wide variety of aspects—the battlefield, the home front, the regional defense, the headquarters—it does not capture the full historical significance of the war. Nor does it plumb the psychology of the men who brought off this miracle.

Other writers chose to represent the war through chronicles, such as Abba Kovner, whose two-volume novel *Face to Face* [*Panim 'el panim*] appeared in 1953–1955. Moshe Shamir also did not depict the war itself, but described other conflicts that preceded it, either by a few years (in *He Walked through the Fields, Under the Sun,* and *With His Own Hands*) or by several thousands of years, as in *The King of Flesh and Blood* and *The Hittite Must Die*. Yizhar's answer to the War of Independence was *Days of Ziklag*. If the Frankel and the Sened novels resembled the memorial books to the obliterated Jewish communities, the War of Independence books resembled the books of the period published in memory of fallen soldiers and the fighting units. Shamir created this quasi-fictional genre in his chapters on his brother Elik in *With His Own Hands*. The warrior sagas appeared in parallel to the memorial books as fictional commentaries designed to give the latter an added dimension.

The expectation that creative artists would give their readership portraits of their sons and comrades in the image of the New Hebrew, the warrior-pioneer, accounts for the proliferation in the 1940s and 1950s of bildungsromans. These generally involved a test of maturity, in which the young man (rather more than the young woman) had to prove his readiness to sacrifice himself for the society, thereby qualifying for membership in it. The emphasis on the test of fighting manhood as a principal qualification limited the range of characters in the realist fiction of the period.

Nonetheless, as early as 1956 a new sort of bildungsroman appeared which served to broaden the form. Uri Orlev's *Lead Soldiers* [*Hayalei 'oferet*, 1956] was a realistic autobiographical account of two children in the Ghetto and concentration camps during the Holocaust. It was not concerned with the New Hebrew, either as a stereotype or an exception. Rather, it dealt with the Old Jewish child in the context of Europe during the Second World War. When the writers of native realism encountered these survivor novels, they found them problematic. The subsequent extension of the subject of the Holocaust into the social realist tradition suggests the sense of guilt experienced by these writers as they came to regard themselves as somehow responsible for the demise of the Old Jew.

Thus were the bildungsromans of Hanoch Bartov informed by the presence of the heretofore banished Old Jew. Severely judging the exilic failings of diaspora Jewry, Bartov nonetheless conveyed an attitude of charitable forgiveness. The following is the reaction of the native-born protagonist in *The Brigade* [*Pitz'ei Bagrut*, 1965, literally: "acne"] when he is confronted with the ruined world of his brethren:

> I heard their lives, and all the while I saw ours. Where was I all these nineteen years—I love, I hate, I achieve, I lose, I am miserable, I am happy. Nothing more than a skin full of hollow words. Let me kiss your wounds, children. Let me run away from you, children, and forget you quickly, at once, and fill with glazier's putty the scratches made by rusty nails. Take chocolate. Take all the money in my pocket. I make you a present of my belt. Only let me get away from here. (p. 142)

The man who speaks these lines serves as a soldier in the Jewish Brigade in Italy. He comes to feel guilt, identification, and an urge to suppress the experience of European Jewry. Despite these feelings, or, rather, in reflection of the ambivalence he feels, he cannot work up vindictive hatred for the Germans. When the Brigade reaches Germany he refuses to join his comrades who plan to wreak vengeance on the Germans. He is ashamed of his impotence as an avenger. However, he is also embarrassed by his prowess as a warrior. Principally, Bartov's novel explores the complexity of the need both to accept the historical continuity with European Jewry and to affirm the dimensions of the new Jewish existence in Eretz Yisrael.

His 1975 novel *The Dissembler* [*Habad'ai*] returned to this conflict. A cross between a spy thriller and a political novel, it follows two life stories: that of a Holocaust survivor, who pretends to be a New Hebrew, and that of a native Israeli who, in the process of uncovering the other's terrible history, discovers in himself a residue of the Old Jew. In a raw attempt to survive, the European Jew disguises himself both as a German and a Frenchman, playing a different role in each guise, and, finally, as a sabra. It is as a sabra that he is killed in one of Israel's wars. The subject of

Israeli identity became one of the central issues of Israeli fiction in general and of the bildungsroman in particular. As Haim Gouri, in *The Interrogation* and *The Story of Reuel* [*Hahakirah; Sipur Re'u'el,* 1980] also showed, the road to the fulfillment of the Zionist standard narrative was far from straight, and the maturation of the native sons was beset by internal and external conflicts.

A literary form related to the bildungsroman, which expressed the disillusion of the War of Independence generation and their resistance to the dominant narrative, was the picaresque novel, with its mischief-making *picaro,* whose uninhibited and wild adventures exposed the failings of Israeli society. These fictions constituted a kind of anti-bildungsroman. They depicted the hero as a reflection of society's own decline. One of the first of these picaresque novels was David Shahar's *Moon of Honey and Gold* [*Yerah hadvash vehazahav,* 1959]. Like the archetype of the modern *picaro* in Thomas Mann's *Felix Krull,* the novel's protagonist, Shmulik, exploits the corruption of his society to his own advantage. Although the standard Zionist narrative flickers in the background of this novel, it serves only as a satirical yardstick by which to measure the diminished realities of the moment. The book presents no positive characters. Shmulik himself is a rogue whose erotic adventures cut a swathe through the society, which is depicted as cynical and parochial. Only some strange and distant force, personified by an aristocratic gentile French lover, can promise any measure of possible remediation.

Another such novel was Benjamin Tammuz's trilogy: *The Life of Elyakum* (1965), *Castle in Spain* [*Besof ma'arav,* 1966, literally: "At the End of the West"], and *Hallucinations* [*Sefer hahazayot,* 1969]. One of the Native Generation of writers, Tammuz never wholly accepted the conventions of his time, as evidenced by his collection of short stories *Sands of Gold,* 1950. The characters of these stories are fine, sensitive individuals who represent no one but themselves. Tammuz's Elyakum, like Shahar's Shmulik, is revolted by Israeli society, and he, too, seeks to flee from the social battlefield into the arms of a highly cultured Swedish noblewoman. In Tammuz's trilogy, however, what begins as comic picaresque gradually becomes pathetic anti-picaresque. During the course of his experiences Elyakum undergoes radical psychological transformation. In the first part of the trilogy he is an easily exploited and abused innocent; in the second he is somewhat wiser; and in the final part he is a miserable lunatic, institutionalized in an asylum, bewailing both past and present. It is almost as if, in the process of developing the logic of his protagonist's personality, Tammuz discovered beneath the surface of the disillusioned New Hebrew the desperate and despairing Old Jew. By the time his novel *Minotaur* was published in 1980 his criticism of Israeli society had become truly sweeping. The protagonist Alexander Abramov falls in love with an English woman he has never met. He feels no connection whatsoever to the country. Never truly a realist to begin with, in *Minotaur* and in *Nightingale and Chameleon* [*Haziqit vehazamir*, 1989] Tammuz approximated the sophisticated neo-realism of Yitzhak Ben-Ner, Yeshayahu Koren, and especially Yehoshua Kenaz.

THE INHERITANCE OF THE PROGENY: DISRUPTIONS AND NEW ERUPTIONS OF SOCIAL REALISM

Two writers who catalyzed the changes in Israeli fiction and transformed the tradition in the post-1950s period, stylistically as well as thematically, were Pinhas Feldman-Sadeh in *Life as a Parable* (1958) and Yehuda Amichai in *Not of This Time, Not of This Place* (1963). Feldman-Sadeh was born in Lvov, Poland, in 1929, came to Palestine in 1934, and died in 1993. He was raised in a kibbutz and was familiar with the social milieu of the War of Independence writers. Rejecting the philosophy of the collective and the semiology of the youth movement, Sadeh's protagonist sets out to create a myth of self that is closer to Jewish heterodox movements such as the Sabbateans and the Frankists, and to Christianity than to conventional Zionism. Written in the style of confession—in the tradition of St. Augustine and Jean-Jacques Rousseau, as well as of Brenner and Feierberg—the text is replete with philosophical speculation, religious enthusiasm, and strange erotic experiences. In the Russia of Dostoyevsky or in Europe or the United States after D. H. Lawrence and Henry Miller the book would not have caused a stir. But in 1950s Israel the novel caused a sensation. It exposed a hidden underbelly of primal urges, not to mention Christian tendencies, that the society had otherwise kept in careful check. And it gave voice to an individualistic, eccentric "I" that seemed the very opposite of the collectively defined, ideologically committed New Hebrew.

In a similar manner Yehuda Amichai's *Not of This Time, Not of This Place* also revealed the darker side of the society. Amichai was born in Würzburg, Germany, in 1924 and came to Palestine in 1934. He fought in the British Army in the Second World War and in the Palmah in the War of Independence and, even though his religious upbringing differed from that of the majority (he was raised in an Orthodox family), he shared the major experiences of his generation. The protagonist of Amichai's novel is a split personality who doubly defies accepted values and norms. One side of him—as presented by the omniscient author—betrays his wife, the daughter of his Palmah commander, with a non-Jewish woman. The other side—as described in the protagonist's own confession—is equally bent on challenging normative assumptions; the hero discovers in his return to his native Germany not an historical monster but simply the scene of his childhood.

The artistic innovation of the two novels lay in Sadeh's revival of the expressionist mode and in the structural complexity of Amichai's novel, which was also rather expressionist. These different artistic qualities corresponded to the changing values expressed in the books. Amichai and Sadeh disrupted the consensus of the Zionist standard narrative and introduced, respectively, a counterplot and a deviant plot. Neither was a realist writer. Amichai's richly metaphorical language raised the vernacular to a higher poetical level, whereas Sadeh achieved stylistic originality, in the rhetorical manner of the poet U. Z. Greenberg, by intensifying the phrasing. These aspects, too, changed the readers' expectations and opened the way for as-yet-unimagined new possibilities. The two poet-novelists had a direct impact on the younger fiction writers, and under their influence the older realist writers also became more receptive to new ideas.

A whole new constellation of literary figures arose, among them poets Zach, Avidan, Dor, Sivan, Pinkas, and Ravikovitch; novelists such as Shahar, Yehoshua, Oz, Kahana-Carmon, Kenaz, Shabtai, Appelfeld, and Orpaz; dramatists such as Nisim Aloni; and critics such as Natan Zach, Binyamin Hrushovsky, Dan Miron, Gabriel Moked, Adi Zemach, Hillel Barzel, and Gershon Shaked. The dominant tendency in fiction became non-realist. New characters emerged. And symbolic, expressionist voice was given to the darker forces that had been suppressed in the national psyche for many years. These winds of change did not pass over the older authors. They too absorbed new influences from outside, and many of them became interested in Anglo-Saxon and French cultures and involved with the modernist movement in Hebrew and world literature.

These changes were gradual and took a variety of forms. As fictional points of view became increasingly subjectivized, the realist writers themselves began to adopt more sophisticated techniques. Some chose complex narrative methods, including diary excerpts, complex time structures, and internarrative associations. Others chose the technique of multiple viewpoints (e.g., Megged, Shaham, Bartov, and Shamir). Some used typographic means to indicate different layers of time or reality (e.g., Bartov and Hendel). For most of these writers, however, it was their themes rather than their styles which underwent the profoundest change, and they did not always succeed in matching the form to the content. Some of the realist authors attempted to adapt themselves to the extra-literary developments by presenting a conventional subject from a new angle. Inevitably, the changing perception affected the form as well, and conversely, the demands of form altered the worldview.

One member of the Native Generation of authors who adapted to the changes in society and literature was Haim Gouri. His novel *The Chocolate Deal* [*'Isqat hashoqolad,* 1965] came out after the Eichmann trial and after Aharon Appelfeld's early works about Holocaust survivors, *Smoke* [*'Ashan,* 1962] and *In the Fertile Valley* [*Bagai haporeh,* 1963]. All the characters of Gouri's novel are diaspora Jews, anti-heroes without a trace of Israeli qualities. The impressionist-atmospheric style matches the novel's modernist tendency. The characters are each intensified to some extent by the romantic effect of the mysterious atmosphere, though they are mainly engaged in black marketeering and in trying to piece together their shattered lives.

By the late 1960s the Seneds had also abandoned the safe ground of realist fiction. Like many other writers they began to experiment with techniques similar to the nouveau roman of Nathalie Sarraute and Alain Robbe-Grillet in order to give a more individual imprint to familiar themes, such as the kibbutz, the Holocaust, and the Ghetto uprisings, and to better express the modern experience. Formally innovative, the Seneds' novel *Another Attempt* [*Hanisayon hanosaf,* 1968], and their novella *Tandu* (1973) combined associative structures, compound dialogues, and other modernist devices. A large part of the text consists of events prior to the action and dialogue. Their later works, *The Land Inhabited* (1981), *Oasis* (1988), and *We'll Call Him Leon* [*Nikra' lo Le'on,* 1985], were modernist recyclings of materials earlier presented in a realist manner.

Also of an older generation, Yehudit Hendel, a contemporary of Shamir, Megged, Bartov, and Shaham, started out as a realist with her collection of short stories *They Are Different People* [*'Anashim 'aherim heim,* 1950]. In the late 1960s, however, she joined the literary revolt with a lyrical-impressionist novel *The Yard of Momo the Great* [*Hahatzer Shel Momo Hagedolah,* 1970]. This book takes place in Haifa's lower city. Its characters are marginalized, despondent, and poverty-stricken Oriental Jews and Holocaust survivors, alone and abandoned, in the twilight period before the 1967 war. At the heart of the novel is a threesome. The main protagonist, Shaul, presumably a Holocaust survivor, is in love with the unhappy Tamara, who has been married three times. Her third husband visits her once a fortnight; the rest of the time she lives with Shaul. The husband, Joachim, is a strange sickly creature who arouses feelings of guilt in Shaul; after Joachim's death in a car crash, which might have been a suicide, Shaul departs from the scene of the novel. The plot develops not in an additive sequence (i.e., as a string of separate scenes linked by the protagonist), nor consecutively. Rather, it compiles diverse subplots that correlate with the main story, producing a fictional world governed by its own laws.

This was a transitional novel in Hendel's work. It revealed her growing preoccupation with morbidity and death. This is manifested in her
prose poem *The Other Power* [*Hakoah ha'aher*, 1984], which is an elegy
for her deceased husband, the painter Zvi Mairovich, and in her short
story collection *Small Change* [*Kesef qatan*, 1988]. In *The Other Power*
Hendel abandoned the usual rules of plot construction to create a half-
documentary, half-poetic prose portrait, wistful and quietly elegaic. The
stories of *Small Change* are lyrical and grotesque. Not only do they explore death, but they also express great bitterness against patriarchal tyr-
anny and general inhumanity.

Although Shulamith Hareven is perhaps one of the most authentic
realist writers, who continued writing in this mode even after other authors had changed their styles of composition, nonetheless she, too,
participated in the general expansion of Hebrew literary forms. Like the
1940s and 1950s realists, Hareven initially wrote in an elevated style. Later
she shifted to a more functional realist register, and finally produced a
stylized non-mimetic prose. In most of her writings she describes the vulnerability of women. Coming before the wave of feminist fiction in Israel,
and simultaneous with the production of male fiction by authors such as
Amos Oz, her perceptive depiction of the world of women is especially
striking.

Her best story collection is *Loneliness* [*Bdidut*, 1980]. Like the short
stories, the novel *City of Many Days* ['*Ir yamim rabim*, 1972] is social
impressionist. It takes place in Jerusalem between the 1920s and the late
1940s and the War of Independence and focuses on social issues from
multiple perspectives. The plot revolves around Sara Amorillo, daughter
of an old Sephardic Jerusalem family, and her relations with her elderly
German-born teacher, Dr. Barzel; with her husband, Elias Amorillo; and
with her past and future lover, Matti. These and other relationships illuminate the social diversity of the country. Although the tensions between
the various ethnic communities (the Ashkenazi newcomers and the established Sephardi community) and among the English, the Arabs, and the
Jews are accorded real attention in the novel, the characters are depicted
positively, with a touch of humor, such that the book does not descend
into pathos and melodrama.

In the 1980s Hareven began to write highly stylized, tightly woven
archaic novellas, modern in their economy of depiction and plot and intense atmospheric effects. The first of these, *The Miracle Hater* [*Sone'
hanisim*, 1983], reinterprets the Israelite exodus from Egypt. The central
character, Eshkhar, nurses an Oedipal attachment to his adoptive mother
Baitah, whose lover he later becomes. Only after her death is he capable of
forming a relationship with another woman, Dinah, and only after the

birth of their son are the two of them mature enough to enter the promised land. Staccato sentences create an archaic atmosphere and dramatic density. They produce a myth in miniature. There is no one-to-one allegorical correlation between biblical events and present realities. Nonetheless, by projecting onto the distant past the polarities of slavery and freedom, individualism and collectivity, backward-looking Oedipality and progenerative sexuality, the novel strongly intimates the relevance of ancient stories for contemporary Jewish-Israeli society. Even so, the alterations in Hareven's writing, as in the writing of the Seneds, seem to constitute a self-conscious change of form rather than to represent an organic evolution.

As we have seen, external developments and the search for new literary techniques caused many writers to modify their themes and styles in similar ways. Thus, for example, the impact of Amos Oz's *Elsewhere, Perhaps* is discernible in such kibbutz fiction as Shaham's *First Person Plural* (1968), Naomi Frankel's *My Beloved Friend* [*Dodi vere'I*, 1973], and Yitzhak Ben-Ner's story "Athalia" (1979). Like Oz, they examine social and sexual mores in the kibbutz; the first two works also use a technique of multiple viewpoints like the technique Oz also uses. What this demonstrates is that the realist writers did not remain set in their ways but strove to adapt themselves by means of new techniques and themes to changing social and cultural conditions. They did this both in response to the new circumstances and by way of emulating the currents which predominated Hebrew fiction after the late 1950s. And since those currents, in their turn, had been influenced by modernist movements in Western literature, the realist writers too were both directly and indirectly affected by developments outside of Israel as well as within it. The local currents broke open new channels, with Western culture remaining the main source of inspiration.

In the 1970s the realist tradition went on the defensive and tried to justify itself in literary and political terms. Despite the pull toward more innovative and experimental forms, the Hebrew writers were not wholly able to put aside the pull toward ideology and the commitment to the collective. Even while celebrating individual experience and feeling, the fiction remained gripped by the embrace of communal ideals. As a mode of representation realism hardly disappeared from the scene, even if it was occasionally put to ideological objectives somewhat different from those of the preceding generation of authors. Writers like Naomi Frankel, Zvi Luz, and Shulamith Lapid in her historical novel *Hgai Oni* (1982) remained faithful to traditional realism, making no attempt to adopt the intellectual and technical sophistication of their contemporaries and the younger writers.

Therefore, the 1970s also saw a return to realism in the form of popular fiction, in novels by Dan Ben-Amotz, Ehud Ben-Ezer, and Shammai Golan, which infused ideological elements into the trivial intrigues of their plots. Ben-Amotz and Ben-Ezer wrote didactic social novels. Like their predecessors Bar-Yosef and Mossinsohn, they observed social issues from the worldview of their protagonists in a naturalist rather than purely realist style. A typical example of this was Ben-Ezer's novel *The Quarry* [*Hamahtsevah*, 1963], which depicted the relations of the Sephardic Jewish immigrants (especially within the Kurdish community) and the settled Ashkenazis as an all-out battle for sex and power. The immigrants in the novel are depicted not as an uprooted community struggling to adapt to new surroundings, but as one which is still dominated by naked primal urges.

Although a contemporary of the War of Independence writers, Ben-Amotz, the most notable of the writers of popular fiction, began in the 1960s to address a readership outside the confines of the literary public. His characteristic blend of pornography and social bitterness met the social-cultural needs of disaffected young people on the left. Ben-Amotz's readers preferred light fiction that expressed anti-establishment ideas and required little mental effort, and his novels enjoyed considerable commercial success. Although lacking psychological depth or poetic power, they offered a new narrative to a mass readership that rejected Zionism. Among Ben-Amotz's popular anti-establishment novels were *To Remember, To Forget* [*Lizkor velishkoah*, 1968], which raised issues about Holocaust memory, and *Don't Give a Damn* [*Lo sam zayin*, 1973], which deals with the heroics of war. In their time these books represented a form of rebellion. But lacking appropriate literary form they ended up as merely commercial ventures. Existing side by side with new modernist writings and with the experiments of the older writers who were trying out new forms, such works, which included adventure and detective stories, romances, and didactic melodramas, were fairly popular in the early 1960s.

Netivah Ben-Yehuda was another novelist who continued the realist tradition. She wrote on the same vernacular level as did Ben-Amotz but did not trivialize her subjects. Her *1948 between the Calendars* [*1948 Bein Hasfirot*, 1981] and *Through the Binding Ropes* [*Miba'ad la'avotot*, 1985] demythologized the Palmah by demolishing the poeticized image created by the realists of the first Native Generation.

Two novels which appeared in 1962 and which mediated between old realist convention and the emerging non-realist genres were *The Fifth Heaven* [*Baraqiya' hahamishi*] by Rachel Eytan and *The Heap* [*Ha'aremah*] by Shlomo Kalo. Eytan's style blended literary diction with the dialect of youngsters in a Tel Aviv institution for homeless children. Better than any of her predecessors she succeeded in reflecting the linguistic pluralism of Israeli society. While remaining faithful to the realist-naturalist tradition, she also focused on a marginal social subject, thus extending the frontiers of fiction. Moreover, some passages in the novel went beyond the ostensibly realistic effect and hinted at other possibilities. In a sense, Eytan laid the groundwork which later neo-realists, such as Kenaz, Ben-Ner, Koren, and Shabtai, would develop further.

Shlomo Kalo's novel *The Heap* marked two turning points in Hebrew literary history: the beginning of modernist fiction in Israel, and the advent of Sephardic and Ashkenazi authors who wrote about the immigrant Sephardic community. *The Heap* has a special place in the history of Hebrew fiction because it is the neo-modernist social protest of an immigrant author. The novel is constructed as a series of spatially related anecdotes about a number of unemployed new immigrants from diverse communities—Czech, Bulgarian, Moroccan, Russian, Turkish, and Indian, among others. Seeking work at the municipal offices, they are told to dispose of a heap of garbage. They all try, together and separately, and they all fail. Before their dislocation to Israel, these people had led uneventful but productive lives. Their present situations reflect existential crises. At the same time, they embody the archetypal experience of human failure. In that sense, Kalo may be closer to A. B. Yehoshua than to his contemporaries, who protested against ethnic discrimination. A novel that attempted to deal with social problems of the late 1970s was Ben-Ner's *A Far Land* [*Eretz Rehokah*, 1981], which, in the context of the decline of the labor movement, the rise of the right-wing Likud, and the visit of Egyptian president Anwar Sadat, dealt with relations between Ashkenazi and Sephardic Jews, resident Israelis, and immigrants.

In general, the social realist tradition survived after the 1960s in the writings from the peripheral immigrant communities, who had become a numerical majority and yet did not enjoy a proportional share of the country's economic, social, and cultural resources. By and large these were people who had been impelled to migrate to Israel by political events in their countries of origin rather than by Zionist motivation. The writers included Shimon Ballas, who published *The Transit Camp* [*Hama'abarah*] in 1964; Sami Michael, *Equal and More Equal* [*Shavim veshavim yoter*, 1974]; Amnon Shamosh, *Michel Ezra Safra and Sons* [*Mishel 'Ezra Safra' uvanav*, 1978]; and Yitzhak Gormezano-Goren, *An Alexandrian Summer* [*Qayits 'Alexandroni*, 1978].

The Transit Camp and *Equal and More Equal* both represented immigrant protests against the patronizing attitudes of Israeli culture. At a time when the dominant literary form was modernism, their social realistic fiction represented a subversive minority voice, thus inverting the direction of Hebrew writing from social realism to modernism. Michael and

Ballas were the two leading immigrant novelists. Both of them had belonged to the young intellectual elite in Iraq. Both had been associated with the Communist Party. When they arrived in Israel they experienced personal as well as communal discrimination. After they had learned Hebrew and could express themselves in it, they voiced their resentment.

In time, however, their writing became less concerned with immigrant problems, and because of their Communist backgrounds and feelings of resentment, they became allied with Israeli-Arab intellectuals. Ballas's novel *A Locked Room* [*Heder na'ul,* 1980] and Michael's *Refuge* [*Hasut,* 1977] and *A Handful of Fog* [*Hofen shel 'arafel,* 1979] depicted this alliance. *Refuge,* for example, dealt with the relations between Arab and Jewish members of the Party during the Yom Kippur War. The Arab protagonists go to the house of a Jewish Communist woman, Shulah, whose husband Mardukh, who had been imprisoned as a Communist in Iraq, has just been called up for military duty. Fathi resents the Jews who, ideologically close to him, also must shelter him. Shulah, on the other hand, cannot reconcile her patriotism, including her feelings for her husband at the front and for a former lover who gets killed in the war, with her Communist loyalties. A critique of the Israeli Communist Party, the book presents the movement as dogmatic, a sect of believers, driven by divisions between Jews and Arabs which their universalist doctrines cannot bridge. In the end, *Refuge,* despite its representation of the views of Palestinian Arabs, Israeli citizens, and inhabitants of the occupied territories, winds up affirming the Zionist consensus. For Michael, as for Ballas, the ideological message was more important than subtleties of characterization or plot.

Amnon Shamosh's *Michel Ezra Safra and Sons* is an entirely different kind of work, in which the writer set out to restore the self-esteem of the immigrants by going back to their roots. The book is a family saga about the Safra family in Aleppo, Syria, before the attacks on the Jewish community during the Israeli War of Independence which necessitated their departure. The book presents a Zionist ideology, but it also makes clear the author's preference for the lost past in Aleppo, where the family was united and where it flourished without any discrimination and without discussions about the status of Eastern Jews in a society in which they felt alienated. Another nostalgic-folkloristic novel, which also appeared in 1978, is Gormezano-Goren's *An Alexandrian Summer.* Alexandria, Egypt, is for Goren what Allepo is for Shamosh. Although his literary technique is more complex and interesting, here too the standard Zionist narrative is set against a secret wish to return to the native land. This nostalgia for roots is also a major subject of Sami Michael's *Victoria* (1993).

In this same tradition of subversive protest against the dominant establishment, Anton Shammas published his novel *Arabesques* [*Arabesqot*] in 1986. A Christian Arab writing in a very rich Hebrew, Shammas became the voice of the major minority in the State of Israel. In a style reminiscent of Yizhar he described the village of his youth. The main protagonist embodies the confrontation between the Jewish colonial establishment and the solitude of the Palestinian citizen of Israel. While the non-Ashkenazi Jewish writers like Ballas and Michael protested against the ruling establishment by writing social realist fictions, Shammas, with even greater sophistication, confronted and subverted the society through their very language.

* * *

The foregoing review of literary realism, which dominated Hebrew writing between the 1940s and the 1980s, delineated some of the structural and thematic patterns which characterized, and differentiated, its various practitioners, especially as the authors of Dor Ba'aretz, the first native generation of writers, came into conflict with the second generation of native writers, Dor Hamedinah, who challenged the basic formal and thematic assumptions of Dor Ba'aretz. As we have seen, the movement did not remain static. Nor did it divide neatly across generational lines. Nonetheless it continued to persist within Hebrew writing of the contemporary period, coexisting with another form of literary production that did actually break ranks with the social realists and produce new and different fictional forms. I now turn to the New Wave of Hebrew writers and to the subversion of the Zionist metaplot that they effected.

11

POLITICAL CRISIS
AND LITERARY REVOLUTION

THE NEW WAVE, 1960–1980

As we have seen, the realist tradition was never homogeneous. Although there were common denominators, there was also a broad range of techniques and themes. Different schools of fiction interacted and the realists themselves changed their role within the evolving literary system as a whole. The realist writers whose careers began in the 1940s and 1950s were no longer the same in the 1970s, and the later realists, who appeared in the 1970s, were unlike their predecessors.

In the 1960s and 1970s the writings of the realists exceeded the primary boundaries of the tradition, some of them producing the most impressive accomplishments in the genre. These included Bartov's *Whose Little Boy Are You?* [*Shel mi 'atah yeled?*, 1970]; Aharon Megged's *The Living on the Dead;* Natan Shaham's *First Person Plural* and *The Rosendorf Quartet;* Yonat and Alexander Senet's *Between the Living and the Dead* (and some of their later works); Mossinsohn's *Judas;* Yehudit Hendel's *The Yard of Momo the Great,* and some other works of hers and of Shulamith Hareven's; and certain of Benjamin Tammuz's writings, such as *Sands of Gold, Minotaur,* and *Nightingale and Chameleon.* At the same time, and appearing almost as a negation of the expressionism, surrealism, and impressionism of the post-1948 period, there developed a school of neo-realists, whose works tried to incorporate and adapt elements of the non-realist tradition to new social demands, which seemed to call, once again, for a direct connection between the literature and the socio-political world. The neo-realists include Yeshayahu Koren, Yitzhak Ben-Ner, Meir Shalev, and, in a way, Yaakov Shabtai as well. Further away from realism were such writers as Ruth Almog and Yehoshua Kenaz, whose writings nonetheless represented a later dialectical development.

For the most part, however, the writers of the second generation of native authors, Dor Hamedinah, challenged and resisted realism, introducing into the literary canon alternative anti-realist modes of representation. As we observe this generation of writers, it seems necessary to say that all of my comments in this chapter and the next are preliminary and incomplete. How Israeli culture will be viewed retrospectively, and how the literature will then seem to have reflected or countered general historical, political, and literary forces, remains to be seen. Also complicating judgment is the academization of literary scholarship over the last several decades, both in Israel and abroad, and the fact that recent writers, in Hebrew at home and in translation abroad, have already been extensively analyzed. With these cautions in place, I want to discuss fiction from the 1950s on.

FROM THE SINAI CAMPAIGN TO THE YOM KIPPUR WAR: POLITICS AND THE LITERARY SUBJECT

As we have noted, post-realist Hebrew fiction was created mainly by writers who were born in the 1930s and 1940s. Nonetheless it must be noted that some of its leading proponents were born earlier but only appeared on the literary scene in the late 1950s and 1960s. The principal names are Benjamin Tammuz, Yitzhak Orpaz, Yehuda Amichai, Nisim Aloni, Amalia Kahana-Carmon, David Shahar, Amos Kenan, and Yoram Kaniuk. The development of these writers and those who were born in the 1930s and 1940s was marked by the major historical events that affected their lives. Although literature is not simply the response of artistic models to social ones, and it is undoubtedly also determined by various internal developmental factors, attention must be paid to the social-historical backdrop of the literary texts. Indeed, a close examination reveals that as early as the late 1950s the attitude of Hebrew fiction toward the Zionist metaplot had begun to change and that texts challenging it were already beginning to appear in print. All the age groups were disillusioned when what used to be a community of voluntary idealists turned into a bureaucratic state swamped by waves of immigration. The writers were reflecting the feelings of the elite, which felt it was losing the cultural identity that the Hebrew community had forged for itself since the 1920s. The Sinai War, the Eichmann trial, the Lavon Affair, the revolt against Ben-Gurion, the Six-Day War, the War of Yom Kippur, and the political upheaval of the late 1970s all left their marks on creative people of all ages, but especially on the younger ones, for whom the Holocaust and the War of Independence had not been formative experiences. As we have seen, the disenchantment was expressed both in the writings of the realists and in some of the later writers of that generation, such as Amichai and Sadeh. In the early 1950s Amos Kenan responded to the "outbreak of the State" in his satirical column Uzi & Co. in the daily *Ha'aretz*. And in 1963 he returned to the subject in a modernist-absurd novel, *At the Station* [*Batahanah*]. The year 1963 became a milestone in the development of non-realist Hebrew fiction. The following lines from the first pages of Kenan's novel reflect the mindset of the 1940s dreamers who became the disillusioned and disaffected individuals of the 1950s and 1960s: "Perhaps to feel nostalgic? Perhaps to dream? Or dream about nostalgia? Or be nostalgic for a dream? I don't know. I don't know. I do know that it can't go on like this" (p. 13).

For those who were born in the 1930s, the Sinai Campaign of 1956 was the experience that changed their relation to the Zionist metaplot. Unlike the war of 1948, this seemed more a war of choice than a matter of survival. It was also the first time that the Israeli armed forces encountered the masses of Arab refugees in the Gaza Strip. As one soldier put it in a volume that appeared in 1967, years later:

> In the last round, in the Sinai war, I was in Gaza, and I remember one picture. . . . We were driving through the main street and the fellows—the inhabitants—stood in the doorways and clapped their hands in a slow, forced sort of beat. It was a filthy picture. . . . I remembered all the pictures from films about conquering armies and I had a really sickening feeling. (*The Seventh Day* [*Si'ah Lohamim*], p. 118)

It was also during the Sinai war that Arab villagers in Kfar Kassem in Israel, returning from their fields after the curfew, were mowed down by soldiers. The massacre of men, women, and children caused moral shock throughout the Jewish community.

The ambivalence engendered by the war brought about changes in the form as well as the content of the fiction. Struggling against imaginary external censors and genuine internal ones, writers produced anti-establishment allegories that to some degree veiled their intentions. This accounts for works such as Aharon Megged's *Fortunes of a Fool* (1959) and *The Escape* [*Habrihah*, 1962] as well as the early allegories of A. B. Yehoshua, which began to appear in the late 1950s in the newspaper *Lamerhav* [*To the Expanse*] and in the periodical *Keshet* [*Spectrum*]. Yehoshua's story "The Last Commander" ["Hamefaqed ha'aharon"], for example, which appeared in the collection *The Death of the Old Man* [*Mot hazaqein*] in 1962, is about a group of soldiers who prefer sleep to fighting. It evokes the weary distaste for war felt by the Sinai generation. A more direct response to the transformations in attitude effected by the Sinai Campaign and the Lavon Affair, in which Israelis plotted, and failed, to blow up Americans and incriminate the Egyptians, was mounted in Yariv Ben-Aharon's book *The Battle* [*Haqrav*], which was published in 1967, the year of the Six-Day War. In *Skin for Skin* ['*Or be'ad 'or,* 1962], Orpaz protested the war and the values that led up to it, as did Amos Oz in one of his major works of fiction, *My Michael* [*Mikha 'el sheli*]. Although the book appeared only in 1968, after the Six-Day War, nonetheless its inner climax corresponds to the Sinai Campaign, which was perceived as discharging tensions that had built up during the years of "living on the edge."

Various aspects of the Holocaust that the Israelis had been unable to contend with directly remained suppressed until the 1960s. The writings of the realist authors of the 1920s generation, for example, Naomi Frankel and Yonat and Alexander Sened, had demonstrated that the period of the Holocaust might reveal the immense spiritual and mental powers of Jewish youth. *Saul and Yohanna* and *Between the Dead and the Living* expressed belief in the human ability to contend even with historical catastrophe. Both novels also affirmed the Zionist metaplot. They implied that, despite the catastrophic defeat of the Jewish people, the metaplot would triumph and that exile would be succeeded by liberation. In like manner, in the minds of many people during the 1950s the Warsaw Ghetto uprising (itself a reenactment of the last Jewish stand in Masada against the Romans) was the ideal to be upheld by the soldiers in their war against the Arab aggressor. Elead Peled, a Palmah commander in beleaguered Safed, referred to this example in his address to his men: "The banner of Israel, which fell in the battles of the ghettoes, will fly anew on the fortress of Safed. Safed, the capital of the Galilee, will be ours. And you warriors, be strong and bold, and let the heroes of the ghettoes be your symbol and landmark on Israel's path to liberty" ("An Open Call").

Following the Eichmann trial in 1961, elements of the Holocaust which had been repressed by Israeli society began to rise to the surface of the national consciousness. Some of these elements had already been touched on in the Kastner trial in 1953, when a man named Malkiel Greenwald accused Rudolph Kastner, who had been a leader of the Hungarian-Jewish community, of collaborating with Nazis. In 1955 a judge concluded that, while Kastner was "a servant of Satan," there was insufficient evidence to convict him. The State appealed, but in 1957 Kastner was murdered by a right-wing extremist. The fact of Israeli ignorance and disregard concerning the extermination of six million fellow Jews became especially painful.

After the Eichmann trial an editorial article in *Moznayim,* the organ of the Writers' Association, put it this way:

A young soldier, born in a *moshavah* in the Sharon, admitted that the knowledge that millions of his people had been exterminated and tortured caused him no feelings of pity, horror or revenge. These . . . young Israeli natives are of course convinced that such a thing could not have happened here. What can we expect of Germany's younger generation, which does not want to reopen past wounds, if our own sons and daughters in our homeland speak like this? The sorrow of the disaster is enormous, but so is the sorrow that some of our own children are viewing it with cold and distant eyes. (*Moznayim*, June 1961)

In his book *The Glass Cage* [*Mul ta' hazkhukhit*, 1962], poet Haim Gouri expressed the national guilt when he said: "We judged them without judging ourselves. . . . Which of us would swear, hand on heart, that the Hebrew community in our country did all it could to alert the world, to uncover the truth, to challenge, to save? Which of us can assert wholeheartedly that our efforts to save were commensurate with that slaughter?" (p. 249). Secular Zionism had rested on the negation of the diaspora and diaspora Judaism. The Eichmann trial revalidated the Old Jew in Israeli eyes. The Jews who had been slaughtered were not guilty of anything, not even of having failed to heed the Zionist message in time. They were innocent victims of a hostile world. Therefore, the Jewish metaplot, of which the Zionist metaplot was one part, had to acknowledge these Jews as equally legitimate protagonists in the unfolding of the national narrative.

What the Eichmann trial did for the Holocaust, the Lavon Affair in 1961 did for the Sinai War. For this reason it galvanized the writers who only began their literary careers in the 1950s. After the affair and Ben-Gurion's attack on his successor, Levi Eshkol, Amos Oz wrote in 1963: "David Ben-Gurion led the State in pathetic times, and grew accustomed to uttering thunders of pathos at all times, which eventually became grotesque and degenerated into irrational cries of 'prophetic' despotic commandments, even in everyday, ultra-secular politics. Pathos has a broad back and helps nourish a variety of bigwigs and little despotic deputies who represent the holy spirit in mundane matters, and the thicker the pathetic fog, the richer the soil of its earthly interpreters" (Amos Oz, article in *Min hayesod* [*From the Foundation*], p. 9). In Oz's view, not only was Ben-Gurion a petty, pathetic despot whose bombast had become grotesque, but his whole generation seemed to become "a monster of redemption," a concept Oz uses in *A Perfect Peace* (1982). Ben-Gurion's decline cast a heavy shadow on Israeli fiction. Yitzhak Orpaz's *Skin for Skin* sharply satirizes the rule of the Labor Party, allegorically representing the authoritarianism of Ben-Gurion through Eliram, the antagonist of the novel's hero Momo. It may not be a coincidence that the landmark year

1961 preceded the first short story collections of A. B. Yehoshua (*The Death of the Old Man*) and Aharon Appelfeld (*Smoke*). The following year Yoram Kaniuk published his first novel, *The Acrophyle* [*Hayored lema' alah*, 1963], followed by Yehoshua Kenaz's first novel, *After the Holidays* [*'Aharei hahagim*, 1964]. Amos Oz's first short story collection, *Where the Jackals Howl* [*'Artsot hatan*, 1965], appeared shortly thereafter.

Exacerbating the trauma of the Holocaust memory was the other major event of the 1960s, the Six-Day War, which became inextricably intertwined with thinking about the Holocaust. The days leading up to the outbreak of the war reawakened in Israelis the terror of Jewish decimation. It revitalized and revivified national myths. B. Y. Michali, a leading figure of the literary establishment, put it this way in a special issue of *Moznayim* devoted to the War:

> The State embodied the dream of generations of suffering and hunted people. The threat to exterminate it, with its Hitlerian inspiration, was a threat against the entire people. The victory of the IDF, the heroism of the soldiers and the fallen, had but one aim: to save the people from annihilation, and to achieve a permanent peace with the Arab states, for their sake and Israel's. . . . The young State of Israel, the rock and the light of the far-flung Diaspora, was not created to satisfy the ambitions of dictators and tyrants. This people, experienced in disaster, bleeding since it was driven from its homeland, deserves to live in security, in undisturbed peace. (*Moznayim*, July 1967, p. 99)

Similar associations between the Holocaust and the war were made by the soldiers quoted in the anthology *The Seventh Day:*

> Shimon: "They talked a lot about this business, that the Holocaust must not happen again, that we must fight well, so that it won't come back, won't happen again to the Jewish people. . . . I remember that they talked about it and that I felt it." (p. 68)

"The children of the generation that saw the crematoria," wrote Haim Gouri, "retained the lesson of that disaster. Many Jews suddenly understood what it meant, and believed the words which had come alive, pierced the heart and ravaged it. . . . The anxious hour. Then, suddenly we were more numerous and stronger, though only the Israelis paid the price of that hour with their sons' blood." ("A Wondrous and Terrible Hour of Grace," p. 175). This connection between the Holocaust and the Six-Day War infiltrated the fiction as well. For example, a character in Kaniuk's novel *The Last Jew* (1982) says this: "They've built themselves an Auschwitz with a philharmonic orchestra and are now sitting and waiting. Why aren't they hitting out?" (p. 347).

Nonetheless, reactions to the victory were mixed. Alongside growing guilt concerning the Palestinian people, whom the war had turned from a potential menace into the victims of Israeli occupation, there was also the euphoria of a nation that believed its victory realized divine promise and the Zionist vision:

> If hitherto we needed to be devout believers to call our enterprise of revival in the past few decades "The Rebirth of Israel," today we can see with our very eyes the auguries of redemption! The warriors of Israel have broken through—westward, eastward, northward and south, and proffered us the whole longed-for Land of the Prophecy, holy Jerusalem and Hebron, Jericho and Bethlehem, the Straits of Tiran and the Golan Heights, the plains and mountains, and the bank of the Jordan river. What more can the Jewish heart hope for, which has not yet been given? What more can seers see, dreamers dream, poets sing, which has not yet been fulfilled? From now on the liberator of Israel has but one commandment left: Arise and inherit! ("The Advent of Redemption")

The response, Sh. Shalom continued, must be widespread settlement:

> Every day which is not employed to this sublime purpose is a wasted day that does not figure in the count of redemption. Every hour which passes without great deeds is an hour of crime against the nation. Every space which remains empty because of our tardiness is an opening for another war. (Ibid.)

Shalom's enthusiasm was shared by a number of writers who signed their name to the "Greater Israel" ["*Eretz Yisrael Hashleimah*," meaning "the whole Israel"] petition, which affirmed the right of Jews to possess all the conquered territories. Among the spokesmen of this group were the novelists and poets S. Y. Agnon, Haim Hazaz, Natan Alterman, Moshe Shamir, Haim Gouri, Dov Sadan, and Menahem Dorman. Although their position was highly controversial and was opposed, from the start, by the Israeli left, which had embraced the writings of the 1930s and 1940s generation, their mood reflected many sectors of the society. These included some of soldiers quoted in *The Seventh Day:*

> Now I can really understand [the Palestinians]. They always cherished a little hope that one day they would return. I think this war was the result of that aspiration. . . . The Arab states fanned it, kept them locked in. Didn't let them mingle in their own countries. There's Palestinian Rafah and Egyptian Rafah. . . . But I don't see any reason—even today, yes . . . let there be Arabs in Zarnuga or Beersheba. . . . Let them say they are the inhabitants of Zarnuga or Beersheba. (pp. 120–121)

The young soldier is willing, as the victor in the war, to be generous, but for him military triumph is Israeli moral victory.

This triumphalism angered many leftist intellectuals, whose outcry struck the dominant post-1967 note. Wrote Meir Wieseltier in 1968: "We are only writers, and the literary cart is becoming bogged down in the sticky morass of nationalist idiocy" (*Ha 'aretz,* 1968). Repelled by the exultant society around her, Ruth Almog presented post-1967 Israel as a land of contractors, snobs, and the newly affluent in her novel *Death in the Rain* [*Mavet bageshem,* 1982]. One of her protagonists, the Greek Yannis, describes these Israelis as "restless, these children of a sick people. An angst-ridden nation" (p. 167).

Not everyone presented such extreme positions. Nonetheless, the country and its literature were divided between those who justified occupation and annexation and those who saw new Israeli power as corrupting. A few months before the Yom Kippur War, in the spring of 1973, an editorial article in the literary avant-garde magazine *'Achshav,* edited by Gabriel Moked and Dan Miron, distinguished between the writers born in the 1920s, who supported the Greater Israel movement, and those born in the 1930s and 1940s, who sought peace:

> It is well known that in the great debate raging in the Israeli public, the literary community is also divided between the annexationists, including the Greater Israel supporters, and those who believe in peace and security, based, inter alia, on avoiding annexation and the recognition of the right of the other nation that lives in this country. . . . Is it a coincidence that in this painful confrontation most of the older writers and those of the "Palmah generation" stand on one side of the barricade (though not the two outstanding ones, S. Yizhar and Amir Gilboa), whereas the great majority of the "State generation" writers support the platform of the movement for peace and security?

The editorial admitted that this division was not cut and dried, but it did demarcate two opposing camps on the central political issue facing Israel from 1967 through the 1990s. In the autumn of 1974, *'Achshav* published a "we told you so" editorial, as if Israel's near-defeat at the hands of the Arabs was a sort of moral victory for avant-garde literature:

> Are we, as writers and intellectuals, supposed to keep silent in the face of this foolish refusal, which harms Israel, to recognize the right of the other nation in this country, namely the Palestinian people, to self-determination at our side?

To this day, Gush Emunim and Peace Now are the visible expressions of the two political ideological worldviews. The struggle for peace of the committed left has also been occupying a central place in the fiction and non-fiction of the 1930s writers and the late bloomers of their company. The most notable are Yehoshua, Oz, Kaniuk, Ruth Almog, and Yitzhak Ben-Ner.

Thus the following passage from Amos Oz's *Touch the Water, Touch the Wind* [*Laga'at bamayim, laga'at baruah*, 1973], published a little before the Yom Kippur War, but set in the moment of 1967. The novel involves two Holocaust survivors, a husband and wife, one of whom (the wife) becomes a high-ranking official in the Communist Party in the Soviet Union, the other of whom survives the war in the forests of Poland and relocates to Israel. The passage concerns Yotam and Audrey, one a kibbutznik who "from childhood . . . had suffered from weak nerves and short sight" and the other an American hippie flower child, both of whom, on the eve of war, try to discover the path of peace:

> [W]ords were not enough. That very night, they resolved, they would get up and walk to the hills across the border, and there try with all their might to meet, to speak, to explain, to convince, to extinguish with the right words the flames of blind hatred. Not that they had much faith that the attempt would succeed. But Yotam and Audry shared the feeling that nothing in the world could measure up to their attempt, even if it failed. (pp. 182–183)

Amos Kenan went still further in his grotesque-satirical novella *Shoah II* (1975). This was nothing less than an elegy for the old Eretz Yisrael, suggesting that occupation would lead to self-destruction, a second Holocaust.

Most of the post-realist fiction belonged on the left side of the political divide, and only a few writers—most of them members of a generation which had passed from the literary and public stage and a handful of the realist writers of the 1920s generation—remained faithful to their right-wing ideology. One way or another, the Yom Kippur War shook the self-image of Israeli society. The culture lost its confidence in the unbeatable New Hebrew, a myth that had been born in the Six-Day War. The writers felt the old anxieties of the Jew, the uncertain fate and the shaky existence, which lurked behind the apparently confident mask of the New Israeli.

Following the change of government in 1977, when the Likud took over from the Labor Party, such responses by the intellectual left grew even stronger. An increasing number of didactic writings warned against the right-wing government, Gush Emunim, and the Orthodox community. Benjamin Tammuz's *Jeremiah's Inn* [*Pundaqo shel Yirmiyahu*, 1984] and Yitzhak Ben-Ner's *Angels Are Coming* [*Mal'akhim ba'im*, 1987] satirized Orthodox Jewry. Amos Kenan's *The Road to Ein Harod* [*Ha-derekh le'Ein Harod*, 1984] was an anti-establishment dystopia, and Kaniuk, Orpaz, and Oz likewise confronted the new political situation in their fiction. All of them issued warnings against an extreme right-wing and Orthodox-Jewish takeover of the State. A novel which attempted to deal with the social as well as the political problems of the late 1970s was Ben-Ner's *A Far Land,* 1981. It ranged over such topics as the decline of the labor movement, the rise of the right-wing Likud, Sadat's visit, relations between Ashkenazi and Sephardi Jews, and emigration and emigrants. A political novel with an element of nostalgia, it assessed the years since the change of government in light of the Zionist metaplot.

All these social and political factors—to which must be added the rise of young people of the so-called Second Israel, the socio-economically disadvantaged sectors of the society—affected the themes of post-realist fiction between the 1950s and 1980s. They also left their imprint on the older writers who remained faithful to the strict realist manner. There were two broad literary responses. On the one hand, there was nostalgia for the old Zionist values (for example, in Moshe Shamir's writings). On the other, the literature challenged some of the basic values of the Zionist metaplot. Fiction had to find a way to represent the social division and its growing conflicts. The revolution in the forms of fiction was an outcome of this social-artistic need.

CRITICISM AND SOCIETY

The group of young writers dubbed the New Wave first made its appearance in the late 1950s. The first to use the term New Wave was Aharon Megged, in the title of a lead article he published in 1962 as the editor of the literary supplement of *Masa'* [*Journey*], *Lamerhav.* Warning against lumping these new writers together, he said: "Let them develop in their own individual ways. Recognize that a new generation is quietly arising, which will make its appearance in a few years and will consist of individuals, each unto himself. As always, they arrive together but make their impact separately."

The ringleaders of the revolt against the existing corpus were writers born in the 1920s, who began to write in the late 1950s. They were joined by the writers born in the 1930s and 1940s: Appelfeld, Yehoshua, Oz, and Kenaz. To these were added in the 1970s Yaakov Shabtai, Yitzhak Ben-Ner, Israel Eliraz, Yeshayahu Koren, Yotam Reuveni, Ruth Almog, David Schutz, Reuven Miran, Israel Hameiri, and others. Their struggle was at once difficult and easy. The difficulty was that they were up against a fairly united front of writers and values with strong links to the dominant social and political establishment and with strict social and literary norms of their own. Following the publication of the anthology *Dor Ba'aretz* [*The Native Generation*] in 1958—which defined the shared characteristics of the writers born in the 1920s—Aharon Megged stressed that "the sharp transitions in our life carry us in new directions before we have finished observing the earlier ones." The clash between the new writers and the entrenched group involved a conflict of individuals versus the public domain. At the same time, the revolt of the New Wave writers was also quite easy. The forces they had to battle with might have been unified, but they were not complex. This is not to suggest that the authors of the 1940s and early 1950s were all alike. As we have seen, each of the writers born in the 1920s was a distinct individual author. Nevertheless, with the exception of S. Yizhar, there were no far-reaching stylistic or even thematic differences between them.

The revolution in poetry preceded the revolution in prose. The Native Generation had been led by prose writers, some of whom later became dramatists. Poetry remained marginal, and only the subsequent innovations of Pinhas Sadeh, Yehuda Amichai, Natan Zach, David Avidan, Dalia Ravikovitch, Israel Pinkas, and others brought it to the forefront. More than any other poets, it was Amichai and Zach who transformed the poetry, Amichai in practice, Zach in practice and theory both. The two poets were associated for a time with the *Likr' at* group, which Zach led with Benjamin Hrushovski-Harshav. The group was the focus of the literary life that evolved at the Hebrew University in Jerusalem in the early 1950s. The principal critics and researchers at the Hebrew University— Gabriel Moked, Dan Miron, Adi Zemach, and Gershon Shaked—were students of Dov Sadan and Shimon Halkin. At Bar-Ilan University, there were the students of Baruch Kurzweil, Hillel Barzel, Zvi Luz, and Yehuda Friedlander, while the most innovative group finally to arise came from the new Department of General Literature at Tel Aviv University, which was founded by B. Harshav, M. Peri, Y. Haefrati, A. Even-Zohar, H. Golomb, and G. Touri. The *Likr 'at* group was divided from the start, essentially between immigrants and sabras. Among the first were Yehuda Amichai, Binyamin Hrushovski-Harshav, Natan Zach, Israel Pinkas, Gabriel Moked, Gershon Shaked, Maxim Ghillan, and Yonah David. These individuals had been influenced by German and English culture rather than by the sources of Shlonsky's poetic heritage, which had been closer to Russian poetics and French symbolism.

Natan Zach produced a transformation in the poetics of his time by preferring T. S. Eliot, Ezra Pound, Rainer Maria Rilke, and Georg Trakl over the Russian-French symbolism and constructivism that had reigned supreme in the days of Shlonsky and Alterman. He was, moreover, like Eliot, a poet-critic who fought against the old poetic tradition and pointed in future directions. He also created new premises for a certain kind of historical study, written for the purpose of distorting, attacking, or revising the past or suppressing parts of it. His critique was in many ways central and preceded that of the academics. As early as 1953, Zach was aware of the need for an artistic revolution. Reviewing an exhibition of paintings for the journal *Ma'avaq* [*Battle*], he wrote the following:

> I visited the exhibition on Saturday. The little hall is a refuge from the heavy heat outside. Scores of people coming and going. I listen to their comments. The lack of comprehension of our average citizens in all matters of art is truly astounding. It would seem that their only criterion for distinguishing a good from a bad painting is their resemblance to nature. Degrees of ability, a different spirit or style—these have no meaning for them. In this area we lag behind other advanced countries, and we must seriously consider how to introduce basic artistic concepts to the interested public.

Zach led his literary companions with manifestos against the generation of the fathers, defining the poetry of his generation and creating a new historical dynasty in which rejected names were brought to the forefront and prominent ones were set aside.

In 1959 Zach published a programmatic theoretical essay attacking the foremost Hebrew poet who had influenced the poetry, prose, and spirit of the age—Natan Alterman. When this manifesto appeared the new poetry already occupied a fairly central position in the literary sphere. Entitled "Thoughts about Alterman's Poetry," the essay—later expanded in the book *Time and Rhythm in Bergson and Modern Poetry* [*Zman veritmus 'etsel Bergson ubashirah hamodernit,* 1966]—listed the norms that Zach's poetry fought against. Also in 1966, he published in the literary supplement of *Ha'aretz* a series of articles, "On the Stylistic Climate of Our Poetry in the Fifties and Sixties" ["Le'akliman hasignoni shel shnot hahamishim vehashishim beshirateinu"], in which he attempted to define the nature of his poetry and that of his generation. Zach stressed that he was not looking for "a homogeneous body, all of a piece, but at most related frames of mind, which express themselves in individual bodies of work that may well be more varied than otherwise. Furthermore, while one stylistic tradition becomes canonized, others may exist on the side, which could well prove more influential in the long term than those which were dominant in their time." Then he spelled out the premises of the new poetics: no four-line verses; a more fluid column; irregular rhyme; a free meter; less rigidity in the architecture of the verse; no excessive figurativeness; deflation of the poetic image; receptivity to the objects, views, and landscapes of the modern world; a more informal language; rejection of rhetoric ("high-flown language is no longer convincing, even in political speeches"); attention to "unrepresentative" side aspects of a given situation (for example, avoidance of its standard signs and symbols, the disruption of formal balance, a preference for imaginary and incomplete tensions, a preference for small lyrical forms, the aspiration to make the poetry express some rapport with reality); the poet's biographical reality or his surroundings; continued use of biblical material (but not posture!), sometimes in novel contexts which completely altered its signification; objection to groups writing in an identical style (regardless of the "stylistic climate").

These premises were especially applicable to the poetic tradition which took shape in the 1950s and matured in the 1960s. They also bear a resemblance to the stylistic and thematic qualities of the new fiction. This fiction began to appear in the periodicals *Keshet* and *'Amot* [*Measures*] and the literary supplements in the late 1950s. It underwent maturation in collections of short stories and novels from 1962 on. Beginning in the late 1950s, the fiction of the New Wave was also characterized by a certain deflation of style and rhetoric. Attention was paid to marginal and unrepresentative aspects of reality. Like the poetry, it began to open up to the modern world, and its plots became more fluid as the narrative shook off the constraints of realist conventions and social realist intentions.

The fiction of the post-realist authors became generally more flexible and complex than the work of most of their predecessors. The rapport with reality (often marginal reality) also became a feature of this fiction—for example, in Kenaz's first novel, *After the Holidays* (1964), which Zach praised highly. Since A. B. Yehoshua's early stories did not exhibit this particular kind of connection to reality, Zach attacked them as lacking credibility (in *Yokhani*, March 1962). What Zach valued, and argued that the poetry and fiction of the age demanded, was a clean break with the stylistic and thematic uniformity which, he believed, characterized the older generation. The younger writers all tried to fashion their own individual forms of expression, "on many windows at side entrances," to use an image from a poem by Yehuda Amichai.

Zach served as a catalyst both in creating a new literary tradition and in reevaluating and revising an old one. He and other critics revived the interest in Mendele, Brenner, Agnon, Gnessin, and Jacob Steinberg. They discovered Aharon Reuveni, David Vogel, Dov Kimhi, Yaacov Hurgin, and others. They pushed forward the new fiction and set aside the old realism. In the spring of 1959 the editor of the literary periodical *'Achshav*, Gabriel Moked, expressed the case as follows:

> We must tackle not only the pseudo-metaphysical view of our reality, but also the attempt to memorialize it as a metaphysical process. Our literature must not be compelled to depict the armed forces, the under-

ground movements, kibbutzim, the desert, immigrant villages, old settlements and new. Altogether, literature must not be obliged to do anything, either in accordance with pseudo-messianic prescriptions, or with mini-Bolshevik, leftist, super-responsible social-democrat prescriptions. There is a whole generation of native writers who produce chiefly folkloristic sketches, rarely literature. The dramatists of that generation are incapable of writing anything higher than commonplace skits, and the prose writers cannot go beyond stories for secondary-school and youth-movement textbooks, or readable childhood memoirs. You can count on the fingers of one hand the genuine poets among the group which arose in the mid '40s. Most of these people became involved in literature by accident, either because they were the first native-born generation, or because of the social-national themes they dealt with—principally the themes of the War of Independence. By and large, they were meant to be youth-movement leaders, senior functionaries of the Broadcasting Corporation, spokesmen for the Ministry of Education, skit-writers for Telem [an establishment organization marketing to villages of new immigrants], public-relations people at the military high command, editors of kibbutzim leaflets. But perhaps now, when the freshness of the newly depicted social phenomena has worn off, our literary world can shake them off, discard their primitive babbling and anachronistic spiritual and cultural affiliations, and return to a healthy, personal, intellectual and literary tension. Only this kind of mental tension, in which every problem is experienced without being first refracted in the metaphysical-ideological prism of the "redemption of Israel," or the social-national prism of "constructive enterprise" and "rebirth of the Homeland"—only such a tension can help us to confront our reality as it is, in literature and philosophy alike.

As far as Moked was concerned, the realist poets and novelists had been mere cultural functionaries. Just as their collective ideology had become obsolete, so also did their realism come to seem low-grade and nonliterary. Moked's assault was one of a series of attacks and debates, like Zach's on Alterman, which accompanied the rise of the New Wave. The magazines *Likr'at, 'Ogdan, 'Achshav,* and *Yokhani* infuriated the old literary establishment. Neither the writer-functionaries of the Writers' Association nor the literary establishment of Dor Ba'aretz had any use for these young people. They attacked them in *M'oznayim,* the Writers' Association's monthly, and in the main organ of the Dor Ba'aretz, *Masa'.* But through their two leading spokesmen, Gabriel Moked and Dan Miron (who used a variety of pseudonyms), the new writers fought back, publishing editorials and satirical writings in the journal *'Achshav* (the satirical page was entitled "Dag Hadeyo" ["Squid"]). Although not a little nonsense was spouted in the course of the confrontation between the establishment and the opposition (which eventually became an establishment in its own right), the battle was fought over real literary values. Each side staked all it had, until eventually the New Wave of writers defeated the old.

For most of the writers of the New Wave the academic nature of their relationship to literature was crucial in the revolutionizing of Israeli fiction. The core of the 1930s generation came from a different social background than did their predecessors. Yizhar, Shamir, Megged, Shaham, Bartov, the Seneds, Nitzan, Gouri, N. Yonatan, and Mossinsohn had all been associated at some point in their lives with youth movements, agricultural settlements, kibbutzim, and one or another of the fighting organizations during the Second World War and the War of Independence. Some of the *Likr'at* group had taken part in the latter war, but except for Amichai, it was not a formative part of their experience. Although most of the authors of the New Wave were born before 1948, they grew up in the State of Israel, and their social and cultural codes differed from those of the war generation. More likely their shared experience would be not their experience on a kibbutz or their having served in the same army unit, but their course of studies at the Hebrew University in Jerusalem, where most of them came from Tel Aviv to study.

RETURN TO THE GRANDFATHERS

The powerful pressure exerted on the mid-century writers to produce a more literary Hebrew literature with an internal aesthetic development that did not depend on historical events, facilitated by the revolution in poetry led by Natan Zach and others, revived interest in earlier generations of Hebrew writers, such as Mendele, Brenner, Agnon, Gnessin, and Yaacov Steinberg. The writers also discovered writers such as Aharon Reuveni, David Vogel, Dov Kimhi, and Yaacov Hurgin. The writer who made the greatest impact on the new writers of non-realist fiction was Agnon. Regarded as the very antithesis of such local writers as Yizhar, Shamir, and Megged, Agnon, it was argued, transcended his time and place. For this reason he could not be narrowly identified with the cultural tradition of the Yishuv and the State of Israel. As Gabriel Moked put it:

> This locality gave Agnon nothing, while he, as a writer, endowed our spiritual reality with dynamic contents, though these have been ignored. Therefore, Israel as a cultural entity cannot boast of Agnon as its prime representative writer. Much the same may be said of Buber. We must get rid of the curious custom which has recently struck root here, of hastily claiming, or nationalizing, important spiritual phenomena whose development owes nothing to the real and typical cultural background of Israel. (*Davar,* 1966)

The influence of Agnon on A. B. Yehoshua is marked. Yehoshua wrote psychoanalytical analyses of Agnon's writing (for example, *A Simple Story*), and, in an article linking his own writing to Agnon's, admitted that Agnon's *The Book of Deeds* had, along with Kurzweil's and Moked's commentaries, influenced his first collection of short stories, *The Death of the Old Man*. Kafkaesque, as well as Agnonesque, *The Death of the Old Man* used non-realist forms which transcended time and place and made possible a metaphorical expression of surreal and subreal worlds that was impossible to express by other literary conventions. But whereas Agnon used materials drawn from concrete local temporal circumstances in order to produce psychological, theological, and philosophical interpretations of that world, Yehoshua's *The Death of the Old Man* (with the exception of the story "Galiah's Wedding" ["Hatunatah shel Galyah"]) concretized and historicized timeless archetypical materials (more in the manner of Kafka than Agnon). In later years William Faulkner (notably with his *As I Lay Dying*) to some degree dislodged Agnon and Kafka as major influences on Yehoshua's fiction.

Nor was Yehoshua the only writer to turn to Agnon. Amos Oz devoted a book to three of Agnon's works ("Tehillah," *A Simple Story,* and *Yesteryear*). He dwelt on the demonic elements in Agnon's writing that he would come to use in his own fiction. For Appelfeld, Agnon, as a pre-Holocaust writer, returned him to the Jewish shtetl of his own youth. *A Guest for the Night,* he wrote, "revealed to me something of the twilight of childhood, of the smells of spacious houses abandoned by the sons to the old parents' sighs" (*First Person Essays* [*Masot beguf rish 'on*]). Discussing experimental fiction in the magazine *Keshet* (Autumn 1965), Yitzhak Orpaz described Agnon's "From Lodging to Lodging" ["Midirah ledirah"] as nothing less than a model of experimental writing. Nor is there any mistaking Agnon's influence on Orpaz's surrealism, as in *The Death of Lysanda* [*Mot Lysanda,* 1964], *The Hunting of the Doe* [*Tzeid hatsviyah,* 1966], *Ants* [*Nemalim,* 1968], and *A Narrow Step* [*Madregah tsarah,* 1972].

Berdyczewski also emerged as an influence on the new fiction, especially in the work of Oz, whose tensions between repression and desire and dense atmosphere and taut style were highly reminiscent of Berdyczewski. "Man is the sum of the sin and the fire in his bones," wrote Oz in an article explicating Berdyczewski's art (*Under This Blazing Light* [*Be 'or hatkhelet ha'azah*]). In his novel *The Last Jew,* Kaniuk actually alludes to Berdyczewski, when the protagonist, Nehemiah Shneorson, foresees the New Hebrew and objects to the morality of the prophets: "Between Elijah and Ahab, choose Ahab. Between Saul and David, choose Saul. He was born amid the destruction, the prophets prophesied me, he said, I shall prophesy their traducers; and the old rabbi wept" (p. 123).

Revived in the 1950s, Brenner also wielded considerable influence, especially in relation to the moral register of the new fiction. In an essay entitled "A Ridiculous Wonder Hanging Overhead" ["Pele' meguhach me'al ler'asheinu"], Oz specifically associated his own writing with Brenner's, while Yehoshua dealt with him in several of his essays. For many of the writers, Brenner emerged as the father of Zionist modernism and existentialism. As Appelfeld put it in an article linking Brenner's Jewish identity with his own: "Brenner is unquestionably one of the strongest manifestations of the Jewish crisis. No one succeeded so well in depicting this complexity which verges on disease and madness. He was famous for sparing neither himself nor anything, nor anyone else. And just as the disease was severe, so too were the longings for the elemental that exists under the garments of culture, beyond the paternal inheritance, and is no less powerful" (*First Person Essays*, pp. 76–77).

Thus, in *Past Continuous* Shabtai both captures the complexity of Brenner's vision and reveals his equally complicated legacy. Dealing, inter alia, with the decline and fall of the labor movement, *Past Continuous* still made the normative distinction (as did Brenner and his contemporaries) between the true pioneer and the individual who fails to obey the call. Nonetheless, Shabtai stresses that the failure of the younger generation is the consequence of the dogmatism (in Goldman Sr.) and greed (in Ervin) of the founding fathers. Similarly, the characters of Kaniuk in *The Acrophyle* and *Himmo, King of Jerusalem* [*Himo, melech Yerushalayim*, 1965] experience Zionism very ambivalently, and are (in the words of a Brenner protagonist) generally "at a loss," however they keep going: "Rivkah's father came in the night, embraced his daughter, touched Nehemiah's arm and said: 'Maybe it's a vision of death, maybe this nation has no future, but go and build me a house there'" (*The Last Jew*, p. 139). This tone also characterized the later writings of Orpaz, which also strike the dominant note of social-moral commitment, as in *A House for One* [*Bayit le'adam 'ehad*, 1975], *The Mistress* [*Hagvirah*, 1983], and *A Charming Traitor* [*Ha'elem*, literally "the youth," 1984]. Even the neo-realism of a writer such as Yitzhak Ben-Ner is suffused with Brennerish ideology and fragmentation. Like Brenner's *From Here and There*, Ben-Ner's *Protocol* (1983) also strives for a documentary effect, incorporating the hero-narrator's experiences and ideologies into the text. But unlike Brenner, Ben-Ner places melodrama and Zionist history side by side.

One of the more marginal writers rediscovered by Natan Zach and others was David Vogel. *Married Life*, which was originally published in 1929–1930, was reissued in 1986 and translated into several European languages. *Facing the Sea* (1934) was reprinted in 1974. Although Vogel's work seemed to stand outside the contours of the Hebrew literary canon, several young Israeli writers, not all of whom knew Vogel, began to take on features of his style. A striking example of this is Dan Tzalka, whose novella *Dr. Barkel and His Son Michael* [*Doktor Barqel uvno Micha'el*, 1967] concerns the lives of assimilated Jews in Poland, far from the Jewish problems of the period of revival or the experience of the young Hebrews in Palestine. This detachment from local issues and national culture, à la Vogel, may also be found in some aspects of the writings of Kenaz and Kahana-Carmon. It becomes especially significant in the postmodernism of the 1990s.

The persistent influence of Uri Nissan Gnessin on elitist writing must also be noted in this context. As a writers' writer who perfected a stream-of-consciousness technique, Gnessin came most powerfully to bear on the writing of Yizhar; while the combination of Yizhar and Gnessin, in the company of such European authors as Proust, Woolf, and Joyce left their imprint on David Shahar, Amalia Kahana-Carmon, and Yaakov Shabtai. In his turn, Gnessin's heir, Yizhar, influenced a number of writers, even the more prosaic authors, such as Yitzhak Orpaz, who evidenced Yizhar's influence in his psychologically fraught landscape depictions:

> Suddenly he felt that the sky was very high and the stars isolated ice crystals which cared for nothing, and the night was vast, very vast, and the strange sensation which he had earlier warmed with a couple of swallows and believed to be melted, now gave a sharp twinge and shrank with terror: This night, this hour, this moment know nothing about you. The stars are cold and self-absorbed, the shadows are blind and the sounds are stragglers. And you, for all your stature (1.88 m.) and weight (85 kgs) are but a small and fearful creature. He walked faster. (*Skin for Skin,* pp. 14–15)

Yehuda Amichai is technically Yizhar's contemporary. Nonetheless, he belongs with the post-realists, and his poetry and prose have had a distinct influence upon that entire generation. Amichai liberated the writers from the high poetical style that had been current. He legitimized the use of vernacular and absurd metaphorical combinations. He also opened the language and the story contents to a new style that permitted both lyrical and grotesque associations. These features came to characterize the writings of several of the new generation of authors. Kaniuk, for example, renounced poetical attempts to create aesthetic associations. He favored the grotesque and the unexpected.

The new fiction was not altogether severed from the realist tradition of Shamir, Bartov, Megged, and Shaham. Indeed, some of the neo-realist writers were quite close to their predecessors. For example, a Yitzhak Ben-Ner novella in *A Far Land* depicted a 1980s Israeli whose roots go back to the 1940s. It is the portrait of a generation which turned its back on its origins, a society in decline. It is essentially a nostalgic elegy for a lost

Eretz Yisrael. In this Ben-Ner resembled the Native Generation that had mourned the lost past and the future. In a similar vein, his novel *Protocol* is a traditional realist melodrama without any particular stylistic innovations. Although the author places in the forefront of the story a small communist community that existed only on the fringe of the Yishuv, the book primarily affirms the values of socialist Zionism.

WINDS FROM THE WEST

Perhaps the most significant element in the literary revolution of the mid-1950s and the 1960s was the growing openness of Israeli culture and literature to Western Europe and the United States. Thematically and stylistically, the influence of Eastern European culture (especially of Russia) waned as Hebrew writing renewed its relationship to the West. This pull of the West is manifest in Yitzhak Orpaz's 1965 literary manifesto, "On the Experimental Story" ["'Al hasipur hanisyoni"], which blended existentialist philosophy and the nouveau roman, Kafka, Agnon, Albert Camus, Jerzy Andrezeiwski, and Alain Robbe-Grillet:

> The experimental story is not a story of despair or nihilism, as it is often described by the proponents of psychological fiction. Perhaps that is what it was like when it first discovered the desolation of a world without God. By now it is inured to the condition. Here and there it even gropes for a new revelation. . . . The experimental story is a revolt against death. It deals with moments. It gives power to the moments. (p. 66)

Orpaz's first book had been a collection of realist stories, *The Wild Plant* ['*Esev pere*']. By 1962 his fiction was plainly more modern (*Skin for Skin*), and he became one of the founding fathers of contemporary Hebrew fiction. Orpaz made no attempt to formulate a new poetics, only to transfer into Hebrew literature the poetics of modern European literature. In addition to the writers cited by Orpaz, Max Frisch (notably *Homo Faber*); the pioneers of stream of consciousness (Virginia Woolf, James Joyce, Marcel Proust and, above all, William Faulkner); the authors of the new grotesque novels and plays (Günter Grass, Friedrich Dürenmatt); and some of the modern American writers, Jews and non-Jews, all left their imprint on the works of Yehoshua, Kaniuk, Kahana-Carmon, Appelfeld, and others. Yehoshua's first short story collection, *The Death of the Old Man*, like Orpaz's *Skin for Skin*, is plainly influenced by Camus, chiefly by his *L'Etranger*.

Of all these influences, the writer who held greatest sway was Franz Kafka. Kafka's surrealism served writers such as Yehoshua and Orpaz well, as they sought to break out of the realist mode of Hebrew writing. In many ways, he fulfilled many of the same functions as Agnon. He provided a kind of mythical foundation for the depiction of the human condition in general and the Jewish condition in particular. As Appelfeld put it,

> Help came from an unexpected source, from a man who had not been in the Holocaust, but had envisioned the nightmare during the serene days of the declining Hapsburg empire, namely, the Jew Franz Kafka. No sooner did we touch the pages of *The Trial* than we felt that he had been with us in all our wanderings. Every line expressed us. In Kafka's language we found the suspicion and doubt as well as the unhealthy yearnings for meaning. (*First Person Essays*, p. 15)

Appelfeld spoke for Kaniuk, Orpaz, and Yehoshua as much as for himself.

A somewhat later influence was Gabriel Garcia Marquez's *One Hundred Years of Solitude*, which appeared in Hebrew translation in 1972. Kaniuk had always been inclined to the fantastic and grotesque. *Rockinghorse* [*Sus'etz*, 1973], *The Story of Aunt Shlomzion the Great* [*Hasipur 'al dodah Shlomtsion hagdolah*, 1976], and, in particular, *The Last Jew* all recall Marquez. So, too, in their blend of folklore, stream of consciousness, and grotesque fantasy, do Shabtai's *Past Continuous*, Yehoshua's *Mr. Mani* (which also bears the imprint of Faulkner), and three novels by Meir Shalev (a writer who began his career in the 1980s and therefore will be dealt with only in the next chapter): *The Blue Mountain* [*Roman Rusi*, 1988], *Esau* [*'Esav*, 1991], and *As a Few Days* [*Keyamim 'ahadim*, 1994]. The writer who most completely conveys the impact of European on Hebrew literature, anticipating Yoel Hoffman in this respect, is Dan Tzalka. His short story, "Aharoni and the Antique Collectors" [" 'Aharoni vehovevei ha'atiqot"] in the collection *Bassoon Wood* [*'etz habasun*, 1973], swarms with European carnivalesque figures (cf. *Dr. Barkel, Philip Arbes* [1977], and *A Thousand Hearts* [*'Elef levavot*, 1991]).

THE LANGUAGE OF LITERATURE

In general the New Wave writers were more self-conscious literary craftsmen and women; many of them (Appelfeld, Yehoshua, Oz, Amichai, and Zach, for example) taught literature at Israeli universities. Amalia Kahana-Carmon concluded her collection of stories *Under One Roof* [*Bikhfifah 'ahat*, 1966] with a poetical manifesto, and her novella *And Moon in the Valley of Ajalon* [*Veyareah be'emeq 'Ayalon*, 1971] concludes with a chapter ("Death Mask") in which the author states her poetic principles in an imaginary interview with a young woman journalist. Orpaz also wrote such manifestos, as in his essay on the experimental story and in *The Secular Pilgrim* [*Hatsalyan hahiloni*, 1982], in which he justified surrealist techniques and an existentialist philosophy. In his collection of essays, *Under This Blazing Light* (1979), Amos Oz discussed a number of authors, revealing more about himself than about his subjects. The same may be said of Appelfeld's *First Person Essays*. Several other writers (Tzalka, Orpaz, Kaniuk) also wrote self-conscious fictions which expressed their craft-conscious aesthetic philosophies.

Dor Hamedinah (the New Wave) was by no means homogeneous. Nevertheless, when categorized by genre and theme as well as by style or school, it becomes clear that a number of the Dor Hamedinah writers bear marked similarities. The period between the late 1950s and the 1960s witnessed a post-realist revolution characterized by a growing tendency toward the non-mimetic and grotesque modes of representation. This radical rejection of social realism and mimetic representation began to achieve equilibrium with its opposite as the fiction tried once again in the late 1960s and early 1970s to connect itself with and reflect social reality. If initially the tone of New Wave fiction was set by such writers as Yehoshua, Orpaz, Kaniuk, Oz, Appelfeld, and Kahana-Carmon, later writers such as Shabtai, Tzalka, Ben-Ner, Koren, the later Kenaz, Ruth Almog, and David Schutz soon intervened to change the tenor of the writing once again.

In the 1960s, as Zach noted, poetry deflated the high style and rhetoric, so it would have been reasonable to expect that prose would do the same. But this was not the general case, and many of the post-realist writers used an elevated diction, though they applied it in different ways. The realists had followed the old formulation using classical phrases and numerous neologisms in the manner of Avraham Shlonsky and his contemporaries. The post-realist writers who went in for high language used other methods of elevating their style. Many used rhythmical sentences and an intricate system of metaphors, while a complex figurative language often served as a high stylistic substitute for the rich classical language of the realists.

Orpaz, who tended toward surrealism, began by using a naturalistic style. He tried to lower the register as much as possible in his dialogues. In this he did not differ from his contemporaries, such as Mossinsohn and Shamir. Here is a passage from *Skin for Skin*, which attempts to represent real speech: "You stupid piece of nothing, goat's shit son of goat's shit, leprous solitary son of a bitch, now take my hand because you are cheeky and bold, you bastard whore's son" (p. 19). This naturalistic style, supposedly reflecting the speech of soldiers going to the Sinai war, is quite unlike the speech of the War of Independence soldiers in, for example, Yizhar's *Days of Ziklag*.

The most stylized of all the post-realist writers whose work is characterized by a high stylistic register is Amalia Kahana-Carmon. In *And Moon in the Valley of Ajalon,* the writer Hiram states his stylistic poetics, and by implication the poetics of his creator: "Words. The army of words the only enemy. Defeat them, word by word. Combine, organize, polish. All by yourself. Only the words and you. No other factor enters the picture. Not the reading public. Not other authors. No one" (p. 202). Kahana-Carmon has little tolerance for her generation's supposed stylistic deflations. Using a fairly elevated diction and intricate figurative language she forces a slow reading that takes into account not only what is said but also what is left unsaid.

While Kahana-Carmon's style is less elevated than that of Yizhar and Shamir, it descends only in order to move up to an even higher poetical register. This is achieved by means of rhythm, elliptical sentences, anaphoric rhetoric, a distinctive vocabulary, and even inner rhymes. At times she used a very high register derived from the ancient sources to achieve exaggerated, semi-grotesque effects by means of archaic linguistic devices:

> The days passed. But did not pass. The State recovered its youth. We have sloughed off the old skin, we said. And to this too one gets accustomed, fast. The city's din. One runs and another saunters. Nets and traps are spread for animals, fowl and fish. Linen is given to the launderer. Light is confined within the blaze of the furnace-house. A stove which has been fired with straw or chaff, or with punk and wood, as one would fire an oven. And those who write with two letters with one missing write on the boards of the sanctum, to inform his spouse. The tablets and the tablets' fragments lie in the ark. Towers hover in the air, and the land is filled with wisdom. And if he be condemned to stoning let him be given good strong wine to drink for that the stoning hurt him not, and with no witnesses present tear off his arms and legs. (*And Moon,* p. 147)

Philip, the stranger to whom the heroine of the story says these words, has returned to Israel following the Six-Day War and admires the changes that have taken place. The heroine's response is hyperbolic, resorting to extracts from the Mishnah in order to heighten the effect of her comments. Ultimately the language takes over from its argument, producing a reality of its own.

Such literary self-consciousness is the dominant feature of Kahana-Carmon's style. She makes extensive use of truncated sentences consisting of only subject and adjective, or inverted sentence structures broken by the personal pronoun ("Did you know that with you I was through years ago?" *And Moon,* p. 103). Her imagery is powerfully metaphorical, as in following examples from *Under One Roof:* "Women like damaged forks, in old coats and button shoes, a coal-basket on their arms" (p. 25), or "Black paving-stones, furrowed like a tyre" (p. 27), or "The Negev, and us wandering over it like flies on a white platter" (p. 59), or "The air was heavy and damp, as in a hothouse" (p. 21).

Amos Oz does not lower the register of language either. Quite the opposite—he heightens rhetorical effect by means of short elliptical sentences and emotive leitmotifs, as in the following: "Total darkness outside. Grasshoppers. Stars. Wind. I shall cease now" (*The Hill of Evil Counsel* [*Har ha'eitsah hara'ah*], p. 81). His *Unto Death* [*'Ad mavet*] is an expressionist historical novella which exhibited various stylistic devices. Adjectival modifiers, for example, underwent intensification—violent, chilly, spiteful, lowly, seething, gloomy, slow, venomous, corrosive, cautious, meticulous, quiet, poisoned; "the autumn, a patient grey friar, would stretch out silent chill fingers and smooth the face of the earth" (p. 122). Oz also treated the landscape symbolically, producing in *Where the Jackals Howl* a virtual menagerie of representational figures: a jackal, a viper, a stormy aquarium, a cat, and an owl. In *Elsewhere, Perhaps* mountains are represented so as to suggest human fornication (pp. 194–195), while in *Touch the Water, Touch the Wind*, Oz presents the following image:

> Standing erect and belligerent on the chest of drawers is an African warrior carved in wood and colored in war-paints. Day and night this savage menaces with his immense, grotesque phallus the frightened girl in the Matisse picture, and above, wonderfully silent, the bear's head looks out. (p. 30; cf. p. 8)

The principal leitmotif in *To Know a Woman* [*Lada'at 'ishah*, 1989] is the statuette of a pouncing cat, which self-consciously reflects the poetics of the novel: "It may, therefore, be asked if the continued agony of an interrupted leap and frozen momentum, a leap and momentum which never cease yet are never achieved, or do not cease because they are unachieved, if such agony is greater or less than a leg smashed once and for all?" (p. 81). And further on: "And is any self-defense possible, let alone a chance of compassion and charity? Or perhaps, not to defend oneself, but simply get up and flee. But the question still remains, how and where will an eyeless animal leap?" (p. 140).

Yoram Kaniuk's writing is also highly expressive, full of awkward metaphors and grotesque combinations of heterogeneous materials that serve to draw attention to the language itself and suggest the intractability and horror of the physical world: "Jugs of cold water, salt and pepper, mustard, anchovies, chili sauce, ketchup, lemon juice, vinegar, raw olive oil" (*Adam Resurrected*, p. 57); or "I'm not Miles Davis. This is a hospital. I am Adam Stein and there are no armed guards anywhere. Dr. Gross will piss on you. His piss stings and is yellow, he has worms, his mother is a whore in Jerusalem. Gina is Adam's girlfriend, she is awful, you'll get to meet her. Once she pricked me, she has pins in her pockets, she pricks" (p. 146); or "An old man selling kvass under Myrna Loy. A girl holding bagels on a string. Under the—I'm crazy about you, Frankie. The Hebrew bookseller peers out. He's looking for me. He always follows me. The bagels are war rings. The Indians on the cinema wall are headless. Someone tore out Ava Gardner's eyes. The innocent violence of the 1940s" (*Rockinghorse*, pp. 45–46). Allusive and pictorial, the language depicts the wholeness of reality in its fragmentariness and implied threat.

By turning his limited knowledge of Hebrew into an advantage, Appelfeld achieved remarkable stylistic innovation in Hebrew fiction. Constrained by his restricted vocabulary and unfamiliarity with the Hebrew sources, he was probably one of the first Israeli writers to try to adapt the language to Western sentence structure and modes of expression, inventing adjectives and adverbs where none existed in the Hebrew. In this, he followed in the footsteps of Gnessin. In later years Appelfeld attempted to stylize his writings, but on the whole he continued to write straightforward simple sentences in which the use of a sudden, unexpected image or action breaks the placidity of the style and startles the reader into attention: "A Jew emerged as from a camouflaged den and stood in the path. He looked like a huge beetle which had lost its way. 'Oh hell,' he shouted. And the Jew fell down on all fours" ("The Flight" ["Habrihah"], from *On the Ground Floor* [*Beqomat haqarqʿa*], p. 12). Or, from the same collection: "Wagons with Jews passed from time to time. They were known by their black garments. Great beetles, exposed in the field. No Jew entered Berdinski's house" ("The Betrayal" ["Habgidah"], ibid., p. 21). "Her face was sturdy, like all her former being. A tree uprooted entirely, so that you can envision the hole it left behind. He thought that's how it is when a man forgets his wife" (*The Skin and the Gown* [*Haʿor vehakutonet*], p. 17). "The light drew back. The glance could retreat no further. And all the years were again lost and all the words became mute; and they were in their own years like prisoners after a brief leave: the guards, the door, the bolt, Grozman's unappeased weeping" (ibid., p. 109). "Snowflakes fell slowly and covered the face of the earth with a grey coat of white. A storm was already thickening on the horizon, and the shorn trees stood shivering, their skin turning blue" (*As the Apple of His Eye* [*Keʾishon haʿayin*], p. 5). And: "I knew: all that had been would return no more. Even the place we had been in, it too was dead" (*The Age of Wonders* [*Tor haplaʾot*], p. 15). Beetles, an uprooted tree, prisoners after leave, the dead place, trees turning blue—the images are taken from sources unrelated to the subjects to which they are applied. Appelfeld's stylistic power rests in these brilliant figurative associations combined with his Western sentence structures. Earlier precedents for this may have been Gnessin, who also adapted Western sentence structure and verb usage, and David Vogel, who used various Western deviations.

Yaakov Shabtai's style in *Past Continuous* resembles what in 1920s Germany was called the "new matter-of-factness" ("*die neue sachlichkeit*"): "And indeed a few weeks later, after Manfred and Elinor had already left the country, Goldman contacted that cheiromantist and arranged an appointment, but he committed suicide a few days earlier and the appointment never took place" (p. 269). This style deflated the pathos and the stylistic excesses that prevailed among the realist writers and even some of the post-realists. Shabtai moderated every extreme emotive expression. He dealt with matters of life and death objectively, without emotion. Whatever emotion does emerge is produced through the text's excisions and omissions.

Shabtai is distinctive for the way in which he achieved emotional impact through stylistic moderation. Each of the writers of his generation, however, compensated differently for deflating the formerly high style of Hebrew prose. Some underscored the poetic function of language itself or elevated the register by other means. Very few, though, tried to stylize the vernacular and make it into a literary language (as did the playwright Hanoch Levin, for example). In most of the texts of this period there remains, as in realist fiction, a gap between the written and the spoken language.

NARRATING THE VISIBLE AND THE CONCEALED

In 1973, on the occasion of the publication of his collected works, Moshe Shamir told an interviewer:

> If we consider Hebrew fiction as a family, we might say that there are two conflicting tendencies running through it. Occasionally they inspire one another, but mostly they block each other. One impulse—let's call it the good one—is drawn to the hidden meaning, to allegory and parable, vision and symbol. What is the meaning of it all? it asks. The other—call it the evil impulse—is attracted to the turbid material of concrete reality, to the visible and tangible, the physical and realistic. What is the nature of all this? it asks. (Eli Mohar, "Novels are a Difficult Business")

Shamir quite correctly distinguished between the poetical principles of most of his contemporaries—namely, the description of the visible—and those of the younger generation of writers, who were drawn to expose what is hidden from view. The techniques which characterized a mystically inclined writer such as David Shahar, a surrealist such as Orpaz, expressionists such as Oz and Kaniuk, lyrical impressionists such as Kahana-

Carmon and Almog, and even neo-realists such as Benjamin Tammuz, Shabtai, and Ben-Ner tended toward symbolization and allegorization. Non-mimetic representation dominated over realism per se. As Aharon Appelfeld formulated this phenomenon, "The plain and the hidden are both in the nature of any expression. But for us, who have known the Holocaust, this nature is the soul. The word stands or falls on the thin wire of utterance and non-utterance" (*First Person Essays,* p. 41).

Symbolization came to dominate many works of fiction, though other techniques were also used to overcome the linearity of the plot that had characterized the realist tradition. These include various techniques of narrative fragmentation and express multiple and frequently mutually contradictory points of view, often through monologues and confessions. There are, for example, Tammuz's *Minotaur* and *Nightingale and Chameleon* and A. B. Yehoshua's fiction; the triptych technique of Kahana-Carmon's *Magnetic Fields* [*Sadot magnetiyim,* 1977]; Appelfeld's retroactive reconstruction of the past; the polyphony of David Shahar's serial novel *The Palace of Shattered Vessels* [*Heichal hakeilim hashvurim*]; and Ben-Ner's novel and stories. Shahar expertly developed the technique of the dual testimony, as in *Nin-Gal* (1983), for example, in which the narrator hears the confession of an old classmate of his, Arik Wissotzky, mainly about his mother Anastasia.

Although the realists had also used some of these techniques, the post-realists took them even further, breaking out of the conventions of realism altogether. For example, in *Days of Ziklag* Yizhar had used a number of perspectives to observe the central phenomena he wished to describe, while in Shamir's *Under the Sun* and *The Border* [*Hagvul*] the plots unfold from a number of angles that are focused by several personae. Megged in *Evyatar Notebooks* and Shaham in *The Rosendorf Quartet* used multiple narrators. However, these texts do not achieve the intricacy of a work such as Tammuz's *Minotaur* or *Nightingale and Chameleon*.

Indeed, of the native writers still active at mid-century, Tammuz emerged as the most important innovator of narrative style. *Minotaur* is an epistolary novel in which the letter-writing lover conceals his identity. The novel's tension is achieved by the opposition between the sentimental epistolary passages and others which are written in a more factual prose. *Nightingale and Chameleon* is even more complex. It is constructed out of discontinuous fragments, anti-religious and anti-establishment sequences interspersed with nostalgic passages and poetic manifestos. The consciousness of the autobiographical narrator, Abramson, continuously merges with other equally strange personalities.

More than any other work of Israeli fiction, David Shahar's series of novels, jointly entitled *The Palace of Shattered Vessels,* recalls Marcel

Proust's *Remembrance of Things Past*. Meaning is constructed through the shifting memories of the narrator, who tells the story of a group of interrelated individuals, all of whom are positioned on the margins of society. The evocation of memory through encounters with physical reality gives Shahar's aesthetic its special quality:

> I have always sensed in my encounters, not only with people but also with houses, trees, alleys, streets, smells and sights, something of the nature of the appearance of memories. They exist no less than do the other things, and have lived their lives through the long years in which they were outside the circles of our routine existence, when they were dead to us, external, moribund. Suddenly, when their routine touches upon ours, they rise before us like Lazarus rising from the dead, proving to us that their having been dead to us was due to the tightness of the lightbeam cast by the torch that illuminates only part of the dirt road along which we walk through the great broad field which is otherwise invisible, because the curtain of darkness excludes its immensities from our sight, even when its gulfs gape within us. (*Summer in the Street of the Prophets* [*Qayits bederekh hanevi'im*], p. 118)

Shahar's protagonist—who stands for the author in the series—is a witness-narrator who often confronts another witness-narrator, who speaks to him as to a confessor and relates his life story or that of another character.

One of the outstanding achievements in Hebrew fiction in recent decades is Shabtai's *Past Continuous*. While each of the characters in this novel is distinctive and singular, together they compose a kind of carved relief on a tombstone for 1970s Israeli society. The novel uses a form of collective stream of consciousness in which the lives of the characters are woven together into a single tapestry of threads. However much the characters try to separate out from one another, they are integrally part of the collective social memory.

Most of the novelists of the period used similarly complex methods of narration. Amos Oz revived the epistolary novel in *Black Box* (1987) and A. B. Yehoshua used alternating points of view as early as 1977 in his first full-length novel, *The Lover*. He further refined this technique in *A Late Divorce* [*Geirushim me'uharim*] in 1982, while *Mr. Mani* was written in the form of half-dialogues, that is, dialogues of which only one side of the conversation is recorded.

Amalia Kahana-Carmon's triptych *Magnetic Fields* produces a different effect; authorial perspective is provided by the analogical associations linking the first two stories and the concluding novella. Ruth Almog's *Death in the Rain* constructs multivocality through the device of a fictional editor, Licht, who incorporates and annotates various journals, letters, stories, and editorial comment. David Schutz's *White Rose, Red Rose*

[*Shoshan lavan, shoshan 'adom,* 1988] continued this trend. It is presented through three different viewpoints with linked intertextual associations. Similarly, Kaniuk's *The Last Jew* has its hero editing taped recordings of the self-conscious narrator and various subsidiary personalities, their individual contours becoming blurred in the course of the narrative, such that they come to represent the single multifaceted personality of the implied author:

> Then I understood that my hundreds of hours of talk, the scores of tape-recordings, had sloughed a high wall off me, and I wondered about my life, if it had been beautiful, if it had been good. I didn't know what to think. It was the first time in years that I was almost free of all the people who had hitherto spoken from inside me, and now I am talking about one moment, I am talking not to an anonymous audience, not in a nightclub, I am talking to Germanisofer and to Hankin, who will hear these words and say, Ah, Evenezer has ceased to be the Last Jew. And surely if I ceased to be the Last Jew they would be able to write the book I had woven for them from the memories which were not mine. (p. 448)

Related to the technique of using multiple points of view, and sometimes combined with it, was the piling up of separate stories within a single volume in order to produce an expanded multidimensional perspective, as in Yitzhak Ben-Ner's *A Far Land* (1981), which presents a number of different responses to the election of the right-wing Likud government in 1977 and the visit of Egypt's President Sadat (1977–1978).

THE GROTESQUE

The grotesque was part of the New Wave right from the beginning. In *Not of This Place, Not of This Time,* Amichai applied many of the same gothic elements that characterized his poetry: stylistically hybrid metaphors, game-playing and punning, the yoking together of the absurd and the implausible, and a series of pathetic-grotesque characters. Another writer of the Native Generation who pioneered this type of literature was Amos Kenan, whose satirical newspaper column appeared throughout the 1950s and who also wrote a number of grotesque-absurd novellas, notably his quasi-poetical *At the Station.* It is difficult to pinpoint the subject, time, and place of this novella, but it appears to be about an exile living in Paris, who suffers constant conflict with the past and is full of "thoughts about the dead" (in Alterman's phrase). It is made up of a series of absurd dialogues between a main speaker and several secondary voices who talk incessantly about death and despair. The images of horror are not unlike the 1990s writings of Orly Castel-Bloom and the dialogues of dramatist

Hanoch Levin. Structurally, the novel develops spatially rather than temporally, through disjointed episodes. The characters are not psychologically developed, nor is there a conventional Aristotelian plot.

A typical stylistic feature of Kenan's writing is the parodic intertextual treatment of canonic material, as for example, the following interpolation of Psalms 137 into the text of his story: "These longings at midday can drive one mad. / By the rivers of Babylon we sat down and wept when we remembered Zion. / In Babylon's rivers there are no fish. You sit all day with the fishing-rod, scattering breadcrumbs on the water, / smoking a pipe, never catching so much as a minnow. . . . That's how it is. All the fish have gone to the big sea. Abandoned mama and papa. No one left at home to warm the chill winter nights. What's left? Only the memories, crying, crying" (*At the Station,* p. 20). Further on the same verses serve in another parody: "Many years passed, many years, and once again we met by the rivers of Babylon. . . . The harps hanging above our heads hummed ceaselessly in the east wind. Enough is enough. If only someone had a new song" (p. 86).

Kenan's text constantly fluctuates from the pathetic to the grotesque to the trivial, and the author's revulsion for the trivial is made obvious. Although the novel appears to stand outside time and place, it satirizes petty bourgeois Jewish-Israeli life in the 1950s. In a way anticipating the later fiction of Kaniuk, Orpaz, Yehoshua, and Oz (in 1975 Kenan published another grotesque-absurd novel entitled *Shoah II*), Kenan plays against each other spiritual-versus-earthly longings, the desire to live and the wish to die, nostalgia for the native land, and a loathing for the ugliness of shattered hopes.

From the beginning of his career A. B. Yehoshua used the literary inventory of the grotesque to structure his plots and configure his social dissent. In general he combines conventional with extraordinary materials, bringing together love and an act of terror in "The Yatir Evening Express" ["Masaʿ haʿerev shel Yatir," also published in English as "An Evening in Yatir Village"], an old man's burial at the hands of another old man in "The Death of the Old Man," and a tongueless Arab guarding the forests of the Jewish National Fund in "Facing the Forests" ["Mul Hayeʿarot"]. Such combinations of the ordinary and the grotesque even characterize such novels as *The Lover, A Late Divorce,* and *Five Seasons* [*Molho*]. The typical Yehoshua plot uses a disintegrating Israeli family as a kind of synecdoche for the deformation of Israeli society as a whole, as in his play *A Night in May* [*Layla bem 'ay,* 1975], which depicts events in the life of an Israeli family in May 1967, the eve of the Six-Day War. In most of the novels a carnivalesque atmosphere prevails. The impression produced is that while the individual or the family may be disintegrating, the tribe and society nonetheless survive, perhaps due to the vitality released by the grotesque-carnivalesque itself.

Aharon Appelfeld, too, incorporated grotesque elements into his fiction, as in *The Searing Light* [*Mikhvat ha'or*, 1980], where he depicted the liberation and the immigration to Eretz Yisrael through a portrayal of its opposite: the transports, concentration camps, and penal colonies of the war itself. Becoming part of the Israeli army emerges as like nothing so much as a form of transport.

Similarly Yoram Kaniuk produced a poetic-grotesque text in *The Acrophyle* and a pathetic-grotesque form in *Himmo, King of Jerusalem, Rockinghorse, The Last Jew, His Daughter* [*Bito*, 1987], and *Post Mortem* (1992). In *Adam Resurrected,* pathos prevails over the grotesque horror; and only in *The Story of Aunt Shlomzion the Great* does Kaniuk produce a kind of humorous, liberated grotesque. In the course of his writing, Kaniuk tackled the two historical melodramas of twentieth-century Jewish history— the Holocaust and the War of Independence.

In this tradition of surrealistic expressionism Orpaz preceded Kaniuk. Grotesque elements already appeared in his earliest semi-realistic writing, as, for example, the following from *Skin for Skin:*

> The fat woman with the swollen legs who lived in the next room kept her skinny little husband permanently at her bedside. She had an enormous mouth, and one wondered absently when she was going to open it and swallow that little prune, complete with his spectacles, necktie and other paraphernalia. (p. 65)

Further on the novel turns sadistic:

> And Mr. Eliram was very glad and the amiable back of his neck became like a fresh honeycomb from the hive, with its color, pores, dampness and sweetness. Momo amuses himself imagining how he would stick the scissors in that nape to the hilt, and bucketfuls of honey would flow out of it, and the following morning all the front pages in the country would print Mr. Eliram's famous photograph framed in black, under the headline: "Died of a honey-hemorrhage in the neck." (p. 175)

Indeed, as writers, Kaniuk and Orpaz strongly resemble each other, and Amichai as well, though without the latter's genuine sense of humor. The tendency toward allegorical grotesque grew in Orpaz's first surrealist series: *The Death of Lysanda* (1964), *The Hunting of the Doe* (1966), *Ants* (1968), *A Narrow Step* (1972). It developed as well in his social-surrealist works: *A House for One* (1975), *The Mistress* (1983), and *A Charming Traitor* (1984). On the whole, Orpaz's grotesque tended toward cruelty and the demonic and lacked humorous balance.

A novella in an early collection of Amos Oz that also approaches the grotesque is *Unto Death* (in the collection by the same name). Set in the time of the Crusades, the story follows a series of grotesque characters as they become embroiled in a twisted plot of romantic yearning and repulsive hatred. The vicious massacre of Jews and the marching of the crusaders toward their ultimate dissolution produce a brilliant pageant of the grotesque. In the story "A Late Love" ["'Ahavah me'uheret"] in the same volume, an itinerant lecturer locked in his single-minded commitment to destroy Russia is likewise a blend of the pathetic and the grotesque. Certain such elements had already appeared in his first collection of stories, *Where the Jackals Howl.* They persisted into the 1990s, as in a more recent novel, *Fima* [*Hamatsav hashlishi,* meaning "the third condition," 1991]. In Oz, the grotesque is associated with the demonic. His hero is often the clever-sickly or clever-ugly character who poisons his environment but also stirs it up. The Arab twins who appear in Hannah's dreams in *My Michael,* Azariah in *A Perfect Peace,* and Gideon (in a more favorable version) in *Black Box* all take after Oz's most outstanding demon, the ugly and clever hunchback Claude in *Unto Death.*

Oz was not the only writer to introduce menacing irrational elements. Supernatural mysterious forces appear also in Orpaz, in Sabi (*A Narrow Step*), and in *Ants.* It also appears as a destructive force in Yehoshua, sometimes in inhuman guise, as in "Galiah's Wedding" and "Flood Tide" ["Ge'ut hayam"]; sometimes in a terrifying human one, as in "The Yatir Evening Express"; or as the downtrodden's cry of revolt, as in "Facing the Forests." In the novel *A Late Divorce* the demonic emerges in the madness of the members of the family, which drives the plot toward its pathetic grotesque climax. Appelfeld disclosed the demonic elements of history as impersonal forces that can dominate human existence in *Badenheim 1939* [*Badenheim: Ir Nofesh,* literally meaning "Badenheim: resort city"], while Kenaz found it in perversion (*After the Holidays* [1964], *The Great Woman of the Dreams* [*Ha'ishah hagdolah min hahalomot,* 1973]).

From his first novel, *After the Holidays,* Yehoshua Kenaz evidenced his tendency toward the grotesque. But the grotesque revulsion reaches its peak in the second novel, *The Great Woman of the Dreams,* which reads like an Israeli version of Mendele's *The Book of Beggars.* Kenaz's characters are the wretched of the earth. They inhabit an apartment house in one of Tel Aviv's poorer neighborhoods. The communal property forces highly disparate types into close proximity with each other's lives, giving rise to tension and mutual revulsion. In this as in other works Kenaz expresses the power and sordidness of the world of physical urges, the repression of which produces grotesque consequences.

Haim Beer followed the same route in his novel *Feathers* [*Notsot,*

1979], which depicts a burial company from the viewpoint of a child who befriends a utopian apocalyptic character. The general impression created by the novel is of a macabre pleasure in death. Beer's second novel, *The Time of Trimming* [*'Et hazamir,* 1988], is a social-grotesque story about the military rabbinate, written as broad satire.

THE RETURN OF THE ROOTLESS HERO

Sociopolitical and aesthetic transformations also put an end to certain popular protagonists, namely, the young Israeli man as idealized figure of an ideological pioneering military elite. This revamping of the hero took two forms. In Nurit Gertz's formula, "in the prose of this generation a passive, unaware hero seeks to establish contact with elements beyond him: human nature, metaphysical nature, society, etc. These elements distort [conventional social norms]. Contact with them is achieved through destruction, violence, collapse." At the same time, she observes, "old her[oes are] introduced into a new structure" and are thus parodied and deflated ("The Role of Parody"). David Shahar (*The Palace of Shattered Vessels*), for example, and Nisim Aloni (*The Owl* [*Hayanshuf,* 1975], first published in the magazine *Keshet* in the 1960s) discovered their heroes, respectively, on the frontier streets of Jerusalem and in the poorer neighborhoods of Tel Aviv. Simultaneous with this introduction of the new anti-hero is the diminished view of an older type of hero, such as the parachutist Gideon Shenhav in Amos Oz's "The Way of the Wind" ["Derekh haruah"] in the collection *Where the Jackal Howls.* Nothing more than an unhappy young man, Gideon is simply not up to performing his assigned national role. A similar figure is A. B. Yehoshua's student/sentinel who, betraying his trust when he enables the Arab guard to burn down the forest, parodies the old figure of the *shomer* or guardian, in whose trust had been placed the safety of his nation. Even the figure of the bereaved father, one of the most sacred figures in Israeli fiction, an Abraham sacrificing his son upon the altar of the homeland, is made to seem ridiculous. Thus it is the father of Oz's Gideon who pushes his son to impossible and fatal heroics. "There is a halo of sanctity about a bereaved father. Naturally, Sheinbaum is not thinking about this halo now. A stunned, speechless entourage accompanies him to the dining-room. It is important to be at the wife's side and mitigate her grief. Indirectly, is how it should be done. Indirectly" ("The Way of the Wind," p. 57). The son may arouse pity. The father, however, evokes pure disgust. Yehoshua, too, in his novella *Early in the Summer of 1970* [*Bithilat Kayitz 1970*] ironizes paternal bereavement. Indeed, he compounds that irony when the father discovers, toward the end of the story, that his son is alive and his bereavement groundless. "But looking at it again, differently, it is as if everything has been reversed. Your disappearance becomes full of meaning, suddenly ablaze. A stirring source to us of wonderful, prolonged inspiration" (p. 48).

Satiric embodiments of once-idealized figures appear in Yitzhak Orpaz's *A House for One* (1975), Avraham Raz's play *Mr. Israel Shefi's Independence Day* [*Yom ha'atzma'ut shel mar Yisra'el Shefi*, 1972], and Yoram Kaniuk's *Himmo, King of Jerusalem*. Hamutal, the heroine of *Himmo*, is a member of the elite of the old Eretz Yisrael community. A hospital nurse in besieged Jerusalem, she falls in love with Himmo, once called "king of Jerusalem" (a phrase recalling Christ), who is now nothing more than a mangled body, barely human, with little hope of recovery. Himmo is attended by his brother Marco, about whom there was "a primitive nobility which Hamutal was somewhat surprised to find in an uneducated man," but also "something in his voice and eyes [which] reminded her of a type of flashy pimp" (pp. 77, 78). By virtue both of their social status (Himmo and Marco come from the old Sephardic community of Jerusalem) and by Himmo's disfigurement, Himmo and Marco represent both a world outside the mythology of the Ashkenazi socialist Zionist youth movement and the victims of its ideology.

The protagonists of Yehoshua Kenaz's *Heart Murmur* [*Hitganvut Yehidim;* the title's literal meaning refers to a method of infiltration taught in the army, 1986] are also diminished versions of former heroes (such as the soldiers of Yizhar's *Days of Ziklag*). Army recruits with non-combat ratings who have been raised on myths of heroism and yet are physically incapable of being heroes, their sole ambition is to survive basic training. Even this goal, however minimalistic, proves too much for one of the young men, who by the end of the book commits suicide. In one of the stories in Yitzhak Ben-Ner's collection, *Rustic Sunset* [*Shki'ah kafrit*, 1976], the central character is a colonel who falls apart during the Yom Kippur War and is indicted by the Agranat Commission. Another of the collection's protagonists describes the collective collapse as follows:

> Everybody is afraid. They all, like me, hide their fears. The catastrophe is waiting for all of us around the corner. They are all trying to ignore it. I can't. I am living the fear. Not of the wars. Of what lies beyond them. Like a prophet. I was in all those wars: Sinai in fifty-six, the Six-Day War. The last war. I am willing to face physical dangers. It's only fear which frightens me. Alone. Alone. ("Eighteen Months" ["Shmonah'asar hodesh"], p. 144)

The writer who more than anyone else altered the image of the hero was Aharon Appelfeld. Himself an immigrant, Appelfeld did not present parodies of the past, nor did he embody the disillusionment of the 1940s and 1950s. Rather, by reintroducing into Hebrew literature the figure of the Old Jew, he undermined the insistence on both the efficacy and spiritual superiority of the New Hebrew. Although many writers such as Shamir, Hendel, Shaham, Megged, and others had tried to represent the immigrant experience, it was Appelfeld who finally incorporated into Hebrew fiction refugees, the elderly, women, children, the uprooted, and those who were persecuted, terrified, and broken. His first collection of stories, *Smoke,* was a revolution without a manifesto. Swarming with survivors who only barely made it through the war and who carry with them wherever they go memories of diaspora and catastrophe, the fiction tells the stories of individuals whose most ardent desire is to return to the scene of their harrowing experiences ("Cold Spring" ["Aviv Kar"]), people who live paralyzed by their memories of wandering (Max in "Smoke," Max in "Bertha," and Zimmer in "A Serious Effort" ["Nisayon retsini"], whose anxieties and terrors eventuate in his death). Appelfeld also depicted the impossible, internal conflicts of Jewish identity that afflicted Jews both before and after the war. There is, for example, the Jew who flees to a monastery and is poisoned by herbal remedies in "The Final Refuge" ["Hamahaseh ha'aharon"] in *In the Fertile Valley* (1963), or Chukhovski, in "In the Isles of St George" ["Be'iyei seint Gorge"] in *Frost on the Land* [*Kfor 'al ha'arets,* 1965], who is uprooted from the land in which he had never been properly settled to begin with. Likewise, the assimilated Jews of *Badenheim 1939* and *The Age of Wonders* try to deny their identity and ignore the signs of impending catastrophe.

In Appelfeld's world, *aliyah* does not solve the problems of the Jewish survivor. Not only do European refugees bring with them their traumas and Jewish ambivalences, but, as portrayed in *Searing Light,* for example, the Israelis perpetuate the victimization of the victims. They insist on indoctrinating them into a cultural philosophy that discredits their experience of suffering and denies their way of being in the world. Precisely by not tackling the socio-political realities of Israel, as did the native-born writers, Appelfeld established the dignity of the survivors and restored the diaspora to Hebrew fiction. This enabled a writer such as Yitzhak Orpaz, who until then had written surrealist local stories, to publish in 1979 a collection of stories entitled *Tomozhena Street* [*Rehov hatomotsena*], which is set in the Jewish ghetto beside the river Bug, and which is told, like Bialik's *Aftergrowth* and the stories of Y. D. Berkowitz, from the viewpoint of a European Jewish child.

But Israeli writers did not need the diaspora to give them figures of alienation and desperation. Shabtai's *Uncle Peretz Takes Off* [*Dod Perets mamri',* 1972] and *Past Perfect* [*Sof Davar,* 1984] feature such characters, as do the novels of Yehoshua Kenaz: *After the Holidays, The Great Woman of the Dreams, Musical Moment* [*Moment musiqali,* 1980], and, above all, *The Way to the Cats* [*Baderekh 'el hahatulim,* 1991].

The fiction of women writers such as Amalia Kahana-Carmon and Ruth Almog also presents figures of human despair. Kahana-Carmon's characters are sensitive women who are constantly defeated in their desire for genuine emotional exchange. Every one of her female characters is an artist or a would-be artist, aching for the poetry of experience and discovering only the most banal of realities: "The secondary buries the primary. The everyday is barren. But why are matters in reality not as they were in the dream. As they were in the dream" (*And Moon in the Valley of Ajalon*, p. 185). So, too, the women in Ruth Almog's fiction, who are victims of the complex relationships with the men in their lives (fathers and spouses) and who rebel against fate (as in *Roots of Light* [*Shorshei 'Avir*, 1987]). Like Kahana-Carmon's heroes, Almog's women indulge in "romantic fantasies" and are disappointed when their love "[shrinks] into petty needs, hunger, loneliness, self-affirmation, an endless effort to become absorbed in the ephemeral, in order to achieve one moment of eternity" (*Death in the Rain*, p. 146).

More diaspora Jews than Israelis, the protagonists in David Shahar's *Nin-Gal* recall the rootlessness of Agnon and turn-of-the-century fiction. Seeing a sign commemorating the Austrian-Jewish writer Josef Roth, the narrator expostulates:

> The moment a person states that he is Austrian, Polish, Italian, Indian or Japanese, it means he belongs to a certain nation which has a certain country of its own, and as such he is obvious and defined and accepted, whereas the Jew is neither here not there, and yet he is everywhere, without belonging to the nation amongst whom he lives, and without the place being his, and there is always something about him that is exceptional and extraordinary, and either a bit too much or a bit too little, and a bit too hidden or a bit too obvious, and a bit too stuck in the throat and a bit too airy-fairy and inscrutable. (p. 45)

Such diaspora types came to populate many mid-century fictions, such as Orpaz's *The Wild Plant* or *Skin for Skin,* in which the character Momo, who lives in Israel during and after the Suez war, is a "hollow being," "apart from everything, even his own mind":

> His whole life hung on him like a tattered, worn, useless rag. He could not find himself anywhere. He did not live himself anywhere. Nowhere did he realize himself. He only sowed troubles and miseries. His love was no love. His hate was no hate. His revenge was no revenge. Even his escapes were not real escapes, but mad chases after something, God knows what. Perhaps after some reason for living, living, dying. And what did he find everywhere? Idiot traps: "Together" . . . "Together" . . . "As one" . . . A monster with one head and many arms. . . . And he wanted to see many heads, Jewish heads, jumping and falling, doing something

in their lives, confronting themselves in some action, even one single action. (pp. 63, 247)

As in the work of Yoram Kaniuk, such rootless New Jews might also be returning emigrees (in *Rockinghorse*), self-hating native Israelis (*Post Mortem*), or half-mad Holocaust survivors (*Adam Resurrected, The Last Jew*); or, as in the work of Dan Tzalka, they might be immigrants. In Tzalka's work, the critique of the old hero took the form of presenting the immigrant as superior to the native-born Israeli (for example, *Dr. Barkel* and *Philip Arbes*). As Tzalka saw it, the confrontation was not between the New Hebrew and the Old Jew, but between Western culture and the Middle East. In this contest, Israel had taken the wrong side.

In *The Last Jew* native-born Yoram Kaniuk dissolved the division between the New Hebrew and the Old Jew. "Did you know then," one of the characters asks,

> that Boaz and Shneorson and Shmuel Lipker were born on the same day and in the same hour? Did you know then that your son Boaz, whom you abandoned in the village, and Shmuel, whom you found in the camp, were two sides of the same coin, almost identical? You told me then that Boaz was your bastard! That Boaz and Shmuel are identical twins born in different places to different mothers, and maybe even to different fathers! (p. 83)

In his autobiographical *Post Mortem* Kaniuk personalizes this sense of haunting doubles and ghosts and reveals that he himself had always preferred the German-Jew represented by his father than the new sabra type that he, the son, was supposed to embody: "It seems that for one rare moment Moshe [his father] wanted to be a Jew among Jews, without pagan Canaan of the Herzlia Secondary School, without the seminar, and pressing flowers, and the wagtail and the flowering squill and 'my plough, only thou', and Trumpeldor" (p. 129). Kaniuk's *The Last Jew* and *Post Mortem* were extreme expressions of a trend which had begun in the early writings of Amichai, Sadeh, Appelfeld, Oz, Yehoshua, Kenaz, and Shabtai. *Post Mortem* was not a new development in fictional portraiture. It was a culmination.

VISIONS AND REVISIONS OF THE ZIONIST METAPLOT

Against the socio-political background of war and the changing relations not only between Arabs and Jews but also among Jews of different socio-economic and ethnic groups, a multifaceted, multivocal literature of resistance to the Zionist metaplot began to emerge. The characters of

Yehuda Amichai, for example, tended to rebel against the collective narrative in order to stress their independence and individuality. The alienated persons of A. B. Yehoshua's fiction penetrated to contradictions in Zionist ideology, while Amalia Kahana-Carmon's individualists viewed reality from so deeply personal a perspective as essentially to eclipse altogether the ideological dimension of their thought. In the fiction of Amos Oz the characters relished abandoning, even demolishing Zionist ideals, which at the very least they perceived paradoxically. Yaakov Shabtai's dysfunctional inheritors of the dreams of the fathers could barely keep themselves, let alone the dreams, alive; while Aharon Appelfeld's refugees are not idealists, but rather are driven to Israel by horrific circumstances beyond their control.

As we have seen, Tammuz never accepted the conventions of his generation, as evidenced by his collection *Sands of Gold*. In 1965 he began writing his socially critical picaresque trilogy *The Life of Elyakum;* and later his social criticism became truly sweeping. The central figure in his 1980 *Minotaur* is Alexander Abramov, whose body is in the East while his heart is in the West. His image of the ideal is the Western woman Thea, who has no connection whatsoever with Israel. Unable to break out of his personal, cultural, and social dead end, the hero dies.

David Shahar, too, wrote a satirical picaresque novella, *Moon of Honey and Gold* (1959), before venturing on his series of novels *The Palace of Shattered Vessels,* which began to appear in 1969. Tracing the history of Eretz Yisrael during the Ottoman period, the British Mandate, and the State period, his characters stand outside the Zionist context and his plots revolve around the singular destinies of various eccentric individuals. The work of both these writers is driven by the tension between the Canaanite experience and the European one:

> It seemed to me certain and obvious that this delight flows from the ancient Canaanite world, that continues to exist imperceptibly in the land of Canaan, and only in the late-late night, alone in the field, the spirit of one of the gods or goddesses passes us by and fills us with that ineffable thrill. That it might come to me not at night but by day, and not alone in the field but in a crowded city, not in Canaan but abroad—I would never have conceived of such a possibility if it had not happened to me on Rue Soufflot in the middle of the Latin Quarter on a rare sunny day. (*Nin-Gal,* p. 85)

Yitzhak Orpaz, in *Skin for Skin,* was one of the first to produce a work of fiction which criticized the regime led by Mapai, which was for years the political embodiment of the Zionist metaplot. His satire about Momo, the rootless individual who rebels against the establishment, criticized the

Suez war and the treatment of new immigrants. Momo's antagonist, Mr. Eliram, caricatured the authoritarianism of Ben-Gurion. Most of the characters of *The Mistress* also enact the anti-Zionist metaplot, but they are set against half-mad heroes, Zionist saints of a sort, who provide the Zionist background against which the society is seen to shed its values.

Directly responding to the expulsion, oppression, and occupation of the Arabs surrounding the events of the Six-Day War, A. B. Yehoshua's "Facing the Forests" tells the story of a student, used as a fire-watcher while working on a paper about the Crusades, who sees his helper, a mute Arab, preparing to set fire to the forest. This forest now covers over a pre-State Arab village. The story eventually comes to justify the act of vandalism. Instead of building and being rebuilt, the book suggests, perhaps one ought to begin by burning up and destroying. Such ideas also circulate in Yehoshua's *Mr. Mani*. Indeed, most of Yehoshua's novels revolve around such anti-metaplots.

In the original Zionist story, the elite heroes were secular pioneering Ashkenazi warriors. In Yehoshua's *The Lover* the elite is Sephardi-Arab. Here the advantage and the final triumph are given to figures who represent all the values the old establishment rejected: Arditi is an emigrant from Israel, a deserter from military service who pretends to be ultra-Orthodox, and Naim is a young Arab who succeeds where the Jews fail. The family is conquered from within by Arditi, the lover of Adam's wife, and Naim, the lover of his daughter. The fact that the readership still kept the old Zionist metaplot in mind sharpened the contrasts and ironies.

Resistance to the Zionist metaplot features just as prominently, if somewhat differently, in Amos Oz's short stories and in his longer fictions, such as *Elsewhere, Perhaps; The Hill of Evil Council; A Perfect Peace; Black Box;* and, especially, the historical novella *Unto Death*. In *Elsewhere, Perhaps* and *My Michael* the author exhibits sympathy for emigrants who sought their salvation in Germany and for a pair of Fatah twins. By contrast, the loyal Israelis of these stories, such as Reuven Harish and Michael Gonen, are not much liked by the author, who is attracted by darker, more elusive forces than they can embody. In Oz's view, the demon lies within the Zionist metaplot itself, in its ideological insistences and in the uneasy combination of romantic yearnings, anxiety, and pragmatism that the founding fathers foisted upon their children.

Despite these powerful elements of Zionist critique, however, Oz also remains one of the most affirmatively Zionistic of the New Wave writers. In many of his works morality is still measured by Zionist standards, especially the standards of the kibbutz. In *A Perfect Peace,* for example, it is the kibbutz secretary Srulik who is both the humanist and the Zionist: "There is enough pain in the world," he insists, "and it is our job to reduce the pain, not to add to it" (p. 362). Similarly, those who desert Zionism do so for ethically problematical reasons. In *Elsewhere, Perhaps* the mysterious and somewhat evil Eva Hamburger deserts the kibbutz to live in Germany; in *The Hill of Evil Council* a mother leaves the country in order to elope with an English officer; in *A Perfect Peace* the man who might serve the young Yonatan as a surrogate father flees to the United States; while in *Black Box* the anti-hero, Gideon Alexander, returns home to Israel to die. Jews, Oz knows, are themselves victims, as he indicates in *Unto Death*, in which the authorial voice ironizes an anti-Semitic account of the Jews during the Crusades.

Yitzhak Ben-Ner remained even more faithful than Oz to the Zionist metaplot. In *A Far Land* Ben-Ner measures the characters against the Zionist beliefs they betray. *Protocol* (1983) similarly applies to the values of settlement and the humanist tenets of the labor movement in order to judge a 1920s Palestine-based communist terrorist group, which is the novel's subject. Ultimately, when the hero and his lover Vera have reached a dead end, Vera returns to essential Zionist doctrine: "This bitter awakening from a great universal dream which failed can only lead to this liberation, my dear, or to destruction. Only such a liberation—realistic, sober, humane, aware of its limitations, seeking to achieve fulfillment without much harm to others" (p. 366).

Resistance to the ideological assumptions of Zionism produced a series of retrospective revisions of Jewish history. Shabtai's *Past Continuous*, Kaniuk's *The Last Jew*, Yehoshua's *Mr. Mani*, and Tzalka's *A Thousand Hearts* were all, in one way or another, historical novels that blended realism and the fantastic in their effort to provide a new genealogy for the nation. In scope and quality they match Agnon's *Yesteryear* (about the Second Aliyah), Hazaz's *Yaish* (about the Yemenite Jewish community), and Yehoshua Bar-Yosef's *Enchanted City* (about nineteenth-century Safed). Like other twentieth-century sagas, they did not depict the rise and flourishing of dynasties, but rather their decline and fall. Considering that they were written in a country and nation which had just been revived, this charting of the spiral downward was especially significant.

Perhaps the most sweeping and powerful of the New Wave critiques of Zionism was Yaakov Shabtai's *Past Continuous*. The novel opens with the death of Goldman senior, one of the fathers of pioneering labor Zionism. It ends with the suicide of his son, an emasculated figure representative of the generation that had witnessed the demise of the dreams of the fathers. The ideals of the parent generation find some representation in the novel, for example, in the younger Goldman's Aunt Zipporah, who believed that "a man must learn to serve himself and to help others as best he could, and . . . that work, any work, was dignified, and that laziness and idleness were the root of all evil, and were sure to corrupt a person and lead him to prurience and decadence and even crime, and so did extravagance and ostentation. . . . She believed that a person must struggle with his troubles and not rush to impose them upon others" (pp. 217, 228). Nonetheless, such ideals as these, which echo the beliefs of the founding fathers Gordon and Brenner, remain in the background of Shabtai's novel. Instead, occupying center stage, and framed by the deaths of father and son, are the struggles of the characters to maintain a mere semblance of normalcy and meaning. It is as if the book is intended to tell the saga of the pioneering family's act of closing its account with the Promised Land.

The novel's technique—it runs unbroken, like a single paragraph, from start to finish, in something like a collective stream of consciousness—underscores its synchronic and diachronic character. There is no differentiating past causes from present realities or reversing their fatal consequences. Goldman junior's literal suicide and the figurative spiritual suicides of his companions Caesar and Israel are nothing more than the inheritance bequeathed by the pioneers to their sons, who can cope neither with their fathers nor with the reality their fathers have constructed:

> And Goldman, continuing to hold the now empty teacup, felt sadly and helplessly that everything wears out and comes to an end—the body and human relations, and that he himself was part of that wearing out process. (p. 214)

Or:

> He meant to go and visit his father's grave for a minute but did not do so, and as he walked away from the place there spread through him, almost delicately, the sense of the death of Uncle Lazar, a sense of finality and loneliness, which turned into a depressing awareness of irreparable loss and longings, and then a sense that his life was already behind him and he was being driven to his death and was parting from everything. (p. 253)

Also recording the history of immigration and settlement, Dan Tzalka's *A Thousand Hearts* puts at the center of its narrative the *Ruslan,* the first ship of the Third Aliyah, whose arrival in Jaffa started a new chapter in the history of Zionism: "Every person who was on the ship, every child, will tell his story, everything to do with that sailing. There were even photographs, and some people kept diaries! I talked with Professor Bogan, the historian. He said that 1919, the year the Ruslan arrived, opened an era in the history of Zionism, of Eretz Israel, the start of the Third Aliyah! It's the period! I already have a cupboard full" (p. 138). Moving along a dual track, the author follows the story of the passengers of the *Ruslan* some twenty years later in tandem with the story of those who remained in Poland, especially one young man who received a Polish decoration on the Soviet home front in Uzbekistan. Multiple interpretations are invited, underscoring the historical parallels linking different waves of Zionist immigration, while the major trope of the novel—its protagonist's desire to create an archive about the ship—suggests something of the self-consciousness of the country's concern with its past.

Even more innovative and original in its interpretation of Zionist history, Yehoshua's *Mr. Mani* is what one might define as an anti-family anti-saga. Moving backward from present to past, it is narrated not by members of the family (except in the final monologue) or even by an omniscient narrator but rather (primarily) by outsiders who are represented in the text as being in conversation with still other non-members of the Mani clan. The principal events that shape the novel's historical sweep are (proceeding backward through the novel's retrogressive chronology) the war in Lebanon, the German occupation of Crete during the Second World War, the British conquest of Palestine and the rise of the Jewish and Arab nationalism in 1917, the third Zionist Congress and the old Sephardi community in Palestine (circa 1898), the revolution of 1848, and the Sephardi community before the advent of Zionist immigration. *Mr. Mani* is not simply historical interpretation. It is psychocultural analysis. It is the spiritual and emotional biography of a people.

In revising the Zionist metaplot the writers could not but recast the interpretation of the Holocaust. The post-realists made no attempt to depict the victims as heroic. Rather, they accepted them as they were, helpless victims driven to their collective deaths. The following passage, from Kaniuk's *Adam Resurrected,* summarizes one post-realist response to the Holocaust:

> And Mrs. Shpring, we are all grumbling and yawning and trying to make a profit, to build houses, to hurry, quick-quick, and all this happens in the daytime. At night we have nightmares and we scream, because Satan has engraved blue numbers on our arms. Do you know, my dear Mrs. Zeisling, what screams are heard in this country in the dead of night? Powerful screams. . . . All these numbers, which scream and cry, who don't know why and wherefore and how and when and in what way and for how long and how far. . . . There is no escape. That is why they scream. Weep. A searing insult. The knowledge, the profound knowledge that they were raw material in Europe's most advanced factory, under the sky in which God sits in exile, like a stranger. . . . This knowledge drives us mad, and we have become a country which is the world's biggest madhouse. (p. 46)

Several other Hebrew authors who tackled this risky subject were Uri Orlev in *Lead Soldiers* and *Till Tomorrow* [*'Ad mahar,* 1959], and Ruth Almog in *The Exile* [*Be'eretz Gzeirah,* 1971]. A new wave of Holocaust novels and stories appeared in the 1980s by David Grossman, Nava Semel, Itamar Levy, Savyon Liebrecht, D. Peleg, and others.

The great writer of Holocaust fiction, who also transformed the metaplot of Jewish history, was Aharon Appelfeld. Appelfeld's metaplot is based on the myth of Ahasverus, the wandering Jew, condemned to wander the earth, unable to live fully or to find rest in death. From the writings of the 1960s, *Smoke, In the Fertile Valley, Frost on the Land,* through later works such as *Searing Light* (1980), *Tzili: The Story of a Life* [*Hakutonet vehapasim,* meaning: "the shirt and the stripes," 1983], *Katerina* (1989), *Abyss* [*Timayon,* 1993], and *Laish* (1994), his protagonists, like Ahasverus, stand outside the possibilities of liberation. For Appelfeld, the teleology of salvation from destruction, which was the premise of Judaism and Zionism both, is an illusion.

Appelfeld's characters are the walking dead. They cannot awake from the horrors of the Holocaust. This attraction toward death and self-destruction occupies a central position in the work of many of the post-realists, A. B. Yehoshua, for example, many of whose protagonists—from *The Death of the Old Man* through *Early in the Summer of 1970* and the macabre *Five Seasons*—seem actually to hanker after extinction. It figures as well in Amos Oz's death-seeking crusaders in *Unto Death* or Kaniuk's figures of despair, from *Himmo, King of Jerusalem* through *Adam Resurrected, Rockinghorse, The Last Jew,* and *Post-Mortem.* Death and bereavement (in Israel) and death and the Holocaust (in the diaspora and among the survivors in Israel) are recurring themes in Yeshayahu Koren, *Funeral at Noon* [*Levayah batsohorayim,* 1974]; Ben-Ner, *Rustic Sunset;* Kenaz, *The Great Woman of the Dreams, Heart Murmur,* and *The Way to the Cats;* Orpaz, *Skin For Skin, The Mistress,* and *A Charming Traitor;* and Almog, *Death in the Rain.*

Nonetheless, Shabtai was the great realizer of this theme of death, as a challenge to the heroism and idealism of earlier Hebrew texts:

> He was hardly willing to listen and look with that frozen gaze at Caesar, who got up and walked about the room and began to speak angrily about Goldman, who two days earlier, when he had hinted at his son's condition, tried to cheer him up and said he should not panic and even the best doctors make mistakes and that he is certain that it will be all right in the end, and as he spoke he changed his tone somewhat and went on to say that life is nothing but a journey to death, as the ancients already knew, and that is the one certainty in it, and furthermore—death is the quintessence of life and becomes progressively embodied in it, hour by hour, until it is fully embodied in the end, like the worm which irresistibly becomes embodied in the pupa, from which the butterfly will emerge. Therefore, man must train himself to accept death, which never comes

too soon, and even when it seems that it has, there is no point in resisting it. (*Past Continuous,* p. 255)

Past Continuous does more than sum up the post-modern position vis-à-vis the Zionist metaplot. It ranges over the many historical events that produced this response: the Sinai (Suez) war, the Eichmann trial, the Lavon Affair, the fall of Ben-Gurion, the Six-Day War, the occupation, and above all, the war of Yom Kippur, in which Israeli society experienced the fall from euphoria into a deep depression.

Needless to say, characters who are drawn to death or are impelled toward death without any heroic cause are not unique to Hebrew fiction. As Natan Zach put it in *Airwaves* [*Qavei 'avir*] in 1983: "How desolate and gloomy are the landscapes of contemporary Hebrew prose. To judge by the books we have examined together (and I don't for a moment suggest that they represent the entire picture!), there is such a lot of strangeness and distress, alienation and loneliness, vapidity and death! How poor it is in passion and vitality in the face of universal pain. How crushed is Eros as a creative, fertile force" (p. 62). Nonetheless, the appearance of such books on the stage of Israeli writing is significant in the history of Hebrew literature. The thematic change affected the form. The difference between ending a story with a heroic death as the climax of the Zionist metaplot and a climax in the form of a slow decline makes for different cathartic effects as in the above passage from *Past Continuous.*

These new transformative sagas of Israeli history and Jewish national consciousness must be read not only against the background of the Holocaust, the War of Independence, the Sinai Campaign, and the Six-Day War, but, as we move into the 1970s, 1980s, and 1990s, also against the Yom Kippur War, the Lebanon War, and, increasingly, the Palestinian uprising (the Intifada) as well. All of these later events cast their shadow retrospectively back over earlier Israeli history, causing a reinterpretation of earlier events. For the fiction writers were not the only ones rewriting the nation's history. Historians and sociologists such as Benny Morris, Tom Segev, Yigal Eilam, Ilan Pape, Amnon Raz, and Baruch Kimmerling were also engaged in a post-Zionist historical revisionism, some of them reinterpreting the past to claim that, already in the War of Independence and the early State period, the Zionists had sinned not only against the Palestinians but against the victims of the Holocaust as well. In a writer such as Kaniuk this emerges as nothing less than prioritizing the victims of the Holocaust over Israel's own fallen, since the heroes of 1948 were people who not only chose to sacrifice themselves and their children but also killed innocent people in the process. Thus, from the 1950s on, the Zionist metaplot is increasingly called into question, as writers—augmenting the fiction's range of characters and introducing into the standard narratives of Israeli history counter-histories of other places, other times, and other Jews—produce a Hebrew fiction responsible not to the reaffirmation of Zionist ideology, but to the unhampered and oftentimes severely critical investigation of the nation's history and culture.

* * *

The expressionism of Sadeh, Oz, Kaniuk, and the early Kenaz; the grotesque surrealism of Yehoshua, Orpaz, and Appelfeld; the lyrical-baroque and feminist thematics of Kahana-Carmon and Almog; Shabtai's generalized, communal stream of consciousness; and perhaps the late impressionism of Kenaz—all of these distinguished Hebrew fiction of the 1960s and 1970s. So did a radical shift away from the Zionist metanarrative to much more hard-hitting confrontations with disappointment and disillusion, both on the public and private levels. It seemed that Hebrew literature had come into its own. But, of course, literary traditions never work this way. By the 1980s, twenty-five years after the rise of the New Wave, literary conventions once more underwent radical transformation, while new political realities on the ground—the war in Lebanon (1982–1985) and the 1987 Palestinian uprising (Intifada)—again shifted the fictional subject.

Many writers took part in left-wing demonstrations, signed petitions, and wrote articles and books opposing government policy. Amos Oz published a collection of political essays in 1983 entitled *In the Land of Israel* [*Po vesham be'eretz Yisra'el*] and wrote about the war in Lebanon in *The Slopes of Lebanon* [*Mimordot halevanon*, 1988]. In 1987 David Grossman published *The Yellow Wind* [*Hazman hatsahov*], detailing conditions in the occupied territories and issuing warnings concerning the continuation of occupation. The main effect of these events on the literary establishment was the further withdrawal of young writers from the dialectics of the Zionist metanarrative. At the same time, the 1980s witnessed the appearance of a number of innovative stylists, who once again radically revised Hebrew literary poetics. Writers such as Yoel Hoffman, Dan Benaya Seri, Avraham Heffner, and Yossl Birstein were of an older generation, making their literary debuts relatively late. But there were younger writers as well, including David Grossman, who were to have a decisive impact on the texture of contemporary Hebrew literature.

12

TOWARD THE 1990s
A GENERATION WITHOUT DREAMS

The legitimate heir of the 1960s generation was David Grossman, who revolutionized the heritage from within. His early stories and novels showed the same social involvement as the novels of Oz and Yehoshua. In *See Under: Love* [*'Ayen 'erekh: 'ahavah,* 1986], however, he declared his independence as a writer. A highly allusive and intertextual work, the book wove together different narratives and literary styles. It disrupted familiar literary boundaries and produced a wholly original work of art. The first part of the novel is a neo-realist rendering of a child's experience of the survivor community in Israel, presented through the child's consciousness. The second and third sections, moving back into the period of the Second World War, are fantastic and parodic-grotesque. The work culminates in a decidedly postmodernist move. Instead of narrative, it provides an encyclopedia of names, terms, events, and concepts, many of them connected to the Holocaust and to events which appear elsewhere in the novel itself. Invoking the real-life figure of Polish-Jewish author and painter Bruno Schultz, who does not belong in the lineage of Hebrew writers and who was killed by the Nazis during the Second World War, the book incorporates features of the German gothic tradition and, in particular, the writings of Günter Grass (*The Tin Drum* and *The Flounder*). Thus, even though the book also carries traces of internal Hebraic influences, such as the Holocaust fiction of Yoram Kaniuk (*Adam Resurrected*) and Oz's metahistorical-grotesque novels *Touch the Water, Touch the Wind* and *The Hill of Evil Council,* it also places itself within an unmistakably European context.

At the same time, it forges new territory in Holocaust fiction. It insists that nothing less than phantasmagoric representation can get at the reality of the death camps. And it proclaims the efficacy of art in its attempts to come to terms with the horror. By dealing with the Holocaust, Grossman violated sacred taboos which held the Holocaust as an inappropriate subject for fiction of any sort, most especially fiction of the wildly imaginative variety Grossman himself produced. Despite its apparent rebellion against the literary tradition of the 1960s, *See Under: Love* also reaffirms an aspect of that tradition, namely the importance of the collective experience as the locus of Hebrew fiction.

The writings of Oz, Yehoshua, Kaniuk, Orpaz, and most of their contemporaries were susceptible to socio-allegorical interpretation because the authors observed and commented on the national scene. In the 1980s writers permitted themselves to turn inward toward more idiosyncratic and sui generis experiences. Thus, for example, in Amos Oz's novella about a child during the War of Independence (*The Hill of Evil Counsel*) the focus is on a confrontation among a British officer, an underground leader, and a terminally ill man who is expending his last energies trying to invent weapons to defend against the Arabs. By contrast, in Grossman's *The Book of Intimate Grammar* [*Sefer hadiqduq hapnimi*, 1991], the Six-Day War serves only as background for an apolitical narrative. Tracing the maturation of a sensitive, introverted young boy growing up in Jerusalem in the 1960s, the novel does not attempt to confront the main issues of the times, such as the Jewish-Arab conflict (as in Grossman's earlier *The Smile of the Lamb* [*Hiyukh hagdi*, 1983]) or the Holocaust and its survivors. Rather, despite its being thoroughly anchored in time and place, it does not presume to define that time and place. Nor is the novel overtly ideological. The protagonists are socially and politically marginalized individuals, going through the ordinary prosaic course of their lives (as in Albert Suissa's novel *Bound* [*'Akud*, 1990]). The children are all familiar with the ins and outs of the buildings, with the gossip that spreads like wildfire through the flats, and with the life that flourishes within its confines. The everyday life of the neighborhood is far more important than large national events.

In this the novel resembles Henry Roth's classic *Call It Sleep*. Whether or not Grossman was familiar with Roth's novel, both *Call It Sleep* and *The Book of Intimate Grammar* recall their original sources of influence, namely, James Joyce's *Portrait of the Artist as a Young Man* and *Ulysses*. In books of this genre, ordinary family life moves to the center, and what appears to be merely bourgeois and banal is made to reveal hidden depths of mental and emotional experience. Grossman's Kleinfelds are both typical and atypical of Israeli families. In the background are the father, once imprisoned in a Soviet labor camp in the steppes, and the mother, an orphaned refugee who brought up her own sisters. Even though these historical backgrounds are important, the novel, unlike *See Under: Love,* is less concerned with the sweep of history and its consequences for the collective consciousness than with the very specific effects of family biography on the family itself. Of primary importance is the distance between the communal and the private. Thus, when "suddenly a shrill siren shrieked," what is more important than the war to fourteen-year-old Aaron is his own, very different, personal liberation. "Maybe their war's begun," he muses. "The siren stopped abruptly" (*Intimate Grammar,* p. 308). "The transistor generation, the yeah-yeah generation," says the protagonist, "what has it got to do with the things that it is in? And maybe, who knows, it no longer has any other life and existence anywhere else" (p. 234).

In focusing on private interpersonal relationships rather than on the group, *The Book of Intimate Grammar* recalls the early novels of Yehoshua Kenaz (*After the Holidays* and *The Great Woman of the Dreams*) and Yeshayahu Koren (*Funeral at Noon,* 1974). Grossman draws on the neorealism of the bildungsroman (Kenaz's *Musical Moment* and *Heart Murmur*) but also introduces grotesque elements, as in the long episode about Edna Blum, whose relationship to the boy's father verges on the absurd. In this the book recalls the example of A. B. Yehoshua. It produces a neorealism committed to flitting on the margins of history.

Two other writers who built on the innovations of the 1960s generation are Meir Shalev and Dan Benaya Seri. Adapting Yehoshua's grotesques to explore as-yet-uncharted territories, Shalev produced socio-historical pageants with nostalgic overtones: *The Blue Mountain,* 1988, *Esau,* 1991, and *As a Few Days,* 1994. The fictions are carnivalesque, almost in the manner of English and French Renaissance writing. They proceed through abundant secondary tales and anecdotes, producing an amazing conjunction of laughter and tears, an uninhibited use of strange and contrasting materials, and tribal rather than personal perspectives on sexual relations. In some ways the obverse of the decadent novels of 1970s Hebrew fiction, Shalev's fiction incorporates myths, legends, rituals, and visions in a *danse macabre* mingled with a dance of life. The author plays endless games with the primary elements—fire, water, and sun—while mixing and leaving unreconciled bizarre and tragic events, such as (in *Esau*) a son who does not return for his mother's funeral, a woman who refuses to return to life after her son's death, a woman who saw her family massacred by an Arab mob, a young girl abandoned by her father and married to a man she was not meant for, two ridiculous short-sighted brothers, and the failed marriages of the two principal couples.

Of the three novels, *Esau* is in all ways the most important. On the face of it, it is about a family of bakers. One of the brothers (Esau) leaves the country, gives up the trade, and writes cookery and baking books. The other brother remains in the country, loses his son in a military incident, and continues his father's trade. But the novel is intertextual and allusive such that the relationships also signify biblical and historical archetypes. This is history as myth, the names of the characters—Abraham and Sarah, Jacob and Esau, Leah and Benjamin—and their various activities making their biblical overtones unmistakable. It is also parody. In the fraternal struggles of the novel, it is Jacob who is the earthy man, not Esau; Leah who is loved by the brothers, not Rachel; and the United States which is the Egypt to which the protagonist emigrates. Parody does not cancel the text's symbolic force. For example, the author insists that fraternal conflict is one of the basic elements of the human condition, especially in the direct descendants of Cain and Abel, Isaac and Ishmael, Jacob and Esau, and Joseph and his brothers. In the biblical tradition, the older brother served the younger, because the younger was more spiritual. In *Esau* the picture is reversed and reversed again. The narrator, Esau, seems to be spiritual but his spirituality is barren. He can write about bread but he cannot bake it. He sleeps with many women but he fathers no children. Jacob is the material brother: an absurd lover and a bereaved father. A baker of bread, it is he who conveys the positive vision of the text.

Dan Benaya Seri is another writer who, like Shalev, adapted the grotesquerie of Yehoshua's fiction to new purposes. Even before Yehoshua had expanded his own techniques in *Five Seasons* and *Mr. Mani*, Seri had turned the grotesque inward to examine the mythical and psychological depths of the communal psyche. "The Thousand Wives of Naftali Siman-Tov" ["'Elef neshotav shel Naftali Siman-Tov"], which opens the collection *Birds of the Shade* [*Tziporei tsel*, 1987], deals with the impossibility of human sexual relations. Its male and female protagonists are incapable of entering into direct conversation about any of the issues that connect them, most especially sexuality itself. Sex, in the world of this text, is outside language. Not only do men and women refrain from conversing either before or after engaging in sexual relations, they do not seem even to understand what is happening to them. For example, one pregnant woman does not even know that she is pregnant. One of the male characters, who does know, cannot tell her, because he also knows that he is not the one who impregnated her, preferring, as he does, masturbation to sexual intercourse. By his use of communal materials, the euphemistic avoidance of the subject, and the grotesque depiction of his protagonists, Seri succeeded in painting a picture of a society that avoided conflict by escaping into its unconscious and repressing its psychosexual needs. In this way, it perverted itself and courted disaster. Seri's writing provides insights into a particular Israeli community. Yet it is not ethnic fiction per se. Rather, the stylized, anti-mimetic quality of the writing produces a universalized portrait of the human condition, cast in Middle Eastern terms.

Quintessentially post-modernist, the fiction of Yoel Hoffman also has discernable roots within the tradition of Hebrew writing. His stories "Katschen" (about a young immigrant boy who eventually gets delivered to a kibbutz) and "The Book of Joseph" ["Sefer Yosef"] (which takes place in Europe before the war), both of which appear in the collection *The Book of Joseph* (1988), have much in common with Appelfeld's inventory of alienated and uprooted immigrants and refugees (as do the figures in David Schutz's *The Grass and the Sand* [*Ha ʿesev vehahol*] and *White Rose, Red Rose*). But whereas Appelfeld downplayed his characters' ethnic origins, Hoffman highlighted them, incorporating German phrases directly into the narrative, with translations provided in the margins of the text. Hoffman's structure is fragmentary in the extreme, creating the sense that something is being suppressed or left unsaid or otherwise cannot be rendered articulate (see Conner, *Postmodernist Culture*). Like Appelfeld, Hoffman is grappling with the forces of Jewish identity and assimilation both before and after the war. But whereas Hoffman's dry alienated style modifies the pathos implicit in both these situations, his depiction of the characters and their plights evidences a greater sympathy and warmth than, for example, the parallel representations in Appelfeld.

In his later fiction, Hoffman became even more experimental. From brief poetical sketches he moved into a novel of snapshots, raising questions about the nature of reality and the continuities and discontinuities of its unfolding. The author uses various typographical techniques, for example, short units of text using the form of Japanese haiku, printed on a single side of the page, in order to stress discontinuity, fragmentariness, and the role of the interpretive imagination in creating order and meaning.

For Hoffman (as for Appelfeld and others), the immigrant is an alien in his homeland. As marginal outsider, he is also, however, the central protagonist of the national story. As he puts it in *Bernhart* (1989):

> In his childhood Bernhart flew over Finland on the back of a wild goose. Many strange things happened to him and Sigmund and Klara. Sigmund and Klara died and Bernhart came to Palestine on his own and married Paula, and Paula too died, and all through those years Bernhart never once said "Ahalan" [an Arabic greeting used by sabras]. He detests those double-chinned types who walk about Palestine saying "Ahalan." He wants to ask: "And Bernhart, Sigmund's son, is he not a human being? Sometimes even skinny, skeptical types say (unnaturally) 'Ahalan.'" And

> when Bernhart sees them he feels uncomfortable, as if they'd showed him their private parts. (p. 37)

The hero remains culturally a part of the world he left behind (signified, for example, by the allusion to Selma Lagerloef's children's classic *The Wonderful Journey of Nils Holgersson with the Wild Geese*, 1907). He loathes immigrants who betray their European origins in their hurry to assimilate. This problematic had been raised earlier by Ben-Zion Tomer in his play *Children of the Shadows* [*Yaldei hatsel*, 1963], and by Appelfeld. It receives a new clarity and sharpness of definition in Hoffman's writing. Hoffman's *The Christ of Fish* [*Qristos shel hadagim*, 1991], is an even more innovative and daring book. No longer dependent on the thematic or stylistic conventions of the 1960s, it represents a wholly new departure in Hebrew fiction. As in *Bernhart* the structure consists of small poetic units. They are parts of an ongoing narrative, yet each is self-defined and autonomous. Representation does not exist apart from interpretation. The whole is fragmentary, its pieces either arbitrarily or inevitably associated—it is impossible to decide. In effect, the novel is a discursive poem, with many gaps, recalling Japanese haiku and the "miniature art" (*Kleinkunst*) of turn-of-the-century Austria, in which the text's caesurae are no less important than the rhythmic units themselves.

As in other of Hoffman's writings, the text is extremely intellectual and allusive, assuming familiarity with Western and German as well as Hebrew culture. The reader is expected to know, for example, who Anton Wildgans was (an Austrian expressionist poet and dramatist, who lived from 1881–1932), and to have knowledge of the myths of Parsifal, Nefertiti, the albatross, the ideas of Spinoza, Moses Mendelssohn, Leibniz, Hume, Ignatius of Loyola, the Bhagavad-Gita, and any number of other mythological, literary, and historical materials. Needless to say, the very title of the book recalls Christian tradition.

As in his earlier fiction, Hoffman mounts a critique of the nation in relation to its unassimilable European immigrants:

> After the war (in winter seventy-four), / the godhead sent chill winds over the world. / The waking-up mechanisms (cuckoos and the like, / in the wall-clocks froze. Aunt Magda ignited / a blue flame in her kerosene heaters and sat down / she and Frau Steir on the old sofa / in tandem. . . . At five Frau Steir said "Ignatius." Did she mean the bishop of Antioch (Antiochos / Theophoros) who in his epistles called for / bishops to be reverenced like god? Did she mean / Ignatius of Loyola who founded in the church of / St Mary in Montmartre / the Society of Jesus?" (pp. 179–80)

Two temporal continuities, one historical, the other natural, and two image fields (wars juxtaposed with cuckoo clocks and kerosene heaters or with the two Ignatiuses) reflect the divergence between the external world in which these women live and the inner contours of their lives. For them Christianity is as much a part of their experience as Judaism is to their immediate environment. This contrast between cultures is often conveyed in comic grotesque images: "In fact, the life-story of Aunt Magda / is the life-story of Aunt Magda in a slip. / Guns shelled the 'Altalena.' Begin cried. / But Aunt Magda stood / (such decisiveness has no equal!) like a lump of earth, beside the harpsichord, in a slip" (p. 98). "Perhaps the English had a mandate on Palestine," the text writes elsewhere, "but my Uncle / Herbert had a mandate on all the worlds" (p. 102). This is an elegiac saga about the decline of a culture and about alienated immigrants in a strange non-homeland.

Hoffman is not the only writer of the 1980s to write post-modern fiction using documentary and pseudo-epistolary texts and self-consciously exposing the fictional devices of fiction-making. Among the prominent examples are Avraham Heffner (*All Inclusive* [*Kolel hakol*, 1987]), and Itamar Levy (*The Legend of the Sad Lakes* [*'Agadat ha 'agamim ha 'atsu-vim*, 1989]). The most interesting of these is Yuval Shimoni. The grandson of the Zionist poet David Shimoni, Yuval Shimoni turned his back on his genealogy, and just as Vogel wrote German novels in Hebrew, Shimoni wrote an American-French novel in Hebrew. Like Hoffman, Shimoni also sought resources outside Hebrew fiction. He also experimented with typographical devices. His novel *The Flight of the Dove* [*Ma 'of hayonah*, 1990] is written in two facing columns, each of which narrates a different story. In the right-hand column the protagonists are an American couple in Paris, though this is of little significance, since they emerge as universal rather than national figures. The left-hand column concerns a lonely Frenchwoman contemplating suicide, who is equally universalized. Though the novel does not offer any obvious links between the two stories, despite its hints toward some interconnection, the novel's patterning ipso facto presupposes the human mind as a synthetic entity, capable of creatively collating and organizing otherwise disparate materials. Symmetries of composition—the room, the metro, the pigeons—emphasize asymmetries. Yet they also construct parallels that hint at the shared humanity of the characters. The tourist couple on the right have both been defeated in the battle of the sexes. Their relations to each other are nothing more than shared space and habit. Yet this fate is not particular to them. It is the destiny of monogamy itself.

Time emerges as the destroyer that marriage vainly attempts to defy but which cannot be held back. Speaking about their children the husband says: "They are our fucking hour-glass. . . . What rises for them goes down for us" (p. 69a). Aging is only an external manifestation of an inner process of change which causes people to draw apart, even to feel repelled by one another: "She turns her face to him, compels him to see the flesh which has thickened and grown flabby. The empty bags under her eyes and the loose skin of the neck" (p. 65a).

In the opposing column a different story goes forward, told in a different style as well. External observation is abandoned and stream of consciousness takes over. We know nothing about the past of the lonely woman protagonist, only her immediate and pitifully mundane present, which is depicted with intensely poetic imagery: "So it should be closed. The lid. The lid of the salt-cellar should be closed. There, now it's closed. It's closed. It has turned and reached the big hole, so it has to go on a bit, to this point. To here. The salt-cellar lid is receding from view, and with it the table under it. The tablecloth has red and white checks" (p. 71b). Objective description and metaphor continuously displace each other, until one can hardly tell if there is, indeed, an external world. If, in Column A we have the depiction of waning libido, the physical world coming to substitute for the world of emotions, and loneliness encroaching on the shared life of the couple, in Column B we have heightened sexuality and emotionality, driven by a death-wish more vital and potent than the couple's commitment to enjoying life and having a good time. For the American couple the compelling existential problem is whether to visit the Centre Pompidou or the Eiffel Tower. "In the end everything falls apart," the wife says. "They don't put it together properly, they give no warranty, so what can you do. Your shoelace" (p. 79). The banality of the words expresses the insignificance and meaninglessness of their lives.

In his book *The Dehumanization of Art,* Jose Ortega y Gasset has described what he has called "the death of the plot." In Shimoni's novel we experience not only the end of the plot, but the end of psychological characterization as such. The assumption is that fiction must find a new position among the media, because its plots cannot compete with the cinema, nor its psychological characterization with psychoanalytic research. What it can do better than any other medium is to depict human behavior more meticulously than even a close-up photograph. Therefore, instead of speeding up the plot, Shimoni slows it down, and instead of building up tension, he depicts the minutiae of everyday life as a drama—or anti-drama—of a couple's life and of the monodrama of a solitary woman.

The isolated lonely woman, even though she is not in dialogue with anyone else, still maintains within herself a kind of internal dialogue, and in this, the book suggests, there is meaning. To be sure, the ending is ambiguous. The flight of the dove may represent the woman's death. But it may also signify only her disappearance or escape from the world. The right-hand column charted the dying of communication; the left—the intensity, madness, and self-destructiveness of internal human monologue.

But a paragraph in the left-hand column on the penultimate page suggests a more optimistic possibility:

> And in lighted rooms, in a bright light gentled by a lampshade; there, subdued even as they approached, were the touches which longed to touch, man touching woman, human to human; hopeful and hesitant, fearful, approaching and clutching each other, there was nothing else but they. Somewhere beyond the crowded mass of buildings, a woman stood at a counter and sprinkled white grains of sugar. Water spouted from a little fountain beside her. A dove, like this one here, strutted towards some breadcrumbs. (p. 96a)

"The ends of the roads are only longings," the text tells us; beyond death-in-life there may be, like a twinkling light, a touch, not merely between people but between the human and the non-human (the dove). In his flight from the Israeli scene and the collective experience, Shimoni finds a certain measure of hope in the intensity of solitude.

Women's fiction, another area of radical revision in the tradition, is a subject that has occupied many scholars of Hebrew literature of late, including Esther Fuchs, Naomi Sokolov, Anne Hoffman, Yael Feldman, and Hanna Naveh. Although women have always assumed a prominent place in poetry, in fiction the situation was somewhat different. The novels and stories of Devorah Baron, Elisheva and Esther Raab, and Leah Goldberg never received sufficient reception, even though Goldberg's *And He Is the Light* is probably the originating text in Hebrew literature's women's tradition.

In the 1940s and 1950s many women writers appeared on the scene. Naomi Frankel wrote the trilogy *Saul and Yohanna,* and Yonat Sened co-wrote (with her husband Alexander) many works of fiction. Yehudit Hendel, who started out as a writer of impressionist-realist fiction, moved on to produce impressionist fiction in *The Other Power, Near Quiet Places* [*Leyad kfarim shkeitim*], and *Small Change.* Rachel Eytan promised great things in her 1962 *The Fifth Heaven,* while Shulamith Hareven contributed short stories, a novel (*A City of Many Days,* 1973), and several historical works of fiction (*The Miracle Hater* and *Prophet* [*Navi',* 1989]).

If there is a single woman writer who set standards, produced a style, and created feminist consciousness, it was Amalia Kahana-Carmon who, though a contemporary of Hendel and Yonat Sened, made her debut only in the late 1950s. One of the most stylized authors since Yizhar, Kahana-Carmon is one of the most significant authors of the 1960s. Thematically, she deals with relations between men and women and family experiences set in various periods, regions, and classes in Israel. Stylistically, her writing is characterized by an intricate lyrical manner, with minute observations of her heroine's emotions and longings. Ruth Almog is also important; she appeared on the literary scene somewhat later and produced unmistakably feminist fiction in her short story collection *Women* [*Nashim,* 1986] and in her novels *The Exile, Death in the Rain,* and *Roots of Light.*

Indeed, in the 1980s a large number of women appeared on the literary scene: Savyon Liebrecht, Leah Aini, Yehudit Katzir, Hannah Bat-Shahar, Dorit Peleg, Nava Semel, Noga Treves, Lilly Perry, Tzipporah Dolan, Orly Castel-Bloom, and many others. The appearance of so many women writers in a short space of time is noteworthy in itself and may have something to do with the tendency, within the literature generally but more pronounced among the women writers, to withdraw from the large dimensions of political scene, or to observe it through miniature synecdochic portraits. Ruth Almog's *Roots of Light,* for example, begins as a family tale about a girl growing up in a small town in Eretz Yisrael, and concludes as a feminist depiction of the young woman's rebellion against her Israeli background—her father and the men who tried to dominate her.

Some of the 1980s women writers (Yehudit Katzir and Savyon Liebrecht, for example) adapted rather than overturned the dominant tradition. Katzir evokes the example of Yaakov Shabtai, while Liebrecht, in *Apples from the Desert* [*Tapuhim min hamidbar,* 1986], reexamined old subjects from new, female perspectives. In "A Room on the Roof" ["Heder ʿal hagag"] she describes Arab-Jewish relations from the viewpoint of a Jewish woman who is alone with Arab workers while they build her new room (recalling Amos Oz's "Nomad and Viper" ["Navadim vatsefaʿ"]), while "Doves" ["Yonim"] concerns a Communist Holocaust-survivor mother struggling to dissuade her son from turning Orthodox.

Hannah Bat-Shahar's *Calling the Bats* [*Likroʾ laʿatalefim,* 1990] presents a collection of bizarre and depressed characters who are extremely lonely, complexly related to their parents, and suffused with unfulfilled erotic desire. As she writes of one of her characters, "[H]er condition is a subject which always causes her gravity and awe. It sets her apart from other people and justifies her strange way of life. It makes her suffer, but she is also attached to it, as to a secret which gives her a different outlook on reality, a different yardstick" (p. 166). Dushka lives in a boarding-house where Paul (whom she secretly loves) is employed. She wants to leave the boarding-house and move to the flat where her mother had lived and committed suicide and of which property her uncle is the executor.

Such peculiar and intricate situations recur in most of Bat-Shahar's fiction. Her characters are crippled by love that cannot be realized because of their personal defects or because of their subjugation by ailing or tyrannical parents, as in "Thy Shaded Apartments" ["Behadarayikh tsel"]. Most of the characters have non-Hebrew names (Lotti, Edith, Dushka,

Teta, Paul, Larry, Laibe, Mensel, Polina, Amalia, Gerda), strengthening the impression that the setting is essentially non-Israeli, a different world from that of the average sabra. Bat-Shahar focuses on erotic frustration; the sexual relations she depicts are unreal and impossible of fulfillment. All of the stories are thickly oppressive, the landscape serving as images of the protagonist's despair and dysfunction.

Women's fiction has also produced more experimental forays into women as the literary subject. Rejecting traditional modes of representation altogether, Lilly Perry and Orly Castel-Bloom have done nothing less than change the face of Hebrew fiction. Castel-Bloom's *Where Am I?* [*Heikhan 'ani nimts'eit?*, 1990] is certainly one of the strangest books to appear in recent years. Whereas a writer like Kahana-Carmon produced a dense poetic prose, Castel-Bloom stripped her text of all cultural allusion and poetic metaphor, producing a comic absurdity out of unrelatedness and the unexpected: "When you dive, all people are equal. You dream you're flirting with a tall Negro as you flirt with your first husband. The Minister of Police looked into my computer and spoke to me in a friendly way" (p. 12). Such unlikely juxtapositions as the Negro, the husband, and the Minister of Police recur on the level of the macrotext. The story revolves around divorce, marriage, a typist's job, cousins who visit from France, an attempt to enter drama school, university studies, an attempted rape, seduction by a pimp trying to get the heroine to act as a "companion" for an unnamed figure, a meeting with the Prime Minister—for whom she is also intended—and similar developments that do not add up to a logical and coherent story. The materials all reflect the genuine realities of Tel Aviv, gleaned from the press, the campus, the underworld or—which is much the same—the secret service. But this reality lacks coherence. There is nothing here about longing for true love, and there are no erotic descriptions. Insofar as there is any sexuality, it is as mechanical as the girl's work at her computer.

This is the anti-romantic antithesis of Kahana-Carmon's writing. Castel-Bloom's character is swept along by her own narrative, which is as prosaic as possible, leading to a post-modern dead end in word and plot. The author seems to be saying, in so many words, that the world she lives in, the world of computers, journalists, politicians, imaginary husbands, and imaginary lovers is devoid of emotions and dead: "It was probably at the beginning of winter. A thunderstorm raged outside. But it had nothing to do with my state of mind, which was as indifferent as a dried-up well in the desert" (p. 22). The heroine's unemotional floundering is the social meaning of the text. It is difficult to identify Castel-Bloom's literary point of departure: perhaps the endings of Shabtai's two novels *Past Continuous* and *Past Perfect*. It is not impossible to imagine her heroine as the daughter of Caesar, Ervin's son. But if Shabtai's Caesar is a child of pioneers, whose dream is being lost, for Castel-Bloom the dream is so long gone it can only be recalled in its absence:

> A relative of mine, he's sixty years old. He has silver hair. I like him. He wrote a book about his life in his native country. His decision to go to Eretz Israel. His activity in Zionist organizations. His wonderful years in a kibbutz in the north. How he joined the banking system. The opening sentence in the book says everything: "I was not always a banker," this relative wrote. I've adopted this opening sentence and write: "I was not always a typist. I did not always know how to touch-type." (p. 21)

The equation between the banker's pre-banking existence (Zionism, pioneering, kibbutz) and the narrator's pre-typing life annuls both nostalgia and the satire of disillusion.

If thematically Castel-Bloom picks up where Shabtai left off, formally she recalls the modernist collages of Yitzhak Oren and Menashe Levin (though she may never have read them) and the bitter satires of Hanoch Levin. A not dissimilar 1960s writer was Yitzhak Orpaz, whose urban trilogy (*A House for One, The Mistress,* and *A Charming Traitor*) was also written in an absurdist prose and contained the kernel of Tel Avivian desperation, though in Orpaz there still remained an aching nostalgia for a lost experience.

Like Hoffman, Shimoni, and, later, Yitzhak Laor, Castel-Bloom communicates the despair of a generation which no longer even dreams the dreams of Zionist history. It is not so much that she writes either for or against the Zionist metaplot. Rather, like others of her generation of Israeli authors, she simply writes outside it.

* * *

We have arrived at the end of a long journey through a literature that set on its way without any natural territory or geographical terrain, without a spoken language, and with little chance of producing an ongoing and flourishing tradition. Yet, what Brenner dubbed a literature "against all odds" succeeded despite those odds, and what was once a literature of the ghetto and of a select group of intellectuals metamorphosed into the cultural voice of an entire modern society, read, in translation, by many non-Israelis as well. The literature without a language not only flourished beyond its own language, it transcended its own national borders. The nation that would build and be rebuilt produced a literature that would itself build and be rebuilt.

GLOSSARY

Aliyah: immigration to the land of Israel

First Immigration: the arrival of approximately 25,000 Jews from Eastern Europe to Palestine (Eretz Yisrael, or the Land of Israel) between 1882 and 1904, after the "Storms in the South" pogroms in Russia. [Major authors: Moshe Smilanski and Nehama Pochachevski]

Second Immigration: approximately 40,000 young Jewish pioneers from Russia between 1904 and 1913, influenced by socialist and *narodniki* ("back to the soil") ideologies. The leaders of this group (David Ben-Gurion, Berel Katznelson) were the founders of the social and cultural establishments of the Jewish population in Ottoman Palestine, such as the trade unions and the diverse social organizations of agricultural settlements (kibbutz, moshav, etc.). The majority of these immigrants left the country between 1914 and 1919. [Major authors: Y. H. Brenner and S. Y. Agnon]

Third Immigration: approximately 35,000 young pioneers from Poland, Lithuania, and Soviet Russia between 1919 and 1923. They established most of the institutions of the labor movement. [Major authors: Y. Shenhar, Israel Zarchi, and Haim Hazaz]

Fourth Immigration: an immigration of middle-class merchants and peddlers from Poland between 1924 and 1926, primarily due to economic crises among Polish Jews and Polish anti-Semitism. The majority of these immigrants settled in Tel Aviv.

Fifth Immigration: the immigration of Jews from Germany between 1933 and 1939, after the rise to power of the Nazis. More than 200,000 legal and illegal immigrants arrived in Mandatory Palestine, radically transforming the culture and economy of the country.

Bund: Jewish-socialist party of the working class. It was founded in Katowitz in 1897, the year of the first Zionist Congress in Basel. The movement grew in Russia, Poland, Lithuania, and, later, in the United States. The members advocated equality and cultural autonomy for the Jews in their homelands. Yiddish, the language of the Eastern European Diaspora, was pronounced the national language of the movement. The Bundists were anti-Zionist and were against any territorial solution to the "Jewish problem."

Dor Ba'aretz [Generation of the Land]: The generation of native-born children of immigrants. Born in the early 1920s, they started to publish their works in the late 1930s and 1940s. Most of them were attached to agricultural settlements and the labor movement. Primarily they wrote social realist fiction. This group is sometimes called *Dor Tashach* (the generation of 1948), after the year of the War of Independence, which was the formative year of their lives; or *Dor Hapalmah* (generation of commando troops), because some of the writers belonged to these military units, or identified with them, during the war. The hero protagonist of their fiction was the New Hebrew, like Moshe Shamir's Elik: the strong, independent, healthy Jew who was to replace the Old Jew of the diaspora. [Major authors: S. Yizhar, Moshe Shamir, and Aharon Megged]

Dor Hamedina [State Generation]: A younger generation, most of them born in the 1930s and 1940s, for whom the declaration of the State in 1948 was the definitive event. Beginning to publish in the sixties, most of them rebelled against the social realist conventions of *Dor Ba'aretz*. For the most part, they wrote expressionist, surrealist, and impressionist fiction. Many of them returned to the character of the Old Jew and parodied the heroic character of the New Hebrew as produced by the previous generation. [Major authors: Amos Oz, A. B. Yehoshua, Amalia Kahana-Carmon, and Aharon Appelfeld]

Drasha [sermon]: Given by a preacher (sermonizer) as an oral interpretation of a canonized text, preserved later in written and printed form.

Frankists: Followers of Jacob Frank (1726–1791), a false messiah, who declared himself heir of Shabbetai Zvi. He initiated mystical sexual orgies, which supposedly functioned to bring redemption through impurity. He and his followers were excommunicated by the rabbis in 1756.

Halutz [pioneer]: The young men and women who prepared themselves in the diaspora for agricultural work in Ottoman and later Mandatory Palestine (Eretz Yisrael). The idea of the *Halutzim* movement was the revival and renewal of the Jew by manual work and affinity with the soil. *HeHalutz*—the pioneer—federation was formed by pioneering youth movements. Groups were created throughout Europe from 1919 and 1921, and were joined into a world organization in 1924. *HeHalutz* supplied the bulk of pioneering labor for the building of Jewish settlements in Palestine.

Hapoʿel Hatzaʿir [The Young Worker]: A Jewish labor party in Palestine founded in 1905 by leaders of the Second Immigration. *Hapoʿel Hatzaʿir* was less influenced by Marxist ideas than its counterpart, *Poʾalei Zion* (Workers of Zion). Their main utopian concern was the redemption of the Jews by manual work and affinity with the soil.

Hashomer Hatzaʿir [The Young Guard]: Started as a youth movement in Galicia, it was influenced by the *Wandervogel* German youth movement and socialist-utopian ideas of the young labor movement in Mandatory Palestine. During the Third Immigration, members of the movement settled in Mandatory Palestine. After the late 1920s, the movement was increasingly influenced by Marxist socialism.

Hasidism: Religious and social movement founded by Israel Baal Shem Tov (1699–1761) in Podolia. The Baal Shem Tov taught that all are equal before the Almighty and that purity of heart was superior to study. The new movement spread rapidly through Eastern Europe. In the eighteenth and nineteenth centuries, it became quite diverse, and each *tzaddik* (righteous person or rebbe) had his own court and doctrines.

Haskalah [Enlightenment]: An intellectual and ideological movement influenced by the European Enlightenment of the seventeenth and eighteenth centuries. The Jewish Enlightenment began at the end of the eighteenth century in Italy and Germany. By the nineteenth century it was one of the dominant movements in Eastern Europe. The movement preached a certain amount of assimilation and acculturation, with the slogan: "Be a Jew at home and a human being outside." The idea of the Haskalah was a new, acculturated Jew who would nonetheless remain part of the ethnic group. The movement opened the way for a secular national Jewish identity which evolved toward Zionism. [Major authors of the Haskalah include Mendele Mokher Seforim, P. Smolenskin, and R. A. Braudes]

Heder [literally: room]: Traditional Jewish primary school for boys.

Hibbat Zion [Love of Zion]: A pre-Zionist movement at the end of the nineteenth century in Russia and Romania. Some of the movement's supporters emigrated to Palestine. At the beginning of the twentieth century the movement joined forces with Herzl's Zionist political movement.

Kastner Affair: In 1953 a man named Malkiel Greenwald accused Rudolph Kastner, who had been a leader of the Hungarian-Jewish community, of collaborating with Nazis (he had negotiated with Eichmann and had saved some Jews from the death camps). In 1955 a judge accepted Greenwald's arguments, but concluded there was insufficient evidence to convict Kastner. The State appealed, but the Supreme Court cleared Kastner, who in the meantime (1957) had been murdered by the extreme right. The trial created a tremendous stir, in the course of which the Israeli public was confronted with the non-heroic aspect of the Holocaust.

Kevutzah [group]: Cooperative agricultural group in Ottoman and later Mandatory Palestine working a farm on national land. The earliest group was formed in Deganyah (1910). Unlike the kibbutzim (see below), they tended to have greater selectivity in admitting members and tried to avoid the hiring of outside wage workers. They also resisted the introduction of industries.

Kibbutz [gathering in]: The main principles of the kibbutz resemble those of the *kevutzah*. The form originated during the Third Immigration, when the creation of large workers' groups who needed contract work and the need to develop wide tracts of land engendered the broadening of the *kevutzah* concept to incorporate industry, wage labor, and the removal of restrictions on the size of the group.

Lavon Affair: The 1954 uncovering of a Jewish underground in Egypt, organized by the Israeli intelligence service, and the hanging of some of its leaders. The question of who had given the order for the operation raised a furor in Israel. A government commission of inquiry led to the resignation of Minister of Defense Pinhas Lavon. In 1960 the testimony of an army officer implicated his superiors in forging relevant documents. Lavon demanded to be cleared and Ben-Gurion demanded that he be dismissed from his post as secretary general of the labor federation (Histadrut).

Melitzah: In biblical Hebrew, an aphorism; in the Middle Ages, elegant style. It now denotes a style popular in the Haskalah period that is based on the artful combination of flowery phrases from the Bible.

Midrash: A method of textual interpretation that elaborated on and expanded the meanings of scriptural texts. Talmudic tradition has formulated certain rules to deduce such hidden meanings. Midrashes were interpolated into the Talmudic text, but there also exist independent midrashic compositions, which retain the order of the verses as found in the scriptures.

Min Hayesod [From the Foundations]: A movement founded by Professor N. Rotenstreich, Amos Oz, and others in 1964, following the Lavon Affair, in which Lavon, the secretary-general of the Histadrut, had been forced to resign by Ben-Gurion (see *Lavon Affair*). They had a weekly publication named after the movement (1962–1965), which endeavored to fight against Ben-Gurion and to reaffirm the basic values of the labor movement. The struggle culminated in Mapai—the leading labor party—splitting up, and in the fall of Ben-Gurion from leadership.

Mishnah: Legal codification containing the core of Jewish oral law. The Mishnah was compiled by Rabbi Yehuda Hanasi on the basis of previous juridical collections. It is divided into six tractates, concluded approximately at the end of the second century C.E.

Mitnagdim [Opponents]: Opponents of the Hasidic movement, so called after a ban against the Hasidism was issued by the Vilna Gaon in 1772. They opposed the Hasidic belief in *tzaddikim* over the dominance of the Talmud scholar.

Moshav 'Ovdim [workers' settlement]: An agricultural village, usually just called a *moshav,* where the inhabitants of the moshav own individual homes and small holdings but cooperate in the purchase of equipment and the sale of produce. The first experiments of this type of agricultural settlement were at Be'er Ya'akov (1907) and 'Ein Ganim (1908).

Moshavah [colony, settlement]: Agricultural villages in which privately owned land is farmed by individuals. The *moshavah* originated during the First Immigration. The earliest settlements were Petach Tikvah (which failed in 1878 and was rebuilt in 1883) and Rishon Le Zion (1882). A number of these villages were founded or assisted by Baron Edmund de Rothschild.

Neologism: Creation of new words by combining existing semantic roots with new configurations of linguistic patterns. After the generation of Mendele and Bialik this was a major device of stylistic renewal in the works of authors such as the poet A. Shlonski and the novelist S. Yizhar.

Neturei Karta [Aramaic: Guardians of the City]: An ultra-Orthodox anti-Zionist group in Jerusalem, living mostly in the Mea Shearim neighborhood, that accepts neither Zionism nor the Jewish state. According to their ideology, redemption must await the times of the Messiah and any attempt to force a secular redemption is sinful.

Nussach: A style developed by Mendele Mokher Sefarim. It is based on a very symmetric syntax, following the parallelistic style of the Bible and the Mishnah. The vocabulary is very rich and uses most sources of the Hebrew language. It is also rich in conventional idioms and intertextual connotations and allusions.

Palmah [shock battalions, abbreviation of the Hebrew: Peluggot Mahatz]: The combat units of the Israeli underground self-defense organization (the Haganah), set up by its high command in 1941. It numbered 5,500 soldiers in 1948. After 1948 it was disbanded and its members became an organic part of the Israeli army.

Sabra [Arabic, lit: prickly pear cactus; in Hebrew: tzabbar]: Jewish native of Israel. The term refers metaphorically to the natives' alleged characteristic prickly exterior that hides a tender interior.

Shabbateans: Followers of the messianic movement led by the so-called false messiah Shabbetai Zevi (born in Smyrna in 1626; died 1676). The Shabbateans maintained their faith in his ideas even after he converted to Islam.

Talmud: Name applied to each of two great compilations, the Babylonian *Talmud* and the Jerusalemite (Palestinian) *Talmud,* in which the records of discussions on Jewish law during the several centuries after the closure of the Mishnah are collected. Structurally, the Talmud (*Gemara*) is a commentary and supplement to the *Mishnah.* Its content, however, exceeds the juridical limits by far. The text is mostly written in Aramaic and most scholars maintain that the Babylonian *Talmud* was "concluded" at the end of the fifth century C.E.

Tzaddik [righteous man]: The Hasidim regarded the *tzaddik* as the intermediary between God and man. He gave his followers advice and counsel, and also treated illness. Some of the *tzaddikim* adopted a luxurious mode of life, which included holding court.

Yeshivah [lit: a conference place]: The highest school for Jewish learning, where students mainly study the law (the Talmud) and its commentaries.

Yishuv [lit: the populated area]: The Jewish population in Palestine at the time of the British Mandate (1919–1947).

LIST OF LITERARY JOURNALS AND NEWSPAPERS

'*Akhshav* [*Now*]: Avant-garde literary journal published irregularly since 1957 in Jerusalem and Tel Aviv. Edited by Gabriel Moked and Baruch Chefetz (with Dan Miron in the sixties). The first issues were published under the name '*Ogdan* (*File*) in 1957–59.

'*Ammot* [*Measurements*]: Highbrow intellectual literary bimonthly, edited by Shlomo Grodsenski in Tel Aviv from 1962 to 1965.

Gilbo'a [name of a mountain near the center of the kibbutzim in the Jezreel valley]: Literary and ideological journal published only once in 1926 in kibbutz Ein Harod. It is important as an expression of the ideology of the pioneers of the Third Immigration.

Ha'adamah [*The Soil*]: Literary monthly edited by Y. H. Brenner in Tel Aviv from 1920 to 1923. The final issues appeared after its editor was murdered.

Hador [*The Generation*]: Literary and aesthetically oriented weekly edited by D. Frischman in 1901 and 1904 in Krakow, Poland.

Hamelitz [*The Eloquent Speaker/The Advocate*]: Weekly and biweekly published in Odessa from 1860, and in St. Petersburg from 1871. It was a daily newspaper from 1881 to 1903. *Hamelitz* was founded by Alexander Zederbaum-Erez, who was its editor until 1893.

Hame'orer [*The Awakener*]: A literary monthly published by Y. H. Brenner in London in 1906–1907. This was one of the most influential journals at the beginning of the century.

Ha'olam [*The World*]: An organ of the World Zionist Organization. This weekly was published in Cologne from 1907 to 1914. From 1919 to 1950 it was also published in Vilna, Odessa, London, Berlin, and Jerusalem.

Ha'omer [*The Sheaf*]: Literary journal published irregularly during 1907–1908, edited by Simcha Ben Zion. S. Y. Agnon published his first Hebrew story in Ottoman Palestine in this journal; Y. Shami also published his first story in this journal.

By permission of the Keter Publishing House, I used the index of Hebrew newspapers and periodicals that is included in the first volume of *Encyclopedia Judaica* (compiled by Mr. Getzel Kressel) for this glossary. I refer only to those journals mentioned in this volume that are of literary and historical importance.

Hapo'el Hatza'ir [*The Young Worker*]: Biweekly, later weekly, organ of the Hapo'el Hatza'ir and the Mapa'i parties from 1907 to 1970; a weekly since 1912. The first editor was Joseph Aharonovitz (1877–1937).

Hashiloah [*The Shiloah Spring*]: The major literary monthly journal in Russia until the end of the First World War. It appeared from 1897 to 1926 in Krakow, Warsaw, Odessa, and Jerusalem. The journal was edited by Ahad Haam and later by Haim Nahman Bialik and Joseph Klausner. Under the auspices of Ahad Haam it was ideologically Jewish in its selections and its literary approach.

Hasifrut [*Literature*]: A literary criticism and literary theory quarterly, published by the department of general literary theory at Tel Aviv University and edited by Binyamin Hrushovsky (Harshav) from 1968 to 1986.

Hatkufah [*The Epoch*]: Literary quarterly, later a yearbook, published from 1918 to 1950 in Moscow, Warsaw, Berlin, Tel Aviv, and New York. The spiritual heir of *Hashiloah* and *Hador*, it was edited by David Frischmann, who published his translations of European literature in the journal. After his death in 1922 several other editors took over.

Hayom [*The Day*]: Hebrew daily that appeared from February 12, 1886 to March 12, 1888 in St. Petersburg.

Hedim [*Echoes*]: A leading bimonthly literary organ published in Tel Aviv from 1922 to 1928; edited by Asher Barash and Yaakov Rabinowitz.

'Itim [*Epochs*]: Left-wing literary weekly published in Tel Aviv from 1946 to 1948; edited by Avraham Shlonski.

'Iton Shiv'im Vashev'a [*Newspaper Seventy Seven*]: Literary monthly published in Tel Aviv since 1977; edited by Yaakov Besser.

Keshet [*Bow, Rainbow*]: Avant-garde literary quarterly published in Tel Aviv from 1958 to 1976; edited by Aharon Amir. Some of the major authors of the New Wave (Yehoshua, Kenaz, and Oz) started their careers in this journal.

Ktuvim [*Texts*]: Literary weekly of a group of young avant-gardists, published in Tel Aviv from 1926 to 1933, edited by Eliezer Steinman, Avraham Shlonski, and Yaakov Horowitz.

Likr'at [*Towards*]: Organ of a group of young writers, students at the Hebrew University in Jerusalem. It was published in 1952–53 and was edited by Natan Zach and Binyamin Hrushovsky.

Massa' [*Journey*]: Literary biweekly published from 1951 to 1954; edited by Aharon Megged and T. Carmi. After 1954, it appeared as the literary supplement of the newspaper *Lamerchav,* which belonged to the leftist activist party Achdut Haavodah. Since 1971 it has appeared as a supplement of the Union's organ, *Davar.*

Mo'znayim [*Scales*]: Publication of the Hebrew Writers Organization. It appeared as a weekly from 1929 to 1933. Its first editor was Y. D. Berkowitz. Since 1933 (with some intermissions), it has been the monthly journal of the association. It is a conservative literary journal.

'Orlogin [*Clock*]: A literary journal published irregularly in 13 issues between 1950 and 1957 by the Workers Publishing House (Sifriat Poalim). It was

edited by Avraham Shlonski and was the mouthpiece of the left in the new state of Israel.

Revivim [*Showers*]: A literary journal published irregularly that wandered with its editor, Y. H. Brenner, from Lvov, Galicia to Jaffa, Eretz Israel. Six volumes were published between 1908 and 1919.

Sadan [*Anvil*]: A literary journal published irregularly and edited by the expressionistic poet U. Z. Greenberg between 1924 and 1926. The journal includes mostly expressionistic manifests and texts.

Siman Kri'ah [*Exclamation Mark*]: Avant-garde literary journal published irregularly in Tel Aviv since 1972 and edited by Manahem Peri. Since 1996 it has not appeared again.

Turim [*Columns*]: Literary weekly of the political left, published in Tel Aviv in 1933–34. From 1938 to 1939, it was edited by Avraham Shlonski.

FOR FURTHER READING

ANTHOLOGIES

Abramson, Glenda, ed. *The Oxford Book of Hebrew Short Stories*. Oxford: Oxford University Press, 1996.
Alter, Robert, ed. *Modern Hebrew Literature*. New York: Behrman House, 1975.
Lelchuk, Alan, and Gershon Shaked, eds. *Eight Great Hebrew Short Novels*. New York: Meridian, 1983.

INDIVIDUAL WORKS

Agnon, Shmuel Yosef. *Ad henah* [*Thus Far*]. Tel Aviv: Schocken, 1953.
———. *Agadat hasofer* [*The Tale of the Scribe*]. In *Eilu va 'eilu* [*Of Such and Such*]. Jerusalem: Schocken, 1941.
———. *Behanuto shel mar Lublin* [*In Mr. Lublin's Shop*]. Tel Aviv: Schocken, 1974.
———. "Bin'areinu uvizkeneinu" ["With Our Youths and with Our Aged"]. In *Al kapot haman'ul* [*At the Handles of the Lock*]. Berlin: Jüdischer Verlag, 1922.
———. *The Bridal Canopy*. Trans. Israel Meir Lask. London: Gollancz, 1968.
———. *Collected Stories*. New York: Schocken, 1970.
———. *A Guest for the Night*. Trans. Misha Louvish. New York: Schocken, 1968.
———. *Me'atsmi 'el 'atsmi* [*From Myself to Myself*]. Jerusalem: Schocken, 1976.
———. *Sefer hama'asim* [*The Book of Deeds*]. Tel Aviv: Schocken, 1941.
———. *Shira*. Trans. Zeva Shapiro. New York: Syracuse University Press, 1997.
———. *A Simple Story*. Trans. Hillel Halkin. New York: Schocken, 1985.
———. *Tmol shilshom* [*Yesteryear*]. Tel Aviv: Schocken, 1966.
———. *Vehayah he'akov lemishor* [*And the Crooked Shall Become Straight*]. In *Eilu va 'eilu*. Jerusalem: Schocken, 1941.
Almog, Ruth. *Death in the Rain*. Trans. Dalya Bilu. Santa Fe: Red Crane, 1993.
Amichai, Yehuda. *Not of This Time, Not of This Place*. Trans. Shlomo Katz. New York: Harper and Row, 1968. Hebrew: *Lo me'akhshav lo mikan*. Jerusalem: Schocken, 1963.
Appelfeld, Aharon. *The Age of Wonders*. Trans. Dalya Bilu. Boston: Godine, 1981.
———. *Ashan* [*Smoke*]. Akhshav, 1962.
———. *Badenheim 1939*. Trans. Dalya Bilu. Boston: Godine, 1980.

——. *Bekomat haqarqa'* [*On the Ground Floor*]. Tel Aviv: Sifrei Daga, 1968.

——. *Ha'or vehakutonet* [*The Skin and the Gown*]. Tel Aviv: Am Oved, 1971.

——. *Ke'ishon ha'ayin* [*As the Apple of His Eye*]. Tel Aviv: Kibbutz Hameuhad, 1972.

——. *Massot beguf rish'on* [*First Person Essays*]. Jerusalem: Hasifria HaZionit Alyad Hahistadrut HaZionit Haolamit, 1979.

Barash, Asher. *Pictures from a Brewery*. Trans. Katie Kaplan. London: Peter Owen, 1972.

Baron, Devorah. "Sunbeams." Trans. Joseph Schachter. In *The Oxford Book of Hebrew Short Stories*, ed. Glenda Abramson, 85–93. Oxford: Oxford University Press, 1996.

Bartov, Hanoch. *The Brigade*. Trans. David Simha Segal. New York: Holt, Rinehart and Winston, 1968.

Bar-Yosef, Yehoshua. *'Ir ksuma* [*Enchanted City*]. Twersky, 1950.

——. *Sukat shalom* [*The Tabernacle of Peace*]. Tel Aviv: Am Oved, 1958.

Bat-Shahar, Hannah. *Likro' la'atalefim* [*Calling the Bats*]. Jerusalem: Keter, 1990.

Ben-Avigdor, Abraham Laib. *Le'ah mocheret hadagim* [*Leah, Fishmonger*]. Warsaw, 1891.

Ben-Ner, Yitzhak. *'Eretz rehoqah* [*A Far Land*]. Jerusalem: Keter, 1981.

——. *Protoqol* [*Protocol*]. Jerusalem: Keter, 1983.

——. *Shki'ah kafrit* [*Rustic Sunset*]. Tel Aviv: Am Oved, 1976.

Berdyczewski, Micha Yoseph. *Kol kitvei* [*Collected Works*]. Tel Aviv: Am Oved, 1951.

——. *Mimekor Yisra'el: Classical Jewish Folktales*. Ed. Emanual Bin. Trans. I. M. Lask. Bloomington: Indiana University Press, 1976.

——. "Without Hope: Beyond the River." Trans. Yael Lotan. In *The Oxford Book of Hebrew Short Stories*, ed. Glenda Abramson, 28–39. Oxford: Oxford University Press, 1996.

Berkowitz, Yitzhak Dov. "Cut Off." Trans. Yael Lotan. In *The Oxford Book of Hebrew Short Stories*, ed. Glenda Abramson, 56–69. Oxford: Oxford University Press, 1996.

Bialik, Haim Nahman. *Aftergrowth and Other Stories*. Trans. I. M. Lask. Philadelphia: Jewish Publication Society of America, 1939.

——. *'Igrot, cerech 'aleph* [*Letters*, vol. 1]. Tel Aviv, 1938.

Brenner, Yosef Haim. *Breakdown and Bereavement*. Trans. Hillel Halkin. Ithaca: Cornell University Press, 1971.

——. *Ktavim II* [*Collected Works II*]. Tel Aviv: Dvir, 1960.

——. *Nerves*. Trans. Hillel Halkin. In *Eight Great Hebrew Short Novels*, ed. Alan Lelchuk and Gershon Shaked, 31–58. New York: Meridian, 1983.

Burla, Yehudah. *'Alilot 'Akavi'a* [*The Adventures of Akavia*]. Mitzpeh, 1939.

Castel-Bloom, Orly. *Heichan 'ani nimts'eit* [*Where Am I?*]. Tel Aviv: Zemora-Bitan, 1990.

Conner, Steven. *Postmodernist Culture*. Oxford: Basil Blackwell, 1989.

Feierberg, Mordechai Zeev. "The Calf." Trans. Hillel Halkin. In *The Oxford Book of Hebrew Short Stories,* ed. Glenda Abramson, 40–44. Oxford: Oxford University Press, 1996.

———. *Whither? and Other Stories.* Trans. Hillel Halkin. Philadelphia: Jewish Publication Society of America, 1973.

Frischmann, David. *Bamidbar* [*In the Desert*]. Jerusalem: Knesset, 1950.

Frye, Northrop. *Anatomy of Criticism.* Princeton: Princeton University Press, 1957.

Gertz, Nurit. "Mekomah shel haparodiyah behilufei hadorot basifrut haʿivrit" ["The Role of Parody in the Changing Generations in Hebrew Fiction"]. *Siman Kriʾah* 12–13 (Feb. 1981): 272–273.

Gnessin, Uri Nissan. *Sideways.* Trans. Hillel Halkin. In *Eight Great Hebrew Short Novels,* ed. Alan Lelchuk and Gershon Shaked, 3–27. New York: Meridian, 1983.

Goldberg, Leah. *Vehu haʾor* [*And He Is the Light*]. Merchavia: Kibbutz Haʾartzi Hashomer Hatzair, 1946.

Gouri, Haim. "Shʿat hesed niflaʾah venoraʾah" ["A Wondrous and Terrible Hour of Grace"]. *Moznayim* 25 (Aug. 3, 1967).

Grossman, David. *The Book of Intimate Grammar.* Trans. Betsy Rosenberg. New York: Farrar, Straus, Giroux, 1994.

———. *See Under: Love.* Trans. Betsy Rosenberg. New York: Farrar, Straus, Giroux, 1989. Hebrew: *ʿAyen ʿerekh: ʾahavah.* Tel Aviv: Hakibbutz Hameuchad, 1986.

Halkin, Shimon. *Ad mashber* [*Crisis*]. Tel Aviv: Am Oved, 1945.

———. *Yehiel Hahagri.* Berlin: A. Y. Shtibl, 1928.

Hareven, Shulamith. *City of Many Days.* Trans. Hillel Halkin. New York: Doubleday, 1977. Hebrew: *ʿIr yamim rabim.* Tel Aviv: Am Oved, 1972.

———. *The Miracle Hater.* Trans. Hillel Halkin. Berkeley: North Point, 1988. Hebrew: *Soneh hanisim.* Jerusalem: Dvir, 1983.

Hazaz, Haim. *The Gates of Bronze.* Trans. S. Gershon Levi. Philadelphia: Jewish Publication Society of America, 1975. Hebrew: *Daltot hanehoshet.* Tel Aviv: Am Oved, 1956.

———. "Rahamim." Trans. I. M. Lask. In *The Oxford Book of Hebrew Short Stories,* ed. Glenda Abramson, 94–101. Oxford: Oxford University Press, 1996.

———. *The Sermon.* Trans. Ben Halpern. Tel Aviv: International Theatre Institute, Israeli Centre, 1981. Hebrew: *Hadrasha.* Tel Aviv: Institute for the Translation of Hebrew Literature, 1981.

Hendel, Yehudit. *Hahatser shel Momo hagdolah* [*The Yard of Momo the Great*]. Tel Aviv: Am Oved, 1969.

Hoffman, Yoel. *Bernhard* [*Berhnart*]. Jerusalem: Keter, 1989.

Horowitz, Yaʿacov. "El mul machbesh hayetsirah" ["Opposite the Furnace of Creation"]. *Sadan* 4 (1925).

Hurgin, Yaacov. *Professor Leonardo.* Jerusalem: Keter, 1990.

Kabak, Aharon Avraham. *The Narrow Path: The Man of Nazareth.* Trans. Julian Louis Meltzer. Tel Aviv: Massada, 1968. Hebrew: *Bamishʿol hatsar.* Tel Aviv: Am Oved, 1949.

———. *Toldot mishpahah 'ahat* [*History of One Family*]. Tel Aviv: Am Oved, 1943–1945.

Kahana-Carmon, Amalia. *Bikhfifah 'ahat* [*Under One Roof*]. Merchavia: Sifrut Hapoalim, 1966.

———. *Veyareah be'emek 'ayalon* [*And Moon in the Valley of Ajalon*]. Tel Aviv: Hakibbutz Hameuchad, 1971.

Kaniuk, Yoram. *Adam Resurrected*. Trans. Seymour Simckes. New York: Atheneum, 1971.

———. *Hayehudi ha'aharon* [*The Last Jew*]. Tel Aviv: Hakibbutz Hameuchad Sifriat Poalim, 1981.

———. *Himmo, King of Jerusalem*. Trans. Joseph Schachter. New York: Atheneum, 1969.

———. *Post mortem* [*Post Mortem*]. Tel Aviv: Hakibbutz Hameuchad/Yedioth Aharonot, 1992.

———. *Rockinghorse*. Trans. Richard Flantz. New York: Harper and Row, 1977.

Kaufman, Yehezkel. *Goleh venechar, cerech sheini* [*Exile and Foreign,* vol. 2]. Tel Aviv: Dvir, 1930.

Kenan, Amos. *Batahanah* [*At the Station*]. Tel Aviv: Hakibbutz Hameuhad, 1992.

Kimhi, Dov. *Beit Heifetz* [*The House of Hefetz*]. Jerusalem: Mosad Bialik, 1951.

Liebrecht, Savyon. *Apples from the Desert*. Trans. Marganit Weinberger-Rotman et al. New York: Feminist Press and the City University of New York, 1998. Hebrew: *Tapuhim min hamidbar*. Tel Aviv: Sifriat Poalim, 1986.

Maletz, David. *Young Hearts: A Novel of Modern Israel*. New York: Schocken, 1950. Hebrew: *Ma'agalot*. Tel Aviv: Am Oved, 1983.

Megged, Aharon. *Fortunes of a Fool*. Trans. Aubrey Hodes. New York: Random House, 1962. Hebrew: *Mikreh haksil*. Tel Aviv: Hakibbutz Hameuchad, 1960.

———. "Hagal hehadash" ["The New Wave"]. *Masa, musaf Lamerchav* (June 29, 1962).

———. *Hedvah and I*. Jerusalem: World Zionist Organization, 1957. Hebrew: *Hedvah ve'ani*. Hakibbutz Hameuchad, 1953.

———. *The Living on the Dead*. Trans. Misha Louvish. London: Jonathan Cape, 1970.

Mendele, Mokher Seforim (S. Y. Abramowitz). "Burned Out." Trans. Jeffrey M. Green. In *The Oxford Book of Hebrew Short Stories,* ed. Glenda Abramson, 17–27. Oxford: Oxford University Press, 1996.

———. "Shem and Japeth on the Train." Trans. Walter Lever. In *Modern Hebrew Literature,* ed. Robert Alter, 19–38. New York: Behrman House, 1975.

———. *Tales of Mendele the Book Peddler: Fishke the Lame and Benjamin the Third*. Trans. Ted Gorelick and Hillel Halkin. New York: Schocken, 1996.

Michael, Sami. *Refuge*. Jewish Publication Society of America, 1988. Hebrew: *Hasut*. Tel Aviv: Am Oved, 1977.

Michali, B. Y. "Bein milhamah veshalom" ["Between War and Peace"]. *Moznaim* 2, no. 25 (July 1967).

Mohar, Eli. "Romanim zeh 'inyan qasheh—re'ayon im Moshe Shamir" ["Novels Are a Difficult Business—An Interview with Moshe Shamir"]. *Dvar Hashavu'a* (Feb. 3, 1973).

Moked, Gabriel. "Ma'amar ma'arekhet" ["Editorial"]. 'Akhshav (Spring 1959).

———. "Sifruteinu bishnot hashishim, hirhurim vetiqvot" ["Our Literature in the Sixties, Thoughts and Hopes"]. Davar (October 7, 1966).

Mossinsohn, Yigal. Judas. New York: St. Martin's, 1963. Hebrew: Yehudah 'ish krayot. Tel Aviv: Am Oved, 1963.

Muir, Edward. The Structure of the Novel. London: Hogarth Press, 1957.

Niger, S., and Nomberg, H. D. Vegen Yiddishe Shreiber, Vol. 2. Warsaw, 1913.

Nitzan, Shlomo. Beino leveinam [Between Him and Them]. Tel Aviv: Hakibbutz Hameuchad, 1953.

———. Tsvat betsvat [Togetherness]. Tel Aviv: Hakibbutz Hameuchad, 1956.

———. Yated la'ohel [Not Even a Tent Peg]. Tel Aviv: Sifriat Poalim, 1960.

Orpaz, Yitzhak. "'Al hasipur hanisyoni" ["On the Experimental Story"]. Keshet (Autumn 1965).

———. 'Or be'ad 'or [Skin for Skin]. Tel Aviv: Massada, 1965.

Ortega y Gasset, Jose. The Dehumanization of Art. Garden City: Doubleday, 1956.

Oz, Amos. Be'or hatkhelet ha'azah [Under This Blazing Light]. Tel Aviv: Sifriat Poalim, 1979.

———. Black Box. Trans. Nicholas De Lange. New York: Harcourt Brace Jovanovich, 1988. Hebrew: Kufsa shehorah. Tel Aviv: Am Oved, 1987.

———. "Drushah te'udat zehut 'ideit" ["An Ideological Identity Card Is Required"]. Min Hayesod 31 (Jan. 8, 1963).

———. Elsewhere, Perhaps. Trans. Nicholas De Lange. New York: Harvest, 1985.

———. The Hill of Evil Counsel. Trans. Nicholas De Lange. New York: Harvest, 1991.

———. To Know a Woman. Trans. Nicholas De Lange. New York: Harcourt Brace Jovanovich, 1991.

———. My Michael. Trans. Nicholas De Lange. London: Chatto and Windus, 1988. Hebrew: Micha'el sheli. Tel Aviv: Am Oved, 1968.

———. A Perfect Peace. Trans. Hillel Halkin. New York: Harcourt Brace Jovanovich, 1985.

———. Touch the Water, Touch the Wind. Trans. Nicholas De Lange. New York: Harcourt Brace Jovanovich, 1974.

———. Unto Death. Trans. Nicholas De Lange. New York: Harvest, 1985.

———. Where the Jackals Howl. Trans. Nicholas De Lange and Philip Simpson. New York: Harcourt Brace Jovanovich, 1981.

Peled, Elead. "Qriy'ah ptuhah mehamefaked hatsvai shel ha'ir" ["An Open Call by the City's Military Commander"]. Kol Tzfat (April 23, 1948).

Peretz, Isaac Leib. Kol kitvei, kerech sheini [Collected Works, Vol. 3]. Tel Aviv: Dvir, 1942–1947.

———. Selections: The I. L. Peretz Reader. Ed. Ruth R. Wisse. New York: Schocken, 1990.

Rabinowitz, Y. "Sifruteinu vehayeinu" ["Our Literature and Our Life"]. In Maslulei Sifrut [Literary Paths]. Jerusalem: Neiman, 1971.

Reuveni, Aharon. Ad Yerushalayim [Unto Jerusalem]. Jerusalem: Keter, 1987.

Sacks, Sheldon. Fiction and the Shape of Belief. Berkeley: University of California Press, 1967.

Sened, Yonat, and Alexander Sened. *Bein hameitim uvein hahayim* [*Between the Dead and the Living*]. Tel Aviv: Hakibbutz Hameuchad, 1964.

Shabtai, Yaakov. *Past Continuous.* Trans. Dalya Bilu. Philadelphia: Jewish Publication Society of America, 1985.

Shaham, Natan. *Guf Rish'on Rabim* [*First Person Plural*]. Tel Aviv: Sifriat Poalim 1968.

———. *Ha'eilim 'atseilim* [*The Gods Are Lazy*]. Merchavia: Hakibbutz Haartzi Hashomer Hatzair, 1949.

———. *The Rosendorf Quartet.* Trans. Dalya Bilu. New York: Grove Weidenfeld, 1991.

Shahar, David. *Nin-Gal.* Tel Aviv: Am Oved, 1983.

———. *Summer in the Street of the Prophets.* Trans. Dalya Bilu. New York: Weidenfeld and Nicolson, 1988.

Shalev, Meir. *Esau.* Trans. Barbara Harshav. New York: Harper Collins, 1994. Hebrew: *Esav.* Tel Aviv: Am Oved, 1991.

Shalom, Sh. "Hitgalut hage'ulah" ["The Advent of Redemption"]. *Moznayim* (July 1967).

Shami, Yitzhak. *The Vengeance of the Fathers.* Trans. Richard Flantz. In *Eight Great Hebrew Short Novels,* ed. Alan Lelchuk and Gershon Shaked, 61–163. New York: Meridian, 1983.

Shamir, Moshe. *The Hittite Must Die.* Trans. Margaret Benaya. New York: East and West Library, 1978. Hebrew: *Kivsat harash.* Tel Aviv: Sifriat Poalim, 1956.

———. *He Walked through the Fields.* Trans. Aubrey Hodes. Jerusalem: W.Z.O, 1959. Hebrew: *Hu halach basadot.* Tel Aviv: Sifriat Poalim, 1948.

———. *The King of Flesh and Blood.* New York: Vanguard, 1958. Hebrew: *Melech basar vadam.* Tel Aviv: Sifriat Poalim, 1954.

———. *With His Own Hands.* Trans. Joseph Schachter. Jerusalem: Institute for the Translation of Hebrew Literature, 1970.

Shapira, Avraham, ed. *The Seventh Day: Soldiers Talk about the Six-Day War.* New York: Scribner, 1971.

Shenhar, Yitzhak. "Prazon" ["Country Town"]. In *Sipurim ktsarim* [*Short Stories*], 3 vols. Jerusalem: Mosad Bialik, 1960.

Shimoni, Yuval. *Ma'of hayonah* [*The Flight of the Dove*]. Tel Aviv: Am Oved, 1990.

Tammuz, Benjamin. *Castle in Spain.* Trans. Joseph Schachter. New York: Bobbs-Merrill, 1973.

———. *Hayei Elyakum* [*The Life of Elyakum*]. Tel Aviv: Am Oved, 1963.

———. *Minotaur.* Trans. Kim Parfitt and Mildred Budny. New York: New American Library, 1981. Hebrew: *Minotaur.* Tel Aviv: Hakibbutz Hameuchad, 1980.

———. *Hazikit vehazamir* [*Chameleon and Nightingale*]. Jerusalem: Keter, 1989.

Tzalka, Dan. *Elef levavot* [*A Thousand Hearts*]. Tel Aviv: Am Oved, 1991.

Vogel, David. *Beveit hamarpe'* [*In the Sanatorium*]. Tarmil, 1975.

———. *Facing the Sea.* Trans. Daniel Silverstone. In *Eight Great Hebrew Short Novels,* ed. Alan Lelchuk and Gershon Shaked, 221–268. New York: Meridian, 1983.

———. *Married Life.* Trans. Dalya Bilu. New York: Grove Press, 1989.

Wallenrod, Reuven. *Dusk in the Catskills*. Trans. Reuven Wallenrod. New York: Reconstructionist Press, 1957. Hebrew: *Ki panah yom, sipur*. Tel Aviv: Neuman, 1946.

Wieseltier, Menachem. "'Ish vede'ato: 'eich hifsadnu 'et milhemet sheshet hay-- amim" ["Each Man's Opinion: How We Lost the Six-Day War"]. *Ha'aretz* (Aug. 9, 1968).

Yaari, Yehuda. *Ke'or yahel* [*When the Candle Was Burning*]. Tel Aviv: Eretz Yisrael, 1937.

Yehoshua, Avraham B. *Bithilat Kayitz—1970* [*Early in the Summer of 1970*]. Jerusalem and Tel Aviv: Schocken, 1971.

———. *The Lover*. Trans. Philip Simpson. New York: Dutton Obelisk, 1985. Hebrew: *Hame'ahev*. Tel Aviv: Schocken, 1981.

———. *Mot hazakein* [*The Death of the Old Man*]. Tel Aviv: Hakibbutz Hameuchad, 1962.

———. *Mr. Mani*. Trans. Hillel Halkin. New York: Doubleday, 1992. Hebrew: *Mar Mani: roman sihot*. Tel Aviv: Hakibbutz Hameuchad, 1990.

Yizhar, S. *Ephraim hozer la'aspeset* [*Ephraim Returns to Alfalfa*]. Hakibbutz Hameuchad, 1978.

———. *Midnight Convoy and Other Stories*. Jerusalem: Israel Universities Press, 1969.

———. *Yemei ziklag* [*Days of Ziklag*]. Tel Aviv: Am Oved, 1958.

Zach, Natan. "Biqoret" ["Review"]. *Ma'avak* (Jan. 9, 1953).

———. *Kavei 'avir* [*Airwaves*]. Jerusalem, 1983.

———. "Le'akliman hasignoni shel shnot hahamishim vehashishim beshirateinu" ["On the Stylistic Climate of Our Poetry in the Fifties and Sixties"]. *Ha'aretz Literary Supplement* (July 29, 1966).

———. *Zman veritmus' etsel bergson ubashirah hamodernit* [*Time and Rhythm in Bergson and Modern Poetry*]. Tel Aviv, 1966.

Zioni, A. "Tarbut ha'avodah" ["Culture of Labor"]. *Hedim* 4, no. 1 (1925).

INDEX

GERSHON SHAKED

is Professor Emeritus of Hebrew Literature at Hebrew University, Jerusalem. He is author of *Die Macht der Identität, The Shadows Within, No Other Place* (Hebrew), *S. Y. Agnon: A Revolutionary Traditionalist,* and *Hebrew Fiction 1880–1980* (5 vols.) (Hebrew).

YAEL LOTAN's

translations from Hebrew include *Persian Brides: A Novel* by Dorit Rabinyan and *Samir and Yonatan* by Daniella Carmi.